D1715489

MOCKINGBIRD
PASSING

MOCKINGBIRD
PASSING

Closeted Traditions
and Sexual Curiosities
in Harper Lee's Novel

HOLLY BLACKFORD

THE UNIVERSITY OF TENNESSEE PRESS / KNOXVILLE

Selections from *To Kill a Mockingbird* by Harper Lee are reprinted by permission of
HarperCollins Publishers. Copyright © 1960 by Harper Lee; renewed © 1988 by Harper
Lee. Foreword copyright © 1993 by Harper Lee.

Selections from *Other Voices, Other Rooms* by Truman Capote are used by permission of
Random House, Inc. Copyright © 1948 by Truman Capote.

Selections from *The Member of the Wedding* by Carson McCullers are used by permis-
sion of Houghton Mifflin Harcourt Publishing Company. Copyright © 1946 by Carson
McCullers; renewed 1973 by Floria V. Lasky, Executrix of the Estate of Carson McCullers.
All rights reserved.

The paper in this book meets the requirements of American National Standards Institute /
National Information Standards Organization specification Z39.48-1992 (Permanence
of Paper). It contains 30 percent post-consumer waste and is certified by the Forest
Stewardship Council.

Library of Congress Cataloging-in-Publication Data

Blackford, Holly Virginia.
Mockingbird passing: closeted traditions and sexual curiosities in Harper Lee's novel /
Holly Blackford.
     p. cm.
Includes bibliographical references and index.
ISBN-13: 978-1-57233-749-7 (hardcover: alk. paper)
ISBN-10: 1-57233-749-4 (hardcover; alk. paper)
1. Lee, Harper. To kill a mockingbird.
2. Passing (Identity) in literature.
I. Title.

PS3562.E353T63335 2010
813'.54—dc22

2011001889

To Todd,

Two together!
Winds blow South, or winds blow North . . . If we two but keep together.
Walt Whitman, "Out of the Cradle Endlessly Rocking"

and to our four Scouts,
cautiously peering, absorbing, translating,

always.

No poet, no artist of any art, has his complete meaning alone. His significance, his appreciation is the appreciation of his relation to the dead poets and artists. You cannot value him alone; you must set him, for contrast and comparison, among the dead. . . . what happens when a new work of art is created is something that happens simultaneously to all the works of art which preceded it. The existing monuments form an ideal order among themselves, which is modified by the introduction of the new (the really new) work of art among them. The existing order is complete before the new work arrives; for order to persist after the supervention of novelty, the *whole* existing order must be, if ever so slightly, altered; and so the relations, proportions, values of each work of art toward the whole are readjusted; and this is conformity between the old and the new.

T. S. Eliot, "Tradition and the Individual Talent," 1920

CONTENTS

ACKNOWLEDGMENTS

This book was born when I went to Monroeville, Alabama, to interview young readers of *To Kill a Mockingbird*. While my manuscript on the fascinating reader responses of teens is still in process, the words of teens drew me further and further into a consideration of how multiple literary canons circulate in Lee's novel. The things teens had to say were so complicated and contradictory that I had to write this book.

Long before I had finished my interviews with young readers, I knew that I had to investigate *Mockingbird*'s literary traditions before I could finish the book that I had gone to Monroeville to research. I wrote chapter 2 on racial melodrama after analyzing the remarkable way young people voiced their pride at "figuring out" the trial and believing they had uncovered Tom's innocence. I wrote chapters 3 and 4 after analyzing how teens said they could see *more* than Scout could see, and how reading *through* or *over the shoulder of* Scout was such a unique experience. The people of Monroeville also proudly promote the career of Truman Capote, which led me to many years teaching and considering Capote so I could better understand the subtext of Dill's story in *Mockingbird*. Although this is not the book that my interviewees in Monroeville expected to see, I wish to thank them here and promise them that now I can finish my book about young readers.

I wish to thank Keith Green, Vibiana Cvetkovic, and Julie Yankanich for reading a full draft. Thanks also to students Carla Meluso and Karen Ogden for volunteering to help with my research on queer theory in relation to novels of child consciousness. Thanks to Rutgers University for a sabbatical that enabled completion of the book, and thanks to the University of Tennessee Press for believing in the project and shepherding it into print. Finally, a supportive family, such as I am blessed to have, makes everything possible.

INTRODUCTION

MISS JEAN LOUISE,
YOUR NOVEL'S ABOUT PASSIN'

"Go ahead and laugh, girl. But you know I really *could* be a Cotillion debutante if I wanted to be. 'Cause I'm so good at passin'. I can be whatever I choose to be, and if I choose to be a rich white girl, honey, that's what I will be."

> —The Lady Chablis, in *Midnight in the Garden of Good and Evil*
> by John Berendt

"Was I sleeping, while the others suffered? Am I sleeping now? To-morrow, when I wake, or think I do, what shall I say of to-day? That with Estragon my friend, at this place, until the fall of night, I waited for Godot? That Pozzo passed, with his carrier, and that he spoke to us? Probably. But in all that what truth will there be? He'll know nothing. He'll tell me about the blows he received and I'll give him a carrot. Astride of a grave and a difficult birth. Down in the hole, lingeringly, the grave-digger puts on the forceps. We have time to grow old. The air is full of our cries. But habit is a great deadener. At me too someone is looking, of me too someone is saying, He is sleeping, he knows nothing, let him sleep on."

> —Vladimir, in *Waiting for Godot*
> by Samuel Beckett

How often does a novel earn its author the Presidential Medal of Freedom, awarded Harper Lee in 2007 by President Bush, and a spot on *Publishing Triangle*'s list of "100 best gay and lesbian novels"? Such incongruent positions of eminence alert us to the diversity of journeys embedded in *To Kill a Mockingbird*. As Claudia Durst Johnson subtitled her 1994 book-length study of *Mockingbird,* Lee's 1960 novel is an exercise in "threatening boundaries." Boundaries only become boundaries when contesting arenas border one another, making collision imminent. Indeed *Mockingbird* has meant a great variety of things to a great variety of "folks," a category that Scout concludes encompasses all of us who are passing through an existential drama called human life.

All great novels, Mikhail Bakhtin has instructed us in *The Dialogic Imagination,* comprise a diversity of voices and points of view, even as they select, exclude, and parody some voices. To look at the voices represented in a novel is to barely skim the surface of what those voices mean and where they have originated. When you start to excavate voices in a complex novel, you often wind up chasing those voices in other novels. This is because literature begets other literature, just as words are used to define words, in an endless chain of signification. The idea of a literary canon, and I use the article "a" rather than "the," is a useful idea insofar as it denotes a way to view texts in relationship to one another, as well as in relation to culture. There are multiple journeys in *Mockingbird* because there are actually multiple canons evoked in and by it.

In his influential essay "Tradition and the Individual Talent," T. S. Eliot defines "the" canon as a relationship between literary objects speaking to one another. When a writer writes, he or she rewrites existent literary objects and the canon is forever altered. Any novel or piece of writing inevitably becomes an independent literary object disconnected from any particular author or reader, which is not to say that it is entirely aesthetic and disconnected from life. But it is to say that a literary object provides a snapshot of life in all its contradictions, a snapshot capturing motion and built upon tension, like one of the moving photographs in *Harry Potter*. A novel bears the contradictions of a culture whether an author intended it to or not, and whether or not every reader can see it. Fredric Jameson calls this inevitable phenomenon "the political unconscious" of a text. The critical environment that has arisen since the publication of Roland Barthes's influential essay

"The Death of the Author" enables us to regard intertextuality as part of a text and its meaning with or without the consent of any particular author or reader, something even Eliot could not have foreseen. Barthes explains the cultural complexity of a text as follows:

> We know now that a text is not a line of words releasing a single "theological" meaning (the "message" of the Author-God) but a multi-dimensional space in which a variety of writings, none of them original, blend and clash. The text is a tissue of quotations drawn from the innumerable centres of culture. . . . Thus is revealed the total existence of writing: a text is made of multiple writings, drawn from many cultures and entering into mutual relations of dialogue, parody, contestation, but there is one place where this multiplicity is focused and that place is the reader, not, as was hitherto said, the author.

Neither reader nor author denotes any particular person. The name "Lee" enables me to simplify sentences about the design of *Mockingbird* in my discussions of how the novel taps into various literary traditions. However, I intend to uncover how *Mockingbird* "is made of multiple writings," revealing "the total existence of the writing" in a broader, cultural sense.

Novel writer and poet Margaret Atwood likewise indicates a piece of writing more as an instance of a cultural unconscious. When the writer writes, he or she creates a double that even the writer may not recognize, own, or know. Atwood uses Alice's journey through the looking glass as analogous to the writer's journey through the underworld:

> It is a false analogy, of course, because Alice is not the writer of the story about her. Nevertheless, here is my best guess, about writers and their elusive doubles, and the question of who does what as far as the actual writing goes. The act of writing takes place at the moment when Alice passes through the mirror. At this one instant, the glass barrier between the doubles dissolves, and Alice is neither here nor there, neither art nor life, neither the one thing nor the other, though at the same time she is all of these at once. At that moment time itself stops, and also stretches out, and both writer and reader have all the time not in the world. (*Negotiating with the Dead* 57)

In Lee's *Mockingbird,* time has stretched out. The novel is both a product of its time and has transcended its time and place. It is both a reflection of the world in the fifties, when it was composed (not to mention the thirties, its setting), and a reflection of a literary underworld, literary conventions and meanings that fuel its power and complexity. Atwood calls writing "negotiating with the dead" because there are a whole lot of writers in the underworld; a writer of any particular text is never identical to a writer we might meet because time has passed. The question becomes the composition of the underworld. We evaluate works of art in comparison with other works. What happens in the minds of writers as they write and rewrite is something only they know, and if you believe in the unconscious, which I do, it is something more than they know. Whether or not Lee intended, her one published novel entered several existent American canons and spoke back to them. Paradoxically, she entered an American underworld of queer literature even as she found favor with those whom such a notion would shock. A text will not tell what it is not asked.

Yet the contesting arenas within *Mockingbird* are embedded in its very title. Apparently, Amasa Lee took credit for teaching his children that it is a sin to kill a mockingbird (Going, "Truman Capote" 142), which indicates the title's status as perhaps a colloquial expression. However the precision of the title took root, its violence (Tavernier-Corbin 58), its overdetermination as symbol (Dave 50; Woodard 580–83), and its status as an American icon, in opposition to the more conventional birds of British romanticism, can hardly be imagined without considering Walt Whitman's elegiac poem about two mockingbirds from Alabama. This allusion stands side by side with a curious and contradictory meaning that Marianne Moates conveys in *A Bridge of Childhood.* Moates relays the tale that Truman Capote in childhood play articulated why it is a sin to kill a mockingbird; he was pretending to give a school lesson when he said it is a sin to kill a mockingbird, "'Because they eat little colored babies' eyes out. . . . With their eyes gone they can't find their mother's nongies. And when they can't see how to nurse their mother's nongies, they'll starve to death. So mockingbirds keep down the colored population'" (147). It would hardly be a sin to kill those mockingbirds. However seriously we can take this anecdote, it reminds us that the idea of killing a mockingbird arises many times in the novel and is reinterpreted by many characters. Atticus first says it, but he does not explain it; Miss Maudie explains it in her own way; Mr. Underwood writes a different version of it; and

Scout finally makes Boo Radley analogous to it. Boo could not be any clearer a symbol of an underworld in the closet. Emphasis on the song of the mockingbird suggests other meanings, such as the perpetually singing Uncle Tom in *Uncle Tom's Cabin*. Ultimately, the mockingbird could provide us with an image of the narrator's voice and the entire novel, which calls upon a diversity of American literary traditions.

The point of a multifaceted symbol like the mockingbird is that it lacks a definitive origin, just as "the voice loses its origin" (Barthes) the very moment something is narrated in writing; mockingbirds are experts at learning the vocal patterns of others and singing them in parody. "Mockingbird" is an apt description for what Lee achieved with her unique coalescence of American canons: allusions to Walt Whitman, Ralph Waldo Emerson, Harriet Beecher Stowe, Nathaniel Hawthorne, Richard Wright, Truman Capote, Carson McCullers, Kate Chopin, Nella Larsen, Edith Wharton, and others not even imagined here penetrate the novel's texture and sharpen our reception. Mapping out these canons in *Mockingbird* helps us understand how a novel can be so many things to so many folks.

The comparative method does not only tell us how texts relate to one another, but it also leads us to broad critical analysis. The deconstruction of *Mockingbird* in relation to other American texts—their forms, their expressions, their ideologies, their visions—teaches us about the interworking of the novel and a culture that continues to find meaning in it. Both overt and embedded meanings emerge when we study how *Mockingbird* speaks to American canons, and if we understand novels as artifacts of culture in all its complexity, then we have also learned something about ourselves and American culture in the process. This book looks extensively at major literary legacies of the nineteenth and twentieth centuries informing *Mockingbird* and giving it not only its lasting power, through fine craft, but also its complexities and contradictions. We like *Mockingbird* because it skillfully leads us into paradoxical responses. It manages to hold within its pages not two years of events but over 150 years of American literary history.

Reading *The Gray Ghost*

This book's journey into *Mockingbird* begins with a question evoked by the novel's ending. After all is said and done, a phantom neighbor unveiled and an innocent African American man executed, Atticus says he is reading

"'One of the few things I haven't read'" (280), a book of Jem's titled *The Gray Ghost*. Lee made up the title, but its genre is fairly clear. It is an archetypal gothic, a type of story beyond Atticus's worldview and in the province of popular children's literature. The book is now Jem's, but it was originally Dill's. And Scout has already read it. The book *The Gray Ghost* has actually circulated among the children Jem, Scout, and Dill, but in ownership it has traveled from Dill to Jem to Atticus. Its content has something to do with Boo, a resemblance of plot revealed when Scout retells the story to Atticus. Historically, Confederate commander John Mosby was known as "The Gray Ghost" because he and his men continually eluded the Union army by blending in with local townspeople, a symbol of "passing" Lee would have seen in the late fifties when a television series *The Grey Ghost*, based on the Mosby Raiders, could be viewed on CBS. Lee turns the title into a children's gothic. What does it mean that Atticus is reading this book?

The implications of this ending are profound, bespeaking fundamental ideas about the fate of the American enlightenment and the poetics of reading, literacy, and interpretation present throughout the novel. I have been haunted by this ending, even as Atticus is clearly being haunted by ghosts, which he has never before considered and about which the children already know. Reading *The Gray Ghost* and thus left reading issues unresolved in *Mockingbird*, Atticus beckons us to consider the destiny of who Atticus is. Atticus is what Ralph Waldo Emerson famously termed *man thinking*. To consider his destiny is no less than to consider the destiny of nineteenth-century ideas about democracy and the nature of man.

Reading in general is a major concern of the novel. Characters are differentiated by their relationship to literacy, major scenes of tensions in reading define relations to knowledge and power, and Atticus, generally perceived as the heroic and shining model of virtue in the novel, is if nothing else a reader. He spends most of his time in the novel reading, at least from the point of view of his children, who might wish he did other things. Who could forget the careful way he packs something to read and an illuminating light on the evening of his vigil outside the local jail, where he—archetypal reader—confronts a lynch mob? Can a reader change the course of human events? Reading and Socratic dialogue, as reflected by his signature question "do you really think so?" are ways of living for Atticus. Scout and Jem spend most of the novel learning to read what Atticus reads with ease and regularity. Atticus regularly practices logic and argument with Jem by presenting reading material, and Jem and Scout experience attachment to their father through ritualistic reading of newspapers and law books. The novel itself has come to signify an important foundation of literacy for countless school-children, thus encoding the enterprise of reading and intellect through its example.

Reading is a broad poetics in the novel, a way of engaging with the world and self, an enterprise of seeking enlightenment and truth, as it has been since the earliest days of theorizing American democracy and citizenship by, for example, Thomas Jefferson and Benjamin Franklin. However, reading isn't everything. Although Scout can read and cannot recall a time she could not read, Scout faces the limits of knowledge in many scenes that she cannot decode. Dill introduces himself to the Finch children as a reader, but of a type of imaginative literature to which most Maycomb children are "immune" (16). Reading is a poetics of the novel, but it is not human empathy and it is not, necessarily, action, as Emerson argued in "The American Scholar" when he announced the need for America to forge a relationship to knowledge that was not completely dependent on reverence for the past.

At the end of *Mockingbird, man thinking* is reading a children's gothic and is perhaps accepting the legitimacy of the children's worldview: a view of the world that includes villainy, evil, irrationality, passion, ghosts, phantoms, and manifestations of the supernatural—of ghosts you cannot see, of gray areas you cannot directly glimpse. The reader of *Mockingbird* knows, too, that the book is not originally Jem's and thus not the worldview of the adolescent most like Atticus. The book comes to Jem from Dill, avid and imaginative reader of the fantastic genre and harbinger of dramatic storytelling. Jem won the book from Dill in the very first chapter, successfully answering a dare to touch the Radley house. The circulating book is thus a recurring subject in *Mockingbird*. We can view *The Gray Ghost* as a sort of bookend in the novel, traveling between boys in chapter 1 and circulating into Atticus's library at the end.

My scholarship on *Mockingbird* is a long journey of uncovering of why *man thinking* is reading *The Gray Ghost* in the last scene of the novel. What phantoms lurk in the margins? First, it is very important that with *The Gray Ghost* Lee gives us no particular book in the real world whose specific story we can explore as an intertext. She does not do what Edith Wharton does with her character Charity Royall, who in an opening scene of *Summer* uses Maria Cummings's *The Lamplighter* to wind her lace. Lee refuses to be that specific in announcing her continuity and difference with literary tradition. Rather, Lee makes up a title that suggests several literary modes as operational and as embedded in her novel. On the most obvious level, she is suggesting that the gothic mode is one operational mode of her work, a mode that has been thoroughly analyzed by Johnson in her book *To Kill a Mockingbird: Threatening Boundaries.* Johnson demonstrates how gothic conventions and a fascination with "the other" define and unify *Mockingbird* aspects, including the various spatial boundaries and crossings in the novel. Hers is a satisfying and deeply meaningful account of what the stories of Boo Radley and Tom Robinson have to do with each other beyond the novel's own account of both as wrongly perceived and persecuted innocents. Charles Chappell names this unity thematic—the theme of learning to see from dual perspectives of self and other. Lee's own naming of Jane Austen as writerly model calls attention to gothic parody, as famously mocked in *Northanger Abbey* (see Blackall). Like Catherine Morland, Scout is erroneously and ridiculously obsessed with mapping a gothic onto everyday life, yet, like Catherine, Scout turns out to be not so very far off.

Second, it is noteworthy that *The Gray Ghost* could be any of a number of popular storytelling modes, opening up the idea that various novel and theatrical traditions inform *Mockingbird.* One such mode would be melodrama, a mode heavily influenced by the gothic. Racial melodrama defines the trial of *Mockingbird,* as I argue by showing the intertextuality of Harriet Beecher Stowe's *Uncle Tom's Cabin.* But the theatricality of the trial has already been practiced in part 1 of *Mockingbird:* in the children's elaborate reenactments of the Radley tragedy, a drama "of their own invention." If we understand the circulation of *The Gray Ghost* from Dill, who imports imaginative literature into a world "immune" to it, to Jem to Atticus, then we can understand this book as a transfer of Dill's intimate knowledge of ghosts. Atticus's Emersonian lens does not include ghosts, and he has to learn that ghosts exist. Dill already knows this; indeed, he is preoccupied with monsters, and we shall uncover why.

Ghosts like Boo Radley disrupt the enterprise of Atticus's reverence for the reading life. The reader learns, by report of Miss Stephanie, that when he stabbed his father with scissors, Boo was in the middle of cutting things out of *The Maycomb Tribune* for a scrapbook, an activity he calmly resumes after his sudden violence (11). We know Jem wins *The Gray Ghost* after touching and thereby imbibing a little bit of Boo and what he represents—madness, violence, disorder, and the unexpected disruption of patriarchy and enlightenment reading rituals—and we also know that Boo has been turned into a ghost, not through physical oppression but through a much more subtle process of psychological oppression: "Atticus said no, it wasn't that sort of thing [of being chained to a bed], that there were other ways of making people into ghosts" (11). Thus *The Gray Ghost* suggests the process whereby people like Tom and Boo, through marginalization, are made into ghosts. It should be noted that our tale-teller above is Miss Stephanie, who represents an oral tradition—a social tongue designed for popular effects, not unlike the popular tradition of melodrama and sentimental sensationalism "beneath the American Renaissance," argues David Reynolds.

Third, we need to explore the basic fact that *The Gray Ghost* is an object circulated "between men," to appropriate Eve Sedgwick's title of her book on women as objects of exchange, in a heavily patriarchal and arguably misogynist novel. We can observe that at the end of the novel Scout knows the story well (she tells Atticus), even though she herself has never owned the book. The book seems to suggest a cultural truth about knowledge owned by men yet known by girls and women, who thus may also be the ghosts mythologized in the book that Atticus has yet to read.

Fourth, we need to press deeply into the fact that *The Gray Ghost* is brought into the *Mockingbird* universe by an artistic outsider named Dill, "a curiosity" whom we know is based on the homosexual and eclectic writer Truman Capote, childhood and lifelong friend and colleague of Harper Lee. Sexual ambiguity preoccupied Capote in his writing, and the relationship between Dill, Boo, and the Finch household will temper our view of Atticus's tolerance.

Fifth, we need to understand the circumstance surrounding the reading of *The Gray Ghost* and the sensual scene of Atticus coming into the worldview of the children and particularly Scout, whom he lovingly undresses and tucks in at the end of *Mockingbird*. If we understand *The Gray Ghost* book as gesturing toward the common gothic mode of many post–World War II southern writers, we might then see alternative "genres" and meanings that Atticus may not understand. Lee tried to define herself against writings of the haunted and grotesque South, but as Jean Frantz Blackall eloquently states, the haunted and grotesque find their way in:

> The world Lee has undertaken to represent includes elements of violence and evil having no counterpart in Austen's fiction. In certain respects Lee's chosen sphere, her small southern town, is that of Mark Twain or William Faulkner or (nearer to home) Truman Capote. Drug addiction, alcoholism, incest, racial violence, an attempted lynching, imprisonment, Tom Robinson's suicidal despair leading to his violent death—all comprise this superficially orderly world. (21)

The valuable and "rich social pattern" of "a very small world," the passing of which Lee said she wanted to lament (Blackall 19), is not the whole story.

Therefore, *The Gray Ghost* quite broadly suggests alternative canons lurking in the subtexts of *Mockingbird*. These alternative canons include canons emerging to include other voices even as American romanticism informs the dominant story of Atticus, and Uncle Tom melodrama is "the book of" Tom Robinson. These alternative canons include nineteenth-century melodrama; southern gothic and deadpan humor; modern novels of unstable consciousness, duplicity, and passing; queer literatures; and modern women's regional novels, like Kate Chopin's *The Awakening*, in which women "awaken" only to become exhausted, sinking into the numbed trance of acquiescence in the end.

Atticus Finch has tended to steal the spotlight in discussions of *Mockingbird*, but the fact that at the end of the novel he is reading a book of the children's tells me there are many stories in his shadow. I hope to bring these stories to light. Atticus's journey as *man thinking* and appointed representative of "the one" in Emerson's philosophy will take us into a discussion of Emerson's "The American Scholar" in chapter 1. Tom Robinson's story will lead us to a consideration of *Uncle Tom's Cabin* in chapter 2. Scout's child consciousness and the older narrator's multivoiced discourse will lead us to consider Henry James's *What Maisie Knew* and Mark Twain's *Adventures of Huckleberry Finn* in chapters 3 and 4. Dill's journey to court Jem and Boo will lead us to the fiction of Truman Capote and Carson McCullers in chapter 5. And Scout's need to pass as a lady, in connection with her tendency to fall asleep in the last third of the novel, will lead us into the canon of modern women's regional writing, especially to Kate Chopin, Nella Larsen, Edith Wharton, and Carson McCullers. Bringing out these canons in the wings of *Mockingbird* ensures that unexpressed journeys in *Mockingbird* find expression. Though often taught for its historical value and its morality, *Mockingbird* is actually far more.

Canons in the Wings

To begin with a question about the end of *Mockingbird* is a fitting structure. After all, Lee chose to begin her retrospective and reflective novel *To Kill a Mockingbird* with the chronological end of her story. Lee's narrator begins the novel by telling us about the crippling of her brother Jem, which she subsequently explains by telling the story of the crippling of national justice and consciousness. Jem and, by extension, youth are clearly a synecdoche for a nation wounded from within. Like a house divided, Jem's broken elbow may heal, but it will always be marked and disabled; Jem's left arm is shorter than his right, just as Tom Robinson is crippled in his left arm, Laurie Champion argues ("Lee's *To Kill a Mockingbird*"), because the righteous like Atticus always shoot "'a little to the right'" (Lee 96), in the words of Heck Tate. The *Mockingbird* story of crippled righteousness has now been appreciated by the American public for fifty years, institutionalized for school-aged youth but remembered far beyond those years.

Yet, disturbingly, the opening passage of Lee's novel offers ambiguity about whether the children can absorb a lasting lesson from what they have witnessed. About his crippled arm, "[Jem] couldn't have cared less, so long as he could pass and punt" (3). At the end of her opening paragraph, then, Lee challenges us with the fundamental problem of human perspective and memory. We are all fundamentally trapped in our selfishness, with hopelessly flawed attention spans: "Maycomb was interested by the news of Tom's death for perhaps two days" (240). She seems to be asking us how long her book would live, given the habits of human beings to be utilitarian, apathetic, and forgetful.

Lee surrounds *man thinking* with characters facing the limitations of human consciousness. Her theory of imperfect humanity is essentially modern. She calls attention to the vexed process of epistemology by foregrounding

a study of child consciousness and of regionalism. Whereas many characters embody the inevitable bias of human perception, her most fully realized
symbol for the closeted nature of humanity is Boo Radley, whose embodiment of "the closet" impresses itself on young Scout.

The view of humanity advanced by modern literature wins, destabilizing Atticus's lessons about stepping into the skin of another, walking in a
man's shoes to really know him, and viewing one's street from another porch.
Succinctly put, the novel asks whether self-transcendence is in fact possible.
In Atticus's worldview, transcendentalism is possible. But the novel demonstrates the overwhelming limits of his worldview, an idealist view of our
connectedness that emerged in the nineteenth century with the philosophy
of the transcendentalists. Published at the crossroads of the civil rights era,
Mockingbird asks unanswered questions about the concept of transcendentalism that helped define the relationship between "the one, [and] the many"
(Emerson, "Plato," *Representative Men* 256) in nature, which a democratic
union would capture and which an independent American literature would
represent, incarnate, and help substantiate.

Mockingbird grapples with legacies of the nineteenth century that found
expression in a variety of American literary forms and that were both pressed
and challenged in the modernist and regional writing of the twentieth century.
The nineteenth century was a formative period for the American novel, for poetry, for the essay, and for an American point of view that would be expressed
in art and literature. Philosophical and literary writing concerned itself with
what the democratic experiment would look like as it came of age culturally
and aesthetically. Whereas Lee named Jane Austen as one of her models, explaining her successful study of social irony most comparable to *Northanger
Abby,* the comic story of a girl's obsession with *Mysteries of Udolpho,* Lee also
condensed many American authors in her unique distillation of national literary history. Lee belongs on a great variety of university syllabi as well as on
surveys of American literature, like *Beloved,* as a capstone.

In her entry on Lee, Carolyn Jones names Lee's literary heroes as Mark
Twain, Nathaniel Hawthorne, and Eudora Welty. We know, too, that Truman
Capote was for Lee an inspiring writer whose early work of southern regionalism must have influenced her, and whose career and prestige were
still rising during the years Lee composed and revised *Mockingbird.* Capote,
who was more open about, well, everything, named many nineteenth- and

twentieth-century American writers as influences, such as Henry James, Mark Twain, Edgar Allen Poe, Nathaniel Hawthorne, Willa Cather, Sarah Orne Jewett, William Faulkner, and Eudora Welty (*Other Voices* x). We can assume a similar canon of influence on Lee, who was collaborating with Capote on the research for *In Cold Blood* even as *Mockingbird* made its debut.

In his recent biography of Lee, Charles Shields observes that Carson McCullers, writing southern novels a decade before Lee, noticed the resemblance between *Mockingbird* and her own play and novel, *The Member of the Wedding*:

> The press had likened *To Kill a Mockingbird*'s nine-year-old narrator Scout to preadolescent Frankie in Carson McCullers's *The Member of the Wedding*, and the film version of McCullers's novel had flopped. (The surface similarities of the two novels were not lost on McCullers, either, who commented acidly about Lee to a cousin, "Well, honey, one thing we know is that she's been poaching on my literary preserves.") (192)

Lee poached on a whole lot of literary preserves, as all great authors do. Lee's debt to McCullers goes deeper than similar hunting ground, and through understanding Capote's and McCullers's concerns with freakishness, queerness, and inversion, we can understand more fully subtexts of *Mockingbird*, such as characters forced to live in drag. Mass adoption of *Mockingbird* for school-aged youth seems to have prevented critics from more openly teaching its frank preoccupation with making a closeted character "come out," even though no one can deny the homosexuality that Dill, who is most obsessed with Boo's coming out, inherently encapsulates. Obsession with freaks, drag, grotesque, and bodily infirmity is a hallmark of southern literature, as avowed by Flannery O'Connor, whose irony and Gothicism presage Lee's and who has some eerily similar child characters in various stages of awakenings and sleepwalking.

Our journey begins with Emerson's *man thinking* and ends with southern and other regional writing, but there are myriad contesting arenas to visit along the way. The influence of Harriet Beecher Stowe is more than obvious in some ways, but close comparison of *Mockingbird* and *Uncle Tom's Cabin* goes far beneath the surface of the ritual murder of the Tom characters.

Then there is the matter of Lee's focus on child consciousness, not only as focalizer but also as indicator of epistemological uncertainty. A term coined by narratologist Gerard Genette, "focalizer" refers to the character through whom a scene is presented, a narrative strategy added to the story to direct our response (Felluga 3). Seymour Chatman believes we can more properly understand focalization through the term "filter" or "slant" (144). Philippe Lejeune characterizes narratives of childhood as indirect freestyle (60). The style, pioneered by Jules Vallès, creates "a perpetual 'dissolve' or a 'double exposure' between the two voices" of older narrator and child filter, "so subtle" a transition that different readers may not agree on which voice is which (56). This sort of exercise in child study comes to the forefront when compared with Henry James's study of Maisie and Mark Twain's study of Huck.

Mental life can hardly be separated from point of view and voice, but Lee manages to separate it. The complex voices and narrative practices of *Mockingbird* have to be analyzed in their own right, both as stemming from a fusion of James and Twain and as taking on a female life of their own in *Mockingbird,* with its uniquely intrusive, manipulative, and comic older narrator. And whereas the arts of Capote's regional gothic about the same small town in *Other Voices, Other Rooms,* which turns comic in *The Grass Harp,* sharpen our reading of the queer Dill and Boo, regional women's writing brings out a different paradigm: a tradition of women who, at the end of textual awakenings, experience some sort of *passing* as passing out. The master writer of this regional novel of manners is not actually southern at all; Edith Wharton, with her similar *The Age of Innocence* and *Summer,* remarkably finds her way as a centerpiece to *Mockingbird* with its Wharton-styled Missionary Society scene and its reincarnation of Mrs. Mingott in Aunt Alexandra. All of these contesting canons, tackling human nature and subjectivity in philosophically distinct ways, find their way into the underpinnings of *Mockingbird.* All bring to the foreground different aspects of Lee's classic novel.

Fred Erisman discusses the correspondence between Atticus and Emerson in his essay on romantic regionalism, and William T. Going advances Lee's technique of child focalization as Jamesian in both his foreword to Alice Petry Hall's collection and his earlier comparison of *Mockingbird* to *The Store* in his *Essays on Alabama Literature* (28). But the amazing way in which both Emersonian theory and Jamesian technique can work their way into *Mockingbird* when they are at odds with each other in terms of their theories of human subjectivity needs to be addressed. Indeed, traditions at odds with one another define the many canons embedded in *Mockingbird*. My first chapter on *Mockingbird* and nineteenth-century philosophy makes it apparent that simply by evoking Emerson and Whitman a conflict occurs about what nature *is* and what about us is transcendent and connected to others. Is it the divinity of God or is it our animal bodies? Complexities upon complexities only proliferate as we disentangle and unfold the contesting nineteenth- and twentieth-century modes informing the multifaceted strands of *Mockingbird* that make it uniquely able to win President Bush's commendation and the endorsement of *Publishing Triangle*.

In chapter 1, "*Mockingbird* and Nineteenth-Century Philosophy: A Test Case for the American Scholar," I chart the presence of Emerson's influential construction of *man thinking* in the representation of Atticus Finch. Specifically, I analyze the way the novel offers "one"-shot Finch as "representative man" in the Emersonian sense of *man thinking* as delegate intellect of the transcendental "one." The chapter in which Atticus is christened One-Shot Finch foregrounds the very questions that Emerson sought to answer in "The American Scholar," where he defines four aspects of *man thinking*: the call to study nature; the call to dialogue study of nature with books; *man thinking* as active and therefore masculine; and the duties of the scholar. Not only does Lee offer Atticus as a divinely appointed "one," using Miss Maudie to interpret his actions as transcendental and as representative, but she also uses the children's questions about his masculinity to test the office of *man thinking* as active duty. Atticus's wisdom about human nature is legendary, but whereas he is *man reading* throughout much of *Mockingbird,* his study of nature and his theory of transcendentalism temper the value he places on reading; books, like law, are not everything, a key theme we see enacted in Scout, who is a fluent reader but as yet inexperienced in the laws of human nature.

I conclude the *man thinking* approach to Atticus by looking at Scout's view of the oversoul when she thinks about communal action while awaiting the verdict. I link the vision she has in that moment with the title's allusion to Whitman, who took a very different approach to people's connectedness and nature in his "body electric" poetry. Waiting for the verdict, the sleepy Scout thinks that if everyone together were to concentrate on setting Tom free, then he might be freed. However, she immediately realizes that if everyone were as tired as she, the action would not work anyway. Any reader would notice that Scout becomes increasingly sleepy in the last third of the novel, which is a convention of more modern literature in which characters "awakening," as paradigmatic in Kate Chopin's *The Awakening* and Nella Larsen's *Quicksand,* languish because there is "nowhere to go," Lee's famous words to describe childhood in Maycomb County. Whereas Atticus desires transparency and "oneness," expressed to Heck Tate when he says, "'I can't live one way in town and another way in my home'" (274), characters who are more identified with their bodies learn to negotiate social worlds through duplicity and passing, the acquisition of an identity that hides or veils a different identity. Characters like Cal who have "bodies that matter," as Judith Butler puts it in her book on how we imagine our bodies to be the root of our identities, lead a "modest double life" (125). They are, as Luce Irigaray put it in her essay about female difference, "this sex which is not one." Characters who are neither white nor male nor upper class are not "the one" representative man.

Virtually any character who is not Atticus lives a very different lifestyle— one embracing passion, body, and the varying requirements of social context. Whitman's poem about Alabama mockingbirds marks the speaker's intimate knowledge of, and duty to sing, the "dark brother's" grief about the sudden disappearance of his soul mate. If the slain mockingbird indicates all oppressed victims whose grief must be sung, the image also suggests all the diverse bodies behind Whitman's *Leaves of Grass,* which sings equally of the slave, the working class, and even the prostitute. Of his diverse bodies waiting to be sung, there is also the unseen gay body of his original *Calamus* sequence, which seems to lurk in the margins of the mockingbird poem's composition. Its presence can be intuited in Whitman's anonymous review of his poem, "All about a mocking-bird," in which he declares his return to his role as American bard after three years' silence. In the silence, he wrote a sequence of poems titled "Live Oak, with Moss," which relays the inadequacy of poetry in light of a gay love affair.

The dispassionate Atticus, who "could make a rape case as dry as a sermon" (169) and who, Scout initially claims, is "satisfactory" because he "treats us" with "a courteous detachment," is revealed to be unsatisfactory to a daughter attempting to gain access to his body and affection. An embedded discourse of passion, emotion, and melodrama becomes apparent when we compare *Mockingbird* to a very different literary tradition popular in the eighteenth and nineteenth centuries—that of the sentimental novel. Specifically, the type of democratic melodrama first glimpsed in Susanna Rowson's 1791 *Charlotte Temple,* a novel of female education, resurrected with a vengeance in Harriet Beecher Stowe's overwhelmingly influential racial melodrama: her 1852 *Uncle Tom's Cabin.* Chapter 2, "*Mockingbird* and the Nineteenth-Century Novel: Testimony to the Mythic Power of *Uncle Tom* Melodrama," charts the intertextuality of Stowe's novel. Because in *Mockingbird* the trial and death of Tom function as stage melodrama, with its tableaux of mute legibility and unrecognized virtue, I will theorize this tradition as a melodramatic mode and demonstrate how the popular form of uncomplicated racial melodrama makes *Mockingbird* particularly accessible, despite its complex narrative tissue, and how the ritualized presence of *Uncle Tom's Cabin* unlocks particular meanings.

The melodramatic persecution of the innocent Tom, "'licked a hundred years before we started,'" says Atticus, literally haunts both transcendentalism—his worldview—and the representation of consciousness in the novel, which I cover in chapter 3. But the comparison between *Mockingbird* and *Uncle Tom's Cabin* goes far beyond the crucifixion of the Tom figures. Ewell is a revised Legree, Mayella a revised Cassy, Atticus a revised Augustine, Aunt Alexandra a revised Aunt Ophelia, and Scout an integrated Eva-Topsy figure in whiteface. The melodramatic unveiling of spectacle and bodies in the trial gives the reader a really different experience from other portions of the novel, which are characterized by a detached, ironic, modern style. The form of melodrama in the *Mockingbird* trial literally overwhelms the earlier style of narration and it exhausts Scout, just as slavery murdered Eva again and again in melodramatic Tom shows. Such shows shaped an archetypal American drama in many twentieth-century texts, from the racist novels of Thomas Dixon Jr. to Richard Wright's *Native Son,* argues James Baldwin. While Tom Robinson and Wright's Bigger Thomas share the impossible position of white girls trying to kiss them, Lee neutralizes Bigger by her resurrection of Tom. She invokes the image of Bigger's powerful arms, which the racist press in *Native Son* views as bestial, only to deflate and diffuse Tom's "powerful shoulders" (185) with the emasculating disability that reifies his innocence.

When we understand the migration of *Uncle Tom's Cabin* into *Mockingbird,* and the updating of racial melodrama in courtroom drama, which was popular in the 1930s, we also have to keep in mind both Hawthorne's theory of the past in romance and his *The Scarlet Letter* as shadowing Topsy and Scout. *The Scarlet Letter* constructed tropes of American sin and the affixing of scarlet letters on single parents whose daughters bear the mark of their environments. Hawthorne's Pearl incarnates sins of American fathers in the same way as Topsy. Scout shares with Topsy and Pearl a witnessing of sin and the "passin'" of fathers whose public eloquence is ineffectual against overwhelming scarlet letters. Scout learns to rise by *passing* just like Topsy and Pearl because these daughters are born of environments and not just parents. Topsy tells Aunt Ophelia, "I spect I grow'd. Don't think nobody never made me" (356), while Pearl tells her examiners "she had not been made at all, but had been plucked by her mother off the bush of wild roses, that grew by the prison-door" (77). In other words, these otherworldly children are hybrids of systemic and sinful environments: the perfect audience for the community's ritual need to slay a mockingbird or "other" someone with scarlet smear.

Young Scout is a synecdoche for environmental conditioning, and thus *Mockingbird* is a study of the formation of child consciousness that can be profitably compared with two novel studies of child minds that marked the transitional period between mid-nineteenth-century literature and modernism: Henry James's *What Maisie Knew* and Mark Twain's *Adventures of Huckleberry Finn*. This is the approach of chapter 3, "*Mockingbird* and Modernist Method: Child Consciousness, or How Scout Knew," which demonstrates that Lee separates a masterful older narrator, who deploys irony, comedy, flashback, prolepsis, and foreshadowing for distancing effects in Scout's everyday world, from young Scout's consciousness, which in scenes beyond Scout's everyday world takes in impressions and sensory details in a less mediated manner. Scout shares with six-year-old Maisie the "long habit of spectatorship" indicative of Maisie's observations of her beloved Sir Claude, along with Maisie's passivity and status as an object; her tendency to focus on unusual, vivid, or familiar details of a scene, which obscures broader meaning; and her internalization of voices from her environment. Twain's Huck reasons in a similar way to Maisie and Scout, finding points of entry into new experiences by passively adapting to environment, by interpreting the people rather than the abstract moral situation, and by reasoning in a way that shows the penetration of his mind by others' voices.

In seeking to understand what Lee achieved with the style of impressionism that emerges whenever Scout's consciousness is the focalizer, we have to situate James's Maisie and Twain's Huck in the context of the inception of developmental psychology, a field that drove the new psychological methods of modernism forward and that was actually born from the insights of Charles Darwin. Darwin published an article about his child's growth of consciousness in 1877, and within thirty years the field had blossomed to the extent that developmental psychology would become the very principle of twentieth-century childhood. By understanding the ideological background to child consciousness in the American novel, we can best interpret why Lee embedded the consciousness of a child in *Mockingbird* and why doing so both gives the novel unique effects and destabilizes earlier literary traditions that implicitly believed knowledge was a stable matter. The representation of child consciousness is the putting forth of the modern view that thought and thinking are inseparable, that the human mind is inherently limited. We must place Scout in the theory of the stream of consciousness that the children Maisie and Huck exemplify.

These children mime and mimic even as they attempt to assert their independence, which is ironically expressed in moments of bargaining with progenitors. *Maisie, Huck,* and *Mockingbird* are ultimately novels about freedom, but final moral decisions become, instead of real freedom, opportunities to select which internalized voices the child will mime. Chapter 4, "*Mockingbird* and Modernist Polyphony: How Scout Tells, How Lee Laughs," presses the modernity of Scout's fusion of Maisie and Huck by focusing on how the older narrator manipulates the young Scout for irony, and how she uses her child self to show the composition of her future storytelling voice. I begin by looking closely at how Scout's bargains with Atticus, regarding reading and later Boo Radley, echo Maisie's bargains with Sir Claude, moments that ironically reveal mimicry for admission to gentlemen's clubs. When Maisie asserts she is free, she is only echoing Sir Claude, as she has increasingly done throughout *What Maisie Knew*. Similarly, Scout in the end must choose to verify the line "he fell on his knife," a scene in which she has become an object in a power struggle between Heck Tate, the local authority, and Atticus, the "one" who transcends the local. Huck's famous decision to help Jim is similarly a study of the limited strides a child can make: Huck manipulates the internalized voices of others by negotiating between Pap and the Widow, then deciding he will embrace hell (the Widow's sentiments) and steal Jim because he was "born to wickedness" (Pap-like sentiments).

These children make moral choices only accidentally, so the issue of freedom is beside the point. The real point is that the child can only think in the ways he or she has been taught to think—that voices penetrate the mind of a child. In comparing Huck and Scout, I make the case that both are changelings and experts at *passing* into various social situations. I then connect this chameleon identity to the older narrator's fascinating blend of languages, which can be sophisticated or blunt, "high" or "low," transcendent or local, depending on how she wishes the reader to feel about her subject.

The older narrator develops a unique insider/outside position in relation to Maycomb, setting herself up as an anthropologist or translator; she often foreshadows, summarizes, renders flashbacks, and interrupts immediate scenes to distance us from young Scout and to develop irony on the child and the region. The narrator thus demonstrates that she, like Cal, also leads a "modest double life," which is precisely why it is Cal, in her kitchen, who has taught Scout to write. If we look at other ladies in the novel, however, we find that womanhood in general is embrace of Huck Finn's chameleon identity and proficiency at passing. The most prominent "chameleon lady" is Miss Maudie, an obvious model for Scout in terms of gender inversion and *drag,* as well as vocal shape-shifting. Miss Maudie can pass with the ladies, but she can also use her voice in very strategic ways, shutting down Miss Stephanie and Mrs. Merriweather when she likes, yet opening up polite conversation when she wishes. The recipe that no one can copy—her fine cake with one *large* cup of sugar—communicates the narrator's admiration of her uniqueness, and it is thus crucial that Miss Maudie touches Scout's hand in the Missionary Society scene, when Scout must learn to pass as a lady by quite literally passing out cookies and hiding her grief for Tom.

The capacity to speak different languages to different communities becomes in *Mockingbird* comic and ironic. Thus, by comparing *Mockingbird* with *Huck,* I suggest that the skillful and comic older narrator of *Mockingbird* draws distance from young and limited Scout in the way that Twain only implies we are to experience Huck. In *Huck,* Twain leaves "deadpan Huck," as Sacvan Bercovitch calls him, on his own as Twain's comic mask, thereby putting the burden of interpretation on the reader, even while the opening notice warns against interpretation. Lee uses her older narrator to sketch her ironic stance in a more accessible way. My chapter on the many voices of Scout gives the image of the mockingbird this meaning: mockingbirds speak in a variety of dialects, you might say. They parody others. Through vocal parody and narrative irony, Lee reveals that she is laughing in the same fashion that O'Connor embraced laughter as a state of grace in her short fiction.

At the end of the chapter, I link the characters who laugh in the novel. The "inverted" characters Miss Maudie, Boo, and Dill all embrace laughter to cope with an intolerant and unfeeling universe. They indicate the mode of *Mockingbird*'s ironic narrator, connected because they enjoy a unique outsider position in relation to the small-town world. In fact, after the trial Dill vows that he will become a new kind of clown, the kind that laughs at people. This image of a comic aesthetic, voiced by the character based on Capote, symbolizes a stance inspirational to Lee and her decision to write *Mockingbird*. I link this to Hélèn Cixous's essay, "The Laugh of the Medusa," in which Cixous argues that women must write because we do not know what woman even is. Woman has not represented herself, but she has been represented as the Gorgon's head in male Western literature. If you just look at the Gorgon, Cixous writes, you will see that she is laughing. Similarly, Boo, at whom Scout is looking, is not frightening, but he is laughing. Lee is laughing and revising gender in the process. Despite the overt misogyny of the novel that makes it conform nicely to "Melodramas of Beset Manhood," defined by Nina Baym as the dramas of American romance critics value, there are subtexts to draw out, and they could be identified with feminist, queer, and postcolonial criticism.

Dill's journey emerges in chapter 5, "*Mockingbird* and Post–World War II Southern Writing: Dill, Capote, and the *Dragging Out* of Boo Radley." A queer theory approach to Dill's journey is logical when we consider both his characterization and his major quest to make Boo "come out," a phrase coined in the early twentieth century to indicate a man's entry into the gay community, appropriated from the debutante (Chauncey 7). After interpreting Boo as "an epistemology" of the closet (see Sedgwick), I look closely at Dill's efforts to "get closer" to Jem at the Radley *Camp* that Dill and Jem engineer for the children to perform, and at the homosexual invitations that Jem has to reject for Atticus's approval and for proper masculinity. We will see why it is that Jem loses his pants in the Radley yard, and why they are repaired but the stitches will always be crooked, and why he might be permanently wounded from events of discrimination and intolerance. Just what lessons does he have to learn from Mrs. Dubose? Jem's journey is inseparable from

Dill's need to come out; Jem has to become the male who doesn't care about his wounded arm "so long as he could pass and punt." Dill cannot become this male, and in a moving scene at the very core of *Mockingbird,* he admits this to Scout.

Closely reading Dill's appearance under Scout's bed as a scene of abjection, as Dill's desire for Atticus's acceptance, and as Dill's confession to Scout that his parents intuit and are repulsed by his queerness, we can compare Capote's core scene between Idabel (based on Lee) and Joel Knox (based on himself) in *Other Rooms, Other Voices.* Capote's view of how Idabel and Joel can enjoy a moment of connection swiftly turns into violence and carnival. In Capote's first published novel, also set in Monroeville, young Joel is haunted by a phantom drag queen, which sheds light on the meaning of Boo Radley, the quest for paternal approval, and the spiritual isolation of Miss Wisteria, with whom Idabel falls in love. Capote's vision of Lee's inversion and refusal to "come out" condemns her to yearn for an image of wounded femininity. Miss Wisteria, with her miniature perfection of the feminine, is the vulnerable, feminine counterpart to the wounded, masculine, and impenetrable Jem; she signifies Capote's view of Idabel (Lee) as stunted in her development. I also look at Capote's commentary on "men-women," gay desire, and wounded heterosexual men in *The Grass Harp,* in which the most horrid "morphodyte" character, Miss Verena, is pining for her lost love, Maudie. Verena's actions against Dolly are unpardonable, requiring a ritual shaming before she is made acceptable. Capote's view of the lesbian who does not understand herself is unkind. It is unlikely to be a coincidence that a lady with a distinctly pronounced masculinity named Miss Maudie appears as a model of passing for Scout in *Mockingbird.*

An understanding of latent homosexuality, passing, and a young girl's perspective can hardly be thorough without consideration of McCullers's *The Member of the Wedding,* which appears in both this chapter and the next. The manifestations of homosexuality and drag in *Member* bring out submerged themes in *Mockingbird,* themes that converge in the violent death of the feminine boy John Henry of *Member,* parallel to Lee's quiet abandonment of Dill. Comfortable with his freakish femininity in a way Frankie, the focalizer, is not, John Henry, once deceased, haunts Frankie like a painted dummy with wax legs escaped from a department store window, just as Lee leaves Dill as the laughing clown. Figures of carnival, art, and freakish bodies, these effeminate boys are not allowed to pass into the social world, whereas the girls will. I conclude the chapter with a deconstruction of all the multifaceted symbolism Boo brings out when he finally appears. Atticus says in reading *The Gray Ghost* that most people are nice when you finally see them. Boo's appearance is not at all nice, and what Scout sees from his porch is, well, herself as Boo's child. But this is her old self, like Frankie looks at her old self, and not the lady self newly acquired. Linking this important textual moment with Linda Williams's film theory, "When the Woman Looks" at monsters in cinema, I conclude that the closeted Boo is simply not an option for Scout anymore. Scout's fantasies of Boo have radically altered in the last chapters of the novel, and when she sees him she is fully the lady, hosting him, ensuring his comfort, using her "best company manners," and putting his arm on hers so he will appear the gentleman when crossing the street—in case Miss Stephanie should see. This radical alteration in Scout only bespeaks how fully she has absorbed lessons taught by the ladies of the Missionary Society, which is because the young lady of Maycomb is actually now in a new canon altogether: the novel of manners, imported into Scout's life when Aunt Alexandra takes her under *her* wing.

My final chapter, "*Mockingbird* and Modern Women's Regional Writing: Awakening, Passing, and Passing Out," takes as its focus a long twentieth-century tradition of women's novels in which regional environments gradually close in on protagonists until they are forced to *pass* or *pass out,* which usually amounts to the same thing. The suicide of Kate Chopin's Edna Pontellier bespeaks her desire for eternal rest from the exhaustion of *passing* in an overwhelming environment. Like Scout, Edna is often falling asleep in the heat, and the intertext of "Rip Van Winkle" clarifies the meaning of the trope. Likewise, rhythms of sleeping and awakening that culminate in a state of final numbness define Nella Larsen's rewriting of Edna in her mulatto character Helga Crane, who experiences vertigo each time she realizes that a particular social role is an inadequate act of *passing* (Cutter 78). Although this exhaustion or final descent, sometimes even madness, closes many modern women's novels as feminist parables, Edith Wharton's novels of manners provide the most influential intertext to Lee's view of the social world as a primitive world thriving on rituals of exclusion and elaborate "tissues of mutual dissimulation." Wharton's *Age of Innocence* shares with *Mockingbird* anthropological language as it studies the caste system of a particular region;

like Wharton, Lee uses words like "tribe," "clan," and family "streaks" not only to identify the narrator as a participant observer engaged in anthropological research, but also to subtly link her Maycomb ladies to the ruling matriarchs of Wharton's New York society. In fact, the "formidable" and corpulent Aunt Alexandra, Lee's comic caricature, is an import from *Age of Innocence,* the reincarnated and transplanted Mrs. Catherine Mingott, whose royal reign of New York society is unquestioned, just as Aunt Alexandra immediately sets up her royal dominion in Maycomb social life.

Understanding Lee's "age of innocence" in the guise of childhood, we can then understand the emergent consciousness of masculine Scout as aligned with Newland Archer, who is able to analyze the social ritual, participate in it, and then laugh at his own participation. In a crucial scene modeled on Wharton's famous dinner parties, Scout takes up the baton to pass as a lady. Deconstruction of the multiple occurrences and symbolism in the Missionary Society scene demonstrates how Maycomb stages elaborate rituals to exclude "the foreign," just as Wharton's New York rallies around its kinswoman May to exclude the "foreign" threat Madame Olenska as well as the Jew, Julius Beaufort. Newland's decision to pass and play at innocence parallels the "modest double" life that Scout takes on in the Missionary Society scene, when she is led across the threshold by Cal, by her mother's coffee pitcher, by Miss Maudie, and ultimately by Aunt Alexandra, of whom the narrator says, "if Aunty could be a lady at a time like this, so could I" (237).

Literally passing out cookies to the ladies and controlling the shaking of her response to Tom's execution, Scout is assuming a state of being that is inherently linked to the trance of being in which we find her in much of the last third of the novel. The awakened simply have to sleep or leave. To understand how this works in the consciousness of a young girl, we have to look back at Wharton's earlier novel *Summer,* which depicts a young girl's lack of opportunities and rewrites the sexuality of *Charlotte Temple* with a frank view of female desire, like *Mockingbird* of Mayella, but closes down Charity Royall's options with the weightiness of North Dormer. Like James, Wharton is a pivotal figure in the transition from the mid-nineteenth-century novel of a girl's growth to the twentieth-century's view of her "inside" response to growth. Charity is in a trance by the end, pregnant and forced to marry her guardian, who initially adopted her from "the Mountain," tantamount to the backwoods of Maycomb, where female desire can be expressed.

A significant scene for Charity occurs during Old Home Week, which is parallel to the community pageant at the end of *Mockingbird*. To understand why these historical pageants are turning points in the lives of girls, we have to historicize the fashion of the historical pageant, which underwent transition in the early twentieth century (see Glassberg). The cheesy historical pageant in the early part of the twentieth century was connected to the summer camp movement, which would put on pageants in an attempt to mythologize "the indigenous"—a word that, Susan Miller argues in her book on girls' organizations like the Girl Scouts, had reached mythic proportions by the twenties and thirties (29). Rural places were trying to survive in the modern period, so measures like the pageant are not surprising. Their mission of civic engagement and appreciation for place, however, makes them darkly parodic spectacles of confinement in *Summer* and *Mockingbird*.

The trope of endless summer in *Summer* and the shutting down of female possibilities can also be located in McCullers's *Member of the Wedding*, which, however, ends ambiguously. My chapter concludes by returning to McCullers's Frankie, who longs for the summer of her discontent to end, and poses questions about the novel's ending—whether it informs the ambiguity of *Mockingbird*'s ending sleep. The African American characters Berenice, with one blue and one brown eye, and Honey, a "man God had not finished" who is internally divided, function as indices of duplicity within Frankie, just as the duplicitous characters in *Mockingbird* do for Scout. After interpreting the ending of *Member*, in which Frances (no longer Frankie or F. Jasmine) is now in a relationship with Mary Littlejohn, and together they appreciate the arts, I posit questions about whether Scout is similarly in what Frankie calls a prison you cannot see. Scout heads to an exhausted sleep, a sort of mini-death, but she affirms Atticus's secure presence at Jem's bedside—not hers, probably because she has passed out of her father's world. She has in some ways tamed Atticus, as shown by his new reading material and his undressing her and tucking her in. However, the ending of *Mockingbird* is a conventional gesture of lying in wait for something. It suggests various postures of "Waiting for Godot," along with worry that one might sleep through it even if he should come, which Jem has done.

Sleeping and Awakening, Snowing and Dragging: History and Theory

Many of the characters in *Mockingbird* actually engage in Maisie's long habit of spectatorship; the mood of watching and waiting prolongs the tension of the novel. Dill patiently waits by the telephone pole for Boo; Atticus waits at the jail, waits for the judgment; Jem waits for Mrs. Dubose to sleep; Scout waits for Jem, waits for Boo, waits for the jury. The tension of waiting and of the winds of change slowly descending, like the town's weak but significant snowfall, defines a predominant mood—like "the waiting place" captured in Dr. Seuss's *Oh the Places You'll Go!* The mood, likely foundational to childhood experience, is often crystallized in young Scout's tendency to nod off while waiting. Just as Chopin's southern novel *The Awakening* repeatedly deployed the tension between sleeping and waking present in the nation's early literature like "Rip Van Winkle," the rhythm of oscillation in *Mockingbird* marks also the tension between the setting of the depression and the awakening era of its publication.

Sleeping is a human reaction to trauma, of course, and the movement between drifting in and out of consciousness describes Scout's state of mind throughout the trial of Tom Robinson. The town of Maycomb is initially presented as a tired and sagging town, and images of stillness pepper the narration of the trial and repeatedly come to Scout's attention. She wonders how it is that even the babies are still, and the imagery of stillness reminds her of the street awaiting the mad dog, when even the mockingbirds were still. Stillness and sleepiness suggest stasis and resistance to development, but they also suggest escape from entrapment in a town where "there was nowhere to go" if one is awake—awake meaning consciousness of confinement.

Yet the mood of stillness throughout *Mockingbird* and in its ending is a tense stillness that amounts to anticipation. We can understand Scout's descent into slumber as a strategy for showing us both that she has been overwhelmed by what she has witnessed and that there is "nowhere to go" for a girl fighting environment. Similarly, we can best understand Atticus's mythical presence, his vigil of bedside waiting, and his reading of *The Gray Ghost* by looking at the anticipatory reading that closes an earlier politically persuasive story: Frederick Douglass's first edition of his slave narrative published in 1845. Douglass's ending anticipates the need for change that has not been realized. Newly settled in New Bedford, Douglass is offered a subscription to the "Liberator," the antislavery publication run by William Lloyd Garrison:

> The paper came, and I read it from week to week with such feelings as it would be quite idle for me to attempt to describe. The paper became my meat and my drink. My soul was set all on fire. Its sympathy for my brethren in bonds—its scathing denunciations of slaveholders—its faithful exposures of slavery—and its powerful attacks upon the upholders of the institution—sent a thrill of joy through my soul, such as I had never felt before! (151)

Literacy is a powerful tool and symbolic trope throughout Douglass's *Narrative,* just as it is in *Mockingbird.* The closing image of Douglass reading is a moving symbol of his access to definitions of American manhood, but it also an anticipatory stance suggesting he is waiting for freedom through necessary social change. The image of Atticus as a man reading and waiting, while Scout sleeps, has a similar resonance and tension. Tension between action and stillness that anticipates action and prolongs suspense is part of aesthetic craft, of course, a way that scenes feel "drawn out" and readers feel suspense. But more than that, the tension between the novel's sleepy setting and time of publication can fuel our retrospective lens at how Lee simultaneously captures the thirties and the fifties.

Critics generally stress the historical context of Lee's childhood, which is important. For example, they might stress the patterning of Atticus on Amasa Lee or Judge Horton, the judge who gave a moving speech to the Scottsboro boys' jurors about unprejudiced justice and who ordered a new trial, generally understood as the most widely publicized trial of the thirties. Certainly the fictional Maycomb sounds like McComb in Mississippi, the state if not precise location of the initial Scottsboro trials. Other specific trials have been discussed in application to *Mockingbird* sources, but as Petry puts it, "as with most works of the imagination, one cannot readily point to a single 'source'" (xxi) as definitive.

Moates in *A Bridge of Childhood* has given us a profound glimpse of Lee's childhood Monroeville through her presentation of the memories of Jennings Faulk Carter, model for Jem (argues Jennings), who spent summer days with his imaginative cousin Capote and the young Nelle Lee. The way life permeates novels is always true but never direct; Lee appropriated many of Capote's experiences in her fiction, including a situation with Sonny Boular (Boo Radley's living counterpart), that ended with him being threatened by the local Klan while in a restrictive robot costume. On the whole, however, we also need to be forever mindful of the civil rights environment into which *Mockingbird* launched. In his essay on *Mockingbird,* Patrick Chura effectively argues for the analogy between Tom Robinson's trial and the trial of Emmett Till, demonstrating the blinders that can cover our eyes if we exclusively focus on the period of the novel's setting. Chura defines the novel as a cross-historical montage (1).

The stagnation trope present in Maycomb's description and in many scenes of watching, waiting, and sleeping represents the setting of 1933 and a depressed economy, whereas the mood of anticipation and tension—something about to happen, which characters are waiting *for*—points toward the civil rights era in which *Mockingbird* made its debut. The style of reminiscence, which can be linked to Whitman's first mockingbird version in "A Child's Reminiscence," must be understood as particularly tense because the memory emerged in a time of escalation, violence, and calls for rights crying out to be heard. In her study of law in *Mockingbird,* Johnson writes, "The three years at the end of the 1950s, when the novel was written, form one of the most turbulent periods of race relations in a state with a turbulent history, a time when a long-standing relationship between blacks and whites, maintained in refutation of the spirit of American democracy, was being tested in the courts" ("Secret Courts" 129), by both the Supreme Court's 1954 ruling that school segregation was unconstitutional and the important events of Rosa Parks refusing to give up her seat for a white passenger in 1955 and Autherine Lucy's enrollment in the University of Alabama in 1956 (130).

The *Brown v. Board of Education* decision, Chura argues, fueled southern anxieties about racial mixing, specifically regarding interracial sex (2). However, the 1955 trial of Emmett Till's murderers, a trial that similarly emphasized Till's disability (his speech impediment) and prosecutors who tried to see justice served despite the jury's quick decision to find the accused not guilty, left many feeling that the courts had not done their office:

By the end of Lee's novel, then, the limitations of a particular and highly historically relevant ideological apparatus have been exposed, and the law is,
even for Atticus, reduced to a ritual in which absolute faith is no longer possible. Through this process we perceive the potential instability of the structure of legal order in the South on the verge of the violent convulsions that
attended the civil rights era. . . . Lee's novel therefore ends where the civil
rights movement begins, with a resolve born of disillusionment to improvise
ways and means of justice both within and outside a system that could convict Tom Robinson and acquit Emmett Till's murderers. (Chura 9)

Johnson looks at patterns of extralegal quests for justice occurring in Alabama
in the late 1950s ("Secret Courts" 138), and Doris Betts sees the two perspectives in *Mockingbird*—the child of the thirties and the narrator's voice of the
fifties—as related to the division between setting and publication: "During
the year *Mockingbird* was published, Dr. King was already leading civil rights
demonstrations. Young black students (always in the press called 'Negroes')
had staged sit-ins at lunch counters that spread from Greensboro to Raleigh,
Charlotte, Atlanta, Birmingham, Little Rock, Nashville, and Montgomery.
That spring there was a race riot in Biloxi, Mississippi" (139). In her view,
Atticus's naming of his inroad as "the shadow of a beginning" is true, despite Harold Bloom's account of *Mockingbird* as provocative of "America's
own lost innocence" before the 1960s (140–41). Oddly, the novel can be both
things—about innocence and violence—depending on your point of view.

The tension between the sleepy past and the awakening present makes
the novel have the effect of an anticipatory pause. As Twain puts it in the more
humorous context of Pudd'nhead Wilson's manipulation of artistic effects in
court, "the stillness gives warning that something is coming" (*Pudd'nhead*
136). *Mockingbird* employs these effects masterfully. Indeed, the continual
obsession with waiting for Boo to come out and expecting to see him, at any
moment, in the light of the sun, or waiting for a mad dog to walk down the
street, is an effective literary representation of the political scene in the 1950s.
It's a southern sort of "Waiting for Godot," the title of Samuel Beckett's existential play that, incidentally, premiered in 1953 and perhaps bears a similar
mood, especially concerning its subtitle of "tragicomedy in two acts," which
accurately describes *Mockingbird*.

Lee puts the Depression in our minds with her mocking voice, "Maycomb County had recently been told it had nothing to fear but fear itself" (6), quoting without citation Franklin D. Roosevelt's address to the nation as he tried to buoy its spirit in the face of extreme poverty, high unemployment, low production, defaulted properties, and in the South continuing activities of the Klan that he chose not to emphasize, much to Eleanor Roosevelt's discontent. Eleanor Roosevelt is named (with disdain) in the Missionary Society scene. She, who resigned from the Daughters of the Revolution when they refused Marian Anderson use of Constitution Hall and who arranged an alternative site for the concert, might have interpreted *The Gray Ghost* as the unresolved issue of violence against African Americans. Atticus, we are informed in the novel, cannot even fathom the possibility of Klan activities in his worldview of the rational human being.

But the scene that Lee entered with her novel looked somewhat different; federal power had altered with the Second World War and was now looking to enforce its powers against states. In 1954 *Brown v. Board of Education* had overturned segregation in public schools as established by *Plessey v. Ferguson* in 1896. As C. Vann Woodward's 1955 *The Strange Career of Jim Crow* ended by observing, the Jim Crow system was beginning to crack. President Truman had desegregated the military; the Montgomery Improvement Association, with the assistance of Martin Luther King Jr., had organized the Montgomery bus boycott in 1955–1956; and in 1957 President Eisenhower determined to enforce federal law in Little Rock. The years of writing *Mockingbird*, composed in New York and revised with the assistance of editors who helped turn Lee's disparate collection of childhood stories into a strong novel with a unifying theme, saw the donning of many crusades for rights that eventually would flower in second-wave feminism and later gay rights.

The cooler winds of change and integration can be found in the snowman the Finch children make when the heavens suddenly open over Maycomb and the sky falls, Apocalyptic fashion. Gerald Early ends his essay on *Mockingbird* with a reflection on the "nigger snowman," which is the term used by the *limited* child-Scout, as "a mixed-race snowman." In a novel of isolates, one of whom is "sickly white," "even in a world where nature is racialized and we have a 'nigger snowman,' we know that the white snow falls upon the black earth. There they become one, and different from what they were separately" (Early 102–3). The symbol, like the novel of 1960, suggests the winds of change in a variety of ways. Heaven and earth seem to be moving. Though an image of mixed race, the snowman is likewise "an uneasy coexistence of femininity and masculinity" (Richards 133); he is a model of Mr. Avery and thus exposes the mockery occurring in the narrative stance. At Atticus's objection to caricature, the children *drag* the snowman, much as Jem has dragged mountains of dirt to make him in the first place. They give him Miss Maudie's hat and garden clippers, and Miss Maudie, the "chameleon lady" who wears britches all morning and becomes a lady after her afternoon bath, is a clear index of the invert.

The snowman passes as white and is whitewashed so he does not resemble a person at all, but this is because there is a subtext in *Mockingbird* of drag and sexual difference, equally important in an era of "McCarthyite witch hunts" (Butt 9). In his study of the role of gossip and underground codes in New York art circles between 1948 and 1963, Gavin Butt discusses how the period ushered in a hermeneutics of suspicion regarding homosexuality. In 1948 Alfred Kinsey had published his report on male sex behavior, in which he asserted that homosexual actions were far more predominant than previously thought, and in which he defined homosexual actions on a variable scale rather than simply "homosexual" or "heterosexual." The report's assertion of the widespread occurrence of male homosexuality, like the vague fears of interracial sex imagined in the wake of the *Brown* decision, made people fear and fantasize about how visibly masculine bodies might harbor latent homosexual tendencies and inversion, the concept—popularized in English by Havelock Ellis—widely applied to the homosexual.

While George Chauncey has documented gay communities in New York that were thriving in the earlier decades of the century—highly visible in the drag balls and pansy craze of the early thirties—what particularly alarmed homophobic Americans after Kinsey's report was the sense that homosexuals were perhaps not visibly gay-coded but were passing as "normal" men. The period of the thirties through the fifties saw a gradual reorganization of men defined as hetero- or homo- because of sexual object-choice, whereas this binary axis was not the predominant one of earlier time periods, when the visible effeminacy of the pansy or the gender "invert" defined the "queer" more than object-choice. The crackdown on homosexuals beginning in the thirties was part of "the crisis in gender arrangements precipitated by the Depression," Chauncey writes: "As many men lost their jobs, their status as breadwinners, and their sense of mastery over their own futures, the central tenets undergirding their gender status were threatened. A plethora of sociological studies of 'The Unemployed Man and His Family' reflected a widespread concern that massive male unemployment and job insecurity had upset gender relations and diminished the status of men in the family" (354). The Depression setting and questions about manhood and aggressive female desire in Lee's novel suggest this crisis in masculinity, given that men such as Mr. Cunningham are indeed having trouble supporting families.

However, the period in which Lee actually composed her novel saw a new reactionary ideal in the postwar boom, following a war in which many people "came out under fire" (Bérubé), of men as domesticated family men. They were idealized as nonaggressive father figures and prototypes of the "organization man," navigating corporate hierarchies by depending "less on personal ambition and individual initiative than on respect for authority, loyalty to one's superiors, and an ability to get along with others—all qualities traditionally associated with femininity" (Corber 5–6). The ending of Lee's novel does, in fact, domesticate Atticus, whose individual conscience threatens his family's security. Corber argues that many men protested this sort of domesticated man in various ways (9), framing his study of authors Tennessee Williams, Gore Vidal, and James Baldwin. *Mockingbird* constructs a range of masculinities, anchoring this range with its core plot of a victimized black man.

Paradoxically, even as this new domestic ideal of manhood was promoted, worries about masculinity and homosexuality became an obsessive concern in Cold War America, when the Senate Subcommittee on Investigations defined homosexuals as a threat to national security (Kaiser 78–79). A 1948 cartoon by Herb Williams, originally appearing in the *New York Times Book Review* and reprinted in *Life,* featured a female reader of the Kinsey report looking suspiciously at her husband as he sits reading the newspaper. The caption reads "New worlds of suspicion . . . were opened to doubting wives by Kinsey's revelations on men" (Butt 33). In his book *Monsters in the Closet,* Harry Benshoff quotes a 1958 article in the men's magazine *Sir!* titled "It's the Day of the Gray Flannel Fag." The article writer, who claimed to be addressing women, though it was, after all, a men's magazine, wrote with paranoia: "They design dresses, decorate homes, sell antiques, make the rounds of Broadway producers' offices. But what throws unsuspecting women is that they also can be found heading Wall Street firms, boxing in Madison Square Garden and playing baseball. There's no telling where a gray flannel he-man fag will turn up" (qtd. in Benshoff 132).

Worries about masculinity and homosexuality were newly organized around the issue of passing, mirroring the Red Scare. Harris Mirkin writes of a typical photo essay on homosexuals in *Life* (1964) that it "began by asking if homosexuals, like Communists, intended to bury us. The problem was that homosexuals were furtive, and for every obvious homosexual there were probably nine undetected ones" (9). Extreme antics of surveillance and tricks were used by police, civil service committees, the FBI, and post office to ensnare homosexuals, who were prohibited from bars and places of entertainment (see Chauncey), from entering the country or having government jobs (Kaiser 80; Mirkin 11), and from being represented in movies.

Homosexuality was at once everywhere and nowhere, rather like the closeted Boo: "Homosexuality was brought into discourse as an object of epistemological doubt: in which it was discursively constituted, by turns, as being both everywhere and nowhere" (Butt 26). Homosexual innuendo was particularly rampant in the art world, which both the snow*man* and Dill's various artifices suggest. Such 1950s gay publications as *One* circulated the assumption that there was a special connection between the homosexual and artistic genius, ruminating in 1954, for example, on Walt Whitman as gay poet. Codes, like having the statue of Michelangelo's *David,* might signal homosexuality in a particular home, all under the guise of high culture. Bronski argues that "the aesthetic contribution" has often functioned as gay men's ticket to social acceptance, an image we can locate in the "quasi-Wildean figure" (Butt 116) of Capote, who takes a leading role in *Mockingbird* and who registers the pain of the trial as if it reflects on himself.

American parents so feared turning their male children into homosexuals that advice columns on discouraging effeminacy flourished. Julia Grant notes that one possible reason is new roles for men in the postwar workplace, roles that did not require "the traditional masculine virtues of strength, courage, and decision-making" (119). *Mockingbird*'s preoccupation with parenting belies the fifties' general preoccupation "with identifying the type of parenting that would perpetuate 'appropriate' sex roles in children and prevent children, especially boys, from growing up to be homosexual" (Minter 12). Scout certainly views Atticus's job as effeminate. With his snowman, Jem, who is deeply concerned with building a more masculine body and whose "soft brown eyes . . . were our mother's" (152), initially designs a crystal clear masculinity, based on Mr. Avery, whom in another scene the children witness urinating with exceptional prowess. At Atticus's pressure, Jem sculpts the invert, paradoxically satisfying Atticus's desire for passing and for revising masculinity. The making of the snowman causes the neighbors to shake their heads at the perceived unruliness of youth, marking the onset of youth culture that would change the cultural landscape and American tolerance in years to come. The sense that the heavens and earth are moving accompanies the craft of human manipulation in the snowman. Through a fifties perspective on Atticus and masculinity set in the thirties, there is a suggestion that many changes are on the horizon, but that masculinity and homosexuality might still be a highly contested area.

Bronski argues that although the connection between, for example, homosexuals and the Harlem Renaissance, or the fondness of gay men for black arts such as the blues, is acknowledged, in general activist groups of the fifties and sixties promoted their causes through excluding people from their identity category. Black civil rights leaders and nationalists tended to deemphasize homosexuals; for example, in the sixties "black nationalists demanded that Harlem's Apollo Theater cease its presentation of drag shows" (Bronski 75). Similarly, women's movements promoted a vision of feminism that seemed insensitive to working-class women and women of color. Homosexual groups like the Mattachine Society, organized in 1953, seemed exclusively focused on whites and men, although the lesbian Daughters of Bilitis was founded in 1955. Showing the interconnectedness of those confined to the closet, those racially persecuted, and the perspective of a girl resisting Maycomb femininity, *Mockingbird* is a truly remarkable novel. It turns a sympathetic lens on characters as diverse as Mayella, mixed-race children, and men like Dolphus Raymond and Atticus who must face questions about their masculinity. And *Mockingbird* gives space to this wide range of individuals by passing with fairly conservative readers who can enjoy the novel for very different reasons.

Recent critical writings have productively examined the intersection of race and queer studies, providing us with a framework for understanding how *Mockingbird* might uniquely combine racial discrimination with construction of the homosexual closet in Cold War America (see Corber), the construction of which began in earnest in the thirties: "To use the modern idiom, the state built a closet in the 1930s and forced gay people to hide in it" (Chauncey 9). In her book *The Color of Sex: Whiteness, Heterosexuality, and the Fictions of White Supremacy,* Mason Stokes examines the construction of whiteness and white supremacy, especially in the racist novel that Thomas Dixon wrote after seeing a stage version of *Uncle Tom's Cabin* in 1901 (5), as dependent on the active construction of white heterosexuality. Following the insights of Sedgwick into the English novel (*Between Men*), Stokes finds that white women and black men are the objects exchanged and controlled to support white manhood in Dixon's *The Leopard's Spots: A Romance of the White Man's Burden, 1865–1900* (1902), "in which homosociality of racial desire and hatred is most transparent":

> At almost every turn in the plot, Dixon finds himself narratively dependent on white women and black men in positions of exchange. In the novel's obsession with alleged black sexual crimes against white women, white men use these women as a battleground for their complicated skirmishes with black men. In the novel's larger allegiance to the conventional romance plot, a white woman is given from white man to white man in marriage, a move that ultimately consolidates white male political power at the expense of both white women and black men, dramatizing the extent to which white supremacy is more properly understood as white-male supremacy. In *The Leopard's Spots,* then, the campaign for white supremacy is more properly understood as white-male supremacy. (134)

The trope of paranoia regarding rape of white women—"the subject *par excellence* of Southern literature in the nineteenth and twentieth centuries" and "a concern as obsessive as that with seduction in eighteenth century England" (Fiedler, "Afterword" 316)—is inseparable from a broader homosocial context in which Mayella and Tom are exchanged. While the latter is feminized in the structure, the former paradoxically exposes the perverse sexuality of the belle in twentieth-century literature (see Seidel, *Southern Belle*), historically denied sexual impulses, even as Lee keeps the upper-class gentleman's daughter (Scout) pure. Like the raped character Mary Clay in *Death in the Deep South* (1936), Mayella is not a belle but is defended as if she were, showing her structural rather than personal importance. The defense of the rapist in a similar trial novel *Act of Darkness* (1935), includes the man's claim (here, white and a gentleman) that *he* and not the woman was ravished. This queering of sexual panic has profound impacts on the young male narrator of the novel, bearing striking similarities to Lee's novel.

Similarly viewing the potential for Sedgwick's later work (*Epistemology*) to apply to race theory in American culture, Maurice O. Wallace innovatively looks at the relationship between architectural metaphor and black male subjectivity in African American men's literature, finding that Sedgwick's metaphor of the closet operates analogously as space into which men withdraw as relief from the pervasive meanings accorded to black male bodies in public space. Innovatively reading the closet into which Frederick Douglass withdraws upon the beating of Hester as an enactment of his own fears of rape, an initiatory scene analogous to young Scout's witnessing of the trial, Wallace goes on to suggest that such closeted moments are desires for interiority, related but not identical to moments of masking in African American literature. African American men have faced a particular crisis in the coordination of inside/outside perspectives; as Baldwin put it in "The Black Boy Looks at the White Boy," "It is still true, alas, that to be an American Negro male is also to be a kind of walking phallic symbol: which means that one pays, in one's own personality, for the sexual insecurity of others" (qtd. in Wallace 150). His comment is particularly ironic given that the FBI put him under surveillance for his political activities and suspected homosexuality (Wallace 138–40). By exposing the black male body as public spectacle with racist sexual meaning, and then replicating Stowe's strategy of castrating it, in Baldwin's words about Stowe "divest[ing]" her "only black man" "of his sex" (17), Lee frames the ravished and handicapped Tom in what Wallace calls spectragraphia. Both Wallace and Baldwin use the metaphor of price or payment extracted from the black man for the sexual paranoia of others, which in *Mockingbird*'s queer perspective enframes not only the principal black male character but also one of the only married ones.

The productive intersection between race and queer studies is especially apparent in the second generation of southern writing following the Southern Renaissance, as extensively analyzed by Gary Richards in his interpretations of sexual otherness in novels by Capote, Lillian Smith, Lee, and McCullers. Like Lee, Capote and McCullers center their fiction on queer white characters (called "gender transitive" rather than "queer" by Richards), who find in both disabled and African American characters similar marginality. African American characters often register violence that, in effect, warns queer characters to closet and pass for "normal" if they can. In her article "'A Mixture of Delicious and Freak': The Queer Fiction of Carson McCullers," Rachel Adams argues that McCullers "engages in a project of social criticism that, at its most penetrating, reveals the links between sexual intolerance and racial bigotry" (553). McCullers continually attacks the intertwining of racism and sexism by featuring deviant or freakish bodies, such as those of Frankie and Berenice in *Member,* and Jester and Sherman in *Clock without Hands.* Freakish bodies reflect young characters intuiting and fearing queer sexualities. In her 1961 novel, *Clock without Hands,* in which critics supposedly spotted the influence of *Mockingbird* and which made Lillian Smith uncomfortable because it too neatly included "'all the ingredients for a New York success'" (interracial sex, politics, adolescence, vague homosexuality, senseless violence) (Richards 159–60), a clearly homosexual character, Jester, has read the Kinsey report and fears being called homosexual. However, he is overwhelmingly attracted to an African American male character with blue eyes. Blue-eyed Sherman dies when his house is burned by the white characters, punishing him for buying into a white neighborhood. Whereas the link between closeted gays and African American characters in McCullers's fiction reflects Cold War politics that policed both, a theme almost cliché in the publishing environment, "the crucial distinction between racial and sexual difference is that queer sexuality has the potential to remain dangerously undetected, whereas race in McCullers's fiction is the visible signifier of difference in spite of her characters' attempts to alter or conceal bodily attributes that make them targets of discrimination and abuse" (Adams 567). The difference is the ability to pass, a major theme of *Mockingbird* that requires some context and definition.

Racial passing, such as George Harris's escape from slavery by passing for Spanish in *Uncle Tom's Cabin* (see Stern 103–27), had long been a concern of white America, which created in the 1896 ruling for *Plessey v. Ferguson* the "one-eighth" legal definition of Negro ancestry, or functionally the "one drop of blood" rule (Ginsberg 6–7; Wald 11–13). In his inquiry into the complex intersection between definitions of homosexual and racialized bodies in sexology texts at the turn of the century, Siobhan Somerville demonstrates the intertwined nature of the fields. Whereas "the supposed need for racial segregation, as it was formalized by the *Plessey v. Ferguson* case in the 1890s, was articulated through a discourse of panic about sexual mobility," evident in editorials expressing horror that a white woman or girl might be sitting next to a black man or teen, the lens of segregation had similarly a marked effect on studies of homosexuality (Somerville 35). The concept of passing, related to trespassing, stems from racial passing but actually encompasses a wide array of social categories, the mixing of which exposes the artifice of those categories as well as incites panic in those who wish to sustain them.

Concepts of passing have been critically applied to people of various identity categories, as theorized by Elaine Ginsberg: "Passing is about identities: their creation or imposition, their adoption or rejection, their accompanying rewards or penalties. Passing is also about the boundaries established between identity categories and about the individual and cultural anxieties induced by boundary crossing. Finally, passing is about specularity: the visible and invisible, the seen and the unseen" (2).

Not always involving deliberate disguise, passing includes a variety of ways in which individuals are presumed to belong to one identity category over another, positing a theoretical complexity, since the "unseen" or cloaked identity is "an individual's presumed 'natural' or 'essential' identity, including class, ethnicity, and sexuality, as well as gender" (Ginsberg 3). The very idea that there is a natural category that one is "not" when one is passing for something else is naive. Judith Butler in *Gender Trouble* has demonstrated that something like gender comprises a stylized set of actions, speeches, behaviors, and accouterments, which are continually performed and repeated for iterative effect. In fact, she argues, men in drag expose the extent to which femininity is a stylized performance. As Ginsberg notes, passing is typically motivated by a desire to gain access to privileges and opportunities accorded to a different social group, but it is also more complicated. In *Midnight in the Garden of Good and Evil,* the famous Lady Chablis makes a comment that reveals how passing can be deeply protective of the self. She says that while she is revered as the Lady, she would be beaten and harassed as a small, effeminate, light-skinned male.

The discourses of racial and sexual passing and discrimination intersect in a variety of ways. For example, Nella Larsen's novel titled *Passing* is a case in point. I briefly summarize the novel because, like Butler, I see it as foundational to theories of passing. The main character Irene is driven to insanity by her mirror-self Clare, who has chosen to pass for white and therefore lives in fear of exposure. On the surface Irene disapproves of Clare's choices, and she does not wish to associate with her; yet every time the indeterminate Clare is in her presence, Irene is overwhelmed by Clare's attractiveness. Not only does Clare ironically evoke Irene's own actions of occasionally passing—they first find each other at a restaurant in which Irene is passing for white—but Clare embodies "a certain kind of sexual daring that Irene defends herself against, for the marriage cannot hold Clare, and Irene finds herself drawn by Clare, wanting to be her, but also wanting her. It is this risk taking, articulated at once as a racial crossing and sexual infidelity, that alternatively entrances Irene and fuels her moral condemnation of Clare" (Butler, *Bodies* 169). In the course of the novel we discover how precariously balanced Irene is because she is actually passing in a different sense; she has committed herself to middle-class black family life, forcing her husband to keep practicing as a physician and raising her two children properly. Her facade might crack at any moment, and it seems to indeed crack when, the novel vaguely suggests, Irene pushes Clare out of a window. Irene's anxious commitment to black family life is political, a commitment to "uplifting the race" and undoing a history in which whites equated rampant sexuality with black women and justified exploiting them (Clare's husband does not know she is "Negro," but he is turned on by her dark skin).

Butler summarizes how critics are divided about whether *Passing* should be read as a story about race or the difficulty of representing black female sexuality, when it is clearly both. Rather than claim that one reading should be privileged over another, it is more logical to view *Passing* as the convergence of racial and sexual issues, just as Somerville has interpreted panic about miscegenation as broader sexual panic. Whether or not Irene is specifically suppressing homosexual desire for Clare (see McDowell and B. Carr), she is definitely suppressing general sexual feelings, which results in very "queer" feelings about Clare (see Butler) and the sexual energies she seems to unleash in everyone. Harlem in the twenties and thirties housed a highly visible gay enclave and hosted the largest gay annual event, the Hamilton Lodge Ball (Chauncey 227–28, 244–66) as well as other places of entertainment, but clergymen such as Adam Clayton Power led a crusade against homosexuality specifically because "the spread of homosexuality threatened the Negro family, the bedrock of social stability" (Chauncey 255). Richards discusses the uneasy relationship between Richard Wright and James Baldwin and notes the paradoxical fact that many titles in Wright's library concern homosexuality; sourcing Barbara Smith's comments on resistance to homosexuality in African American communities, Richards says that homosexuality is sometimes perceived as "an infection of white culture" (67–68), contextualizing the conjunction of racial and sexual passing in Larsen's Irene. Given the way racially marked bodies are interpreted, characters are driven to pass.

Larsen's position on the multiple ways an individual can pass becomes even clearer in her novel *Quicksand,* a rewriting of *The Awakening* that I link to the pattern of *Mockingbird* and women's regional writing in chapter 6. Through Helga Crane, Larsen demonstrates that passing is far more than racial passing; it is the acquisition of any social role through which one feels that the complexity of the self is not fulfilled. Clarifying Larsen's point about the political necessity of suppressing sexuality, Helga fears her sexual attraction to Dr. Anderson, just as she fears "the jungle" (59) of ecstasy she experiences with the music in Harlem. Helga tries to pass into many social groups: as fiancé to James Vayle; as teacher in a school modeled on Booker T. Washington's Tuskegee, where "everyone must 'pass'" (Cutter 77) as subordinate to whites; as black in Harlem, where she must veil her white ancestry; as exotic object in Denmark, where she stays with relatives; and as model wife to Reverend Mr. Pleasant Green in a "tiny Alabama town" (118). This latter is her final passing role, after which she descends into numbed sleep and perennial childbearing, depicted as the same death-stupor of Charity in *Summer* and Scout in *Mockingbird.*

We can understand *passing* as threat, as mode, as survival, or as death. By giving us a glimpse of multiple characters who lead double lives, the dominant way homosexuals, for example, understood their lives before the closet came into use as metaphor (Chauncey 6–7), Lee has given us a vision of the interconnected categories of people who pass. As also discussed by Fine ("Structuring" 73), Dolphus Raymond, who first literally passes by the children "on his thoroughbred" and is decoded as a drunk by Jem as he recites to "Dill the histories" (159) of eclectic *Mockingbird* folks, *passes* by emulating the drag of an alcoholic, enabling whites to stomach his "closeted" sober preference for "the company of Negroes" (192). As the figure haunting the margins of the courthouse, he is like a Shakespearean fool commenting on the play, demonstrating that he has ways around the system that Mayella, "because she didn't own a riverbank and she wasn't from a fine old family" (192), does not. His ticket to passing is his masked Coca-Cola drink, offered to Dill as the drink Dill in particular seems to need after his moment of effeminate tears; tellingly, this lesson in dishonest social navigation directly responds to Scout's pride, voiced to Dill, that "'[Atticus's] the same in the courtroom as he is on the public streets'" (199), a oneness only the privileged maintain.

From Mayella, Scout learns that any transgressions in desire or sexuality must be punished, but as I explore at the end of chapter 1, the trial becomes a queer staging of multiple sexual transgressions for a child learning about sex and slipping into the liminal state between sleeping and waking that typically opens the human mind to unconscious sexual intuitions. The trial deconstructs the fiction of white southern femininity as pure and points to Mayella's aggressive sexual impulses. Likewise, Scout learns that some version of passing characterizes any life of the nonwhite or nonmale; Cal leads a double life that evokes a long and complex history of black domestics who "cross the line" into white homes every day, often crossing spatial dividing lines, and take on cultural differences by compromising their home self and altering themselves into something whites wish to employ, as described by Trudier Harris in her book *From Mammies to Militants: Domestics in Black American Literature* (14–15). In *Mockingbird,* there is one lone voice that objects to passing and exposes the power differential: Lula, who "seemed seven feet high" to Scout and who evokes colonized history with her "Indian-bow mouth" (119). She is quickly silenced by "a solid mass of colored people" (119) who understand passing as survival. Nevertheless Lee plants this voice to expose her project in a momentary flash.

We can define passing on a broad spectrum in *Mockingbird.* Scout and the other children pass into black space (in church, in court), displacing black people, and they are identified with Negro speech and/or behavior at several points in the novel. Reverend Sykes refers to Atticus "passin'" in court, and Jem does not care about his wounds so long as he can *pass* and *punt,* or play the social game. In her discussion of why critics prefer the word "passing" to other words, such as impersonation, masquerade, drag, or crossing, Marion Rust argues that the word's association with death allows us to conceptualize it in the terms of loss: "passing describes an act of simulation, in which two states, being and not-being, assumption and revocation, inhere. . . . passing foregrounds what is *between*—between origin and enactment, body and gesture—calling into question all such fixed ways of determining identity" (23). We can mark *Mockingbird* itself as passing its first fifty years, in which it has passed into a canonical status in public schools. Like Larsen's novels, which have invited new critical interest in their views of passing as multiple, contested sites of identity, and as queer sites of sexual dilemmas rooted in history, Lee's novel could be at the forefront of new inquiries from varied fields, whiteness and race studies, masculinity and gender/queer studies, narratological and regional studies, disabilities and childhood studies.

By writing a reflective novel on her childhood of the thirties in Monroeville, Alabama, Lee managed to convey a feeling of nostalgia for a state of sleepiness, even while showing the dire consequences of sleepy-eyed folks who resist change. She thus tapped into a paradox that we find in most substantial American literature: the machine in the garden, a useful concept in a fifty-year reflection. Readers can feel contradictory things when reading. In his famous book, *The Machine in the Garden: Technology and the Pastoral Ideal in America,* Leo Marx explained that American authors have been preoccupied with America as a fresh and uncorrupted Garden of Eden, but at the same time that they revere this America with nostalgia, they embrace a national narrative of historical progress, which paradoxically is destroying the garden of innocent yesteryear. Perhaps the most famous example of this in literature is in Henry David Thoreau's pastoral *Walden,* a treatise of the American good life as simple living with the land, in the woods and on a pond, rejecting the need for imported European products and the values of commercialism and materialism. Yet in the midst of his Edenic narrative, his blood rushes as the train goes by and he evinces a startling moment of excitement at the train as a symbol of national progress. *Mockingbird* seems to long for a communal, precommercial past even while it voices dissatisfactions.

The tension between the machine and the garden, or looking forward and backward, is particularly poignant in literature about childhood, which often takes a mythic look at the historical and personal past, rendering its story concurrently with a Christian narrative of lost innocence, even when that innocence is highly contrived, like in Wharton's *Age of Innocence.* It is a paradox frequently present when people recall the past or when modern/ urban people idealize country life, as Miller has found in her study of the popular Girl Scouts and Campfire Girls movements that in the 1910s–1930s gained ground and sought to celebrate indigenous landscapes of America. The nickname of the central protagonist of *Mockingbird* is Scout, the name that in the period of Lee's childhood would have been synonymous with girls' organizations that were updating the transcendental nature movement for the young, who, Scout leaders believed, had been "disconnected" from rural, Walden-like simple living.

The author herself perpetuated the myth that she only wished to write an account of small-town life that was regrettably passing, but Scout's early "Garden of Eden" is actually about the very subject of passing—passing as the only way to go forward. What accounts for readers' paradoxical responses, however, is the play of contradictions in the novel. The most daunting contradiction in *Mockingbird* is the way it draws from nineteenth-century literary forms and presents them alongside techniques from twentieth-century modernist writers, which challenged the worldview of the nineteenth century as reflected in literary aesthetics and ideas. Modernist texts that find expression in *Mockingbird* pull against nineteenth-century antecedents that are given equal constructive space in the novel. This book is an attempt to sort out these antecedents and their meanings.

CHAPTER 1

MOCKINGBIRD AND NINETEENTH-CENTURY PHILOSOPHY: A TEST CASE FOR THE AMERICAN SCHOLAR

> There is throughout nature something mocking, something
> that leads us on and on, but arrives nowhere, keeps no faith
> with us. All promise outruns the performance. We live in a
> system of approximations. Every end is prospective of some
> other end, which is also temporary; a round and final suc-
> cess nowhere. We are encamped in nature.
>
> Ralph Waldo Emerson, *Nature*

The canonization of Lee's *Mockingbird* can be at least partially, if not mostly, attributed to its refinement of the American romance. Aspects of its style are congruent with the symbolism-infused romances of Nathaniel Hawthorne and Herman Melville, observes Robert Butler (124), as is its content. A long line of nineteenth-century texts in which men have followed individual conscience and pursued independence at the expense of their social reputation stands behind *Mockingbird*'s "democratic vista." Millions of readers have celebrated Atticus Finch for his heroism and Gregory Peck's strong performance of him in the film. In her critical essay on which American writings have been favored by critics and why, Nina Baym identifies a "Melodrama of Beset Manhood" as the central mythos of how critics have understood the American romance. To the neglect of men and women writing social novels (the latter scorned by Hawthorne as a "damn'd mob of scribbling women"), critics such as F. O. Matthiessen, Lionel Trilling, Leslie Fiedler, Richard Chase, Henry Nash Smith, and R.W.B. Lewis have located the "most American" and therefore "excellent" story in dramas in which men oppose "the encroaching, constricting, destroying society" (Baym 133) by privileging individuality and nature. "Society" in such texts is more than likely female-identified, and *Mockingbird* is no exception.

The protagonist of the American romance typically casts women "in the melodramatic role of temptress, antagonist, obstacle" (Baym 133), and anyone familiar with Mayella Ewell's starring role in *Mockingbird*'s rape trial must admit how nicely the novel conforms to the myth. As Baym discusses, the American man defined in opposition to society demands his celibacy, as put forth by Richard Chase. Atticus Finch "could make a rape case as dry as a sermon" (169) with his disembodied yet romantic manner, as if he transcends the sordid details of having a body or desire. When Atticus merely takes off his coat in the courtroom, the result is "the equivalent of him standing before us stark naked" (202). Just as Twain's Huck and Jim experience their brief democratic brotherhood by swimming naked in the river, Atticus's brief moment of nakedness takes the form of his impassioned appeal for the African American man. The beset man Atticus more than obviously conforms to a series of nineteenth-century romances in which white men and racial others embody authors' constructions of democratic possibility, such as we find in *The Last of the Mohicans, Moby-Dick,* and *Adventures of Huckleberry Finn.* These romantic texts depend on binary oppositions between the white man forging his freedom by and through, though supposedly on behalf of, "the Africanist presence," which has been analyzed by Toni Morrison as the symbol for "the not-free" and applied to *Mockingbird* by Diann Baecker. Further, in *Mockingbird,* the wholeness of Atticus as a man emerges in opposition to Tom, who, "If he had been whole, he would have been a fine specimen of a man" (192). However, the maimed Africanist presence notwithstanding, the character of Atticus can be more specifically analyzed as suggestive of a legacy of nineteenth-century philosophy.

Although he was not a writer of fiction, no one had a greater effect on how we think about American letters and the romantic spirit than essayist, orator, and poet Ralph Waldo Emerson. A resident of Concord, Massachusetts, which took a leading role in the American Revolution, and increasingly dissatisfied with Christianity's reverence for Christ—merely the first *representative* man who proved the presence of God within every man (Loving 36)—Emerson was more than poised to become a leading figure in theorizing American independence in terms of the intellect, heart, and mind. Indeed, he made these things become one and the same, and he transformed them into facets of masculinity, just as John de Crevecoeur's farmer had stood for American manhood in the prior century. The philosophy of Emerson and his circle, including the civil disobedience articulated by Henry David Thoreau and the educational ideas advanced by Bronson Alcott, provides the backbone of Atticus's worldview as well as his manhood. *Mockingbird* privileges the intellectual and not the farmer, who becomes the comic backwoods bumpkin ready to turn his back on democracy and justice. In short, *Mockingbird* is the story of Emerson's "The American Scholar." With a deep respect for human nature as well as a romantic sense of what human nature is; with devotional, intellectual, and representational roles in the community; with an obsessive concern that he achieve a transparent oneness for his children; and with an embedded narrative of manhood and transcendent love ("I love everybody") that challenges other definitions of masculinity; Atticus presents to us a test case for what *action* is possible in Emerson's definition of *Man Thinking*.

In this chapter, I trace the character of Atticus and questions raised about him in the novel to Emerson's seminal essay, which is structured similarly to Atticus's gradual transformation from *man reading* to *man thinking* to *action* and *duty*. Not only is Atticus a "representative man" in the Emersonian sense of being delegated by the community; he is also an embodiment of the principles outlined in "The American Scholar" and refined in related essays. In Emerson's philosophy, *man thinking* was to be equally influenced by the study of nature and of texts from the past, thus balancing understanding of human nature with reading, which we can extend to a balance between case law and legal precedent. *Man thinking* was to be nonconformist, self-reliant, and, importantly, *active*. Emerson deconstructs cultural stereotypes of the scholar as feminine because inactive or celibate, and he seeks to counteract those stereotypes with his own definition of the how *man thinking* is always *active*.

The question of whether *man thinking/man reading* "does anything" is overtly raised by Scout in the novel. The question cannot be dismissed as a child's gender stereotype when compared to Emerson's essay and when we consider the violence that erupts against the intellectual in the novel. Emerson always regretted the fact that he did not write an essay on the farmer as representative man, but his failure to do so signifies an important shift in American manhood. For characters like Scout, Miss Maudie, or Cal, it would be unimaginable to take Bob Ewell's challenge calmly. For *man thinking*, the farmer's prowess is nothing. Figured several times in the comic terms of a strutting, red rooster, Ewell is meant to lampoon showy displays of masculine prowess that write themselves on the bodies of others. The correspondence between Atticus and Emersonian principles strikes the core issues of gender, masculinity, and sexuality at issue throughout *Mockingbird*. Atticus answers the test case of the scholar's *activity* with an Emersonian-styled oral address in which he uses the freighted word that Emerson names as the scholar's final contribution—that of his *duty*. In his closing remarks, Atticus discusses human equality and the natural diversity of people's abilities before calling upon the jury's duty to restore the black man to his family; his remarks, like his character throughout the novel, allude to the flow of Emerson's essay, which moves from understanding nature to the scholar's activity and duty.

It is important to explore Atticus's Emersonian roots and his evocation of transparency and "oneness" across public and private space as we move in later chapters to other literary traditions circulating in *Mockingbird*. The other literary traditions upon which Lee called to construct her novel destabilize transcendentalism as a worldview and make clear the fate of Emersonian ideas in the twentieth century as more voices and materialist positions sought to make themselves heard. Not only does the novel overtly show the limits of an Emersonian worldview; it also posits Emersonian idealism as a site of critique. The more passionate and embodied characters of the novel are not white and not male, and thus they are "bodies that matter," as Judith Butler articulates the role of the material body in the performance and construction of identity. Nonwhite and female characters cannot countenance an idealist transcendental position. The disembodied, celibate, and thereby "courteously detached" Atticus can hardly imagine the challenges to his ideology presented by those deeply identified with their gender, class, race, or sexual orientation.

Lee's concern with those excluded from nineteenth-century philosophies of transcendental being enables her to draw from a range of literary influences that represent alternative points of view and philosophies. For example, as I show in chapter 2, she deploys nineteenth-century racial melodrama to capture the ritualized exclusion of African Americans and a tradition of texts concerned with how sins of American fathers fail their daughters. As I show in chapters 3 and 4, she evokes early modern novels that represent the complexities of consciousness to explore epistemology, subjectivity, and environmental conditioning. As I show in chapter 5, she gestures to queer literature and southern grotesque to communicate the plight of homosexuals who cannot "come out" in patriarchal cultures. And, as I show in chapter 6, she writes in the tradition of modern women's regional writing to render the plight of *female* coming-of-age in the novel of manners.

Lee selects the image of the mockingbird as multifaceted symbol. The mockingbird stands for the embodied and persecuted singer who never sings in its own voice but who becomes expert at imitation. Calvin Woodard argues that the mockingbird is Lee's view of the southern mind, possibly losing its will to others or possibly learning from others (581–82); the violence of the bird and of the title are duly noted by Jacqueline Tavernier-Courbin (58) and R. A. Dave: "As we find the mockingbird fluttering and singing time and again, the whole of Maycomb seems to be turning before our eyes into a wilderness full of senseless slaughter" (50). In effect, the mockingbird negotiates the world in a manner antithetical to Atticus's "oneness" across social and discursive situations. Lee draws the mockingbird image from an important source, or two important sources, if we count Marianne Moates's communication of Truman Capote's use of the mockingbird in a childhood anecdote. Whereas the young Truman communicated a chilling account of the mockingbird as "keeping down the colored population" by pecking out the eyes of newborns so they cannot nurse, we can find elegiac poetry of the Alabama mockingbird in Walt Whitman's *Leaves of Grass,* as Dave (51) comments when he also observes the technical kinship between Lee's novel and Whitman's poetic reminiscence. Whitman's ever-growing leaves embody the younger man's answer to Emerson's call for an American poetry. At the end of this chapter, I explore what it might mean that Emerson and Whitman share space in the novel, particularly in light of their differences.

Emerson found in Whitman the promise of the democratic poet yet was uncomfortable with Whitman's "body electric." Whitman's tropes of democratic brotherhood through adhesion, comradery, and masturbatory pleasure have long lent him status as a controversial poet, specifically as endorsing an androgynous if not homosexual love. For example, "both Wilde and Carpenter had found encouragement in Whitman" (Beaver 108), and many men found in Whitman's *Calamus* "a love for other men that was unquestionably masculine" (Chauncey 105). Emerson had trouble lending to Whitman's poetry his full endorsement and even asked Whitman to remove some of the more explicit content. The poem of the mockingbird, variously titled in different versions but finally given the title "Out of the Cradle Endlessly Rocking," represents Whitman's return to proclaiming himself America's bard after a period of crisis, which can be seen as a political crisis before the Civil War or as a personal crisis of a failed homosexual affair. The *Calamus* sequence that depicts a homosexual affair, written just before his mockingbird poem, strongly affects the tone and content of the mockingbird poem, which communicates a young boy's witnessing of an Alabama mockingbird who has lost his mate and sings his agony. The translation of the reference from Capote to Whitman makes a lot of sense, given Whitman's voiced commitment to sing the pain of dark brothers who grieve, along with his broader sense in *Leaves of Grass* that all Americans of *all* social classes and identity positions deserve a place in the body electric.

Although homosexuality is thoroughly addressed in chapter 5 on Dill, Capote, and Boo Radley, the Whitman allusion gives us the opportunity to conclude this chapter with a meditation on the qualities Atticus's Emersonianism excludes. Thus we shall discover that Atticus is reading *The Gray Ghost* at the end of *Mockingbird* because there are a whole lot of ghosts pushed to the margins of the light by his philosophy of American transcendence and possibility. After we discuss Atticus as Emerson's *man thinking,* so celebrated a character that a plaque to his name rests on the town square of Monroeville and is visited by tourists from all around the world each spring, we will spend the remainder of this book bringing from the shadows those gray ghosts.

The "One" of One-Shot Finch, the Man of *Man Thinking*

One of the many intertexts informing our understanding and appreciation of *Mockingbird* is the general legacy of Emerson, whose patterns of thought on heroism, self-reliance and nonconformity, nature and transcendentalism, coalesce in Atticus and explain his unfailing popularity even in the face of critics who point out the plain fact that the novel remains a white perspective: "It might be argued that the structure of the book contradicts its own message. The presence of blacks in the book, mediated through Scout's narrative, is never equal to that of whites. Readers are never permitted to walk in the shoes of Tom Robinson, his family, Calpurnia, or any of the other black characters. On the other hand, that may be the point of the novel"

(Early 100). The gentlemanly noble named Atticus invokes, argues Joseph Crespino, the liberal stance identified in C. Vann Woodward's *The Strange Career of Jim Crow*. But as appointed representative and elected legislator of even the unjust Maycomb, Atticus embodies what Emerson meant when he looked at prominent men such as Plato, Goethe, Shakespeare, Montaigne, and Napoleon as "representative" men.

Men of a specific talent, Emerson argued, become great because they *represent* that particular talent as it would manifest itself in the conglomerate whole of mankind, a sort of Platonic ideal form that could only be fully present in the conglomerate of the oversoul—never in any particular individual. Emerson's idea of great men as representative men can be contemplated in opposition to his friend Thomas Carlyle's ideas in "On Heroes, Hero-Worship, and the Heroic in History." In Emerson's view, a man like Shakespeare would have risen without the particular man called Shakespeare; similarly, "When we are exalted by ideas, we do not owe this to Plato, but to the idea, to which, also, Plato was debtor. . . . Mankind have, in all ages, attached themselves to a few persons, who, either by the quality of that idea they embodied, or by the largeness of their reception, were entitled to the position of leaders and lawgivers. These teach us the qualities of primary nature, —admit us to the constitution of things" (Emerson, "Uses of Great Men," *Representative Men* 237). To Emerson, the *one* man is always a partial glimpse of the many—the conglomerate—whereas the *many* lends energy and representational value to the one. In some wondrous way, we are supposed to see in Atticus the many in the one, and when we are confused about seeing it, we have Miss Maudie, handmaiden to God's great outdoors, to clarify it for us.

The general correspondence between Atticus and Emerson is easy to spot. As Fred Erisman argues, even the most cursory knowledge of Emerson would enable a reader to see echoes of Emersonian individualism, belief in higher laws, and conscience, which, Atticus claims, does not abide by majority rule. The translation of conscience into action is also Henry David Thoreau's, as sketched, for example, in "Civil Disobedience," the essay reflecting on his being jailed for refusing to pay taxes to a government countenancing slavery: "Can there not be a government in which majorities do not virtually decide right and wrong, but conscience? . . . Why has every man a conscience, then?" (387). Pledging allegiance to conscience was a common aspect of life in Emerson's Concord, where the Alcotts, for example, declined to use any products made with slave labor, where Thoreau took up residence at Walden to prove that dependency on the marketplace and fashion could be broken, and where Alcott and others experimented with unity between ideals and private living at Fruitlands.

It is "oneness" in every fullest sense of the word that Atticus seeks. He is the "one man" who is the same in public and in private, observes Miss Maudie on not only one occasion; he believes that if he is not a unified "one," he cannot hold his head up and his children need not listen to him. He strives for transparency—what Emerson terms the transparent eyeball. He symbolically and concretely dissolves boundaries. Whereas in a novel such as *Adventures of Huckleberry Finn,* another influence on *Mockingbird* at which we arrive in another chapter, conscience is socially constructed and thus perverse, in *Mockingbird* conscience raises the individual above social majority to higher divinity and "spiritual law," the oft-used term of Emerson's. To Atticus, law is indeed spiritual. When he admits that equality under the law is no ideal to him, but a living, working reality, we glean a glimpse of his understanding that he is actually idealist—an ideal form. Atticus's sense that he could not hold his head up or govern his children if he did not obey his conscience embodies Emerson's metaphor of achieving transcendence of body and social circumstance through self-trust and the commitment to personal principle. Atticus has become for the American public "representative man" and, for legal commentators (see Johnson, *Threatening* 20; Petry xxii–xxviii), the lawyer as divinely appointed to represent the many in the one.

Emerson more fully theorized what he meant by the "one" in a much later essay, in which he clarifies the concept of an oversoul, an understanding of which helps us understand why Atticus seeks unity: "We live in succession, in division, in parts, in particles. Meantime within man is the soul of the whole; the wise silence; the universal beauty, to which every part and particle is equally related; the eternal ONE. . . . We see the world piece by piece, as the sun, the moon, the animal, the tree; but the whole, of which these are shining parts, is the soul" ("The Over-soul" 173). In other words, the truth uncovered by Atticus "beyond any reasonable doubt" is far more than a plea for equality and blind justice; it is to be understood as a test of the ONE that comprises the immortal portion of the various limbs that make up the original "whole" man. Tom Robinson is only an example of the "not whole"—the parts and particles through which the elusive whole man is glimpsed.

While the general sketch of Atticus "as a Southern version of Emerson-ian man" (Erisman 43) rings true, the analogy also opens up the issue that *Mockingbird* tests the figuration of *man thinking*. Emerson articulated the office of *man thinking* in his famous address to the Phi Beta Kappa Society at Cambridge on 31 August 1837. Intending to deliver his thoughts about what it means to be a scholar, he presented the scholar as the "delegated intellect" of a community and in the process delivered a new version of the independent American man. Independent man is not solipsistic and apart from commu-nity so much as he embodies a community's highest aspiration. One cannot understand Emersonian self-reliance without understanding his broader philosophy of man and a wholeness of spirit communicated through each individual man.

The year before this oratory, Emerson had published his first book, *Nature*, which made him known to the public. The effects of these two works, *Nature* and "The American Scholar," would by the 1890s be celebrated as Emerson's greatness in textbooks. I will quote one such textbook published by Brander Matthews in 1896 to exemplify not only the identification of these two works as launching Emerson's influence, but also as stimulating the reputation of Emerson's ability to see from the points of view of others, which is Atticus's creed:

> Hitherto little had happened to him except the commonplaces of existence; thereafter [1837], though his life remained tranquil, he was known to the world at large ... [recognized also for] his willingness always to put himself in the place of others and to try to see things from their point of view. An in-stance of this sympathetic faculty, and of his abiding simplicity, was his com-ment on the minister who went up to the pulpit after Emerson had lectured, and who prayed that they might be delivered from ever again hearing such "transcendental nonsense." Emerson listened to this, and remarked quietly, "He seems a very conscientious, plain-spoken man." (Matthews 97, 103)

Mockingbird insists on Atticus's sympathetic faculty, his quiet calmness, his self-reliance and adherence to a higher law, and his ability to study human nature as well as books. The questions raised in *Mockingbird* about Atticus's virility, masculinity, and activity are the same questions addressed by Emerson in "The American Scholar." But these questions quickly become a matter of Atticus's embodiment of the many in his one-shot persona.

In his essay, Emerson carefully discusses the role of books, experience, and study of nature for the scholar, interactive forces that are implicit in *Mockingbird,* mostly through interactions between the children and Atticus about what it means to understand people and what it means to represent them. The scholarly way that Atticus studies people is inherently tied to his appointment to represent them. We can best understand the way in which Atticus is a "representative man" in the way that Emerson understood great men to be representative of the larger forces uniting all mankind. This explains the peculiar way that the novel understands Atticus as representative man. Although Maycomb is expressly racist, Atticus is undefeated in his election to legislature, noted by Scout. Miss Maudie asserts his actions as his missionary answer to the community's call to be Christian, which confuses Scout a bit (as it should): "'We're so rarely called on to be Christians, but when we are, we've got men like Atticus to go for us'" (215). The confusion of the "we" behind the sentiment goes noted by Jem, who wishes "'the rest of the county thought that'" (215), to which Miss Maudie answers, "'You'd be surprised how many of us do.'" Jem demands the meaning of the *who*—the many behind the one, and Miss Maudie explains the Judge's appointment and the backing suggested by it. But it is clear that the "who" is not supposed to be literal people, but rather a divine appointment of Atticus's to represent the very idea of a whole man, which is how Emerson begins his essay.

In the opening of "The American Scholar," Emerson gives us a fable of how "the gods, in the beginning, divided Man into men, that he might be more helpful to himself; just as the hand was divided into fingers, the better to answer its end. The old fable covers a doctrine ever new and sublime; that there is One Man,—present to all particular men only partially, or through one faculty; and that you must take the whole society to find the whole man" (1). This suggestion of there being an ever-elusive oneness called Man, synonymous with God or Nature (later the oversoul) when unified in ideal form, underlies Atticus's system of knowledge: that you can access the souls of other men by imaginatively walking in their skin. To some extent, Atticus does not seem to recognize his separateness from other men; he seems to believe that in essence he can imagine their feelings and predict their behaviors. See things from his point of view, he instructs Scout of Ewell. This can only be possible because of some sort of transcendental faith, whatever the sort.

In other words, Atticus believes that transcendentalism is possible because he implicitly believes in an overriding category of Man that he can access. He goes so far as to try on the skin of Ewell and theorize Ewell's anger at being shamed. When Scout comes to the conclusion that there are not different kinds of folks but "'just one kind of folks. Folks'" (227), she has made colloquial Atticus's Emersonian teachings, even though it is not a conclusion she can maintain. In very obvious ways, Atticus is the "delegate intellect" of the "one man" or body politic. This is what Miss Maudie means when she says that Atticus is appointed to do the community's Christian duty for them; her reference to religion and his appointment taps into the idea of divinity or what Emerson would later call the oversoul in his teachings of the transcendental oneness of Man. To Emerson, the role of the scholar is inherently both communal and religious, based on a history of priests and monks being designated readers, writers, and scholars. It is not a subtle theme in *Mockingbird,* which repeatedly mocks church preachers as obsessed with doctrines of sin and female pollution, whereas Atticus transforms the subject of pollution into the dryness of a sermon. The significance of Atticus's appointment becomes apparent at the church of Reverend Sykes, who introduces Scout and Jem to the congregation with, "'You all know their father'" (120). On one level, he is pointing out the "white" implied in Miss Maudie's "we"—"their father," in contrast to the phrase "our father" typically used in church. Yet in contrast to other pulpit figures whom the narrator mocks with her bored tone at "again" hearing "the Impurity of Women doctrine that seemed to preoccupy all clergymen" (122), Atticus is the Christian luminary of the novel, which explains why "he liked to be by himself in church" (148). He is the designated keeper of souls in many ways, as I discuss below.

The ideal of Atticus's appointment as representative man is articulated to Aunt Alexandra in the missionary society scene, a scene contrasting a false mission (the Mrunas) with a true mission:

"—what else do they want from him, Maudie, what else?"

[...]

"Whether Maycomb knows it or not, we're paying the highest tribute we can pay a man. We trust him to do right. It's that simple."

"Who?" Aunt Alexandra never knew she was echoing her twelve-year-old nephew.

"The handful of people in this town who say that fair play is not marked White Only; the handful of people who say a fair trial is for everybody, not just us; the handful of people with enough humility to think, when they look at a Negro, there but for the Lord's kindness am I." (236)

Lee's selection of Miss Maudie as Atticus's transcendentalism interpreter for the children corresponds to Miss Maudie's own love of nature: "She loved everything that grew in God's earth, even the weeds" (42). In her defense of the town's "need" of Atticus as a high tribute in a spiritual economy, Miss Maudie espouses the thesis of a transcendental connection between the African American and the white, phrasing her words carefully, "'there but for the Lord's kindness am I.'" She sees not division and inherent difference but connective possibility and a random interchangeability of self. She believes she could easily be Negro, and the Negro could easily be her. It is thus meaningful that Miss Maudie christens Atticus, for the children, "one-shot Finch" when he shoots the mad dog, a clear and overdetermined symbol for how sane people "go mad" when anything involving a black man arises, Atticus says. We shall return to this scene because, as Carolyn Jones demonstrates in her reading of the novel's structure, it provides a paradigm for understanding Atticus's role throughout the novel. In my view, the paradigm involves Lee's suggestion of Atticus as the "one" delegate elect.

The mad dog scene, an emblem of Atticus's appointment as delegate "right," is heightened by Heck's abdication of the role and Miss Maudie's discussion of marksmanship as a gift from God. The vision of masculinity in the scene rests upon the interpretation by Miss Maudie; she offers the view that masculine prowess is *inherent* in Atticus—it is God's gift to him. This concurrence between inherent nature and community service conveys how *Mockingbird* refines the American romance. The wilderness errand of a pioneer character like Cooper's Natty would show his prowess in the same way, but Lee follows Emerson closely in seeing no distinction between romantic masculinity and service to community, between wilderness (the mad dog) and civilization. In effect, the American romance opportunity comes straight to his doorstep; the dog, like the community's racism, is nature gone awry. Atticus's choice not to exercise his unfair advantage over other living things is the civilized choice of his heart, Miss Maudie interprets, as if Atticus were a text of divine nature needing her gloss. In another part of the novel, Miss Maudie explains Atticus's peculiar sentiments about not shooting a mockingbird; she immediately understands his cryptic commentary about sin and thus solidifies her role as translator of his divine ideals to the people.

Imagery continually suggests that Atticus's appointment to defend Tom Robinson is the weighty task of a divine appointment: a religious, spiritual, and transcendental obligation to man and self-reliance. We can also best understand the "preachings" of Atticus in light of Emerson's ideas, but we can point specifically to "The American Scholar" as anchoring the novel's concern for deconstructing Atticus's brand of activity and masculinity, given the children's questions about him: whether he actually *does* anything.

The frame of "American" in "The American Scholar" is important because in 1837 the subject of the American is undergoing construction. It cannot help but be an important intertext in any novel of any era that takes as its issue race relations and the exclusion of a people from democracy and justice. Just as Whitman's pre–Civil War poem about a mockingbird emphasizes *Two together! / Winds blow South, or winds blow North* as national unity of the traveling birds, in Emerson's philosophy the spiritual accordance of the one in the many and the many in the one defines national unity. A representational jury is a natural and logical outgrowth of Emerson's principle, but short of that possibility Atticus espouses his faith in "the oneness" of the courts and the judicial process. Literature often figures legal judgment as a spiritual endeavor, and the correspondence between secular and spiritual law is easy to see in *Mockingbird,* particularly in its evocation of sin. Early in his essay, Emerson states that "one more chapter of his biography" is being written "year by year" in the life of the American scholar, a biography to which we must add *Mockingbird*'s depiction of its lawyer as delegated intellect.

The dispassionate Atticus exemplifies what Emerson calls "the right state" of *man thinking:* "In this distribution of functions, the scholar is the delegated intellect. In the right state, he is, *Man Thinking.* In the degenerate state, when the victim of society, he tends to become a mere thinker, or, still worse, the parrot of other men's thinking" (2). Emerson means that *man thinking* is a spiritual appointment, the part of the "One Man" that reveals to other parts truth. It is clear from the beginning of *Mockingbird* that Atticus's role in people's lives is more intellectual and spiritual than material. Developing immediate distaste for criminal law but being present "at the departure" of his first clients, he is described by Miss Maudie, in response to the children's accusations that he does not *do* anything, as able to make someone's will airtight. He seems in charge of orchestrating Mrs. Dubose's clean exit, and he is continually associated with spiritual exits, from the Radleys to the mad dog. A minister of last rites so often that we should suspect Tom's passing long before we hear news of it, Atticus and his words in court are indeed a sermon (169). Perhaps the most obvious symbol of Atticus's spiritual role is the analogy made between court and church when the community awaits Tom's judgment, "the grown people sat as if they were in church. In the balcony, the Negroes sat and stood around us with biblical patience" (209). The judgment involves everyone.

In a different novel, the biblical reverence of the African American community for Atticus Finch would enable horrid abuse. It is hard to consider Lee's description of Atticus's settlement in Maycomb—his office containing "little more than a hat rack, a spittoon, a checkerboard and an unsullied Code of Alabama" (4)—without recalling Mark Twain's viciously comic *Pudd'nhead Wilson,* in which the intellectual lawyer "Pudd'nhead" settles in a small town that alienates and mocks him, much like the disjunction between the noble Atticus and his sparse office with little business. Both novels share revelatory scenes of lawyers melodramatically unveiling truths about race. Twain's novel overtly addresses the theme of lawyers and judges appropriating divine functions over the lives of others, but inappropriately and dangerously. In *Pudd'nhead* the only level-headed character is the lawyer, and his level-headedness fuels his odd obsession with fingerprinting—body evidence that, like Tom's useless arm, unmasks truth. This obsession proves the truth of characters whose racial identities are in question, but the overall novel is "The Tragedy of Pudd'nhead" because he ultimately capitulates to the ruling southern order and becomes best friends with people like Judge Driscoll, who threatens to sell his slaves down the river and then shows mercy, which his slaves interpret as being saved from damnation. Without the Emersonian emphasis on principles connecting all mankind, the synonymous role of the court and divine judgment is, in fact, quite dangerous.

It is not dangerous in Emersonian philosophy because human nature is inherently good. Atticus embodies an expansive sense of Emersonian transcendentalism. The circulating spiritual self of transcendentalism, which goes into nature as a "transparent eyeball" and returns with a transcendent vision of its broader and transparent self, most overtly corresponds to the economy of gifts that circulate in *Mockingbird*. They symbolize the circulation of soul and elevate Atticus into a godlike position, most offerings being laid on his doorstep. The gifts are often distributed in the shroud of night, suggesting Atticus's otherworldliness and even his death after his "passing" in court, after which he wakes to find the abundance of gifts from African Americans. It is as if he is pure spirit. The gifts, analyzed as a trading economy by John Carlos Rowe, also suggest a spiritual economy that stands in place of a cash economy because the cash economy is depressed.

The way in which Atticus is initially described as settling in Maycomb and practicing "economy more than anything" (5) suggests the example of Thoreau's settlement at Walden. Thoreau's first chapter is titled "Economy," and it offers a model of virtuous living that exemplifies Emerson's call in *Nature* to stop being beholden to excessive creature comforts. Thoreau's point is that a greater transcendental virtue can emerge by lessening material ties. Certainly Lee reveals her concern with national origins when she gives us quite a bit of background on Finch ancestry, as humorous as it is that Simon Finch migrated from England for religious freedom and then promptly forgot his virtuous purposes. But it is nonetheless noteworthy that Atticus left the lifestyle of a plantation to practice economy, and details such as the fact that he walks to work evoke choices equated with virtue in nineteenth-century writing. At any rate, the concerns of Thoreau for rejecting and mocking the frivolous concerns of women, who represent the antithesis to economy and the simple life of virtue and books, are mirrored in Lee's novel. Atticus seems a lone economist on a street of ladies who distract real missions with their "missionary societies." Economy in the transcendental mindset *is* a mission and a public model. The recurrent description of Atticus as the same in public and private suggests a quasi-textual life always on display; like in Benjamin Franklin's autobiography, virtues extolled for the public are to be practiced in the private life. The circulating value of Atticus as indicated by the gifts and allusions to his divinity signifies the fact that, like many earlier

transcendentalists, he makes his transcendental oneness public. As he artic-
ulates to Heck Tate, echoing sentiments espoused earlier by him and Miss
Maudie, "'I can't live one way in town and another way in my home'" (274).
Nearly every other character experiences divisions based on social situations.

To Emerson, a priestly role and scholarly role are one and the same
thing—one grand appointment to function as delegate intellect. This is precisely what he means by his fable of the "One Man" who was apportioned into
various functions, *man thinking* being of a particular sort. The most compelling analogy between Atticus and Emerson's idea of the American Scholar
lies in the various facets of study that Emerson says the *man thinking* must
consider in his office. Emerson enumerates four aspects of *man thinking* as
he sketches out a "theory of his office." The first influence on *man thinking*, Emerson states, is nature, which includes "every day, men and women,
conversing, beholding and beholden. The scholar is he of all men whom this
spectacle most engages" (2). As a "continuity of this web of God," nature has
no boundaries and thus encompasses human nature. Emerson uses the word
"law" often in his remarks, arguing that the laws of nature are also the laws
of the scholar's mind; "know thyself" and "study nature" are for Emerson
the same because there are no boundaries between the self that learns from
observing nature and the self that intuits truth from within.

Lee's Atticus is named after Titus Pomponius Atticus, close friend of
Cicero's who alienated few because impartial and hospitable to all; the importance of Cicero's admiration for stoicism, argues Kathryn Lee Seidel
("Growing Up"), can also be found throughout American literature and in
Scout's development. But whereas Cicero's Atticus entertained and paid ex-
penses of many to earn good will and friendship, Lee's Atticus, though also
impartial, is a horse of a different color. Throughout much of the novel, Atticus
is *man reading* and *man thinking* by decoding for his children the complexities of human nature. Atticus studies people and explains to his children how
to see from their eyes. The practice of studying human nature is necessary
because, Emerson moves on to discuss, books represent the mind of the past,
and, while important and transcendental in themselves, they are incomplete studies without the study of living nature. In "The American Scholar,"
Emerson puts reading in its place; while *man reading* is also *man thinking*,
man thinking is not synonymous with *man reading*. An important facet of
Mockingbird, which seeks to separate reading and understanding just as it

shows the unfortunate separation between the law of the land and its living application, is the incompleteness of reading.

The tension between reading and studying nature that circulates throughout *Mockingbird,* particularly in Scout and all she learns from directly witnessing "this spectacle" of "men and women," makes "The American Scholar" a particularly applicable selection from Emerson. After arguing that the scholar must first study nature, Emerson tackles the subject of books and reading. Books, while a major means of transcendence and the immortality of the scholar, are only one of the forces that the scholar must accommodate. Emerson, however, is careful to sketch a theory of critical or creative reading through eschewing uncritical acceptance of the thoughts in books: "Books are the best of things, well used; abused, among the worst. . . . The one thing in the world, of value, is the active soul. . . . The soul active sees absolute truth" (4). Not only is Atticus a reader, but he is also a "representative man" who finds truths in study of the world and himself. Someone like Atticus recognizes the difference between law and the application of law in social practice. Nature demands accommodation and consideration.

For example, early in the novel we hear a discussion of whether the legal requirement of going to school can be bent for Scout, following a discussion of how the law is perennially bent for the Ewells, unaccountably "members of an exclusive society made up of Ewells" (30). Atticus's application of the books and what they represent (as precedent) is not rigid and universal but based on the other forces Emerson states, such as study of nature, self, and social context. We see the study of nature in his assertion that it is silly to force people like the Ewells into a new environment (30)—recognition that Mr. Ewell will "'never change his ways'" (31)—and we see a study of self when he says that no one prosecutes the hunting infraction because no one begrudges those children "'any game their father can hit'" (31). He presumes the attitudes of others based on introspection, "'I don't know of any landowner around here who begrudges those children any game'" (31). Atticus thus gives equal weight to his understanding of man and his own conscience as he does to the law. In a model of *man thinking,* rather than parroting the ideas of others he dialogues these scholarly forces, not allowing any to ascend over others.

The Emersonian intertext of "The American Scholar" gives us some understanding of how the "rescue" of Arthur (Boo) Radley, who presumably killed Ewell to save the children, is supposed to resolve the novel. The cover-up by Heck Tate and Atticus has been the subject of some discussion among legal critics who worry, rightly, that it represents the failure of law and the reification of an extralegal southern law tradition, as explored by critic Cramer Cauthen. This extralegal tradition of taking the law into one's own hands enables acts of lynching and other abuses. Again referencing *Pudd'nhead*, Twain provides a humorous parody of this tradition when he has Judge Driscoll deeply ashamed that his own son would settle a dispute in court rather than in a duel. While not written in the comic mode of other parts of *Mockingbird*, the cover-up of Boo's "crime" earns the novel its title, as Scout concludes that prosecuting Boo would amount to killing a mockingbird. Why the law can be bent for whites, as indeed it is for the Ewells, demands critical explanation and evaluation. On the one hand, argues Johnson in "The Secret Courts of Men's Hearts: Code and Law in Harper Lee's *To Kill a Mockingbird*," the entire novel is a study of legal and social codes that define various small communities of which the court is only a small portion, and Atticus's vexed decision to turn away from law parallels precisely the historical reality of the 1950s when civil rights activists were doing precisely that. Chura argues that the trial of the murderers of Emmett Till, which bears many similarities to the trial of Tom Robinson, left many with the feeling that justice had not been served by the courts. I will give only a partial account of Atticus's law-bending here and save the rest of it for chapter 3, when I use the intertext of *What Maisie Knew* to shed light on why it is that daughters must strike particular bargains with fathers in terms of how to construct knowledge.

The reluctance of Atticus to agree to Heck's account keeps him virtuous, but it also echoes his initial reluctance to defend Tom; he says he hoped to get through life without such a case. In some ways, Atticus's cover-up of Boo is a return to status quo—"the return" portion of the hero's journey, given his arc to defend an African American and his "passing" glory while doing so. However much the scene embodies a problem, in that two powerful white men conspire to author their own version of the truth—"he fell on his knife," repeated several times to make it so—the bending of the law in deference to what is learned about human nature is not without precedent in Atticus's earlier, Emersonian code of ethics. If the law of nature is for Boo to be reclusive and private, then, Atticus feels, he has a right to that nature. Similarly, if the law of nature for Ewell is to be evil, which sounds a lot like the word

"Ewell," notes R. Butler (124), then Atticus as scholar over lawyer has the right to privilege the integrity of these natures. The court, in contrast, has failed to recognize what Atticus reads as simple nature—Mayella's desire, Ewell's rage and shame, Tom's simple innocence. They are "natures" insofar as they are neither complexified in the text nor challenged by Atticus: "no one, including the exemplar of moral probity himself, Atticus, thinks of bringing charges against the rapist father" (Fine, "Gender" 125). They just *are;* they are transparent truth.

Emerson's theory of the precedence of nature can accommodate *any* sort of nature: "'if I am the Devil's child, I will live then from the Devil.' No law can be sacred to me but that of my nature. . . . A man is to carry himself in the presence of all opposition as if every thing were titular and ephemeral but he. I am ashamed to think how easily we capitulate to badges and names, to large societies and dead institutions" ("Self-reliance" 34). In some ways, being a lawyer and being *man thinking* of "The American Scholar" are paradoxical states of being, one social and the other spiritual (though equally communal). If Atticus is looked at solely as a lawyer, then the ending is deeply disturbing. Yet, in fact, there are a wide variety of responses to the ending's desertion of truth and human law. In one such compelling interpretation, R. Butler views Boo as a spiritual force throughout the novel (123) and explains his exemption from the law as the special case of grace in the fallen world of the novel (126), for Boo's innate goodness overcomes evil (Ewell). If read as an Emersonian test case, then integrity of nature is paramount, and Boo's nature, though veiled, is quite different. It demands sacred protection, although I will offer a different explanation of why in chapter 5.

Emerson's thesis of the incompleteness of reading recurs in *Mockingbird* as a test for the young scholar Scout, who continually experiences a gap between her excellent reading skills and her knowledge of the world. The two practices of reading and interpreting knowledge are actually quite distinct. For example, in her first day of school Scout already reads fluently and knowledgably, ridiculing her teacher and getting into trouble. In the next breath, however, through careful irony and distance between the older narrator and the inexperienced Scout, we see Scout ridiculed as she attempts her appointment representing Walter Cunningham and acting a mini-Atticus. We receive a flashback of how she learned her special knowledge of the Cunningham "tribe" (20), which results not only in a gap between Scout's reading fluency and understanding of humanity, but also in an even larger gap between her knowledge and articulation skills: "If I could have explained these things to Miss Caroline, I would have saved myself some inconvenience and Miss Caroline subsequent mortification, but it was beyond my ability to explain things as well as Atticus" (21). It is one thing to read, another thing to understand, and quite another altogether to preach.

Atticus later points out Scout's mistake in failing not in any of these things but in her sympathetic faculty, her ability to see from the point of view of others. Voicing his famous lessons about walking in the skin and shoes of others, Atticus faults Scout: "We could not expect [Miss Caroline] to learn all Maycomb's ways in one day, and we could not hold her responsible when she knew no better" (30). In this scene, Atticus argues that Scout's sympathetic faculty is, as yet, undeveloped; that there are "kinds" of folks to study and understand for improved connection; that Maycomb's ways are an unchanging human phenomenon to learn rather than transform; and that innocence in a quasi-legal sense is ignorance of the fundamental human laws embodied by complexities of nature. Scout does not accept his critique, as she often does not accept Atticus's teachings; her path takes the form of a very different novel tradition, as I demonstrate in chapter 5. Her disinclination to accept either Miss Caroline's exemption based on ignorance or Atticus's preference for understanding Ewell nature over truancy law provides a critical viewpoint on *man thinking* and what "diverse" forms of nature he unequivocally accepts.

We see this theme of the gap between reading and understanding many times when Scout encounters scenes beyond her everyday world, such as when she overhears the sheriff and other men discuss threats to Tom Robinson on her porch—the conversation streaming through the window as if an unmediated and uninterpretable stream of consciousness—or in her trip to Cal's church, where raw impressions and surprises about "linin'" teach her about worlds beyond books. The detail that the memoirs of Joshua St. Clair are the memoirs of a madman mirrors the mad dog in such a way as to convey a suspicion of books and the bias of those who write them. Perhaps we see this most of all in the trial itself because law and the theatrical spectacle unfolding before her eyes conflict. Afterward, Scout notes the gap between her teacher's prejudice against African Americans and sentiments on

Hitler. ABCs are not everything, just as law is not everything, but knowledge is a continual negotiation between these various facets of scholarship.

In his "office," which Emerson shows is a loaded word emblematic of the scholar's spiritual and communal mission, Atticus has a law book *and* a checkerboard. This is important because the game is a continually invoked symbol of social calculation. For example, Scout recognizes Atticus's signature question, "do you really think so?" as one he uses both in playing checkers and in questioning the logic of others' arguments. The child-Scout (as distinct from the older narrator) is poised on the threshold of formal schooling to heighten the point that books and human nature are different. It is all the more remarkable that *Mockingbird* has received the recognition it has in American schools, given its critique of formal instruction and its hostility to the idea of a universal curriculum. *Mockingbird* prefers Emerson's earlier sentiments about what literacy is. Sitting down with men at a checkerboard can teach as much about human nature as texts from the past.

Perhaps the most important element of Emerson's "The American Scholar," in application to Atticus and *Mockingbird*, is his section about whether—and how and when—the scholar is *active*. The presumed inactivity of Atticus is directly addressed by the children quite early in the novel, and the way in which Atticus turns away from violence and offers a different theory of courage makes him most memorable to readers. He offers Mrs. Dubose as an extreme example of courage and self-trust. And he offers this lesson to Jem. It is a signature lesson of an Emersonian type, teaching that being pushed to action because of a social situation is not transcendentalism. Transcendentalism is rising above the social body; in some ways its goal is death as it strives to reach beyond the partial man—the illusory self that acts in the world—for the whole soul. Jem has to learn a healthy disgust for the body and admiration for transcending it. In an essay on heroism, which the parable of Mrs. Dubose invokes, Emerson described heroism as being ashamed of its body: "Self-trust is the essence of heroism. It is the state of the soul at war; . . . Heroism, like Plotinus, is almost ashamed of its body" ("Heroism" 162). Shame of the body is writ large on the body of Mrs. Dubose, whose wax camellia sent posthumously gives Jem a toxic shock. The female of *Mockingbird* is always the tale of the body; although the narrator mocks the doctrine of "the Impurity of Women" obsessing clergy, the doctrine shines through *Mockingbird,* most expressly revealed in the corpulent, "formidable" body of Aunt Alexandra. In the thoughtful scholarly form of Atticus and in the dying days of Mrs. Dubose, the body achieves transcendence. Only the half-man, half-woman "chameleon lady"—Miss Maudie—has the privilege of seeing and interpreting the oversoul that Atticus incarnates.

If *Mockingbird* is arguably misogynistic, attributes of masculinity are very much in question in the novel. Emerson tackles the presumed impracticality and feminization of the scholar in a way that seems as defensive as Atticus's "defense" of manhood in *Mockingbird:*

> There goes in the world a notion, that the scholar should be a recluse, a valetudinarian,—as unfit for any handiwork or public labor, as a penknife for an axe. The so-called "practical men" sneer at speculative men, as if, because they speculate or *see,* they could do nothing. I have heard it said that the clergy,—who are always, more universally than any other class, the scholars of their day,—are addressed as women; that the rough, spontaneous conversation of men they do not hear, but only a mincing and diluted speech. They are often virtually disfranchised; and, indeed, there are advocates for their celibacy. As far as this is true of the studious classes, it is not just and wise. Action is with the scholar subordinate, but it is essential. Without it, he is not yet man. Without it, thought can never ripen into truth. (5)

Action and manhood are inextricably bound together. Lee seems overtly invested in presenting Atticus as a test case for ideologies of masculinity and action. Atticus refuses the conventions of masculinity in Maycomb, much to the embarrassment of the children and especially Jem. Whereas the possibilities of action are accessibly performed for the children when he shoots the mad dog, it is the questioning of Atticus's masculinity that more importantly corresponds to Emerson's defensive comments.

Questions about Atticus's definition of manhood are significant in a novel largely devoted to the construction of gender and gentlemanliness. We find questions of masculinity expressed in the rape trial, where the sympathetic faculty gets Tom into trouble and where Tom's debilitation exempts him from the type of masculinity aspired to by "a little bantam cock of a man" (169–70) named Bob Ewell. Ewell seeks to use his daughter as a ticket to masculinity, showing us that masculinity is tied to a discourse of southern womanhood and a chivalric code of defending it. Similarly, Jem and Dill begin to exclude Scout based on her gender, and accusations about acting like a girl abound as insults. The sexually ambiguous figure of Dill, based on Truman Capote, finds expression in an obsession with Boo Radley, evoking further questions about masculinity, violence, and homosexuality. Lee's representation of Atticus provides an overarching unity of man and scholar from which all other sites of masculinity are measured.

Just as Atticus becomes an emblem of Emerson's visions of self-reliance, heroism, and *man thinking,* Atticus also presents us with Emerson's defense of the scholar as representative (embodying "the many") but not feminine; in fact, he is inherently an active man by the way he *sees.* What is noteworthy about the mad dog incident is that Atticus takes off his glasses to see, exchanging the role of scholar for the role of transcendent, masculine see-er. The question of Atticus's potential for action is overtly addressed by Scout at the beginning of the mad dog chapter. Scout begins by bemoaning the fact that her father does not *do* anything, which in the narrator's passage is linked to his corrective lenses and his propensity for reading:

> Our father didn't do anything. He worked in an office, not in a drugstore. Atticus did not drive a dump-truck for the county, he was not the sheriff, he did not farm, work in a garage, or do anything that could possibly arouse the admiration of anyone.
>
> Besides that, he wore glasses. . . . He did not do the things our schoolmates' fathers did. . . . He sat in the livingroom and read. (89)

As humorous as her child's view of activity is, and as limited as her view of masculinity is, Scout's challenge frames the character of Atticus as needing to prove his manhood in a way that others can understand. As *man reading,* Atticus is also the eye of the community, something interfered with by his status as a southern Finch. But his "right eye" is beyond the tribalism suggested by kinship, politics discussed by Laurie Champion.

Atticus's masculinity unfolds in the chapter later as a matter of class; Jem pronounces him a gentleman, which is a distinct category that suggests the discourse of class and chivalry backing Atticus's stance, particularly toward women. As Kathryn Lee Seidel argues in her book *The Southern Belle in the American Novel,* medieval feudalism provided nineteenth-century southern writers with a symbol of "southern men not simply as country squires but as gallant knights. The immense popularity in the South of the novels of Sir Walter Scott is logical in this context" (5). Jem reads *Ivanhoe* to Mrs. Dubose. Much later in *Mockingbird,* the narrator distinguishes Atticus as "only a man" (134) when confronting the social world of female frivolity, also the Finch work energetically undertaken by his sister. Although Atticus's manhood unfolds in a specific binary opposition against ladies, and although her father's world will be distinguished from the "novel of manners" that Scout must navigate because she is female, early on the question of Atticus's manhood is couched as a matter of action. What does the *man thinking* actually do but see and read?

Aside from the politics of Atticus's ability to look from his right eye as the eye of nature rather than family, culture, and tradition, the detail that he wears glasses, like John Henry in *Member of the Wedding,* whose gender is very much a question, aligns him with the position of calm scholar, which in *Mockingbird* is a matter of dispassion and everything opposed to sexuality. During the trial, Scout observes the role of Atticus in dispelling ghosts and passions. He exorcises sexual and other dangers that emerge in the night:

Atticus was proceeding amiably, as if he were involved in a title dispute. With his infinite capacity for calming turbulent seas, he could make a rape case as dry as a sermon. Gone was the terror in my mind of stale whiskey and barnyard smells, of sleepy-eyed sullen men, of a husky voice calling in the night, "Mr. Finch? They gone?" Our nightmare had gone. (169)

It becomes clear that Lee wishes to construct real manhood as dispassionate action, the "infinite capacity for calming" and thereby expelling the passions of others. This, therefore, is what the shooting of the mad dog really means; Atticus strikes down madness and even emotion because they are irrational qualities, exemplifying what Emerson meant when he said that heroism is ashamed of its own body.

Atticus exemplifies the privileging of sight as a quality of transcendence. The ability for sight is always fraught with symbolism in literature; for example, in *Member of the Wedding*, Frankie wants to be seen, and it disconcerts her that her African American caregiver, Berenice, has one glass eye that sparkles a bright blue and that looks away from its partner eye. The importance of seeing is, of course, encoded in the name Scout, which, in her case, remains distinct from interpretation and understanding. Of course, in the incident of the mad dog, it is Cal who correctly interprets the madness first; she is a more passionate figure who does things Atticus would never do, such as spit, hit, and reprimand the children with force enough that her grammar becomes erratic. Atticus's role is not to recognize passion but to quell it; while he studies and understands human feelings, he is the romantic, the poetic practice of which Wordsworth described as "emotion recollected in tranquility" (Wordsworth 444). The depiction of romantic dispassion in the midst of other distinctly tempestuous characters echoes Margaret Mitchell's depiction of the gentleman Ashley Wilkes in *Gone with the Wind*, whom Betina Entzminger views as the novel's dreamer-artist figure, and who, Seidel observes, "represents a spiritual man, unconcerned with the physical passion that [Scarlett] fears in herself" (*Southern Belle* 54). The ungovernable passions of Scout and others replicate this binary opposition as well as "Ashley's complex ennui" (54) shared with Atticus, who fully realizes his tragic destiny.

The mad dog incident, which is a recurrent motif of the entire novel (see Jones), is also noteworthy because the action taken by Atticus lifts him from his typical posture of *man reading*. The dog may seem to suggest the madness of cultural prejudice, but it is also, if anything, an emblem of nature—the Emersonian definition of nature as encompassing the peculiar habits of human beings. This is studied by Atticus in the way Emerson suggests it can be. Atticus only reluctantly takes the weapon from Heck Tate, just as he reluctantly assumes the appointment to defend Tom Robinson, and just as the instance of his defense will recall in Scout's mind the mad dog scene, rewritten as an empty gun. Whereas critics of Atticus such as Monroe Freedman have magnified the fact that Atticus only reluctantly takes the case and that failure to take the judge's appointment would be punishable with a prison sentence, it is clear that Lee has specific narrative conventions to follow. The hero of a mythical journey must always be reluctant to take "the call" to duty, and duty must be experienced as a burden rather than a joy. Atticus's health must suffer as a result. As made specific in Emerson's "The American

Scholar," the scholar's duty, like Atticus's, is the "slow, unhonored, unpaid" task of revealing truth:

> I have now spoken of the education of the scholar by nature, by books, and by action. It remains to say somewhat of his duties.
>
> They are such as become Man Thinking. They may all be comprised in self-trust. The office of the scholar is to cheer, to raise, and to guide men by showing them facts amidst appearances. He plies the slow, unhonored, and unpaid task of observation. . . . he must accept,—how often! poverty and solitude . . . and the state of virtual hostility in which he seems to stand to society, and especially to educated society. For all this loss and scorn, what offset? He is to find consolation in exercising the highest functions of human nature. He is one, who raises himself from private considerations, and breathes and lives on public and illustrious thoughts. He is the world's eye. He is the world's heart. . . . These being his functions, it becomes him to feel all confidence in himself, and to defer never to the popular cry. (7)

In the mad dog chapter, which is invoked again in the trial as the people await Tom's judgment, Atticus is presented as the community's eye and civilized heart, thus the representative man. Poverty, which is very much an issue in *Mockingbird,* is an inherent part of his implicit heroism, embedded by both Emerson and Thoreau in their moral visions. Poverty is not really poverty because the transcendental self that circulates into nature always returns with a greater sense of spirit, which the gifts on Atticus's doorstep convey.

"Only a Man": Emerson, Whitman, and the Many

In Erisman's viewpoint, Lee presents the romanticism of Emerson to counteract her view of the American South, which is "a dual view":

> On the one hand, [Lee] sees the South as still in the grip of the traditions and habits so amply documented by Davis, Dollard, and others—caste division along strictly color lines, hierarchical class stratification within castes, and exaggerated regard for kin-group relations within particular classes, especially the upper and middle classes of the white caste. On the other hand,

she argues that the South has within itself the potential for progressive change, stimulated by the incorporation of the New England romanticism of an Emerson, and characterized by the pragmatism, principles, and wisdom of Atticus Finch. (46)

Atticus retains appeal because he precisely represents Emerson's radical emphasis on self-reliance, "Whoso would be a man must be a nonconformist" ("Self-reliance" 33), but his self-reliance is not opposed to society because of its Emersonian faith in the many in the one. However, in social life, as I will explore in the next chapter, Atticus retains a healthy dose of the southern gentleman detached and ironic toward worlds that Scout cannot transcend: worlds of women. A curious blend of the romantic dreamer Ashley Wilkes and the sarcastic, plainspoken Rhett Butler immortalized by Margaret Mitchell, Atticus is often contrary in dialog and happy to get a rise out of ladies like Aunt Alexandra. In the next chapter, I will name another likely model for Atticus in Harriet Beecher Stowe's Augustine St. Clare, which brings out other characteristics of Atticus that emerge in his social interactions.

Later in the novel, as Lee turns her focus to mocking the social world of female hypocrisy, the narrator observes that Atticus fails to instill in the children respect for family and lineage, those specific traditions the American transcendentalists were rejecting, because he was "only a man." She thus signals the fact that in the early part of the novel she is constructing the masculinity of *man thinking,* whereas in the latter part of the novel she is demonstrating the limits of *man thinking,* especially against mobs of women. If transcendence of self and body is indeed Atticus's platform of being, Aunt Alexandra is all body. Although Aunt Alexandra is a comic figure whom we are supposed to laugh at until the end, when she is somewhat redeemed, *Mockingbird* actually launches a multifaceted critique of the transcendent posture by showing how many people identified with their bodies cannot possibly achieve scholarly disembodiment. Dean Shackelford argues that Scout strongly identifies with her father (122–23), and Seidel argues that Scout identifies with her father's stoicism. Although she is at risk of "becoming a southerner," embodying "all the faults of the old South when we first meet her" (81), the narrator grows up to emulate Atticus and revises the role of lady (Seidel, "Growing Up" 90). Johnson, who believes Scout grows up to be a lawyer ("Secret Courts" 130), and Woodard, who believes the narrator's style mirrors a law professor's (568), seem to agree. In my mind, this is only half the story. In many ways, the narrator wishes us to understand that the "one" of one-shot Finch fails as an inclusive philosophy. The many are not necessarily represented by the one, who is "only *a* man" after all.

As Toni Morrison puts it, "what seemed to be on the 'mind' of the literature of the United States [in the nineteenth century] was the self-conscious but highly problematic construction of the American as a new white man. Emerson's call for that new man in 'The American Scholar' indicates the deliberateness of the construction, the conscious necessity for establishing difference" (39). Like Leslie Fiedler, who points out the repetitive pattern of white men and racial others engaged in homosocial quests for democracy in nineteenth-century literature (*Love and Death*), Morrison argues that the matter of American difference called forth by Emerson and other nineteenth-century thinkers became a matter of distinction from the Africanist presence in the nation, rather than merely a matter of difference from Europe. Just as the Mohican figured in Cooper's construction of manhood in Natty Bumppo; just as blackness figured in Poe's pursuit of whiteness in *The Narrative of Arthur Gordon Pym;* just as Queequeg became an instrumental subordinate player in *Moby-Dick;* and just as Jim became intrinsically part of Huck's quest for freedom in Twain's work; so, too, Tom Robinson is the crucially embedded Africanist presence intertwined in *Mockingbird*'s exploration of Atticus's masculinity and active heroism.

Tom's disability, which emasculates him and makes him perceived as a "safe" and asexual innocent in what I argue in chapter 2 is a manifestation of Uncle Tom melodrama and neutralization of Richard Wright's Bigger Thomas, becomes the counterpart to what Crespino calls Atticus's platform of paternalism. It hardly destabilizes racism. Atticus's noble defense of Tom falls into a later tradition of white lawyers defending black men and, as in *Native Son,* attempting to give expression to black male defendants who are "seen" as spectacles and who pervasively experience themselves "as if . . . 'acting upon a stage'" (Wallace 35). This "spectragraphia," theorized by Maurice Wallace in *Constructing the Black Masculine* as the difficulty of black male subjectivity in the face of pervasive visual images of what black manhood *is,* precludes speaking: "Much has been made by Wright scholars of Bigger's inability to articulate the absurdity of his life in Book III of *Native Son*" (41). Atticus's ability to eloquently speak for civil rights depends upon a similar framing of Tom's lack of manhood and speech. Likewise, Atticus's rising action falls into two traditions that Seidel enumerates as frequent tropes of "Southern Belle" literature—literature in which rape suggests "the ravaging of the South" and the destruction of southern illusions (147), and literature of "the belle on trial," popular in the 1930s, in which "there is a sense of ambiguousness about who is guilty and who is innocent; guilt is usually communal and southern society becomes the real defendant" (157). Atticus's chivalry emerges from his crusade against southern paranoia about black men, but it does so by ironically calling upon the same knightly conventions as spelled out in, for example, the racist novels of Thomas Dixon, which, Mason Stokes argues in *The Color of Sex: Whiteness, Heterosexuality, and the Fictions of White Supremacy*, deepen the applicability of Sedgwick's *Between Men* to racial politics in American culture. In American novels, the triangulated desire between a woman and two rival suitors has frequently hinged upon race. White manhood emerges by abjecting and controlling not only women but also the potential pairing of white women and black men, which in *Mockingbird* becomes the specular event on trial and which is spelled out in Mayella's beaten body and Tom's useless arm.

Ironically enough, there are challenges to Atticus's paternalism from other fronts *in* the novel, which bring home the novel's theme in more subtle ways. There are challenges in terms of gender, most evident in Scout, Cal, and their more vexed relation to transcendental ideals; there are challenges in terms of sexuality, most evident in Dill and Boo's vexed relation to masculinity; and there are challenges in terms of regionalism and its role as "nature" limiting rather than expanding the self and consciousness. These important challenges explain why Lee drew her image of the mockingbird from a poem by Whitman, who was perhaps the most important disciple of Emersonian ideas in American literature but who explored some possibilities and implications that Emerson did not really like: that of the embodied, sexual self embracing body and passion, thus the "baser" instincts of nature connecting American people. Mayella, figured as the loneliest character in the novel, sets in motion the chain of events leading to Tom's death by trying to make a sexual connection. People who make transgressive sexual connections, people like Dolphus Raymond, do not transcend anything; rather, they either disappear, like Boo and eventually Dill, or they live in disguise. They *pass*.

Whitman's ever-expanding *Leaves of Grass* embraced all Americans by listing its many types and thus incarnating an ever-widening democratic poetry. He heard Emerson lecture on "The Poet" and became convinced that he would become the bard of the New World in a much fuller way than the intellectual Emerson could foresee. Whitman publicized Emerson's endorsement of his poetry by printing, without permission and to the annoyance of Emerson, a letter from Emerson commending him on his achievement. Emerson also became annoyed at the continual allusions to sexuality and the generative organ "all men possess" which, in Whitman, demands "the writing." Whereas Jerome Loving believes Emerson's recommendation that Whitman not publish the "Children of Adam" sequence was more practical than moral, Lee Gentry comments on "why Emerson could not accept all of what Whitman had to say in his poetry" (1) and concludes that "it was difficult for Emerson to accept Whitman's belief that (his) own celebrated sexuality was (for him) his assertion of self" (1). Nevertheless the self-reliance and transcendent ideal of nature in Whitman's vibrant poetry gave Emerson joy.

Throughout *Song of Myself* Whitman located in sexuality the regenerative forces of nature and a transcendent wholeness. Thoreau, too, objected to some of the "simply sensual" ("Transcendental Legacy" 1) poems, although he, too, celebrated Whitman's truth and exhilaration. Whitman's shifting perspective on Emerson can be found in Kenneth Price's discussion of Whitman's 1856 open "master" letter acknowledging Emerson as inspirer. In the 1870s, Whitman commented on Emerson as "too aristocratic to capture the distinctive characteristics of American life" (86), and he noted in an unpublished manuscript, "We want freedom, faith self-support, clearness[.] What have we? Instead of the storm beating, the wind blowing, the savage throat, the ecstasy and abandon of the prairie, the dashing sea, we have always a polite person, amid a well-pressed assembly, in a parlor, talking about Plutarch, Astronomy and evidently dominated by the English" (Price 86). Whitman's growing sense that Emerson, who had initially articulated himself in the figure of *man thinking* and who had initially taken up the purposeful stance of infidel (Loving 120–21), had softened over time was true. One reason why Atticus may be reading *The Gray Ghost* at the end is because Emerson himself had become hopeless about the way in which we are all trapped in our own visions, doomed to glimpse only partial aspects of whole Man: "Sleep lingers all our lifetime about our eyes, as night hovers all day in the boughs of the fir-tree. All things swim and glitter. Our life is not so much threatened as our perception. Ghostlike we glide through nature, and should not know our place again" (Emerson, "Experience," 267).

Jerome Loving discusses the duality within Emerson that Whitman sensed, "a view of Emerson that Stephen Whicher later defined as the Emerson of Freedom and the Emerson of Fate" (13) emerging in later essays and oratories. This duality of Atticus, who never expects to win the case and thus seems the Emerson of "Experience" even while modeling *man thinking,* is puzzling to Scout. Atticus seems resigned to the mind-set of Maycomb "nature" (the mad dog) even while he espouses Emersonian faith in the individual, rather than in activism, which dissatisfied the abolitionists in Emerson's time. Whitman was the more political of the two, and he held more admiration for statesmen than intellectuals. But tellingly, it is from Whitman's uncharacteristic 1859–60 poetry about death and "experience" from which Lee seems to have drawn her central image of the mockingbird.

The poem from which Lee drew her title and image was variously titled "A Child's Reminiscence" in 1859, "A Word from the Sea" in 1860, and "Out of the Cradle Endlessly Rocking" in 1871. Each title gives a slightly different emphasis to the poem's subject, which is the artist as a young child. When young, the artist witnesses the "two guests" from Alabama turn into one "solitary" "brother" singing for its likely deceased mate; the speaker has an intimate connection to the elegiac message, "He poured fourth the meanings which now I, of all men, know" ("A Child's Reminiscence" VIII). The first title emphasizes the structure of memory and the man's becoming a child again through tears and poetic song; the second emphasizes mortality as the word continually whispered by the sea is "Death, Death, Death, Death, Death" (XXXIII); the third title emphasizes regeneration and rebirth, the theme of coming into the role of poet through the burden and responsibility of artistically rendering what has been witnessed—the "dark brother's" grief. All apply to the "child's reminiscence" voiced by Lee's Scout, who, like Whitman's boy, is never again to be free after witnessing loss and who becomes American bard through her artistic obligation to mark the mockingbird's elegy.

The earlier versions of Whitman's speaker's panic are the most expansive:

O throes!
O you demon, singing by yourself! Projecting me!
O solitary me, listening—never more shall I cease imitating, perpetuating you,

Never more shall I escape,

Never more shall the reverberations,

Never more the cries of unsatisfied love be absent from me,

Never again leave me to be the peaceful child I was before what there, in the night,

By the sea, under the yellow and sagging moon,

The dusky demon aroused, the fire, the sweet hell within,

The unknown want, the destiny of me.

O give me some clew!

O if I am to have so much, let me have more!

O a word! O what is my destination?

O I fear it is henceforth chaos!

O how joys, dreads, convolutions, human shapes, and all shapes, spring as from graves around me!

O phantoms! You cover all the land and all the sea!

O I cannot see in the dimness whether you smile or frown upon me!

O vapor, a look, a word! O well-beloved!

O you dear women's and men's phantoms! ("A Word Out of the Sea" XXX, XXXI)

In Whitman's apostrophe, we find a combination of torture and privilege at witnessing phantoms; he fears yet longs for more pain. Whitman's outburst denotes all the immediate emotion specifically repressed by Atticus Finch, who countenances no spiritual crisis and foresees no threat to his children. Indeed it is eerie to read Emerson's sentiments on the death of his son in "Experience": "In the death of my son, now more than two years ago, I seem to have lost a beautiful estate, --no more. I cannot get it nearer to me. . . . it does not touch me; something which I fancied was a part of me, which could not be torn away without tearing me, nor enlarged without enriching me, falls off from me, and leaves no scar" (270). This detachment is like the first paragraph of Lee's novel, in which the permanence of Jem's scar is questionable. From this intertext, we can understand why Atticus's shooting of the mad dog functions as a primal scene for Scout; whereas the definition of a primal scene is usually witnessing of parental sexuality, in some form Scout's primal scene is her father's expulsion of all irrational qualities and bodies. Whitman's poem embodies the exuberance of grief excommunicated to the margins in *Mockingbird,* along with everything a six-year-old reminiscence cannot say because of the novel's deep resistance to passion, equated as it is with poor whites of the backwoods. As I show in chapter 6, the primitive violence lurking in polite civilization is a strong theme in *Mockingbird,* a theme derived from Edith Wharton's *The Age of Innocence.* But the outbursts of people like Scout and Cal, who both spit, yell, hit, and name-call, seem understated when compared to Whitman's outburst for the mockingbird.

The poem is much darker than Whitman's earlier celebration of self, body, sexuality, and all Americans in *Leaves.* While positing an artistic crisis that is relatively conventional in romantic poetry, it also suggests some personal crisis in finding poetry meaningful. The loneliness and isolation in the poem, Loving argues, render the same theme as the *Calamus* poems, which were written just prior to "A Child's Reminiscence." In his anonymous review of his poem, titled "All about a mocking-bird," Whitman equates the poem with his announcement that he has returned to the role of New World bard after three years of silence. This is certainly consonant with its subject of crisis and chaos that loss and loneliness threaten—almost the dark consequence of self-reliance. Indeed, Loving locates in both Emerson's later work and Whitman's *Calamus* and "Out of the Cradle" the paradox of transcendentalism, most expressly revealed in "As I Ebb'd with the Ocean of Life": "Its subject is the tension that self-reliance produces between the mortal self and its lover on the other side of death. For self-reliance effectively blurs the mortal vision, dissolves the impact of death. It sees beyond or through death to the other half . . . abnegation [of the mortal self] calls for the denial of personal love as well" (169). It is this paradox of detachment that lies at the heart of *Mockingbird:* Atticus's respect for nature and the integrity of the individual's point of view, regardless of that individual, leads to the novel's recognition of hopelessness and death; death, glimpsed in Mrs. Dubose and in Tom, is only the endpoint of the partial man.

We are now in a better position to understand the discourse of masculinity and wholeness in *Mockingbird:* Tom, "if he had been whole, he would have been a fine specimen of a man" (192). There are no whole men; even the man most innocent and thereby most identified with nature, Tom, is not Emerson's whole man. In fact, Tom runs and his outburst is systematically punished. The novel recognizes the deeply problematic theory of respecting everyone's nature since no one is whole and no one can aspire to transcendental detachment because it leads to a hopeless passivity. Atticus is so Emersonian that he cannot integrate Ewell into his consciousness. Whereas Atticus insists that Ewell was out of his mind, Heck says that Ewell is simply "'mean as hell'" (269). Importantly, Atticus insists that he cannot believe such a man exists, but Heck, who later says he himself is not a very good man, says that some men are simply unworthy. Atticus really cannot give up his position in the scene. The implication is that the good man can only recognize "good man," whereas the "not very good man" can recognize meanness. Therefore, *The Gray Ghost* could be the story of everyone in the end—the story of mortals with blind spots. Atticus even sees the point of view of the prison guards; understanding quenches outrage.

In stark contrast, Whitman's poem conveys a strong and passionate commitment to forever sing what the child witnesses and announces the child-artist's role as translator, which is the role into which Lee writes her narrator. Whitman's speaker is initially detached but also curious: "every day I, a curious boy, never too close, never disturbing them, / Cautiously peering, absorbing, translating" ("A Child's Reminiscence" I). The speaker's youthful curiosity about the monogamous birds suggests he is curious about sexuality and union, which mirrors Scout's curiosity about the trial, poignant because she has no other monogamous models to study. Betsy Erkhilla reads the ideal of union presented by Whitman's narrator in the mockingbirds "two together" as the union of North and South. The lines suggest this by announcing unity of opposites such as North/South, black/white:

> *Two together!*
> *Winds blow South, or winds blow North,*
> *Day come white, or night come black,*
> *Home, or rivers and mountains from home,*
> *Singing all time, minding no time,*
> *If we two but keep together.* ("A Child's Reminiscence" III)

The sudden disappearance of the she-bird, which is similar to the off-stage death of Tom, and the ensuing song of grief and death can be interpreted in two ways: one political, the other personal, just as *Mockingbird* can be interpreted politically or personally—in the sexual journeys of Scout and Dill. Erkhilla makes the case that the panic of the speaker once he hears the song of separation, lines mostly deleted in the later 1871 version, parallels the way Whitman would have felt in the years leading up to the Civil War, when the dissolution of union seemed imminent. The growing conflict in 1960 between state and federal power certainly feels similar. However, Atticus's detachment and Scout's commitment to tell her story suggests a more intimate connection, which critics such as Laura Fine in "The Narrator's Rebellion" argue is the connection between various types of outsiders—from Tom to Boo to Mayella to Dill to Scout—the outsider that could very easily denote the homosexual.

The typical reading of Whitman's panic and elegiac tone includes his personal crisis of love, as represented in the male-male love of the *Calamus* poems. Whitman even alludes to his "Calamus" experience in the mockingbird poem (Loving 167). The twelve-poem sequence "Live Oak, with Moss," which would later be dispersed in the published *Calamus* poems, depicts a man awakening to a glorious male-male love affair and after its end, finding himself in hopeless isolation, which indeed makes him someone who would understand the mockingbird's loss of soul mate:

Sullen and suffering hours! (I am ashamed—but it is useless—I am what I am;)

Hours of torment—I wonder if other men ever have the like, out of the like feelings?

Is there even one other like me—distracted—his friend, his lover, lost to him?

Is he too as I am now? Does he still rise in the morning, dejected, thinking who is lost to him? and at night awaking, think of who is lost? (qtd. in Killingsworth 5)

The "Live Oak, with Moss" sequence, focusing on passion for a man that the speaker "dare not tell" (1.85), conveys the speaker's sense that writing poetry now feels an empty ambition because it is enough to "be with the man he loves" (Parker 1). Whether a real love affair or an artistic composition of homosexual desire, the sequence and its content, which James Killingsworth argues alter the relationship to nature in future poems, and which Hershel Parker calls a gay manifesto, suggest a very personal meaning to why the speaker of the mockingbird poem so intimately knows the "dark brother's" pain: "Yes, my brother, I know, / The rest might not—but I have treasured every note" ("A Child's Reminiscence" IX.1–2).

Similarly, this volume takes the position that the ones who know the brother's pain in *Mockingbird* know it because they inhabit a position of spiritual loneliness from having homosexual tendencies (see also Fine, "Structuring"). Spiritual isolation characterizes many protagonists in southern fiction after the earlier Renaissance, but it is particularly pronounced in influential *Mockingbird* intertexts such as Truman Capote's Joel Knox (*Other Voices, Other Rooms*), a homosexual boy desperate to be loved, and Carson McCullers's Frankie (*Member of the Wedding*), who more than anything seeks connection. When she imagines becoming a member of the wedding, she imagines becoming a member of love. To do so, she has to become a sort of drag queen; she becomes F. Jasmine and wears an orange evening gown with sparkling silver slippers. The discourse of *drag* and *passing* lies in the margins of *Mockingbird*—consider Dolphus, Miss Maudie the chameleon, and Scout, who will learn to pass out cookies with the ladies—just as homosexuality lurks in the intimate silences of Whitman's mockingbird poem. There has to be a reason that "Boo's children" (279) bear intimate witness to the grief of the mockingbird. Boo and his "children" share concerns about not being men at all, much less being whole men.

Whitman's poem as an embedded intertext of *Mockingbird*, with its translation of what occurred in Alabama to separate soul mates, seems to point to some precise reason that the narrator of *Mockingbird* would bear the social obligation to record what is *not* Whitman's natural and organic "Death, Death, Death, Death, Death," whispered eternally by the sea, but murder. Punishment and violence in the novel emerge from what was initially someone's attempt at love. There is in Whitman's mockingbird poem a longing to return to a state before the onset of knowledge. Although Scout was hardly a peaceful child to begin with, and in fact lives with two male figures mourning a woman, the connection suggests that Scout is somehow the "I" who "of all men, know" the meanings of the mockingbird's song. Homosexuality could well provide the answer, especially since the overt oppression of Scout in terms of female accouterments seems hardly comparable to the sort of intimate knowledge of the "sad brother's" pain required for the song to be sung. Scout is singing not only Tom and Helen's pain, but also the pain of Dill,

Boo, Mayella, and mixed children, who, like Whitman's *Calamus* speaker or McCullers's Frankie, belong nowhere (observes Jem).

Scholars of gay studies view Whitman's terms like "amativeness" and "adhesiveness" as codified words for male-male love (Sedgwick, *Between Men* 204); Killingsworth discusses Whitman's notebook, in which, in 1870, he urged suppression of a "'diseased, feverish, disproportionate adhesiveness'" (2). Whitman's elegiac themes and images of male "friendship" or comradery have long been understood as codes for homoeroticism (see Lynch). Killingsworth points out that Whitman emphasizes secrets and confessions throughout the *Calamus* poems, whereas candor and nakedness are ruling principles of earlier work. *Mockingbird,* too, transforms innocence and Atticus's quest for transparency into secrets, especially bringing into sharp focus the closeted Boo, who somehow bears a direct correspondence to both Dill and Scout, and a symbolic correspondence to the lonely Mayella. In the end, *The Gray Ghost* could be the Good Gray Poet whom post-Stonewall gay liberationists christened the Good Gay Poet and who had throughout the twentieth century been a way that gay men embraced the legacy of homosexuality in arts and culture (Chauncey 104, 285).

Let us now conclude, then, that the mockingbird title not only alludes to a general body electric that Atticus, our American Scholar, cannot countenance, but also to the grief of losing a mate and being unable to express this loss except through veiled allusions to homosexuality and loneliness. In other words, homosexuality cannot even be sung aloud by Lee in 1960, although if we trace her inspiration to Capote's candid treatment of various characters in drag, then we can see she shares his concerns with the consequences of the "love that dare not speak its name." The fact that Whitman's "Live Oak, with Moss" sequence went unremarked by scholars and teachers of Whitman in the 1950s and 1960s, Hershel Parker argues, can be traced to teachers' reluctance to deal with the subject, a reluctance that we find in teaching manuals of *Mockingbird* that do not even address Lee's telegraphing of sympathy for Dill/Capote as a gay youth. Whitman's possible homosexuality was acknowledged by Havelock Ellis in 1897: "As early as 1897, Havelock Ellis included in his pioneering book, *Sexual Inversion,* a list of famous homosexuals to give a history and a degree of respectability to his new, radical theories about sexuality. His list included Christopher Marlowe, Sir Frances Bacon, Oscar Wilde, and Walt Whitman" (Bronski 11). Whitman's homoerotic imagery influenced Edward Carpenter to come out aesthetically, politically, and sexually (Bronski 22–25). As Sedgwick discusses in her book *Between Men*, "Whitman—visiting Whitman, liking Whitman, giving gifts of 'Whitman'—was of course a Victorian homosexual shibboleth, and much more than that, a step in consciousness and self-formation of many members of that new Victorian class, the bourgeois homosexual" (28). Like statues of Michelangelo's *David* functioned for New Yorkers in the 1950s, Whitman photographs, gifts, specimens, and references were "badges of homosexual recognition . . . the currency of a new community that saw itself as created in Whitman's image" (Sedgwick 206). The most extensive treatment of Whitman's homosexuality can be found in Robert Martin's 1992 collection *The Continuing Presence of Walt Whitman*. Our understanding throughout the rest of *Mockingbird Passing*, that voices of dissatisfaction are murmuring around Atticus, will hopefully deepen the song of the mockingbird for us, just as Whitman's song continues to deepen and grow even after its last edition. What Lee achieved with her story of "beset manhood," told from the drama of the one who *knows* the mockingbird's notes, was nonetheless a Song of Many Selves that lurk in the shadows of the American Scholar and await his study.

Conclusion: The Tired Oversoul

The limits of the oversoul are quite literally addressed when the sleepy Scout awaits the verdict. In the passage that defines the sleepy town waiting for judgment, the slumbering consciousness too tired to execute the nineteenth-century promise, the narrator brings together the majors ways the novel comments upon transcendentalism:

> I had never seen a packed courtroom so still. . . . the grown people sat as if they were in church. In the balcony, the Negroes sat and stood around us with biblical patience.
>
> The old courthouse clock suffered its preliminary strain and struck the hour, eight deafening bongs that shook our bones.
>
> When it bonged eleven times I was past feeling: tired from fighting sleep, I allowed myself a short nap against Reverend Sykes's comfortable arm and shoulder. I jerked awake and made an honest effort to remain so, by looking down and concentrating on the heads below: there were sixteen

bald ones, fourteen men that could pass for rednecks, forty heads varying between brown and black, and—I remembered something Jem had once explained to me when he went through a brief period of psychical research: he said if enough people—a stadium full, maybe—were to concentrate on one thing, such as setting a tree afire in the woods, that the tree would ignite of its own accord. I toyed with the idea of asking everyone below to concentrate on setting Tom Robinson free, but thought if they were as tired as I, it wouldn't work. (209–10)

Scout points out the churchlike setting and "waiting for Godot" fashion of the community, which in imagery echoes the initial description of Maycomb as a tired old town with a sagging courthouse. The bell tolls, just as Atticus continues to consult his watch throughout the novel, gesturing toward the community's inevitable mortality. Scout has offered her father's closing speech as a sort of gospel, and she experiences the comfort of a reverend's arm, much as she experiences the comforting presence of Atticus at the end of the novel as she drifts to sleep. The trope of sleepiness and the insightful connections made in a preconscious state, as analyzed by Chura as well (9), is in chapter 6 linked to the many ironic "awakenings" and slumberings in modern women's regional writing. In the passage above, the sleepy Scout voices the novel's insightful thesis that the idea of "one" whole man simply cannot accommodate the diversity of heads that she sees even in the white-only section. It is, after all, completely fictional to categorize whiteness as a unity, whether soaked with lye or not.

The sleepy town embeds diversity and renders transcendentalism yesteryear—"passing." As if counting sheep, Scout counts the clock, which seems to make progress but in fact merely repeats. Then she counts heads as she drifts off, identifying the same span of color that Hawthorne would identify in "My Kinsman, Major Molineax" as American—white, red, and black. She then cites the status of the oversoul and its active agency; she wants to believe in its potential, as advanced by Atticus's disciple, Jem, but she also thinks it is too tired to operate effectively. Succinctly put, people are too weighed down to self-transcend. Rip Van Winkle has drifted back to sleep after all.

It could be argued that Scout has achieved a personal transcendence above the heads of others, an argument supported by the very existence of the reflective older narrator. This structure of "the child's reminiscence" as the witnessing of rape, not firsthand but in the surreal, secondhand and therefore communal ritual of the courtroom, similarly marks John Peale Bishop's southern novel *Act of Darkness,* in which the narrator is a teen boy indelibly scarred by the trial and conviction of Charlie. Like Scout, who adopts the transgendered and cross-race role that witnessing the trial invites, John learns that the courtroom is a perverse mirror of transcendentalism in that the viewer is rather democratically *forced* to experience the points of view of others:

> I had learned now nearly everything I was ever to know about the act in the woods, for I had listened throughout the trial. But even before I entered the courtroom, while it was still being consummated in my imagination, already it was an act of darkness. It had become a portion of my memory, so that I could no longer evade it, but must take, now one, now the other part, or even, since it was all in my imaginings, be both Charlie and Virginia, body and mind. (262)

John's reflection on the courtroom suggests it as an inherently queer space in which he imagines both parts, Charlie and Virginia, especially as Charlie claims that *he* was ravished, similarly to Tom's defense that he was "grabbed," "jumped on," "hugged," and "kissed" (193–94) by an aggressive, aroused female teen. The depiction of the trial entering the terrain of "dreamlike quality" and "nightmare" invites Freudian consideration of how the child's consciousness is sexually impressed. Role-playing yields multiple possibilities, including identification with the aggressive Mayella, which would accompany Scout's generally aggressive character and rejection of the "pure" southern feminine; identification with Tom, therefore in the position of being ravished by an older girl; fantasies about being touched by the father, which accords with Scout's other desires for her father's touch, which is a common daughterly fantasy, and which would qualify as a permutation of her father's "nigger-loving" and "naked" passion for Tom, at odds with his courteous detachment toward Scout; identification with bruised and maimed bodies both as punishment for these various identifications and as desire for how they register loss of innocence. The queer space of looking upon the trial evokes Whitman's rather than Emerson's model of transcendence, radical imagination of inhabiting the bodies of others rather than intellectually and spiritually recollecting emotion "in tranquility." The queer perspective encouraged here seems to result in a fluid narrator who equally observes Tom's "velvet" skin and attractive body, how pretty Miss Caroline is, or the heavenly smell of the missionary society ladies. Lee suggests the same lens of Bishop's "act in the woods" as consummated in the child's imagination.

Other similarities between the two novels, such as Bishop's judge, who "listened languidly, without ever seeming to see the witness or even hear her" (218), the boy's shock that sexual actions are dryly discussed in court, and the crowd's tense expectancy (234), suggest that Lee could have been inspired by Bishop's use of the child perspective on a rape trial. One passage in which John considers the mood of stillness and delay in court prefigures Scout's observations of Atticus's ability to dispel passions, connected with images of time that Scout perceives as unnaturally slowing down the stillness of human life. Bishop uses the perspective to argue that the southern crowd witnessing the trial is trapped by "an atmosphere of past judgments" (234–35):

> I had supposed that a courtroom was an exciting place; always they were so in books. But what struck me was the meticulous dullness of the proceedings, the lifelessness of the law. The day of the crime, that summer day, had been brought before the judge, before the jury, as though it had been a clock, conscientiously taken apart. Fragments had been passed back and forth, its wheels and springs examined; its cogs were shown to the gaping stupor of the jurors. Down to the last screw, the lawyers, by their tedious and trivial method, intended to explain the last pinion of its mechanism. But their clock had stopped. At best, it had been only a metal contrivance for measuring living time. It was no longer, as that day had been when two beings intensely lived, clashed, suffered, composed of that dark and burning element—their day was no longer time. (235)

The point is the irreconcilability of passionate nature and "the American Scholar's" method of study. The child cannot reconcile living, clashing, suffering nature with the weighty effect of history, the "gaping stupor" of those in the position of passing judgment, and the clock as a means for measuring lived experience. While the trope of broken clocks is prominent enough throughout southern literature, and a very important motif in novels of childhood that can be seen in Jem's acquisition of a "watch that wouldn't run" (60), the clock in the passage above is an extended metaphor for the failure of translating the elements of human nature into the realm of reflective consciousness.

This is precisely what Scout means when she cites the failure of communal concentration to overpower the rules of the clock. The clock with "deafening bongs" that "shook our bones" demands the action of counting, measuring, and parceling up connective nature ("bones") into different numbers, different color heads, different spaces for those of different races. It deafens and moves Scout "past feeling," slowing down her usually active mind in a way that is distinctly reminiscent of Mrs. Dubose's clock, the manipulation of which makes Scout feel "hopelessly trapped" (109).

Mockingbird documents the failure of transcendentalism and the limits of Atticus's worldview, not only through the trial but also through his inability to really step into the ways of other partial-men. The clarity of Atticus's role in expelling drama gives way to juror verdicts that mirror Scout's "dreamlike quality" as they move into her consciousness "like underwater swimmers" (210–11), but it is noteworthy that Atticus never thought he could win. Like Frederick Douglass's ending to his first autobiography, which has similar discourses of reading and manhood, Atticus is left reading and waiting for a brighter day. But he is reading something he has not read before: Jem's *The Gray Ghost*. Although Atticus has repeatedly been associated with light, signaling enlightenment, his new reading material suggests darkness that he has yet to theorize. The reading material suggests alternative canons that are equally important in the construction of *Mockingbird*.

The ghosts are many. The forms with which he is left reading include the gothic, which always undercut the enlightenment by representing everything it repressed. The form includes ghosts of color, the African, female, and gay presences that Atticus, "only a man" in the end, has yet to theorize. The ghost evokes John Mosby and therefore Confederate sentiment that has gone underground and even become masked as something else. The book was originally Dill's, whose real life inspiration was in 1960 perfecting southern gothic and comic aspects of living a life in drag. The title suggests a character from a gray landscape and twice figured as "ghost-gray" after death: John Henry in McCullers's *Member of the Wedding*. The child dies a horrid death after functioning as the gay muse for the female protagonist in the same way that Dill is the gay muse for Scout, Capote for Lee. There are many ghosts for us to address in a nation that strove for unity and in the process excluded women, African Americans, homosexuals, and children, to whom the ghost story is already known.

When Lee constructed her novel and put at its center the American Scholar to anchor its vision of rights crusades, she did not end the matter with a new romanticism. Other voices emerge in the shadows, and it is to these shadows that we now turn. Before uncovering shadows of the many who are not whole men for various reasons, we must look at the first man deemed not quite whole: Tom Robinson. He, Atticus says, was licked one hundred years before Atticus even began. This is because his journey has been predestined by 100 years of literary history; the ritualized murder of Tom had been playing its role in American drama since it first debuted in 1852. It is to Harriet Beecher Stowe's *Uncle Tom's Cabin* and related texts to which we now must turn in our uncovering of the many literary journeys uniquely coalescing in Lee's classic.

CHAPTER 2

MOCKINGBIRD AND THE NINETEENTH-CENTURY NOVEL: TESTIMONY TO THE MYTHIC POWER OF *UNCLE TOM* MELODRAMA

Not only does "A Child's Reminiscence" characterize the style and "back-thrust" (Dave 53) rhythm of *Mockingbird,* but Whitman's refrain of pending "Death, Death, Death, Death, Death" becomes the relentless song sung by the novel, as if a regenerative cycle "out of the cradle endlessly rocking." The popularity of *Mockingbird's* dark, ironic vision of American history, the fate of transcendentalism, and the sleepwalking state of justice is curious, given that the novel's narrative style, most pronounced in Scout's everyday world, is modern. As I explore in chapters 3 and 4, the narration is fraught with ironic commentary, prolepsis, fragmentation, flashback, juxtaposition, stream of consciousness, and obfuscation. Nevertheless determining the meaning of the story gives pleasure to quite a wide and even young readership. A broad analysis of form, however, can illuminate the novel's accessibility. Partaking of a long history of stage melodrama as manifested in American fiction, *Mockingbird,* with its modern roots in naive child consciousness, actually veils its true mode for mythologizing race relations: Tom show melodrama. No wonder Tom Robinson is "'licked a hundred years before we started'" (76), says Atticus.

Harriet Beecher Stowe's *Uncle Tom's Cabin* was indeed published 108 years earlier, and the novel most famous for revealing how the sins of American fathers incarnate in feral daughters, *The Scarlet Letter,* was published in 1850. If nineteenth-century philosophy forges its transcendental pathway through *Mockingbird,* so does the nineteenth-century novel. Reading *Mockingbird* through the latter's nexus of meaning enables us to more thoroughly understand why a young daughter is the witness to the American romance—to all it excludes and affects. If we view *Mockingbird* through the lens of melodrama, we find that pantomime in the trial overwhelms the literary form of the novel's earlier emphasis on consciousness and irony. Pantomime and spectacle shut down Scout's usually perceptive mind, explaining her increasing sleepiness.

Stylized melodrama has often been used by American writers to simplify and powerfully render social issues, history, and race relations in mythic terms. Melodrama defines some of the earliest popular American novels of female education, such as *Charlotte Temple* (American edition 1794) and *The Coquette* (1797); it defines the working trope of the Native American as innocent noble savage in novels such as *The Last of the Mohicans* (1826), *Hobomok* (1824), and *Hope Leslie* (1827); it defines the vision of the American past expressed in *The Scarlet Letter;* and it defines the modus operandi of *Uncle Tom's Cabin,* the most predominant intertext to *Mockingbird.* This chapter explores *Uncle Tom's Cabin* as an obvious model for Lee's novel of social protest and complements this model with discussion of melodramatic aspects and thematic correspondences in *The Scarlet Letter,* particularly in regard to "wild" daughters who cry out for recognition from their public fathers, fathers gifted with oratory and communal respect. Further, Richard Wright's *Native Son* and James Baldwin's comments about it and Stowe's novel inform my discussion of court as melodramatic theater. Through exploration of these as well as other well-known melodramas, we find surprising insights into how Lee's evokes the concept of sin. R. A. Dave describes the patterning of *Mockingbird* as that of the morality play (56), and Early in passing notes the analogy between Tom Robinson and Uncle Tom (100). By updating Uncle Tom melodrama, Lee taps into a thriving American literary tradition to which readers have been conditioned to react: they must not only think about but also *feel* the outrage of persecuting innocence. It is ultimately the reader who must experience Whitman's passionate outburst at the mockingbird's grief, a response assured by Lee's skillful deployment of Stowe's theatrical tableaux.

Stylized melodrama evolved from pantomime and a variety of theatrical influences in eighteenth-century France and England, as historicized by Frank Rahill in *The World of Melodrama.* Its "inevitably moral tone" developed from the *drame sérieux* of Diderot and his school (Rahill 9), which influenced Guilbert de Pixerécourt, whose illustrious career earned him the title of father of melodrama (Rahill xiv, 3–10, 40–52). Concerned with situation, plot, mimed action, spectacle, suffering heroines and heroes, misunderstood virtue, unregenerate villains, improbable coincidences, and "in the nick of time" saving and punishment, melodrama renders emotion through external and therefore mute means (Mercer and Shingler 22–23).

This muteness is important in *Mockingbird* because voices—who can use them and how—carry authority, as apparent in the wider Maycomb community as well as in Atticus, Scout, Calpurnia, and the Ewells, whose dialect in court becomes an issue, just as Cal's various dialects are observed. In court, Mayella believes Atticus is mocking her because she has no access to his chivalric address. On the most basic level, the image of the mockingbird is an image of voice and what it can do—imitate, parody, sing, praise, and create irony. The performance of voices and the complex style of narration, which I anatomize in the next chapter, jar against stunning tableaux of silences: the revelations of actual bodies that carry meaning by virtue of their legible muteness. Looking at the noteworthy silence of the mockingbirds in the scene of the mad dog, Dave observes the eloquence of the novel's many moments of meaningful silences (50). Melodrama features conflicts of good and evil "within the world" rather than "within the soul"—the latter, Robert Heilman argues, the terrain of tragedy (97). The conflicts of soul in *Mockingbird* are not racial as they are in William Faulkner's fiction; there *are* conflicts within the soul, but they are sexual and developmental ones in white characters, as I articulate in later chapters of this book. Racial conflicts in *Mockingbird* are a matter of pure melodrama, and as such they ironically reinforce popular culture's resistance to complexity and, by extension, miscegenation and integration.

The Past as Pantomime

Although she did not give permission for or receive royalties from melodramatic adaptations of her novel, Stowe shaped American melodrama and likely early cinema with her immensely popular *Uncle Tom's Cabin,* which by the mid-1880s had become a Tom show industry and even in the 1930s enjoyed a brief revival (Rahill 247–53), fully documented in Sarah Meer's *Uncle Tom Mania: Slavery, Minstrelsy, and Transatlantic Culture in the 1850s.* Because melodrama renders meaning through music, mise-en-scène, gesture, tableau, and other nonverbal signs, it has enjoyed a widespread tradition in cinema and thus has been most productively theorized by recent film critics as a mode, a rhetoric, and a sensibility rather than simply a genre or style. For example, scholars such as Christine Gledhill in 1986, influenced by Peter Brooks's 1976 *The Melodramatic Imagination: Balzac, Henry James, Melodrama, and the Mode of Excess,* and Linda Williams in 1998 anatomized melodramatic aspects of emotional excess across films, genres, styles, and media (Mercer and Shingler 79–90). Williams says that melodrama features lost innocence, misunderstood but eventually recognized virtue, an aesthetics of astonishment, a dialectic of pathos and action such that a tension of being "too late" and of something lost provokes tears, and Manichean conflicts of good and evil between relatively monopathic characters (Mercer and Shingler 93–94).

The trial of *Mockingbird,* with its "astonishing" revelation of mute truth, in the form of a disabled and therefore mute but legible arm, should spring to mind when we ponder Williams's definition of the melodramatic *dénouement:*

> Following Peter Brooks' line of argument, Williams asserted that a "quest for a hidden moral legibility is crucial to melodrama." This often results in big sensation scenes that present moral truths (often in gesture). These are never fully spoken in words, they constitute the "unspeakable truth." Revelation occurs as spectacular moving sensation (usually as gesture accompanied by music) sustained through physical action without dialogue. Thus, Williams wrote that, "Melodrama dénouement is typically some version of this public or private recognition of virtue prolonged in the frozen tableau whose picture speaks more powerfully than words." (Mercer and Shingler 93)

In novels, various devices take the place of music and prolong the tableau; it may be the narrator of *Charlotte Temple* or *Uncle Tom's Cabin* pleading for our sympathy as their characters stagger in deplorable postures of victimization (see Warhol); it may be a glowing "A" appearing in the sky to broadcast Dimmesdale's guilt (Hawthorne, *The Scarlet Letter* 107, 109); or, in the case of the mute revelation of Tom Robinson's useless arm, it may be the choral function of the children who enact "a swift mental pantomime" (178) to emphasize the details of Mayella's beating and then reveal the "astonishing" juxtaposition between Tom Robinson's "powerful shoulders" (185) and his "dead" arm, his "small shriveled hand" (186). The spectacle is legible "from as far away as the balcony" (186), as if in an open theater where there are no obstructed views.

Although Lee's irony throughout the novel creates humor, she does not use any irony in the court revelation, which we can see if we compare Twain's *Pudd'nhead,* in which there is a similar revelation, but the emphasis is different. To make the scene comic, Twain emphasizes Wilson's theatrical control of court spectators and the all-too-apparently-manipulated effects of pausing and building anticipation:

> Wilson stopped and stood silent. Inattention dies a quick and sure death when a speaker does that. The stillness gives warning that something is coming. . . . then he said, in a level and passionless voice:
>
> "Upon this haft stands the assassin's natal autograph . . . . and please God we will produce that man in this room before the clock strikes noon!"
>
> Stunned, distraught, unconscious of its own movement, the house half rose, as if expecting to see the murderer appear at the door, and a breeze of muttered ejaculations swept the place. (136–37)

Lee's unveiling of Tom is marked by court stillness rather than "muttered ejaculations." Spectator reactions, in contrast, occur when Ewell uses slang, which makes him comic and "lower" than the reader. In Richard Wright's trial in *Native Son,* a woman screams upon seeing Bigger, distinguishing an internal (racist) audience from the reader. Lee removes ironic commentary about the people's response to Tom because she wants to remove an interpretive layer between reader and action. The older narrator who calls attention to herself in other scenes mostly stands aside during the trial, and thus we experience the melodrama in a far less ironic manner. The revelation of Tom's arm is spectacle *for us.* Although transcribed through Scout, the transcription makes little difference. The revelation of his innocence has little effect on the public actually *in* the novel. If they had reacted, we would not *feel.*

Because of its dialectic of pathos and action "in the nick of time" or "just too late," Williams argues, melodrama renders the feeling of nostalgia for lost innocence and time as "the ultimate object of loss," even while suspenseful action builds tension (Mercer and Shingler 94). George Shelby's "just too late" rescue of Uncle Tom, or Dimmesdale's death on the eve of escape and revelation, are melodramatic instances that Hawthorne, for example, defined as fidelity not to life's complexities but to the truth of the human heart: "If [the novelist] think fit, also, he may so manage his atmospherical medium as to bring out or mellow the lights and deepen and enrich the shadows of the picture" ("Preface" vii). Romance in the melodramatic mode lends a particularly mythic cast to American history throughout texts of the eighteenth and nineteenth centuries. It has enabled American authors to replay the trauma and meaning of national history in the terms that Marx called "the machine in the garden," a simultaneous reverence for America as a pastoral space along with its opposite: embrace of national progress. Just as Stowe argued for progress through the abolition of slavery, yet managed to create nostalgia for plantation life and essentialize African Americans as childlike or as sentimental property (Brown 40–42), so, too, *Mockingbird* simultaneously appeals to America's nostalgia for small-town childhood and its embrace of liberal progress. This paradox provides the context to the novel's mythic emphasis on a persecuted innocent African American Tom, which updates *Uncle Tom* melodrama.

Hawthorne's own style of romance, which Richard Chase describes as "a tendency towards melodrama and idyll" (ix), informs Lee's approach to her subject, setting, and historical timeframe. In his preface to *The House of the Seven Gables,* Hawthorne maintains that romance involves point of view and, more important, the theme of the past's refusal to stay past:

> The point of view in which this tale comes under the Romantic definition lies in the attempt to connect a bygone time with the very present that is flitting away from us. It is a legend prolonging itself, from an epoch now gray in the distance, down into our own broad daylight, and bringing along with it some of its legendary mist . . . the author has provided himself with a moral,—the truth, namely, that the wrongdoing of one generation lives into the successive ones. ("Preface" vii)

In an interview with Roy Newquist, Lee said she wished "to leave some record of the kind of life that existed in a very small world" (qtd. in Shields 117), a world she and other regional writers felt to be disappearing. Capote had documented this sort of world several times with stories set in small-town Monroeville; he described "A Christmas Memory" as the perfect short story, his *Other Voices, Other Rooms* is an updated "My Kinsman, Major Molineux," and in *The Grass Harp* the estranged narrator asks for the gift of his childhood kitchen in a bottle, from someone who might wish to give him the most perfect gift. Lee is addressing not only the past generation of the 1930s, but also the mists of much older American pasts that were preoccupying Hawthorne even as Emerson forged American idealism. This paradoxical pull between idealism and hostility about past American sins, at once a yearning for past and progress, is one that readers of *Adventures of Huckleberry Finn* recognize. It is foundational to the mythos of American literature.

Uncle Tom's Cabin is a powerful melodramatic intertext that has peppered representations of American race relations since its debut in 1852, a little over one hundred years before Lee's composition and only two years after the publication of Hawthorne's *The Scarlet Letter*. As Linda Williams writes in her book about racial melodrama, *Playing the Race Card: Melodramas of Black and White from Uncle Tom to O. J. Simpson*, *Uncle Tom's Cabin* almost immediately became a touchstone for Victorian melodrama on the stage, and it certainly became a framework by which all subsequent racial melodrama on stage, screen, and television would be understood. Henry James described Stowe's novel as "a leaping fish" that refused to stay in one genre and instead went "leaping about the American cultural landscape" (Williams 6). Due to its mythic power and flexibility for adaptation into virtually any political agenda, from minstrel shows (see Meer) to popular film, it leapt with equal agility into even televised trials, Williams argues. It is hard not to notice the *Uncle Tom* antecedent in early films such as *Birth of a Nation* (see Williams), in Shirley Temple films of the 1930s (see Hébert), and in contemporary films such as *The Green Mile* (Williams 301–7), *Amistad*, *A Time to Kill*, and *Man on Fire*. Susan Gillman's book *Blood Talk: American Race Melodrama and the Culture of the Occult* shows how Stowe's mythos informed later writers such as Twain and Kate Chopin, as well as ritualistic ideologies and practices of groups such as the Klan. When Morrison discusses the Africanist presence in American romantic literature, she is affixing a different name to ritualized racial melodrama. She is saying that racial melodrama is the very stuff upon which romance dreams have been made. Certainly the performance of ritualized exclusions brings a community together, in *Mockingbird* as in most nineteenth-century romance in which democratic brotherhood so often involves the sacrifice of the noble "savage"—the mute innocent.

The extent to which *Mockingbird* draws upon *Uncle Tom's Cabin* demands the closest analysis. The similarity goes far beyond the persecution of Tom. Comparing the two novels allows us to unpack the meaningful interworkings of Lee's novel and explain why Lee's novel *moves* its readers while pretending detachment and irony on the part of the narrator. Just as Stowe claimed *Uncle Tom's Cabin* was partially intended for children, *Mockingbird* became part of a children's canon, as Flannery O'Connor thought it was intended to be, because of its deeply embedded working mythos. Like Stowe's novel, it features the crucifixion of a virtuous and innocent African American character named Tom. In melodramatic fashion, it depicts this persecution as the fall of the black family and home, calls upon us to restore Christian ethics and combat the sin of white law, identifies evil with lower-class characters who refuse domestic order and live beyond civilized boundaries, and yet admits that these lowly characters are merely scapegoats for what the law encodes. Simon Legree finds his parallel in Bob Ewell; both characters harbor young, light-skinned women who embody miscegenation and tempt the Toms to their doom.

However, just as the Finch household is a revised St. Clare household, Scout is a revised Eva who partakes of a historical conflation between tomboyism and racialization. Michelle Abate has shown that as early as *The Hidden Hand* (1859), tomboyism became associated with blackness and passing. Further, she has demonstrated that appropriation of the Topsy role allowed white women to explore their distaste for traditional gender codes, as revealed by Louisa May Alcott's "Topsy-Jo." Critic Kimberly Hébert makes the case that films of the 1930s featuring Shirley Temple continually demonstrate "whiteface" appropriation of the mischievous Topsy, which would suggest acceptance of the topsy-tomboy white figure in the broader cultural arena of the thirties, the period of Lee's childhood. Scout is an integrated Eva-Topsy, who, like Topsy, confronts the difficulty of converting a fiercely prejudiced aunt who disapproves of the girl's lifestyle.

It is appropriate that an integrated Eva-Topsy figure (Scout) should be the one to witness the replay of the scene of racial melodrama, for, as I will argue, Lee's children embody the nineteenth-century trope of children replaying the original sins of the fathers, sins that sink into their hearts, just as Hawthorne's Pearl incarnated the scarlet letter and just as Pearl's similarly feral and fatherless counterpart, Topsy, substantiated the fallen and godless state of her creation. The children melodramatically and implausibly "spring" from prejudice and jails, just as Pearl says "she had not been made at all, but had been plucked by her mother off the bush of wild roses, that grew by the prison-door" (77). The scene in which Scout "springs" onto Maycomb's prison stairs to save Atticus and unknowingly address a lynch mob seems almost a direct response to Hawthorne's jail scenes. Securely in the tradition of feral children who substantiate the original sin of slavery and racism, Scout, like her nineteenth-century sisters, embodies the sin of America's exclusion of others from its Eden. In perhaps the second-most "blood-and-thunder" scene, next to the trial, Scout is dressed as a ham and thus quite literally becomes an emblem of what her sinful community has pinned on her and her single father.

Lee's *Mockingbird* updates *Uncle Tom* melodrama with what both Williams and Carol Clover argue is its logical twentieth-century permutation: courtroom drama. Trial fiction, such as William Faulkner's 1931 *Sanctuary* and 1951 *Requiem for a Nun,* John Peale Bishop's 1935 *Act of Darkness,* and Ward Greene's 1936 *Death in the Deep South,* which became a popular film, uses rape as a test case for southern purity (Seidel, *Southern Belle* 157–64). Like earlier melodrama in which the spectator possesses greater knowledge than the characters and thus develops pathos for the misrecognized innocent (Mercer and Shingler 80), courtroom drama requires the active participation of the viewer, specifically as a judge or juror witnessing the adversarial structure of the courtroom and evaluating characters and eyewitness testimony. Greene's novel is akin to Lee's in that a lower-class white woman of questionable character, who is raped and murdered, is fictively transformed by the community into "the innocent" and therefore "pure and beautiful representation of southern womanhood" (Seidel, *Southern Belle* 158), although she is not part of this discourse when alive. Rather, she lives in the slums: "in a cocoon of frying grease, soot, factory whistles, noisy radios and Saturday night brawls, Mary grew.... Once her father beat her for slipping out to a dance with another girl" (Greene 17). It is rather her role in the melodramatic theater of the court that alters her persona: "The chatter ran, the cameras clicked, the reporters wrote furiously. Out of those scrawls was to rise the legend—the lily child, the innocent; the ewe lamb whose slaughter would cry to millions for atonement" (Greene 53). The press takes a similar role in *Native Son*, demonstrating how the trial must be made to conform to a Christian morality play.

Thus, in a profound sense Lee's child narrator literally bears witness to the way in which racial melodrama (as spectacle) replays the sins of American culture—literally, the sin of killing the mockingbird in the novel's Stowe-influenced Christian ethos. In "Everybody's Protest Novel," Baldwin charges Stowe's sentimentality with "the mark of dishonesty, the inability to feel," its "ostentatious parading of excessive and spurious emotion" replacing feeling entirely (14); what she achieves is, rather, "theological terror, the terror of damnation" (17) at being party to the great sin of slavery. The sin of racism similarly activates Lee's trial, not unlike the trial in Faulkner's sequel to *Sanctuary, Requiem for a Nun*. Temple Drake pleas to the governor on behalf of the black woman who killed her child, not because she cares about Nancy but because she needs to expatiate the sin of a longer history: "Because you aren't going to save her, are you? Because all this [confession] was not for the sake of her soul because her soul doesn't need it, but for mine" (196).

Changes in literary taste require that contemporary novels veil their melodramatic roots and tropes by introducing a modernist, psychologically complex point of view. Scout's psychological processing partakes of the modern achievements of authors who pioneered the perspectives of "innocents" such as Mark Twain with Huck, Henry James with Maisie, William Faulkner with Benji, and Carson McCullers with Frankie. Lee cleverly controls our responses to scenes by vacillating between distanced narration run by the intrusive presence of an older narrator, who ironically comments on the young Scout's perceptions, and engaging narration when irony recedes and a more immediate, stream-of-consciousness style takes us *into* the scene.

In scenes beyond her everyday Maycomb world, Scout reads bodies and tableaux for understanding. Thus she often does "mental pantomime" to make sense of adult social scenes. During the trial in particular we experience the older narrator Scout only now and then, and we experience far more of the young Scout transcribing the immediately unfolding pantomime. The effect is an alteration in style. The trial's narrative practice dissolves the earlier narrative style into a relatively unmediated account of good versus evil, Tom Robinson versus Bob Ewell or Uncle Tom versus Simon Legree, along with all the values they embody. The unregenerate villain, discussed by Rahill as the hallmark of melodrama, must be applied, in the least complicated way, to the man who stalks Atticus's children as ruthlessly as Chillingsworth stalks Dimmesdale. In fact, Atticus is being eaten away by the trial, just as Dimmesdale is being internally devoured by the community's scarlet letter. In melodramatic terms, cultural memory and mourning for American sins lead us back to white fathers who, try as they might, fail Uncle Toms and Hesters, Evas and Pearls.

The melodrama that takes over the novel renders formally as well as explains thematically another reason why the novel ends with Atticus reading the children's book *The Gray Ghost*. As Heilman extensively argues, melodrama operates in the social world of action, whereas internal forms like tragedy render the divided nature of the soul, turned, by the end of *Mockingbird*, into ghost. The melodramatic persecution of Tom literally haunts and to some extent shuts down the representation of Scout's consciousness that preoccupied the earlier sections in intriguing demonstrations of psychology and introspection. Theatrical spectacle in court *replaces* interiority, explaining why Scout drifts in and out of consciousness during the trial and why an overwhelming sense of stillness pervades the imagery. As Early observes and Dave articulates, "about a century divides *Mockingbird* from Harriet Beecher Stowe's *Uncle Tom's Cabin,* but there is no fundamental difference either about the content or the technique of the novels. In both we see an astonishing streak of sentimentality, an irresistible love of melodrama and the same age-old pity for the underdog" (57). *Mockingbird* demonstrates the formal failure of Scout's consciousness and voice when confronted with the mythic melodrama of yesteryear recurring on her doorstep, just as slavery murdered Eva again and again in archetypal American stage drama.

Very cleverly, by training us in the first half to read the distinction between an older narrating Scout and a limited young Scout, Lee veils the racial melodrama occurring in the scenes of the town that are slowly building and plotting against Scout's childhood and subjectivity. Lee ironically makes young Scout an expert reader—she cannot remember a time when she could not read—who actually cannot read the easily understood mode of racial melodrama increasingly replaying before her eyes. We are asked to believe that the racial melodrama occurring through the persecution of innocence— a disabled family man named Tom—is beyond her because it occupies the complex and uninterpretable world of adulthood. It is as if the sins of the past surprise her, when even Atticus has admitted, early in the novel, that the doom is inevitable.

The novel's Eva-Topsy integration into one observant character named Scout, she herself a transparent eyeball, coordinates with other themes of white "passing" and mixed households in *Mockingbird*. Yet Lee's novel fears both miscegenation and passion, qualities embodied by young Scout and antithetical to the dispassionate attitudes of adults. As Scout observes, Atticus "could make a rape case as dry as a sermon" (169), a comment revealing a narrator who, as an adult, can match his dryness but who does not completely want to, as revealed by her next comment evoking past sexual feelings about the rape case: "Gone was the terror in my mind of stale whiskey and barnyard smells, of sleepy-eyed sullen men, of a husky voice calling in the night, 'Mr. Finch? They gone?'" (169). Young Scout is always losing her head, is attracted to Tom, and is rampantly curious about Mayella, which, Laura Fine argues ("Gender Conflicts"), is because Mayella and Bob Ewell signify "dark doubles" of Scout and Atticus. Scout craves affection from her father, who, when she crawls into his lap, says to her, "'You're mighty big to be rocked'" (104), just as Pearl pleads for recognition from Dimmesdale and Topsy performs antics for love and attention. Like Dimmesdale and like Augustine St. Clare, Atticus enjoys a rare moment of passion when he makes a stunning speech, right before he "passes." At home he is detached; although the adult narrator introduces the "satisfactory" nature of Atticus's "courteous detachment" (6), the needs of the child-Scout and her satisfaction at his attentions in the last scene of the novel reveal otherwise. Whereas in young Scout's worldview passion is the human spirit, in Atticus's worldview passion is typically discouraged. Passion is passing and passion will pass.

Thus *Mockingbird* features a rather paradoxical instantiation of Stowe's passionate racial melodrama. Like the modern style of detached psychological narration, the modern "passing" tomboy Scout disintegrates or clashes against the melodramatic style of the trial, against which no symbols of modernity or integration can compete. The trial is simply innocence (black) against evil (white). Scout's "passing," her "integration," and her discursive code-switching throughout the novel reveal that she is as much Cal's child as she is Atticus's. She speaks in a mix of local and transcendent language, just as Cal switches back and forth in different communities, as analyzed by

Natalie Hess. However, young Scout does not actually learn that much in the novel—something many adults misremember. In one key scene after Tom has been treated awfully by the prosecuting attorney, Dill is crying about it and Scout reprimands him with the callous words, "'Well, Dill, after all he's just a Negro'" (199). This comment is characteristic of Scout both in her "know-it-all" interactions with Dill and in her communal role as a child who continually stereotypes others and acts without thinking. But it is also the effect of a trial that simplifies issues into two sides, black and white, defendant and prosecutor. Significantly, the courtroom has only two floors for two races. Dolphus Raymond, a figure of miscegenation, is outside of it, and although Scout is "passing" in the upper balcony, she is less and less conscious and more and more stagnant there. The trial's melodrama relies upon fixed categories that essentially cut short the potential development of Scout *and* the form of the modern novel that her narrative practice embodies, just as racism killed Evangeline one hundred years earlier.

Racial Melodrama in
Uncle Tom's Cabin and *Mockingbird*

"Melodrama" fuses the Greek word for song, "melos," with drama, a theatrical form. The term was originally used to denote musical plays, according to M. H. Abrams. Over time, however, it has become more general; we use the term "melodrama" to denote dramatic plots that privilege emotional excess, intrigue, action, and violence over complex character: "the hero and heroine are pure as the driven snow and the villain a monster of malignity" (Abrams 99). Melodrama enjoys a particular appeal in mass media and popular entertainment, and has done so since the nation's earliest literature. The melodramatic *Charlotte Temple*, written to direct sympathy for the seduced young girl excluded from the American dream, became a bestseller when the American edition was published in 1794. Like Stowe, its author Susanna Rowson employs direct address to the reader, a style analyzed by Robyn Warhol as one that disrupts the fictional pretense and thereby exempts the novel from our standards for realism. Cathy Davidson points out that *Charlotte Temple*'s broad appeal made it particularly democratic, used by the less literate to improve reading skills and develop a relationship with reading. This usage is instructive in the treatment of *Mockingbird*, which is commonly used to appeal to students' preference for mystery stories and in the meantime expose them to history, racial issues, complex symbolism, and perspective.

Ann Douglas, in her introduction to the Penguin edition of *Charlotte Temple,* theorizes the way in which the early American novel sought to educate young girls about a corrupt world, which is the story in Lee's novel as well. Douglas argues that the melodramatic mode gives power to the viewer:

> But if early novels told the story of their young protagonists' education by the world, early melodrama depicted their battles against it, and within it. Where the novel taught, melodrama excited. Melodrama dealt not in the written word but in "subliterate myths" marketed to that "feeling heart." . . . If the novel made the reader the author's equal, melodrama gave its audience precedence, top billing, so to speak, over the author—indeed, over all established authority. (xiii)

As Douglas points out (xlii), the quintessentially melodramatic moment of Charlotte fleeing into the icy winter night, to essentially be cast out and die in childbirth, is reimagined by Stowe through Eliza, who flees across the icy floes of the Ohio to save her child from slavery. This important archetype of flight distills an American myth of nation formation; thus "the scene would live yet again in D. W. Griffith's hugely popular masterpiece, the silent film *Way Down East* of 1920" (Douglas xlii). Williams also analyzes this important moment of melodramatic tableau. This sort of moment characterizes the flight of the young Scout from Ewell at the end of *Mockingbird,* a flight bent on exposing the limitations of Atticus's progressive worldview of rational individuals. Atticus's views do not hold water in the real world of popular, social theater. It is social melodrama that through ritual draws together a sleepy town, a dispassionate and in social situations sarcastic father, and a detached narrator imported from a modern tradition.

Mockingbird literally replays the history of the melodramatic novel in this country by educating a young girl through her awakening to the melodrama she witnesses, and by even melodramatically implicating her as she herself flees the villain at the end of the novel. In that flight, she is surreptitiously dressed as a ham because she has been in a pageant celebrating local products, a symbol for how she is vulnerable *because* she is a product of her local, prejudiced community, and yet she is shrouded or protected by being enclosed in her small-town world. As usual, she is in the center of her nation's racial melodrama but isn't really sure what she is seeing, unclearly giving us various impressions to be puzzled over later as evidence is collected. The melodrama in *Mockingbird* is always scrambled, with the effect that an even greater top billing is given its audience, who get to imagine that they are determining meaning. Really, meaning has been predetermined—reader response carefully calculated—by a long tradition of authors translating American history into a mythological landscape.

The character of Uncle Tom, brutally used and eventually murdered by the evil Simon Legree, sings and preaches the Gospel throughout his sojourn from Kentucky to Louisiana and down the Red River. As Jane Tompkins writes in her chapter about Stowe's large-scale plans to restructure the nation and heaven according to matriarchy, "there are only three places to be in this story: heaven, hell, or Kentucky, which represents the earthly middle ground in Stowe's geography" (138). When Lee set out to write her novel of social protest against race relations in America, *Uncle Tom's Cabin* would have been an obvious if unconscious model. Several critics have noted the tendency of melodrama to dramatize social problems and thus popularize social debate (Williams 18–19). In fact, the title *Mockingbird* is relatively opaque unless we consider that the analogy between the victimized Tom Robinson and the mockingbird, which does nothing but sing and thus is a sin to kill, evokes in addition to Whitman the song of Uncle Tom. The singing Uncle Tom is the hero "as pure as the driven snow"; his Christian song symbolizes what to Stowe was the purest relationship to God, uncorrupted by worlds of writing or formal churches—a kind of direct and instinctive faith from the heart. Stowe equates Uncle Tom with Eva, who similarly can read but cannot write, to indicate the purity and simplicity of the Christian receptive to, but not constructive in, literacy, thus uncorrupted by cultural prejudices.

Lee has a similar song to sing about how "'only the children weep'" (213) over the black man's exclusion from full citizenship. Critics of Lee's novel object to her equation of African Americans with mockingbirds (Saney 102), but the idea of the murdered songbird retains mythic power because it melodramatically embodies an ideal of purity beyond or before acculturation, equated with sin in the Christian ethic of both novels. Both novels seek to establish a narrative of Genesis, establishing the innocence of children who "fall" when they discover the sins of adults and racist cultural traditions. The Finch children find it striking that Atticus, who is not inclined to speak of sin, claims that it is a sin to kill a mockingbird. Both novels attempt to show that the sins of adults imprint themselves into the hearts of children, inherently a melodrama that mirrors the Christian master plot of persecuted innocents. Williams points out that melodrama performs a particular cultural function by identifying suffering and pain as virtue (29). In both *Uncle Tom's Cabin* and *Mockingbird*, we are to understand the suffering of the black characters named Tom as a recurrent and thus ritual sacrifice for the sins of white culture: "'They've done it before and they did it tonight and they'll do it again and when they do it—seems that only children weep,'" argues Atticus in his home court (213).

When Lee named her black victim Tom, she tapped into the cultural icon of Uncle Tom. It is nearly impossible to consider the wrongful persecution of Tom Robinson without evoking the excessive violence perpetrated against Uncle Tom. Uncle Tom has become virtually synonymous with passivity and the desexualization of the black man: "Tom, therefore, [Stowe's] only black man, has been robbed of his humanity and divested of his sex. It is the price for that darkness with which he has been branded" (Baldwin 17). Baldwin says that Tom is Stowe's *only* black man because he is the only developed black character, amidst what Baldwin views as stereotypes and mulatto figures who are essentially white. Victorian audiences looked upon Uncle Tom with sympathy because he neutralized white paranoia about the sexualized black man who, at any moment, could rise up and act upon his rage. Yet Stowe introduces Tom as "a large, broad-chested, powerfully-made man, of a full glossy black" (68), before describing his grave face and suggestion of simplicity. Stowe thus suggests that his subsequent acquiescence to oppression is a choice; he certainly could, physically, become the overseer Legree wishes him to be, and he certainly could have slain Legree when Cassy tempts him to do so.

Like Stowe, Lee inherited a dilemma in her project. White audiences' paranoia about black male bestiality had to be balanced against the fact that audiences would hardly be moved by the persecution of a nonentity. Lee follows Stowe's pattern. However, Lee had a much harder act to follow: Richard Wright's Bigger Thomas, created shortly after his success with *Uncle Tom's*

Children. Wright presents Bigger as a dichotomy. He is an angry anti-Tom, whom Sterling Brown called an example of the "bad nigger" stereotype (Rampersad xiv), and whom Baldwin faulted for being exposed in the raw: "If, as I believe, no American Negro exists who does not have his private Bigger Thomas living in the skull, then what most significantly fails to be illuminated here is the paradoxical adjustment which is perpetually made" (Baldwin 40). The deeper structure of the novel and the concordant trial, in which a Marxist lawyer at length explains Bigger's guilt and argues against the death penalty much like Temple Drake pleas for Nancy, point to Bigger as an inevitable product or victim of segregation, racism, and white paranoia about rape of white women. So terrified about how it will *look* if he is caught in a white girl's bedroom, Bigger kills, slices, and burns the body, then flees, but he is followed by the inescapable cultural image of himself in the newspaper, which he reads obsessively as he checks the furnace to see if whiteness can be burned. Book 2, titled *Flight*, and book 3, titled *Fate,* principles that similarly define the story of Tom Robinson, feature the relentless pursuit not of the police so much as the press. For example, even in glossing a headline about him fainting at the inquest, the press constructs his body as savage threat:

> His arms are long, hanging in a dangling fashion to his knees. It is easy to imagine how this man, in the grip of a brain-numbing sex passion, overpowered little Mary Dalton, raped her, murdered her, beheaded her, then stuffed her body into a roaring furnace to destroy the evidence of his crime. His shoulders are huge, muscular, and he keeps them hunched, as if about to spring upon you at any moment. He looks at the world with a strange, sullen, fixed-from-under stare, as though defying all efforts of compassion.
>
> All in all, he seems a beast utterly untouched by the softening influences of modern civilization. In speech and manner he lacks the charm of the average, harmless, genial, grinning southern darky so beloved by the American people. (323)

Invoking Bigger only to neutralize him, Scout's first glimpse of Tom includes a focus on his "powerful shoulders" (186), but it soon deflates when she sees his useless arm, symbolically lost to a cotton gin. Nevertheless Scout dwells on his physical appeal: "Tom was a black-velvet Negro, not shiny, but soft black velvet.... If he had been whole, he would have been a fine specimen of a man" (192). Tom's disability is a crucial component of the trial; the revelation of Tom's useless arm—an inversion of Bigger's ape arms—is the means by which the truth is melodramatically revealed. Ironically, his upstanding character and kindness to Mayella become secondary to the more clear fact that he physically could not have raped and beaten Mayella—well, on the right side of her body, at least. The prosecuting attorney makes the case that Tom could do a substantial amount of labor with his body, and it is clear that Scout is attracted to his physical presence, as if a sensory desire for "velvet," a word used twice to describe his skin as touchable.

Mockingbird operates with the same paradoxical appeal as Uncle Tom's Cabin, suggesting a strong adult African American man and a white daughter "poised at the threshold of intimacy ... only to contain these errant fantasies by emasculating Tom and eulogizing Eva" (Morgan 11). These words by Jo-Ann Morgan appear in her account of Uncle Tom's Cabin's illustration history. In her essay Morgan discusses the popular images of courtship and romantic garden scenes between Eva and Tom. Early illustrations that recalled "instances of courtship" (8) were so suggestive that a subsequent transformation would occur, gradually aging Tom and introducing white authority figures to supervise interactions between Eva and Tom. However, "of all the scenes and all of the characters, 'Little Eva ensconced in old Tom's lap' was uppermost in Birdoff's recollection. From 1852–1947, and even longer Tom and Eva in the garden not only endured but became the quintessential enactment of the story" (Morgan 16). Attraction to Tom titillated as much as it refused pleasure. The suggestion of rape along with innocence in Mockingbird operates by the same contradictory mechanism.

The working trope of a romantic Tom and Eva is displaced but still recognizable in Mockingbird, where the parallels between Scout and Mayella are very clear (Fine, "Gender" 124; Johnson, Threatening 89), explaining the pathos with which the narrator treats Mayella. Through vilification of Bob Ewell and Mr. Radley, argues Fine, Scout expresses rage against male power structures that she cannot express at home with a saintly father ("Gender Conflicts" 124–25). She also projects her sexual curiosity onto the trial, using the occasion to ask Cal and Atticus about rape and using Tom to ponder Mayella's frank sexual desires. Extending Fine's argument, we can also see how Scout's need for affection from her father, who really likes to detach and read, is not being met except through her curiosity about Tom, a "husky voice calling in the night" (169) amidst the smells of whiskey and barnyards. Scout repeatedly "acts out" for her father's attention, often in the name of "defending" him. In an economy of passion, she triumphs at the end of the novel; after almost losing her, Atticus (rather than Cal) attends to his children affectionately: "He unhooked my overalls, leaned me against him, and pulled them off. He held me up with one hand and reached for my pajamas with the other. . . . He guided me to the bed and sat me down. He lifted my legs and put me under the cover. . . . His hands were under my chin, pulling up the cover, tucking it around me" (281). Tom Robinson and Bob Ewell become Scout's ticket to Atticus's affection.

Both Uncle Tom and Tom Robinson thus straddle interesting boundaries. They are given youth, vigor, appeal, and bodies that are able to do hard labor; yet both are rendered "safe," impotent male figures. They do not threaten the status quo with their anger or agency, as, for example, George Harris does, and yet both become worthy melodramatic subjects largely because they do resist their oppression. Compared to Cal, for example, Tom Robinson dares to do and feel something for a white woman. Both Stowe and Lee seem to feel that white audiences would only view the black man as a sacrifice for white sins if sacrifice is a choice, virtue more than obligatory. While Uncle Tom has been equated with passivity, probably the result of changes in illustrations and in subsequent stage representations that made him older and less virile, he actually takes quite a stand in Stowe's novel by refusing to whip other slaves and advance his "career" to overseer; he refuses to turn against his own community, refusing also to report information on Cassy. Uncle Tom has an important rhetorical function in Stowe's novel, continually articulating his spiritual superiority and converting others. He takes up the work that Eva cannot finish. Even as he dies, he forgives the slaves who beat him for not knowing what they have done, gaining two Christian converts. He draws together the black community much like Tom Robinson draws together the black community in Maycomb, glimpsed in parallel scenes of the black church and the black section of the courthouse, where, significantly, the Finch children sit with, and are instructed by, the black preacher Reverend Sykes. Sykes is the commanding voice and protector of Helen that Tom Robinson cannot quite articulate, robbed as he is of Uncle Tom's rhetorical freedom.

In *Mockingbird* we see much less of Tom Robinson than we do of Uncle Tom in Stowe's novel. Yet Tom Robinson's subtle resistance is similar. His predicament is similar to Uncle Tom's, where choices are not really valid choices. Tom Robinson's resistance comes out in the trial when he repeatedly insists that Mayella is not lying but "mistaken in her mind"; his very careful answers in the trial confirm his heroism for the readers, and the cross-examination by the prosecuting attorney acts as the counterpart to Uncle Tom's physical crucifixion, as Dill's tears sentimentally convey. This substitutes for his murder because his actual murder takes place off stage, similarly to the offstage quality of violence against Uncle Tom in adaptations for children. Nevertheless, both novels use melodrama to achieve "moral legibility" (Williams, *Playing* 29), which Williams identifies as the key to melodrama's function.

Like Uncle Tom, Tom Robinson is depicted as simple goodness; his useless arm slips off the Bible when he tries to be sworn in, demonstrating the inaccessibility of the Bible to him and his plight. Both Stowe and Lee dwell on the *preliterate* faith of the black community, associated with a certain heartfelt simplicity because real faith, in sinful cultures, must be preliterate. Much of *Uncle Tom's Cabin* focuses on Tom's endeavors to read, a project in which he is guided by white children (young George Shelby and Eva). Similarly, Scout learns that in the black church, worship is conducted through "linin'," through which the preacher calls out the line and the congregation repeats and responds. The novels thus offer a highly critical view of literacy. Real knowledge is found in life and in intuitive understandings of Christianity. Although Scout cannot remember a time when she could not read, *Mockingbird* reveals the uselessness of formal literacy instruction and how little Scout actually knows, given that real understanding lies beyond books and law. This trope is, in fact, drawn from *Charlotte Temple,* a novel in which the young girl is corrupted as much by a schoolteacher as by a man. Images of reading and writing are important in both *Uncle Tom's Cabin* and *Mockingbird* because the theme of opening oneself up to sympathy through feeling conflicts with literacy. The one way in which Scout can legitimately climb into Atticus's lap is by reading whatever he is reading, which is why she fears her teacher's command to stop reading, but it is not literacy that she is after.

Literacy has often taken on a life of its own in adaptations of *Uncle Tom's Cabin.* The figuration of Eva reading to Tom was popular in advertising, for example, both because it kept Eva in charge (Morgan 22) and because it advanced an educational agenda (MacGregor 299). Although images of Eva reading to Tom are popular, they miss the point that both characters are in a particular stage of literacy; in a very important scene, Augustine fixes a letter to Chloe that Tom and Eva tried to coauthor but could not. Literacy goes only so far in a culture condemned to repeat "subliterate" melodramatic social structures. *Mockingbird,* in early school scenes, critiques the very concept of a universal curriculum and repeatedly demonstrates that although Scout is a fluent reader, she is utterly at a loss in decoding the black world with which she comes into contact; with understanding the (to her) inscrutable nature of the trial, a symbol for how life's trials exceed legal rationality; with understanding why Tom isn't freed; and with interpreting her own feelings toward Tom and the "dark" mysteries he represents. Like other writers of melodrama, Lee continually suggests, as Tompkins terms it, "sentimental power" beyond literature, law, and consciousness. With this theme, we can see Lee's doubt about the efficacy of *Brown v. Board of Education* and ensuing integration in schools.

Stowe and Lee contrast the simplicity and innocence of the Toms with the pure evil incarnated in the uneducated, lower-class white characters Simon Legree and Bob Ewell. However, the rhetoric of Christian sacrifice implies that Legree and Ewell are also only scapegoats. The real culprit is American law, implicated for giving people the power to inflict evil. As Woodard writes, "The worst villains are themselves easily seen as pathetic victims of something larger and more evil than their own venality: they are all victims of the existing social order itself, based on hallowed tradition sustained by an elaborate network of personal relationships, custom and conventions, and ultimately enforced by law" (568). In their goodness and simplicity, both Toms refuse to fight back, although they take their stands; they are thus sacrificed like Christ for white sins. In Stowe's novel, the sin is slavery, the "thing itself" opposed by Augustine St. Clare; in Lee's novel, the sin is a court that allows only white men who are typically uneducated to serve as jurors. The way in which both authors empty innocence and evil from literacy and writing announces their interest in the song- and stage-form of melodrama as a popular and accessible strategy for feeling over merely reading. Reading and writing require a certain detachment, and I will argue that stances of detachment are embodied by the two characters of Augustine St. Clare and Atticus Finch. Their detachment conflicts with the reactions of the passionate children, who model for the reader the hoped-for, Christian response to suffering. The feeling reader is the soul to be converted.

Both novels maintain a fiercely Christian stance. The failure of the community toward the black man is a failed Christian duty. As Miss Maudie articulates, "'We're so rarely called upon to be Christians, but when we are, we've got men like Atticus to go for us'" (215). Atticus exhorts the jury to, by God, do their duty and restore Tom to his family, equating protection of the black family with Christian duty, just as Stowe's evangelical, sentimental novel does. It is not so much that the novels indict white culture for refusing the black man's equality and individuality; rather, they emphasize that white prejudice destroys the black family. Both use the Christian narrative to plot the fall of the black family, further rendering the black male figures safe and wrongfully persecuted because they are primarily domestic characters. This is similar to the strategy by which Mark Twain made Jim sympathetic—primarily through scenes that highlight his role as a father. The tradition, however, is really a sentimental one; consider Harriet Jacobs's *Incidents in the Life of a Slave Girl* (1861), for example, which deploys an ethos of motherhood, suspicion of literacy, and narrative devices reminiscent of Stowe's novel. Jacobs knows her genre is the domestic novel rather than the slave narrative, arguing at the end, "Reader, my story ends with freedom; not in the usual way, with marriage" (370). Stowe's novel, like Lee's, ends with a melodramatic reconstruction of a threatened family (the Finches), rather than with freedom, because the family is the melodramatic subject. Even *Charlotte Temple* ends not with punishing the deserting lover or with the death of Charlotte but with the melodramatic reconstitution of Charlotte's parents and the newborn Lucy. Falls and resurrections occur to injure and regenerate the family.

Stowe titles her novel *Uncle Tom's Cabin* and introduces the cabin setting of Chloe and Uncle Tom to equate the black family with a New England sense of the origin of the nation's Christian goodness. As Williams argues, melodrama typically begins by constructing home as a space of innocence and "virtue taking pleasure in itself" (28). Uncle Tom's cabin features a portrait of George Washington, tapping into cultural foundations, and gives us an image of domestic bliss. In his analysis of how private and architectural space figures in the writings of black men, Wallace argues that "the more particular iconicity of black Uncle Tom's gardenpatch cabin" embodies a broader project of men seeking relief from relentless public images (111). Chloe's cooking, Tom's cabin preaching, young Master George's reading, and all the children filling the home evoke an image of a temporary Garden of Eden that the institution of slavery contradicts and causes to fall. The novel particularly dwells on the presence of a female baby who unselfconsciously plays with Tom's face even on the very day he is to be handed to the trader. Similarly, Lee dwells on the family image of Tom's residence when Atticus has to tell Helen that Tom has been murdered. Atticus carefully assists Tom and Helen's baby girl down the stairs, just before Helen "drops to the ground" upon news of Tom's death. Richards writes of this cabin scene, "such images are only slightly removed from those of happy plantation darkies that permeate earlier southern literature" (138). The baby girl emphasizes the destruction of innocence, Atticus's role in easing the fall, and the impossibility of saving the black cabin.

Both novels thus narrate the fall of the black cabin, a neat, domestic, and female-identified space located on the margins of white society. Stowe's cabin lies on the margin of the Shelby residence and Lee's cabin beyond the town dump. The cabin is idyllic but has no stability given surrounding conditions. Stowe's novel begins with images of the cabin, while Lee's novel ends with it. In fact, Lee's novel concludes by showing a kind of fall to the Finch home, the fate of which has become intertwined with the fate of the Robinson home. Atticus Finch will no longer have security, just as Jem Finch mirrors Tom Robinson with his crippled arm. Jem is parallel to young George Shelby in his presence as a witness to the fall of the black cabin. The young are models for the reader to feel the pain of the Toms and fall with the cabins.

The Christian melodrama in both novels depicts the fall of the black domestic family by pitting innocence against evil, a binary opposition that structures many other associations—children against adults, individuals against social conventions, the upper against lower classes, black against white, and the subliterate heart or conscience against law—the great shadow of evil in both novels. In Uncle Tom's Cabin, "the shadow of law" (51) lurks behind even the most idyllic plantation setting, ready at any moment to "exchange a life of kind protection and indulgence for one of hopeless misery and toil" (51). Similarly, the shadow of legal inequality affects even the best of trial circumstances in Maycomb—a fair judge, an eloquent and fair defense, and support from those with "background," as Miss Maudie puts it. No matter how just individuals are, the structure of the law itself prevents justice from being served because it puts power in the hands of white men and leaves the just use of that power to individual integrity.

Stowe takes great pains to show how someone like Senator Bird might have mistakenly voted for the Fugitive Slave Law yet is "but a man" (chapter 9) when faced with real runaways in need of assistance (law against heart), as emphasized by Marianne Noble. Similarly, *Mockingbird* is obsessed with Atticus's thesis that to understand people you need to walk around in their skin or see the view from their porch. Throughout the novel we see lessons on the worldview of the Cunninghams, the Ewells, and even the mean Mrs. Dubose, who inoculates Jem against being called a "nigger-lover" by saying it on a daily basis. Even the psychology of the prison guards—to them, Tom was merely an escaping prisoner—is a point of view to be respected, in Atticus's rational and Emersonian philosophy of individualism. The doctrine of individualism embodied by the law fails not only Tom but also Atticus himself; the attack upon his children demonstrates the limits to his philosophy of rationality and liberal understanding of others. When Ewell presents the limitations of Atticus's detached view of people, the novel moves away from law and into extralegal realms of justice. Cramer Cauthen notes that this extralegal tradition is common in southern literature, but in this case it has a precedent in Stowe's novel, where law and legal arguments, particularly justifying slavery, are too abstract to be of any use to real human beings and too dependent on the rationality of individuals.

The novels both equate public and private space, character with domestic lifestyle. Lee's novel extols the virtues of how Atticus is the same at home as he is in public. Individuals that threaten domestic order are those that are evil and live irrationally. Simon Legree and Bob Ewell inhabit similarly chaotic and dilapidated spaces that indicate their hopeless heathen condition, as domestic order is a model of godliness and good governance, Tompkins observes regarding Rachel Halliday's kitchen. Disordered kitchens such as Dinah's indicate, argues Gillian Brown, the way in which a disordered market economy has infected the private sphere (22–25), an infection that reveals the fundamental instability of even the Edenic Kentucky cabin. If the simple well-maintained cabin is the heart of a Christian nation, the dilapidated and chaotic home is everything opposed to it. It harbors uncontrolled passion rather than proper feeling and sympathy. The counterpart to Chloe in *Uncle*

Tom's Cabin is Calpurnia, who keeps domestic order in the Finch home and rules, quite literally, with a strong hand (Scout feels it more than once).

Stowe juxtaposes the meticulous order of the Shelby plantation and the decadent but beautiful classical beauty of the St. Clare plantation with Simon Legree's dilapidated home and yard:

> [Legree's] estate had formerly belonged to a gentleman of opulence and taste. . . . The place had that ragged, forlorn appearance, which is always produced by the evidence that the care of the former owner has been left to go to utter decay.
>
> What was once a smooth-shaven lawn before the house, dotted here and there with ornamental shrubs, was now covered with frowsy tangled grass, with horse-posts set up, here and there, in it, where the turf was stamped away, and the ground littered with broken pails, cobs of corn, and other slovenly remains. Here and there, a mildewed jessamine or honeysuckle hung raggedly from some ornamental support, which had been pushed to one side by being used as a horse-post. What once was a large garden was now all grown over with weeds, through which, here and there, some solitary exotic reared its forsaken head. What had been a conservatory had now no window-shades, and on the mouldering shelves stood some dry, forsaken flowerpots, with sticks in them, whose dried leaves showed they had once been plants. . . . some windows stopped up with boards, some with shattered panes, and shutters hanging by a single hinge,—all telling of coarse neglect and discomfort.
>
> Bits of board, straw, old decayed barrels and boxes, garnished the ground in all directions. (491–92)

In Stowe's New England imagination, in which equality, harmony, and goodness are epitomized by the Quaker kitchen and by Uncle Tom's cabin, the great sin of sloth in Legree's yard indicates and foreshadows the sins to follow. There is no godliness in this yard of slovenly living and chaotic remains, mapped onto a yard that was once a place of high class. Opposed to the virtuous space of innocence, then, is the evil of disordered households. These yards signify disturbed sexual relations as well, similarly perceived as transgressions of physical boundaries and improper housekeeping.

Scout gives us a portrait of the Ewell yard in the very middle of the trial, indicating that a portrait of one's domestic life illuminates character. The Ewell yard was also once neat—once a Negro cabin, reminiscent of the cultural associations of "negro" and "cabin":

> Maycomb's Ewells lived behind the town garbage dump in what was once a Negro cabin. The cabin's plank walls were supplemented with sheets of corrugated iron, its roof shingled with tin cans hammered flat, so only its general shape suggested its original design . . . the cabin rested uneasily upon four irregular lumps of limestone . . . the plot of ground around the cabin look[ed] like the playhouse of an insane child: what passed for a fence was bits of tree-limbs, broomsticks and tool shafts, all tipped with rusty hammerheads, snaggle-toothed rake heads, shovels, axes and grubbing hoes, held on with pieces of barbed wire. Enclosed by this barricade was a dirty yard containing the remains of a Model-T Ford (on blocks), a discarded dentist's chair, an ancient icebox, plus lesser items. . . . One corner of the yard, though, bewildered Maycomb. Against the fence, in a line, were six chipped-enamel slop jars holding brilliant red geraniums, cared for [. . .] tenderly . . . People said they were Mayella Ewell's. (170–71)

These yards are literally and symbolically dumping grounds for white culture's refuse—all that it abjects. The Ewell residence is a Negro cabin already "uneasily" fallen. *Mockingbird*'s yard places more emphasis on broken tools and technologies, signifying perverted industry, while both yards contain raw materials that could signify potential and that maintain the ghostly presence of past wholeness. Significantly, both yards harbor flowers struggling to grow and be cultivated amidst the chaos of slovenly living. Those flowers are Mayella and Cassy, who have similar functions in both novels and for both Toms.

The innocence of the Toms can only be understood as a choice, given temptations to "cross over" to evil—into these refuse-littered yards. These yards signify places of darkness for the hero—what to John Bunyan's Christian would be the Slough of Despair or Vanity Fair, what to Pinocchio would be Pleasure Island, what to any hero crossing a threshold would be a Dark Forest. Temptations to cross these thresholds come in the form of women. Two parallel characters from both novels tempt the pure, untainted

Toms to cross into these yards, exemplifying the novels' associations of lower-class evil with female sexuality. Ultimately, both Toms are sacrificed for women, whether or not the women are worth it. Cassy is a pseudoromantic heroine entombed in Legree's house, just as Mayella is a pseudoromantic heroine entombed in her father's house. Both have lost their innocence from the slovenly living of their patriarchs. Both tempt the "innocent Toms" with plans that would taint their characters. Mayella tempts Tom into a sexual relationship, while Cassy tempts Tom into killing Legree. Both Toms resist but are damned the moment that the women select them for temptation. Both Mayella and Cassy are "window" figures who, although evil temptresses, are worthy of sympathy. It is sympathy for them that gets the Toms into trouble. Uncle Tom dies protecting knowledge of Cassy's escape, and Tom Robinson is a dead man once Mayella invites him in. Uncle Tom is sacrificed so that Cassy, "her life . . . a textbook on domestic violation" (Brown 33), can see the sins of her ways and redeem herself by helping Emmeline escape; Tom Robinson is sacrificed to assuage Mayella's guilt for breaking the code of miscegenation. One could argue that Cassy has broken this code as well, several times in fact. Both "passing" women symbolically murder the purer black family and the "black velvet" men who remain pure of the taint of black-white sexual relations.

But why is the Ewell yard also represented as the yard of an insane child? Much of the novel features children playing and crossing various yards. The Finch and Radley yards are far from sane; consider how the children move yards of dirt and snow to make a "nigger-snowman." Both novels draw topographies associated with degrees of goodness; Stowe moves from the most idyllic of slave situations in Kentucky to the middle ground, part chaos and part kindness (part laziness) of Louisiana, to down the Red River, associated with increasing evil and bloodshed at Legree's plantation. Claudia Durst Johnson has unpacked *Mockingbird*'s obsession with spatial boundaries, arguing that the novel participates in a gothic fear of, yet desire for knowledge of, "the other." Lee's novel is preoccupied with where the children can and cannot walk, with the path they must take to school to avoid the Radleys, and with their illicit transgressions into various yards. As it turns out, the children's obsession with spatial boundaries merely reflects the town's sense of boundaries, the division between town and country folks, the division between the black and white sections, and the distinction between the dump and the Negroes beyond the dump. Lower-class whites who cross boundaries into town present the greatest challenge. For example, the sleepy farmers not used to late hours are the ones threatening to lynch Tom Robinson, and the country children have certain characteristics but have to cross into town for school, with town children and teachers who do not understand country folk.

The Finch children transgress many boundaries—into the Radley yard, into the black church, into the black section of the courthouse, etc., just as the white child, young master George Shelby, crosses boundaries into black space, and Eva crosses boundaries in her affection for Uncle Tom, which Aunt Ophelia cannot countenance. Just as there is an ironic affinity between the preliterate goodness or evil of characters who feel rather than think, there is an ironic affinity between those who cross boundaries as bringing the potential for good or ill.

The Finch yard and unconventional household provide an inverse mirror of the Ewell yard. As Fine suggests in her article on southern female coming-of-age literature, the Ewell family provides us with a double for the Finch family ("Gender Conflicts" 124–25); like many southern belles in American literature (Seidel, *Southern Belle* 6), both Mayella and Scout lack mothers and female friends, and Scout seems to project her sexual issues and her rage at patriarchy onto the villainous fathers Bob Ewell and Mr. Radley (Fine, "Gender Conflicts" 124). Scout mentally compares Mayella to Boo and to mixed-race children, just as Scout seems to have her own intimate connection with Boo, being the one to hear him laugh and to receive his presents. In melodrama, the good and bad are two sides of the same coin; the symmetry between the Ewell and Finch yards—and domestic situations and father-daughter connections—strengthens a mirroring effect between them, particularly given the ungovernable aggressiveness of the daughters. Ultimately, the doubling of these spaces and families stem from Lee's recognition that the St. Clare and Legree spaces are inversions of the central theme of white-black "mixing" and "loving."

Many times the Finch children are equated with "Negroes" and "Negro behavior." When they quote folkloric beliefs in spirits and ghosts, Calpurnia accuses them of "nigger-talk"; when Jem is shot at, Mr. Radley claims that a Negro broke into his yard; when they sit in the black section of the courthouse and the preacher tells them to rise because their father is passing, the word passing has associations not only with death (the failure of his cause) but with racial disguise. The Finch family stands accused of "nigger-loving" and thus transgressing the same boundaries that Mayella has transgressed, and for which Eva stands because she loves everyone—especially Uncle Tom and Topsy. Like Eva, Atticus claims to love everybody when Scout asks him to explain the meaning of these accusations of "nigger-loving." The children regularly cross boundaries because they do not respect adult boundaries and space. In many ways, the children are paradoxical because although the reader is supposed to equate them with a pre-prejudiced innocence, they continually transgress and replicate adult "games." They serve both to parody (or "mock") and question as much as learn. In their yard they enact melodramas of the Radleys and community; the parody nature of melodrama is a language they naturally speak, playing out the sins of their environment. The children are so smart they know how to perform plausible parts for adults and reveal just enough to not be accused. For example, rather than admit they broke into the Radley yard, they claim to have been playing cards, exploiting perceived levels of mischief until they find one acceptable for their purposes. While the children are thus the innocents who weep, they are also the ones who parody and in some sense deconstruct the terms of the melodrama by showing how intimately they understand and can author it.

Just as there are three important child characters in *Mockingbird,* there are three important child characters in *Uncle Tom's Cabin,* representing a possible spectrum of color and character. We first meet the young Harry, who is light skinned and beautiful, and apparently skilled at parodying adult gestures and behavior. We then meet young (very white, golden-haired) Eva, who, like Atticus, loves everybody and who dies because slavery sinks into her heart. We also meet young Topsy, an incorrigible (and very black) mischief maker who is resistant to discipline because the system has treated her harshly and deprived her of the capacity for love, attachment, and guilt (until Eva reforms her). Similarly, in *Mockingbird* we have the most feminine and sensitive character, Dill, who, like the cross-dressed Harry, floats in and out of the novel; he is the smallest, although older than Scout, and he weeps the most at the treatment of Tom in the trial. Scout is less affected than Dill and the moody adolescent Jem, who, like Eva, is moving out of childhood (though not into heaven) and most affected by what he witnesses. Like Eva, Jem takes social inequalities to heart in a different way from Scout and is permanently debilitated by what he witnesses. Scout, with her continual fighting and disruptive behavior, is more like Topsy, echoing the associations between tomboyism and racial passing that Abate has found throughout nineteenth-century literature.

Lee's appropriation of Topsy in her "Eva substitute" is both modern and deliberate. Like Topsy, Scout with her tough demeanor comes out the most unscathed; although continually chastised by her aunt, she is practically adopted by her aunt in the Missionary Society scene. In that scene, Scout, Aunt Alexandra, and Calpurnia hear from Atticus of Tom's death. Calpurnia and Atticus depart to inform Helen, while Scout and Aunt Alexandra return to the ladies. Scout, for the first time, sees the toughness required in acting the lady part; in a telling moment that will concern us in chapter 6, she resolves that, "after all, if Aunty could be a lady at a time like this, so could I" (237). Topsy is the only slave to emerge unscathed from the decadent St. Clare household; she is adopted by Aunt Ophelia, who like Scout's "Aunty" is somewhat transformed. Both novels use the children not only to suggest the corruption of innocence, which is always a suggestion, given that the Finch children are hardly innocent and Scout is hardly unprejudiced, but also to demonstrate that just as the law is only as good as individual men, children are only as good as their environment teaches them to be. Children are the ones most affected by the melodramatic theater occurring before their eyes.

Lee has no use for the division between Eva and Topsy, but she seems to have likened aspects of Eva's relationship to St. Clare and aspects of Ophelia's frustration with Topsy, setting up Scout's relationship to Atticus and Aunt Alexandra's frustration with Scout. Scout is more like Topsy than Eva, but she is Eva in relation to her articulate and gentlemanly father, who despises racism. Eva's initial playfulness on the river parallels Scout's playfulness, but Eva alters considerably from a state of unselfconsciousness to an evangelical influence. Eva is innocent of her privilege, but she begins to "fall" when she acquires knowledge of slave treatment, just as increasing commentary about Tom's trial awakens Scout from her childhood. Both Eva and Scout feel the ills of racism when they also learn of female sexuality—Eva of Prue, Scout of Mayella. Eva and Scout are the same age; both authors position them at the beginning of formal literacy instruction to show what lessons are *really* learned in the world. However, Scout partakes of Eva's function and Topsy's character, complicit with Lee's representation of the Finch children and Atticus as "passin'."

It is significant that Scout evokes both Topsy and Hawthorne's Pearl in her wildness and in the way she challenges a single parent because both Topsy and Pearl claim to have been made not by God but by a more organic environment. Topsy tells Aunt Ophelia, "I spect I grow'd. Don't think nobody never made me" (356), while Pearl tells her examiners that "she had not been made at all, but had been plucked by her mother off the bush of wild roses, that grew by the prison-door" (Hawthorne 77). In other words, these otherworldly children symbolize an outgrowth of an entire community rather than the reproduction of a progenitor (one parent or God). They spring from systemic environments and reflect a corrupt world back to itself. Topsy is not only a signifier of stereotypical racism and minstrelsy, but also a manifestation of an earlier theme of the untamable nature of childhood, particularly for a struggling single parent (Ophelia) who is in exile or shunned by the community. These intertexts are relevant because they highlight Atticus as a single parent whose child, Scout, is quite unmanageable, distinct from him and his ethos, and "grown" in the image of her environment (Maycomb) rather than solely his. The wildness, otherworldliness, elvishness, and heathen quality of Pearl embodies the original sin of community fathers' treatment of her and her mother, just as Topsy's wildness embodies the sin of slavery. Scout's wildness embodies and performs the way in which Atticus is given a scarlet letter by his community. His vigil before the town prison oddly rebirths Pearl from the shadows.

Pearl, Eva/Topsy, and Scout embody passion and raw emotion, qualities in conflict with the eloquent public figures Dimmesdale, Augustine, and Atticus. This theme of conflict between passionate daughters and dry men of the public sphere deeply affects the shape of the melodrama. It is Pearl, Topsy, and Scout who rise while the fathers "pass." All of these daughters have various mother figures who cross proper boundaries and leave their imprint on these daughters; in Scout's case, one of these mother figures is Cal, a passionate character herself, one who, like Scout, engages in physical violence when prompted. Dimmesdale, Augustine, and Atticus, though detached and dry men, all have parallel moments of great oratory in specific settings, moments that stand out because they are distinct from their usual modes of living life relatively passively and even cynically. All these men fail their daughters, black, white, or red, which, if you take a broad view, could symbolize the nation of America itself, just as Hawthorne's "wild man" in "My Kinsman, Major Molineux" appears half black and half red.

Scout's difference from Eva is less important than the striking way in which Lee appropriated the Eva–Augustine St. Clare relationship and similarly framed it with problematic cousins and aunts from the South. Both Eva and Scout cross codes and boundaries without understanding why the boundaries exist. Both novels thus use children as sites of innocence who can destabilize long-established traditions simply by ignorance. Eva loves Tom and all the slaves; "Negro-loving" is the issue of Scout's family's transgression, as seen through the eyes of the community. Scout loves Calpurnia as Eva loves her mammy; these are matters their aunts cannot fathom.

Through Eva, who trusts and loves her papa but poses several questions of and about him, Stowe paints a unique portrait of the southern gentleman who feels slavery is wrong but who feels that it cannot be fought by one man. Augustine St. Clare falls into a tragic passivity and laissez-faire detachment that, eventually, causes him to suffer the loss of his daughter and his own life. Quite similarly, Lee gives us quite a bit of background on Atticus and demonstrates how intrinsically bound he is to a system that was once slaveholding and hence holds certain attitudes to hierarchies. Lee gives us background on his ancestor, Simon Finch (reminiscent of Simon Legree), and his plantation; Finch's Landing represents the origin of Atticus's prominent social position, but also his difference from tradition. The narrator makes the specific point that Atticus departs from a long tradition of plantation life at the Landing; nevertheless, Atticus is internally and externally bound to Maycomb County: "He liked Maycomb, he was Maycomb County born and bred; he knew his people, they knew him, and because of Simon Finch's industry, Atticus was related by blood or marriage to nearly every family in town" (4–5). When he goes against his town, Atticus in fact goes against relatives. Miss Maudie says those "with background" champion Atticus's actions, but his "background" is precisely his cross to bear. In fact, we find out that Calpurnia was first employed at Finch's Landing, suggesting that her ancestors were his family's slaves. Like Stowe, who gives us a rendition of Augustine's origin myth when he explains his inheritance of the slave system he abhors, Lee dwells on the Finch's family background to explain Atticus's acquiescence to many social codes, including gentlemanliness and courtesy to all, even to those who vocally condemn him. Atticus's failure to take a more active stand against his community, along with his dismissal of lynching, his dismissal of Ewell's death, his reluctance to take the case he is assigned, and his classism, result in Monroe Freedman's denunciation of Atticus Finch as a legal hero, a denunciation that shocked and angered the legal world that had mythologized him.

In an ironic manner, Atticus's resignation to fight the case that he was assigned, even when he is resigned to lose, mirrors the resignation of Augustine to slavery despite his own distaste for the system. Atticus realizes his powerlessness, given the enormity of his background, which the narrator stresses when she describes the "three hundred and sixty-six steps" of Finch's Landing, the loads of produce historically delivered there, and its heavy physical characteristics (79–80). Simon Finch was not southern born but a refugee from England; similarly, Stowe gives us background on Augustine St. Clare, an origin myth of plantation foundation, from which two brothers separated into northern and southern lifestyles: "Augustine St. Clare was the son of a wealthy planter of Louisiana. The family had its origin in Canada. Of two brothers, very similar in temperament and character, one had settled on a flourishing farm in Vermont, and the other became an opulent planter in Louisiana" (239). Both novelists take pains to demonstrate that the southern gentleman are who they are purely by accident. Both men have chosen to depart from their landed traditions but cannot turn away from who they are. Augustine chooses to depart from his brother's plantation after they run a plantation together for several years. Both authors thus dwell on southern slaveholding origin myths to demonstrate the fact that both men inherit their positions and "cases" and thus are reluctantly trapped by them.

The chapter in which Augustine critiques slavery to his sister stands parallel to Atticus's closing arguments, particularly since both will "pass" and fail to implement their ideals. Augustine's failure to free Tom, who affects him personally, just as Atticus says the case of Tom Robinson does him, suggests that the system will always win, regardless of any individual case. Atticus understands his defeat from the beginning; he tells Scout they will not win. Atticus evinces a similar fatalism as Augustine St. Clare. Both men are complacent until circumstances—Aunt Ophelia in Augustine's case, the judge in Atticus's case—exhort them to do something. Both men are relatively powerless because their worlds are controlled by social opinion and social opinion is largely female. As St. Clare dies before he can complete his duty, and is thus punished for passivity, it is left to young George Shelby to act. Young George and Jem both learn from their chivalrous but ultimately ineffectual fathers.

The fatalism of both Augustine and Atticus is expressed through similar "gentlemanly" detachment and sarcasm in everyday life, juxtaposed with rare but great illocutionary moments of passionate rhetoric. To live within the system he does, Augustine St. Clare often merely sits around and offers cynical commentary on situations that matter quite a bit to Ophelia or Marie, his wife. He is often reading until Eva demands affection, similarly to the tableaux of Scout demanding attention from Atticus, typically also reading. Remarkably, dry cynicism is a trademark of Atticus's. He offers cynical comments on how Mrs. Dubose's house should stimulate the children's imagination since they can pretend it's the Radley house; how Miss Maudie is in "great peril" when one of his children points a gun at her; how he and Scout will seal their reading deal without the "usual formality" of spitting; and how the children will have to disguise their snowman or the family will stand accused of libel. When the children melodramatically react to the Radley blanket suddenly discovered around Scout's shoulders, a discovery that makes Scout ill and Jem eager to torment her, "Atticus said dryly, 'Do not let this inspire you to further glory, Jeremy'" (72). Atticus uses sarcasm with his sister, like Augustine does with his. In response to her thesis that families have family streaks, he asks if, considering that Finches typically marry their cousins, the Finch family has an incestuous streak? When he is under the most stress, he becomes the most cynical. Scout asks him if she must mind Jem, and Atticus answers that she must mind whenever Jem can make her mind; when Dill appears to trouble an already troubled day, Atticus tells Dill to "'put some of the country back where it belongs'" (141) since soil erosion is bad enough.

Atticus's detached dryness furthers the sense that he is extremely reluctant to fight his community; when challenged, he is polite and gentlemanly before turning the other cheek. The child-Scout challenges his values, just as Topsy challenges everything Aunt Ophelia knows about childrearing. Aunt Ophelia is rather like Catharine Beecher in viewing childrearing as an arm of domestic economy, politically dysfunctional in St. Clare's plantation (see Brown 13–22). Scout does not cope through detachment, and she certainly does not turn the other cheek. She is passionate and craves affection. Augustine and Atticus are odd characters in melodramatic plots; they are detached viewers largely immune to the subliterate, mythic power of the drama, demonstrating sound judgment of events but serving as a poor model for the reader, who is supposed to be open and passionate like the boundary-crossing children.

Both Augustine and Atticus are virtually on their own as parents, and both are harshly criticized by women for the way in which they manage their homes. The inability of single parents to control otherworldly children is present even in the poem "The Sinless Child" by Elizabeth Oakes Smith, Stowe's source for the character Eva. Augustine does not organize Eva's things or life, and he allows a significant amount of housekeeping waste and expense, bemoans his sister, Ophelia. Atticus is continually criticized for letting his children run wild; he pleads that he does the best that he can. Just as Ophelia objects to the way in which Augustine lets his house descend into chaos and allows Eva intimacy with slaves, abhorrent to her, Scout writes that "Aunt Alexandra was fanatical on the subject of my attire... furthermore, I should be a ray of sunshine in my father's lonely life. . . . but when I asked Atticus about it, he said there were already enough sunbeams in the family and to go on about my business, he didn't mind me much the way I was" (81). Both sisters are actually well-intentioned; Aunt Ophelia is merely trying to help Augustine, given his impossible hypochondriac wife, Marie, and Aunt Alexandra is trying to help protect the family and ease her brother's stress by lending her assistance. We are asked to sympathize with her by the end, when she reacts strongly to the death of Tom and feels angry that the town demands so much from her brother. Aunt Alexandra offers Scout a clean pair of overalls at the end of the novel, just as Aunt Ophelia takes Topsy under her wing. But the presence of both aunts also suggests a critical lens on the men as fathers. Even Atticus's fan Miss Maudie tells him he'll "'never raise 'em.'"

Both men refuse to impose any sense of order or management on their households; Atticus refuses to interfere, for example, when Scout begins swearing. The aunts Alexandra and Ophelia view the men as allowing a dangerous amount of autonomy—as misapplying to the home relations from the pubic sphere and even transcendental principles. Both aunts harbor objections to the domestic management of the men, which is primarily to let servants run matters as they please and leave the men free to lead a more public life. Aunt Alexandra objects to Calpurnia's cooking and rarely lets her serve important guests; she also wishes that her brother would not speak freely of his case in front of Calpurnia, wishing to keep strict boundaries, rather like Ophelia believes there should be strict boundaries between black and white (she is repelled by black people). Alexandra even wishes to dismiss Calpurnia, largely because Cal's presence as a mother figure threatens her own dominance. Atticus defends Calpurnia, just as Augustine defends his household liberties from the prying eyes of Ophelia, who is equally racist as Alexandra, but who is, ironically, a northern woman opposed to slavery.

Both aunts try to impose their proper sense of childrearing, Ophelia on Topsy and Alexandra on Scout. In other words, the melodrama is more than a racial one; it is a theater of socializing children. Ophelia tries to instill a proper sense of Christianity and domestic order in Topsy, who thwarts her at every turn, while Alexandra's main mission is to instill more proper gender behavior and family pride in Scout. Both object to the girls' associations with black people; Alexandra objects to Scout visiting Calpurnia and reacts with concern when Scout and Jem go to the black church. Ophelia reacts with horror at Eva's closeness to Tom and her mammy. Both in their own way, one northern and one very traditionally southern, essentially react to the danger of "Negro-loving," which in both books is associated with the sin of miscegenation, permitted for white men but not for white women or girls. Eva's love of Tom is spiritual and filial (he gives her something her father cannot—a Christian and biblical connection), Atticus's "love" of Tom is professional and thus asexual; but whereas spiritual love is permitted and desired in both texts, miscegenation remains much more problematic. Passion must be controlled.

Eschewing passion, both Augustine and Atticus espouse a rhetoric of gentlemanliness and class that tempers their rhetoric of racial equality. Atticus tells Scout, "'Don't say nigger, Scout. That's common'" (75). Ironically, after Dill cries at Tom's treatment by the prosecuting attorney and Scout retorts "'he's just a Negro,'" she demonstrates she has learned Atticus's lesson of diction to the letter. Atticus exhorts Jem to be a gentleman and hold his head high despite what names are leveled at him, even by the meanest character, Mrs. Dubose. Jem proclaims to Scout that he will emulate Atticus's gentlemanly behavior, which takes him into a world from which she is excluded. Atticus's impenetrable gentlemanliness infuriates the Ewells (Mayella and her father), and probably stimulates Bob Ewell to consider the children as Atticus's one vulnerability. Similarly, in *Uncle Tom's Cabin,* Stowe demonstrates that gentlemanly behavior does not affect everyone equally; the only way to win Legree's respect is to knock him down, which George Shelby finally does. Atticus finally realizes he has miscalculated Bob Ewell and put his own children at risk. The gentlemanly lens presumes, analyzes, and unfortunately depends upon everyone's recognition of certain social codes. Ultimately, the greatest problems with Atticus and Augustine are their detachment and gentlemanliness, which make them relatively cynical about the melodrama unfolding before their eyes.

Yet the passions of Eva and Scout are ineffectual. Both have similar encounters with cousins whose value systems are distinctly different. These cousin encounters serve to exemplify the way their families have broken with tradition but have inherited systems in which, at the end of the day, the white community is all they have. Eva witnesses her cousin whip a slave, stimulating her efforts to reform him, while Scout "reforms" her cousin Francis when Francis taunts her about Atticus's participation in the trial. Scout's reformation style is to punch Francis. Scout's scene takes place at Finch's Landing, the place of the Finch slaveholding past. To both aunts and cousins, the behavior of the girls suggests further proof of the lax lifestyles preferred by Augustine and Atticus. Augustine soon plays backgammon with his brother, and although Atticus departs speedily, we are aware that he never has and never will desert the Christmas tradition of visiting the Landing. Both novels thus demonstrate the complexity of taking a stand or acting on beliefs, given family tradition and the pressure of a community. I believe Lee tips her hat directly to Stowe when Alexandra presents to Scout a book to instill family pride—the memoirs of St. Clair. Alexandra claims it is beautiful, but Scout claims that Joshua St. Clair was a madman. The book represents the complexity of "background": is it madness or beauty? Both Augustine and Atticus have, after all, been placed in positions of power that neither want to use. For these men, the melodrama is internal, and their passionate daughters are manifestations of all they have repressed to live in the system they do.

Conclusion:
The Gray Ghost as Melodrama

In melodrama the villain must be punished. Although Simon Legree and Bob Ewell are both disgraced, the houses of the gentleman, notably, fall as well. Both Atticus and Augustine fail to free the Toms, just as they fail as parents, because their assumptions do not apply in a world that is really quite cruel.

In some ironic sense, the children are threatened by the sins of their own fathers because their own fathers live and uphold impossible standards in intolerable settings. It is up to the children for full conversion, but while Stowe develops the young George to ensure that Tom has not died in vain, *Mockingbird* is bleak. Jem is most converted by what he witnesses, but he is the most bitter, scarred, and numb. He, like Scout began, winds up a passionate and angry character. However, passion is the mechanism by which the melodramatic plot is processed, and thus the presence of the passionate children ultimately destabilizes and problematizes the detachment of the adult white gentlemen as well as the nature of innocence and the feeling reader of the racial melodrama.

Atticus's stoicism only lets down a few times in quiet glimpses, such as when we learn that he often gets up in the night to check on his children, or the final scene of the novel when he watches at the bedside of Jem. I believe that the ending of the novel indicates that the more passionate and melodramatic Scout and Jem have in some sense tamed Atticus. Atticus is reading Jem's gothic plots for once, something on which Scout also has expertise, and the children have triumphed as readers with authority and frameworks by which to understand events. We must remember that the narrator of the story is Scout and that she, as character and narrator retrospectively looking back on the events, offers an alternative model to Atticus.

Scout's final response to Atticus's reading of *The Gray Ghost* tells us everything we need to know about the paradoxical appeal of melodrama in the novel's recycling of it. As Atticus tells Scout what he is reading, the narrator reflects that young Scout felt all of a sudden awakened (280). Melodrama awakens an otherwise sleepy town, of which Scout is a synecdoche, until then in "no hurry . . . nowhere to go, nothing to buy and no money to buy it with, nothing to see outside the boundaries of Maycomb County" (5). Scout begs Atticus to read *The Gray Ghost* aloud—to perform it—which is odd because she can read for herself and she admits she knows the story already, telling Atticus that the story is "'real scary'" (280). Hearing the story is not about discovering something new but about connecting to others through a common, shared host of tropes. In fact, as he reads, Scout's wakefulness turns into soothing sleepiness. She tries to keep awake, but the sound of his voice acts as a lullaby. The presence of this type of genre is soothing because it is familiar. It is intimately known, requiring only the slightest attention.

Meaning is entirely predetermined. Scout's sleepiness mirrors her condition throughout most of the trial, where she drifts in and out of sleep, thus serving as the most objective "reader" of melodrama. The endless repetition of American melodrama paradoxically awakens passions and soothing feelings of "already knowing," deep down, how it operates. It is the same paradox with which adults regard the novel—its evocation of sleepy small-town childhood (American yesteryear) and its progressive awakening.

But Scout, like the town, remains in her same sleepy place because the melodramatic style shuts down the complexity of her voice and subjectivity, which preoccupies scenes prior to the trial. The most perspective she achieves is through her confrontation with Boo. But she also "already knows" Boo within, and he allows her to "cross the street" in perception, which is really not so very far away. The multivoiced quality of Scout's narration, which vacillates between a transcendent, detached language and a local, colloquial one, reveals her as a particular sort of progeny. She is part Atticus, part Cal, who code switches comfortably according to context, and part Maycomb itself, as revealed by her unique mix of vocabularies, which I discuss in chapter 4. If Scout is like the town in being unable to hold onto thoughts very long, so is the wounded Jem in the novel's opening paragraph—disfigured and not whole, but not particularly grieved about it.

The point seems to be that the white mind cannot really *remember* Uncle Tom as it should, but it loves to hear the story. *Uncle Tom* has achieved the level of a political unconscious, as Fredric Jameson would define it and as Baldwin exclaimed in frustration at Wright's response:

> Below the surface of [*Native Son*] there lies, as it seems to me, a continuation, a complement of that monstrous legend it was written to destroy. Bigger is Uncle Tom's descendant, flesh of his flesh, so exactly opposite a portrait that, when the books are placed together, it seems that the contemporary Negro novelist and the dead New England woman are locked together in a deadly, timeless battle; the one uttering merciless exhortations, the other shouting curses. . . . For Bigger's tragedy is not that he is cold or black or hungry, not even that he is American, black; but that he has accepted a theology that denies him life, that he admits the possibility of his being sub-human and feels constrained, therefore, to battle for his humanity according to those brutal criteria bequeathed him at his birth. But our humanity is our burden,

our life; we need not battle for it; we need only to do what is infinitely more difficult—that is, accept it. The failure of the protest novel lies in its rejection of life, the human being, the denial of his beauty, dread, power, in its insistence that it is his categorization alone which is real and which cannot be transcended. (21–22)

Uncle Tom, Bigger, and Tom Robinson are not so much individuals as typological roles in a broader theology; just as Wright uses Bigger to advance his Marxist attack of the Dalton's liberal stance—Mr. Dalton builds gyms and does nothing about structural inequality—Lee uses the trial participants to show that Mayella's bruises are caused as much by Maycomb as anybody else: "Maycomb gave them Christmas baskets, welfare money, and the back of its hand" (192). Lee's effort to undo a history of paranoia about sexual desire of black men for white women, just like Wright's, creates the same queer effects that we find in Bishop's trial of a white gentleman for rape. Such queer effects can likewise be traced in Greene's "mock" trial and lynching of a northerner for rape, and, as I discussed in my introduction, Larsen's attempts to undo a history of viewing black women sexually, which fall apart when Irene *sees* Clare. Wright's Bigger rapes and kills his girlfriend after she says people will *think* he raped Mary Dalton, which is the stage version of race relations that Bessie knows. The broader discourse of sin and theology revolves around sexual panic, and attempts to rewrite the script only heighten the queerness of that panic.

Yet Lee offers a self-conscious version of what Wright describes by shifting so radically from early sections of the novel to the trial's pantomime. Her vacillations in form echo Faulkner's in *Requiem for a Nun*, in which the trial scenes are expressly equated to a stage play. Faulkner labels the novel's sections "act one," "act two," and "act three." He splices together novel exposition with trial scenes formatted like a play and including instructions on lighting and stage directions; for example, "Scene I: Courtroom. 5:30 P.M. November thirteenth. The curtain is down. As the lights begin to go up . . . The curtain rises" (49). In "Scene I" of "Act Two," he writes stage directions to introduce the office of the governor:

The whole bottom of the stage is in darkness, as in Scene I, Act One, so that the visible scene has the effect of being held in the beam of a spotlight.

Suspended too, since it is upper left and even higher above the shadow of the stage proper than the same in Scene I, Act One, carrying still further the symbolism of the still higher, the last, the ultimate seat of judgment. (112)

In contrast, the narrative portions of the novel give background and offer the characters as typological examples of the South; the combination of novel and trial-as-stage play comments on the ludicrous nature of assigning blame or equating murder with the actual person who smothered the infant. Lee accomplishes in her novel a less glaring self-consciousness about melodrama; nevertheless, her radical alteration in form and narrative irony parallels Faulkner's more fractured styles in *Requiem*.

This self-conscious quality of courtroom melodrama is present in earlier trial fiction as well, not only in the role of the press that writes Bigger Thomas into the role of beast or Mary Clay (symbol of malleable material) into the role of innocent lamb, but also in the theatricality of the prosecuting attorney of *Act of Darkness*, who "took at once a protective air, which made him like a noble hero in a melodrama" (213). The narrator writes of him, "Cleon O'Connor seemed to be playing some private melodrama. He was the hero whose duty it was to protect Virginia; he displayed nobility and discretion; it was all done like an actor" (213). If the trial is actually a play, it makes even more sense that to John the role of viewer would be a queer space in which he could imagine being either rapist or raped. Unlike her predecessors, Lee does not explicitly mark her trial a performance, but by lessening much of the narrator's earlier humor to which we become accustomed, and which returns outside the courtroom, Lee makes the same point about her "'Roman carnival,'" so called by Miss Maudie, who typically explains matters to the children without mincing words. Lee also brings the style alteration of her novel home by changing Scout from the feisty girl of the early pages to the sleepy child of final scenes.

Knowing the story and finding its tropes comfortable and safe, the white brain (Scout's) relaxes by virtue of melodrama's predictable and compulsive repetition. Just as Atticus does not succeed in his transcendental mission in the public sphere, Scout domesticates history into a gothic form and privatizes Atticus in the end: "He turned out the light and went into Jem's room. He would be there all night, and he would be there when Jem waked up in the morning" (281). With these final lines, we find a vision of comfort in a sleepy place all too reminiscent of the sleepy town with which the novel began and all too primed for the endlessly ritualistic repetition of melodrama. But, of course, the novel is bleak, so the reader wakes up to its landscape of hopelessness. And adult memories of *Mockingbird,* as a novel that impacted them, are perhaps greater testimony to its clever use of melodrama for the purpose of social reform. The hope of reform is ultimately transferred to the young reader, who feels a tremendous sense of accomplishment in seeing more than Scout can see. Just as *Charlotte Temple* gave its readers top billing and thereby functioned to embody democracy in a new republic, paradoxically rendering its theme of the disenfranchised, *Mockingbird*'s embedding of Uncle Tom inspires its readers with a sense of empowerment through its formal embodiment of democratic principle. There are no real mysteries to solve in the trial, which is more than melodramatically legible. But as a reader, it is certainly fun to imagine you solved the case of Tom's innocence.

CHAPTER 3

MOCKINGBIRD AND MODERNIST METHOD: CHILD CONSCIOUSNESS, OR HOW SCOUT KNEW

Stowe's novel is characterized by an omniscient Victorian narrator overtly in control of the story's presentation. Like a stage director, she invites us to revisit certain characters, tells us she will leave certain others to their activities for awhile, and pleads directly for our sympathies in a passionate second address, in the fashion of Susanna Rowson's *Charlotte Temple*. The narrator cuts from one scene to another and directly addresses the reader about why and what point the reader is to take away from the tragic stories the narrator is relating. Over time, as Robyn Warhol discusses, the narrator's tendency to "break the frame" of fiction was considered crass and disruptive to a text's realism, especially if breaking the frame for didactic purposes. Louisa May Alcott's self-conscious frame-breaking in *Little Women* is tolerated because the story is autobiographical and thus the narrator is usually perceived as an adult Jo, gently mocking herself and her sisters. In contrast, Hawthorne's self-scrutiny as an artist and narrator takes the form of "The Custom-House" sketch in front of *The Scarlet Letter*, separated from the fiction itself and advancing thoughts about technique rather than social purpose. With Henry James, the fashion for showing over telling was solidified, although the convention of second-person address never fully died out in children's literature.

With modernism, human consciousness became a subject in its own right. *Mockingbird* not only puts consciousness in its artistic center, but also sketches an impressionist portrait of a child's mind. "What happens to the artist's consciousness," Dave writes of *Mockingbird*, "is more important than the actual happening itself" (51). Scout engages in the "long habit of spectatorship" that readers will recognize as the influence of Henry James's Maisie. Further, the consciousness of the child becomes an artistic mask behind which stands a comic artist whom readers of Mark Twain's *Adventures of Huckleberry Finn* should recognize.

With James and Twain came an entirely new form of narration. Even as the narrator speaking directly to the reader went out of fashion, a new experimentation with point of view arose with the incarnation of child consciousness in the American novel. The view from a child would be limited and unique, naive and ironic as needed, and, without overt didacticism or disruption to a text's aesthetic space, it would teach readers a wide variety of things. Child focalization would show readers not only what we know, but how we come to know what we know. It would be an exercise in the uncovering of human cognition. Child consciousness had the advantage of showing response to and conditioning of environment, thereby exploring the possibilities and limits of social change, given that change must take root in the young human mind. In short, the representation of child consciousness in American literature would put forth a view of epistemology.

Mockingbird is effectively co-narrated by an older Scout, looking back on the events and her younger self, and a younger Scout, filtering the events through her consciousness, sometimes objectively and sometimes with a misplaced or skewed emphasis. The two different Scouts come to the foreground at different times and thus Lee tightly controls our experience of various scenes. The two Scouts have a relationship; the older Scout offers self-mockery on the younger Scout, which gives us permission to laugh at the young Scout's feelings and concerns. The character (as opposed to the thoughts) of the young Scout is revealed more in interactions with others, particularly in action and dialogue, adding a third layer to the mix—how others actually view Scout and how discourse situations define her. Lee carefully controls which Scouts are in the foreground in different scenes, depending on whether she wants us to be distanced from the event or immediately engaged by it (see Wyile).

Some of the early reviewers felt that vacillation in point of view was a technical flaw in the novel. In his biography of Lee, Charles Shields reviews the criticism launched at Lee for switching between narrator and focalizer: "W. J. Stuckey, in *The Pulitzer Prize Novels: A Critical Backward Look*, attributed Lee's 'rhetorical trick' to a failure to solve 'the technical problems raised by her story and whenever she gets into difficulties with one point of view, she switches to the other'" (qtd. in Shields 128). Shields agrees that Lee might have "floundered" since she wrote the original draft in third person, the second in first person, and later blended the two (128). I find the blend unique, compelling, and well executed—a way to complexify the simplicity of the trial. I agree with Going (*Essays* 28) that the technique is Jamesian, but the technique also makes interpretation of irony tricky, similar to the trickiness of interpreting irony in Vallès's narratives of childhood, Lejeune finds (64–66). It is difficult to sort out whether the irony depends on a secret between narrator and narratee, at the expense of the child, or between child and narratee. However, in the same way that the novel's shift from irony to melodrama can be understood as a tactical contribution to meaning, the fluctuations in perspective control reader response.

The novel vacillates between deploying the distancing type of ironic, colorful child voice first glimpsed in Twain's *Adventures of Huckleberry Finn* and the more immediate, unmediated stream-of-consciousness technique pioneered by modernist writers such as James in *What Maisie Knew*. Lee deploys the former style for everyday scenes in Scout's world, to construct comic distance from the young Scout and to set up a contrast in scenes that take Scout beyond her everyday world. In other words, Lee uses the young Scout to acknowledge what white eyes can and cannot see, continually negotiating between local and transcendent perspective. We are continually reminded how Scout makes mental associations between things in surprising and dexterous ways, putting us in mind of how consciousness operates and how streams of experience are processed.

In the novel, we effectively meet three different Scouts. There is a six-year-old Scout revealed to the reader, without narrative comment, in action and dialogue. *This* Scout is complex enough. She is passionate, headstrong, impulsive, childish, feisty, and endearing. She craves affection, gets upset easily, distorts and misunderstands situations, shows her brains and resourcefulness, hates restriction, notices far more than she can explain, and both reasons and applies her prior knowledge and experience. She changes with her social context, following the model of Calpurnia, who, Natalie Hess argues, exemplifies liminality and marginality with her code- and style-shifting. With Atticus Scout is an innocent questioner, with Jem she is assertive and grumpy, with Miss Maudie she is respectful, with Walter Cunningham and Cecil Jacobs she is a bully, and with her new teacher she is superior and wise. But then a more sophisticated side of Scout is revealed through the narrator's rendition of the six-year-old's immediate thoughts. With Scout as focalizer, Lee places the unique attentions, thoughts, and interpretations of Scout alongside a more direct transcription of adult behaviors and dialogue that are beyond her understanding. For example, Scout's thoughts might focus on how something Atticus is doing differs from his usual custom, upon which she is an anthropological expert, placed alongside snippets of conversations that she overhears, allowing the reader to put it all together.

In addition, there is the distinct presence of an older, reflective Scout who introduces the novel and intermittently inserts herself throughout the story, rather reminiscent of Stowe's self-conscious storyteller. This narrator-Scout provides background on people, places, and customs, often disrupting and controlling the meaning of an immediate scene. She provides humorous commentary on the young Scout's behaviors, through a gentle irony revealed in description. Like Stowe's omniscient narrator, she manipulates narrative time, deploying flashbacks and foreshadowing the significance of a scene with a summary. She typically directs our understanding of Scout's everyday contexts, but then she fades into the background when the young Scout confronts new adult behaviors and scenes that she cannot easily interpolate. The key scenes that challenge Scout's understanding are the trial, her voyage to Cal's church, and the near-lynching at the jail, which is presaged by the conversation of men on her front porch; in those scenes, the masterful, ironic older Scout abandons the young Scout so that we feel a different style of telling emerge. In those scenes that foreground emergent child consciousness, we feel less narrative control and we miss the comic irony to which we have become accustomed from earlier scenes.

The older Scout abruptly breaks the frame only occasionally to comment on what she did not understand at the time, and she provides local background even during the trial. But throughout the novel we are asked to regard child consciousness as the imperative it is in the tradition of modernist writers who were concerned, even in regional writings, with point of view, alienation, and the unstable nature of knowledge and the human mind. Modernism challenged the ideology of omniscience and objective knowledge put forth in a Victorian novel like Stowe's; Lee's narration challenges even as it deploys Stowe's melodrama, just as its multivoiced discourse challenges the stability and "oneness" embodied by the Emersonian Atticus.

To understand how the novel works by assembling a multivoiced narrator-Scout, a focalizing Scout that explores epistemological matters, and an interactive child-Scout whom Lee can manipulate for various effects, we have to consider the modern roots of child consciousness in American literature. By understanding these roots and comparing to them *Mockingbird*'s concern with Scout's reasoning, we arrive at various insights that most profoundly explain how the novel crafted with nineteenth-century tools simultaneously undoes the nineteenth-century novel's view of a more or less ordered universe. The modern novel challenged nineteenth-century certainties about man's place in the cosmos, turning attentions to the way in which our psychologies, our subjectivities, and our subject-positions are dynamic forces that stand between us and the world, between us and other people.

In his 1903 *Souls of Black Folk,* W.E.B. Du Bois dubbed double consciousness a veil through which marginalized subjects like African Americans view themselves:

> After the Egyptian and Indian, the Greek and Roman, the Teuton and Mongolian, the Negro is a sort of seventh son, born with a veil, and gifted with second-sight in this American world,—a world which yields him no true self-consciousness, but only lets him see himself through the revelation of the other world. It is a peculiar sensation, this double-consciousness, this sense of always looking at one's self through the eyes of others, of measuring one's soul by the tape of a world that looks on in amused contempt and pity. One ever feels his twoness,—an American, a Negro; two warring souls, two thoughts, two unreconciled strivings; two warring ideals in one dark body, whose dogged strength alone keeps it from being torn asunder.

In the late nineteenth century, double consciousness, earlier discussed by philosophers like Emerson in "Experience," was viewed as an artifact of developmental psychology. The field's growth and search for methods drove the new methods of modernists in their efforts to capture human consciousness. Lee's presentation of Scout's consciousness has literary correspondents with both six-year-old Maisie and teenage Huck, who entered the literary scene as the field of developmental psychology was born of evolutionary theory. Scout increasingly becomes an instance of double consciousness, split between an observing and acting self through Maisie's long habit of spectatorship. By investigating first "how Scout knows" in this chapter and "how Scout tells" in chapter 4, we arrive at *Mockingbird*'s philosophy of how the human mind and environment interact in both consciousness and in voice, notwithstanding the attractive legacy of America's earlier romanticism. Atticus's old-fashioned worldview of truth and sympathy is impossible in a world of fractured selves who linguistically perform their identities and who can only process knowledge through a limited lens.

How Scout Knows

Like *Uncle Tom's Cabin,* with its inquiring Eva and its liberal though ineffectual St. Clare, James's *What Maisie Knew* provides a model for a relationship between a six-year-old girl and a father figure who is also her equal match: the gentlemanly Sir Claude. Like young Scout, Maisie is the focalizing consciousness struggling to comprehend an immoral adult society full of prejudice and discriminatory practices that threaten to subsume her. Like Atticus, Sir Claude occupies the center of a slew of ladies who compete for ascendancy over Maisie, but Maisie only has eyes for Sir Claude. She questions, mimics, and "reads" him, and both her questions and astute observations function like Scout's do—to challenge and mock by slicing through hypocrisy and immorality. The finest example is when Maisie "innocently" asks whether the new man hanging about her mother could not be her tutor, just as Miss Overmore is currently her tutor but primarily hangs about with Sir Claude. James is exploring the subject of how the child "knows" through analogical reasoning; to Maisie, if Miss Overmore (whom we understand to be Sir Claude's lover) is posing as her "governess," then surely a man accompanying her mother could take the same role. Maisie is *explicitly* drawing an analogy to prestigious schools with male instructors, arguing that a male tutor would simply be a prestigious move. But, implicitly, she is questioning Miss Overmore's role and showing her unconscious understanding of Miss Overmore as Sir Claude's paramour. Probably the most similar moment in *Mockingbird* is when Scout asks Atticus why she must go to school when other children can attend the first day and then disappear. This is Socratic logic, the deployment of a question that exposes hypocrisy and the way law does not always define practice, which is a recurrent theme in *Mockingbird.* In *Mockingbird,* Lee uses child focalization and interaction to similarly convey "what Scout knew" and, more important, how.

In reading *Maisie,* the reader has to read between the lines of the child's analogies to decode what she intuits and what is beyond her comprehension. Maisie becomes more and more astute, learning, like Scout, to conceal and to look for clues in social situations for determining how to feel. Both Maisie and Scout survive hostile worlds by becoming expert interpreters of people familiar to them, and thus decoding the incomprehensible adult world by reading gestures, bodily cues, and habits of familiar people. Scout's widening world and perspective are achieved through a particular child epistemology modeled in Maisie's ever-increasing knowledge: to read adult "games" and to know how to feel about the scenes and words streaming through her consciousness, Scout deploys her expertise on reading the bodies that, to her, matter most: Jem, Atticus, and Calpurnia. This crucial point of entry into unfamiliar scenes will focus our analysis after we uncover the philosophical background to Lee's emphasis on the child as observer.

James's 1897 *What Maisie Knew* presents a study of child consciousness that has more in common than immediately apparent with Twain's study of Huck published thirteen years earlier, explicitly titled "adventures" rather than call attention to the accumulation of knowledge. But Huck actually navigates unfamiliar social worlds in the same way that Maisie and Scout do. The reason that James and Twain shared developmental concerns is that a new scholarly field was blossoming around them in the late-Victorian period. Developmental psychology had recently taken root from evolutionary inquiry, and thus what was then known as child study had become of new philosophical importance in a culture obsessed with its origins and seeking illumination about the ascent of man, viewed also as the uniqueness of the Western mind. Both James and Twain used children to explore the suggestibility of the human mind in rather damning, Darwinian environments in which survival is definitely not assured, and in which innocence is only protective ignorance. Both authors were concerned with the principle of adaptability and educatability of the human race. Both explore the limitations of human reasoning by showing that the child can only think through the voices planted by others in the mind, and both show how influences in the environment are both imitated and internalized, destabilizing the emergence of an authentic self.

Both Twain and James used a distinct narrative practice in *Huck* and *Maisie* to show that the human mind learns by analogical reasoning, which is often misleading but sometimes perceptive, and by focusing on only select, salient features of a situation rather than on the abstract whole. Both focused on the impressionability and suggestibility of children to both satirize the sins of society and to worry about the future state of morality, given the very limitations of how the mind can think on its own. Ultimately, both used the child to show the limits of human consciousness and the impossibility of objective epistemology. They both reflected and contributed to the emerging idea that the child embodies the alien unconscious of culture, which would gain even more inertia in the later modern period. In her book *Strange Dislocations,* Carolyn Steedman demonstrates that by the modern period, developmental psychology and other fields had begun to equate childhood with interiority and that the narrations of personal and historical pasts had coalesced in the field of psychoanalysis. Given the anthropological and evolutionary perspective of late-Victorian psychologists and of Freud in particular, it is not surprising that child study was intended to convey the "real" essence of Western man.

Importantly, *Maisie* and *Huck* are responding to a very specific new mode for accumulating knowledge about the human mind. Child study, now known as developmental psychology, had called for turning the cold eye of science on observing childhood apart from pure "moral reference" (Henry James's words for the artist's right in his 1908 preface to *The Portrait of a Lady*). The movement, which coordinated with the increasing popularity of the kindergarten movement started earlier by Friedrich Fröbel and spread by Johann Pestalozzi, was very much tied to educational philosophy. Researchers believed that study of child nature would yield a science of the impressions, sensations, perceptions, and consciousness through which the child really learned, rather than through formal instruction of schooling. Real children, scientists were starting to theorize, decoded the text of the world—the book of nature. It is in this book that Scout has the most to read, notwithstanding her status as a fluent reader of books and her need to perhaps learn algebra in the end. By the time of Maisie and Huck, it had become fairly clear that formal instruction and decoding the book of life were at odds with one another; the characters around Maisie joke about all she is not learning, an obvious result of attracting governesses who keep falling in love with her stepfather. But the crux of the joke is that Maisie is learning everything *except* perhaps algebra too.

The point of view in *Mockingbird* is calculated to show us the fallibility of human subjectivity and the need for us to understand that the individual's point of view is an inescapable by-product of the social world. It is a meaningful detail that Scout, in the key climactic scene of being attacked by Ewell and thus vulnerable to backwoods penetration, is dressed as a ham, having played that part in a local pageant. Her point of view is quite clouded by the shroud of a costume, but the "very slowly" (262) registering of impressions in the scene—the sounds, the stillness, the unclear feelings—are paradigmatic of many scenes in which local men penetrate her mind. The scene is a concretization of other scenes in which incomprehensible local conversations stream through doors and windows at her, or when the jury comes in like "underwater swimmers," indicating a stream-of-consciousness experience. At such times, when her vision of the whole fails, she is left processing sensory information or reading the bodies and habits of familiar people. As symbol of a local product, the ham is important; the shiny material on it makes her vulnerable by attracting Ewell in the night, but it is also made of sturdy chicken wire and thus protects her from his knife. As a symbol for the veil of her regional consciousness, echoing other scenes in which she knows something is happening but cannot explain what, the ham also signifies her object status "between men," to appropriate Eve Sedgwick's description of the way women in novels function as items of exchange in male power struggles. As a girl-ham, Scout throughout the novel is also a pawn in a power struggle between women and men as distinct forces of socialization, just as Mayella is more object between Atticus and Ewell than subject in the trial. In Scout is imprinted a power struggle between the way Maycomb can shape a local product and the way Atticus could lift her out of it, which is extremely similar to the question of whether Jim, depicted as a possible wise father and teacher, could uplift Huck from the other forces that penetrate his mind— Pap, Tom Sawyer, and the Widow, who are continually dialogic presences in his thoughts.

Like James's Maisie and Twain's Huck, Lee's Scout is a study of the human subject as it adapts to a specific environment, a mode of inquiry that we can historicize by looking at pioneering studies of authors who explored the consequences of Charles Darwin's insights in the movement of child study that he pioneered in 1877. Studies of child consciousness in American literature were part of a broader movement in science, philosophy, psychology, and art in the late Victorian and early modern period. In 1877 Darwin published "A Biographical Sketch of an Infant," drawn from a diary that he wrote thirty-seven years earlier; it embodied his quest to understand the ascent of man, through daily observation of his child's movements. Throughout the sketch, he endeavors to accurately describe those movements and interpret them as instinctual or voluntary. Throughout Britain, France, Germany, Italy, and America, researchers would follow Darwin's lead with observations of children. They pioneered a new observational method, which required interpretation, to tackle questions such as when and how did sensation become perception? When did the individual become conscious of its thoughts, and when did it begin to express its will? How, and by what mechanism, did the individual adapt to, or make its own, environment?

Darwin published his diary in response to a publication by M. Taine on his child's language acquisition, which featured a record of his child's sound and tried to sort out rote imitation from human creativity and experimentation. Taine and Darwin launched a fruitful period of child study that would involve psychologists as diverse as William Preyer, Bernard Perez, G. Stanley Hall, Frederick Tracy, Alfred Binet, M. Gabriel Compayré, James Baldwin, and James Sully, whose ideas of the imagination drew upon the work of authors remembering childhood, such as George Sand and Robert Louis Stevenson, and whose ideas about child reasoning would weave their way into the narrative technique of many authors and artists. The figure of the child gradually but irrecoverably assumed a new importance as the theory of evolution, natural selection, and adaptation influenced "the new psychology" and new methods for understanding the human being. As John Dewey put it in his 1884 "The New Psychology," Darwin made possible the study of an organism in its environment, which would eventually culminate in the interpretive work of Freud and in modernist methods by authors who similarly pioneered narrative methods for representing the streaming mind, emergent consciousness, and the onset of volition.

The influence of this movement on Henry James carries it into theories of the novel, about which he meditated. The legacy of Jamesian novel theory, Dorothy Hale traces in her book *Social Formalism: The Novel in Theory from James to the Present,* would carry into the work of Du Bois on subaltern double consciousness and into Bakhtin's work on the heteroglossic voices of the novel form. Henry James's brother William James, known for his pioneering work in the stream of consciousness, had studied with Hall at Harvard. Hall would become perhaps the most prolific American psychologist of childhood and adolescence, virtually inventing the latter as a special period of life that put the individual and society at great risk. James recommended Hall's appointment as professor of psychology and pedagogy at Johns Hopkins, claiming that of all the psychologists in the States, only he and Hall were qualified to teach "the new psychology" (S. White 110). Hall founded the journal *Pedagogical Seminary,* which would take a leading role in turn-of-the-century child study by 1898, annually reporting on the progress of the movement and thus enabling researchers to share knowledge. Hall would invite Freud to lecture in 1909 (S. White 109), and Freud's studies of infant sexuality appeared in 1905. But the groundwork for Freud's studies of the child mind had been laid by a fruitful thirty years of ideas circulating about child consciousness, not least of which could be found in the growth of children's literature after Lewis Carroll's *Alice* books.

The influence of Darwin's ideas on Freud is obvious, as argued by James Sulloway and practically spelled out in *Totem and Taboo.* But belief in the older psychological method of introspection and faith in an ordered mind, composed of discrete parts and capable of observing itself, had pretty much already been eroded by the time Freud published. Child study had given researchers a vision of the "primitive" (so they called it) and dynamic mind as always in flux and engaged in the process of thinking, which could not be separated from thought, as William James clarifies in his discussion of stream of consciousness. The theory of an impressionist stream began to manifest itself in modern literature as relatively passive characters, often trapped in confining environments compensated with rich interior universes of thought. Chapter 42 of Henry James's *Portrait of a Lady* (1880–1881) embodies a pioneering movement inward as Isabel sits by the fire and reflects on her circumstances: "She could live it over again, the incredulous terror with which she had taken measure of her dwelling. Between those four walls she had lived ever since; they were to surround her for the rest of her life. It was the house of darkness, the house of dumbness, the house of suffocation" (160). You could say that the gothic plot was becoming internal. As her perception of walls closing in on her increases, so her interior journey into reflective consciousness begins. In *Mockingbird,* Boo Radley functions as the internal gothic, much as *Mysteries of Udolpho* does for Catherine in Jane Austen's influential *Northanger Abbey.* The difference between the novels of

Austen and Lee lies in the narrative practice and focalization, which transforms Scout's fear and dim recognition of evil into a swirl of vagueness and unclear sensory intuitions surrounding her mind.

James in his 1908 preface to the New York edition of *Portrait* formalized his aesthetic method, writing against those who accused him of "not having 'story' enough" (5). It is interesting that Lee's editors had the same initial reaction to her first draft. As I have argued elsewhere ("Apertures"), James's 1908 account of the artist echoes the observational and interpretive method of piercing windows on the social scene that had already been circulating among researchers of childhood, who felt the study of child consciousness vexed traditional psychological methods and that a window separated what children see from what adults see. What James establishes with Isabel and expands fully with his 1897 publication of Maisie, who becomes an exercise in unique focalization because she is treated as a passive object by adults in her environment, is a way to filter a story without directly telling it at all. This is precisely what occurs in scenes of danger and exploration in *Mockingbird*.

Late-Victorian psychologists were busy studying how children "naturally" learn by deploying myths and "primitive" thought patterns, and how they reason by making analogies and comparisons. Contemporary critics of Twain see racism in Jim's voicing of superstition, but late-Victorian readers would have viewed Jim and Huck's folkloric and anthropomorphic reasoning as "natural" cognitive processes because child researchers equated the child with what they saw as "the savage" or "primitive" man. Both child and "primitive," they felt, were instances of pre-civilized intelligence. When Cal says "that's nigger-talk" about Scout's reasoning regarding the Radleys, she is giving voice to one hundred years of developmentalism that equated myth-making with primitive thought. Sully claimed that "a number of the child's hypotheses are strikingly similar to those shared by older and more primitive cultures" (xxix), and that "this anthropocentric tendency again is shared by the child with the uncultured adult. Primitive man looks on wind, rain, thunder, as sent by some angry spirit" (82).

The "what" of James's *What Maisie Knew* is never clear, just as it never is for Scout, because it is a study of not so much *what* as *how*. As L. M. Montgomery humorously remarked, she had read *What Maisie Knew* but still "couldn't discover what grisly knowledge Maisie *did* possess" (Gammel 55). James's text deliberately leaves "the what" veiled by Maisie's emergent consciousness because that is his point: the process of knowing is inseparable from the knowledge, as articulated by his brother. *Maisie* is carefully calculated to give us a vision of psychological theories gaining inertia at the time. For example, psychologists were devoting much written space to determining the role of consciousness as a liminal quality between involuntary and voluntary actions, between receiving sensations from the environment, transforming sensations into impressions, and then transforming impressions into perceptions, which would then evolve into willful action. Lee uses the young Scout for the same purpose; her consciousness is the liminal sphere between rote repetition of environmental habits and choices that might exceed them.

Maisie and Scout are around the same age. Both are pawns in settings that seek to influence them in different ways and that give them mixed messages. Both romanticize one particular father figure whom they interact with as if at a gentleman's club, seeking access to a gentleman's world (Sir Claude, Atticus). Both demonstrate the conclusions of child researchers that textbook and real-life knowledge greatly differ. Both observe far more than understand what they see. Both deflect scenes with concrete focus on unusual aspects to obfuscate meaning. Both reason in similar ways to decode emotions when we would think emotion would be intuitive. Both inadvertently intervene and create irony in scenes when they ask questions of those who are "supposed to know better." Most evidently, Scout is a Maisie-like observer, more and more so as the madness of racism takes over the town. The role of observer carries with it a certain stance of hopeless passivity, as revealed by more and more instances of Scout's sleepiness, not least of which happens when she is indeed dressed as a ham. She misses her stage entrance because she has been lulled into sleep, partly as escape. But, typically, Scout makes her most creative and insightful cognitive associations when she is drifting off to sleep, as discussed by Patrick Chura (9); for example, the significance of the near-lynching only comes to her when she is going to sleep, and when she sleepily awaits the verdict she free associates Atticus's role in the trial with his role in the empty waiting street, about to confront a mad dog. The equivalent of Atticus taking off his glasses to see "right" is Scout dozing off, when she returns to a fluid and open state of liminal consciousness.

The enterprise of passive spectatorship in *Maisie* nicely exemplifies the aesthetic technique of James's "pierced aperture" into the house of fiction, as articulated in his 1908 preface. This technique should be understood as an ideal in many modernist enterprises at the time, as explored by Juliet Dusinberre in her book about the influence of children's literature like Carroll's *Alice* on modernism:

> [Roger Fry] found in children a capacity to observe without interpreting, which he believed that the Post-Impressionists, and particularly Cézanne, recaptured: "We learn to read the prophetic message, and, for the sake of economy, to neglect all else. Children have not learned it fully, and so they look at things with some passion. Even the grown man keeps something of his unbiological, disinterested vision with regard to a few things. He still looks at flowers, and does not merely see them." (22)

The recapturing of a "primitive" point of view was an ideal in many arts, in reaction to the sentimental and moral weightiness of an earlier era. In her lectures on place in fiction, Eudora Welty observes of the modern revolution in art, "Impressionism brought not the likeness-to-life, but the mystery of place onto canvas; it was the method, not the subject, that told this." But we can locate the distinction between looking and seeing in many texts of child psychology in the period leading up to modernism. As Stevenson had earlier discussed in his influential essay "Child's Play," "Children, for instance, are able enough to see, but they have no great faculty for looking" (1). Philosophic discussions about *what* children see came from an ideological imperative to understand our origins, "the beginnings of things" (Drummond 14), because child development must "correspond to stages in his ancestral history" (Drummond 15):

> We are learning that the child does not see *as* we see, and therefore does not quite see *what* we see. . . . Side by side with direct observation of the child must go interpretation. This is the province of the science of psychology. This is the most difficult branch of child study and the most fascinating. He who would undertake it must be gifted not only with the power of observing with scientific accuracy, but with what has been called his scientific imagination. (Drummond 16)

Lee takes this modern ideological imperative as a national one by tying a child's faculty for seeing but not looking to the question of race: "All the little man on the witness stand had that made him any better than his nearest neighbors was, that if scrubbed with lye soap in very hot water, his skin was white" (171). Sight and seeing are important subjects in the novel, related but not identical to reading, and related but not identical to witnessing. The insertion of the modifying clause ("if scrubbed with lye soap in very hot water") demonstrates the clever way Lee manages to insert a mocking older narrator to control but not completely reveal the interpretation of what is observed—ostensibly by a young Scout who, in the trial, mostly sees while the older narrator looks.

The idea that child study practitioners should observe and interpret with scientific eyes is closely related to James's assertion in his 1908 preface that the artist is bounded by, but somewhat free of, moral reference. Child researchers in James's period were arguing that to really uncover the truth of human consciousness, the child had to be separated from concerns of morality and socialization. This is another reason that neither James nor Twain present their children as primarily moral agents; rather, the children's relationship with morality is always qualified, always partial, always complicated and tied in with environmental factors and techniques of astute observation. As observers of humankind, these literary children are on their own, without the benefit of omniscient narrators or the security of retrospective *bildungsroman* accounts of growth. Maisie and her sister, focalizer Scout, both exemplify Darwinian insight into the nature of the human mind: its infinite and unique (among primates) capacity for adaptability. Sully would call this trait the child's *suggestibility,* which most adequately defines the process of social adaptation in both Maisie and Huck. Huck is practically a model of Darwin's vision of human nature, infinitely adaptable and "suggested" into a wide variety of roles, giving little care to the prior role as a new setting assigns him a new role (see also Blackford, "Child Consciousness"). Maisie, too, quickly forgets about her former ties as she shifts settings, just as Huck forgets about Jim when the demands of, for example, the Grangerfords take precedence in his immediate environment. Maisie exists in the perpetual present: "In that lively sense of the immediate which is the very air of a child's mind the past, on each occasion, became for her as indistinct as the future" (24). When

Maisie lives with Mrs. Wix, the memory of Miss Overmore fades; when she chooses to stay with Mrs. Beale, she fails to consider Mrs. Wix. After she has lived with her father, the memory of her mother becomes "as a memory of other years the rattle of her trinkets and the scratch of her endearments, the odour of her clothes and the jumps of her conversation" (59).

Scout is similarly a changeling; Cecil Jacobs, for example, "made her forget" her promise to Atticus not to fight. She can troublingly say "[Tom's] just a Negro" when the demands of conversing with Dill override lessons learned in the trial. After Cal's "stinging smack" at Scout for embarrassing Walter at lunch, Scout "hated Calpurnia steadily until a sudden shriek shattered my resentments" (25); the line mocks Scout's inability to "steadily" hold onto an emotion. The older Scout mocks the young Scout's attention span: "without [Dill], life was unbearable. I stayed miserable for two days" (116). Yet the purpose of this self-irony is only to suggest the point of the novel: the white characters are entirely trapped in their skewed sense of self-worth and proportion: "Maycomb was interested by the news of Tom's death for perhaps two days" (240). In other words, *Mockingbird* deploys Jamesian study of child consciousness for particular purposes, viewing the child mind as a synecdoche for human egocentricity, just as the study of the child mind was supposed to provide an index to the origins of "civilization." Just as Maisie and Huck are, Scout is journeying toward something we call civilization, where she will "watch herself" pass out cookies to the ladies (237) and display impeccable manners to Mr. Arthur Radley. The initial observation offered in Lee's opening—Jem's inability to care about his arm "so long as he could pass and punt" (1)—offers uncertainty about memory and change for a poignant reason. Children and childhood are destined to *pass*.

James and Twain used child focalizers to separate the real human mind from romantic ideas about shaping one's destiny, which is precisely why both authors overtly explore the question of freedom alongside the problematic matter of child consciousness. Any growth in consciousness, they demonstrate, is really a matter of choosing between various internalized discourses embedded there by others. There is not so much a unique individual personality in Maisie and Huck as there is a variety of roles played by the child in various social situations, which compete for ascendancy in the child's subjectivity. Sorting out these environmental influences becomes the internal drama rendered in these texts. None of these characters can be particularly introspective, and thus they explore the consequences of what developmental psychologists had discovered about the adaptive child mind, the attention of which would be seized by the most vivid objects, quite apart from their moral value.

What impresses Maisie, like Huck and Scout, is not the moral situation unfolding in front of her eyes but the way people she knows feel and react to it. Without full knowledge, the emotions of others are the textbook for the child. For example, "Maisie was not at the moment so fully conscious of [her parents] as of the wonder of Moddle's sudden disrespect and crimson face" (23). Maisie reads the manner of others for her information: "Her [mother's] manner at that instant gave the child a glimpse more vivid than any yet enjoyed of the attraction that papa, in remarkable language, always denied she could put forth" (74). In attempting to interpret the presence of Mr. Perriam in her mother's house, Maisie learns not to ask but to read the situation and gain knowledge that way. Maisie is sensitive to the body languages and performances of others: "It took her pupil but a moment to feel that [Mrs. Wix] quivered with insecurity" (79). It is Sir Claude's change in tone (108) that impacts her when they meet her mother and a lover in the park. In other words, Maisie's experience of herself is entirely mediated by others. She has few raw reactions, but she interprets others to understand how to feel. She becomes an expert at interpreting other people, even to the extent that she can quote how she *thinks* they perceive things; she hears the unspoken words of her father's desires to be let off the hook rather than actually take her with him to America, and she hears those words in his own voice. She thus navigates the world by interpreting the inner emotions of others, as if she has direct access to their unconscious; like Huck, whose interpretive acuity I discuss below, she is sensitive to the living book of nature.

Similarly, the intimate knowledge of those she knows well becomes Scout's lone knowledge in scenes that challenge her comprehension. For example, during the scene in which the sheriff calls Atticus outside and expresses reservations about Tom's safety, Scout reads Atticus and presents in raw form snippets of the adult conversation, occurring outside, which she does not understand. The words of the adults come through the window of the house and take the effect of stream of consciousness. None of the adult sentences is quite finished; rather, the sentences break off and begin with multiple ellipses, one phrase overrunning another. The passage conveys the sense that the men are all speaking over one another, but it also conveys the confusion of consciousness that occurs upon witnessing adult cacophony. The children listen at the windows, literally separated from the adult world by a barrier, which proves thin and slightly permeable, as if about to cave:

> They all seemed to be talking at once.
> "... movin' him to the county jail tomorrow," Mr. Tate was saying, "I don't look for any trouble, but I can't guarantee there won't be any...."
> [...]
> "... know how they do when they get shinnied up."
> "They don't usually drink on Sunday, they go to church most of the day ...," Atticus said.
> "This is a special occasion, though ...," someone said.
> They murmured and buzzed until Aunty said if Jem didn't turn on the livingroom lights he would disgrace the family. Jem didn't hear her.
> "—don't see why you touched it in the first place," Mr. Link Deas was saying. "You've got everything to lose from this, Atticus. I mean everything."
> "Do you really think so?"
> This was Atticus's dangerous question. "Do you really think you want to move there, Scout?" Bam, bam, bam, and the checkerboard was swept clean of my men. "Do you really think that, son? Then read this." Jem would struggle the rest of an evening through the speeches of Henry W. Grady. (145–46)

The adult words are transcribed through Scout as an "aperture" rather than shaped by the older narrator. The words come through as sensory data: pure sound crossing the listening brain and occupying the liminal area between raw stimulus and actual perception. The proliferation of ellipsis and hyphens makes this windowed moment unique and gives us the feeling of discomfort because so many thoughts are unfinished. There are only a few other such moments in *Mockingbird*, such as when the children's reactions to Miss Caroline's scream run over one another, when Jem conveys his streaming surprise at Atticus's one-shot, and, significantly, when Scout overhears the missionary society ladies chatting from behind the swinging door to the kitchen. It is important that Scout's eavesdropping on the front porch men and the missionary society ladies results in similar narrative technique. Both are "streams" from behind thresholds, and they convey the sense that adult worlds are, as yet, behind a cognitive window.

I draw attention to the windows as Jamesian "apertures" because the design is artistic—what James described as registering the posted presence of the artist who uniquely observes the social scene. The trope of the child separated from the adult world by glass or similar surface comes from *Maisie;* Maisie's view of the adult social world is like looking at "the slide of a magic lantern" (21), walking "a long, long corridor with rows of closed doors" (36–37), and "flattening her nose against a pane of glass" (82). The metaphor of the window as a permeable barrier between child and adult perception was first discussed by Stevenson in "Child's Play," published in his 1884 *Virginibus Puerisque.* Stevenson claimed that adults see things through the windows of theories and associations that they have developed through life, whereas children can look at objects more directly. Scout in this scene of threatening men is quite literally pressing her nose against the pane of glass that separates her known and familiar world from the wider world coming to her porch. The porches themselves are liminal spheres between public and private in *Mockingbird,* places where adults and children often come together and where Scout strikes several law-bending bargains with Atticus, which I discuss in chapter 4. What Scout *does* understand in this scene, similarly to how Maisie reasons, is Atticus's question—his "'do you really think so?'" addressed to the men. She knows that this is something he characteristically says just before "the checkerboard was swept clean of my men" (146) or before challenging a flawed opinion of Jem's. Lee's theory of the consciousness "stream" indicates the mind's connective tissue as it makes analogies and recognitions by focusing only on partial aspects of a scene. This is precisely the process identified and theorized by William James: "Consciousness is always interested more in one part of its object than in another, and welcomes and rejects, or chooses, all the while it thinks." What is crucial to note, however, is that William James is not only describing the liquidity of the human brain but also the process of the artist. The artist does not so much create something as suppress partial aspects of the stream to achieve unity. Lee shows that human cognition is the result of suppression and association; as Welty argues, "The human mind is a mass of associations—associations more poetic even than actual." Associations can only arise from the stream through suppressing quite a bit of data and selecting particulars, which concurs with Lee's focus on a child who must suppress various environmental stimuli in order to pass at all.

The metaphor of the checkerboard game to define social relations is also James's. He continually describes adult games in *Maisie* as parlor games Maisie does not yet know how to play (see 17, 45, 51, 67, 76, 78, 107, 112, 136, 205), although she learns to eventually, primarily through observing and imitating Sir Claude. When she uses Claude's word "draw" to mean extract, the narrator observes, "it was astonishing how many [of Sir Claude's words] she gathered in" (64); Maisie and Sir Claude tend to mime each other—for example, going back and forth with "'you said so'" "as if they were playing a game" (67). James makes explicit the importance of the child watching this game of social maneuvering: "[Maisie] found in her mind a collection of images and echoes . . . kept for her in the childish dusk, the dim closet, the high drawers, like games she wasn't yet big enough to play. . . . A wonderful assortment of objects of this kind she was to discover there later, all tumbled up too with the things, shuffled into the same receptacle, that her mother had said about her father" (22–23). Scout is similarly watching adult games and later, when half asleep, the assortment of objects filed in her consciousness often gains new meaning by virtue of their relations with one another.

James peppers his novel with metaphors for the child mind, which, in his view, stores images and echoes as sense memories that can then be interpreted much later. His vision of how impressions come before perceptions seems to come mostly from the work of James Sully on the child's imagination; Jenny Bourne Taylor views Sully as a crucial transition figure between Victorian child psychology and Freud's new interpretation of Darwin. In an 1893 article, Sully links childhood, evolution, and dreams; his article was later cited by Freud in *Interpretation of Dreams* (Taylor 93). Like James, Lee suggests the dreamlike state through which Scout processes many, to her, incomprehensible adult games, which she, like Maisie in the end, will in fact successfully learn to play when the dilemma of Boo confronts her and she agrees with iterative male language, "'he fell on his knife.'"

Continuing the representation of impressionist consciousness, Scout's intimate knowledge of others' habits comes to the foreground when Atticus heads to the jail; she knows something is amiss because he drives rather than walks, and the paragraph in which we learn this establishes both the value and limits of her knowledge:

> "He's takin' the car," said Jem.
>
> Our father had a few particularities: one was, he never ate desserts; another was that he liked to walk. As far back as I could remember, there was always a Chevrolet in excellent condition in the carhouse, and Atticus put many miles on it in business trips, but in Maycomb he walked to and from his office four times a day, covering about two miles. He said his only exercise was walking. In Maycomb, if one went for a walk with no definite purpose in mind, it was correct to believe one's mind incapable of definite purpose.
>
> Later on, I bade my aunt and brother good night and was well into a book when I heard Jem rattling around in his room. His go-to-bed noises were so familiar to me that I knocked on his door: "Why ain't you going to bed?" (148–49)

These paragraphs are designed to draw attention to "what Scout knew" and yet distinguish Scout's expertise from her inexperience, which also builds suspense. What remains interesting about the paragraph on Atticus is the way in which the young Scout and the older Scout, with the vocabulary to express her broad knowledge of Maycomb sentiments, become indistinguishable. The young Scout reads Atticus and Jem, interpreting their habits. But the focalizer who detects a change in Jem's sound and whose suspicions are aroused by Atticus driving rather than walking smoothly transforms into an anthropological expert on Maycomb's feelings about walkers. We do not know which Scout, young or older, knows Maycomb feels this way about walking; it could be the case that young Scout knows this and the older Scout is just giving the thought her vocabulary. This is because Lee wants us to understand both six-year-old and older Scout, whoever she is "when enough years had gone by to enable us to look back" (3), as sharing an anthropological stance.

Both young and older Scout are really participant-observers, which is how modern consciousness operates. This anthropological stance intervenes in our expectations; we expect to learn what young Scout's intuitions of Atticus and Jem suggest. We expect a conclusion and a choice, such as

"I decided to follow them," which might be what we would get in *Huck;* instead, we get the researcher and the incisive question, voiced in dialect, "'Why ain't you going to bed?'" In other words, we witness the rupture in the child between blind acceptance and query. Young Scout is probably not aware of knowing so much about Atticus's and Jem's usual customs until she detects an alteration from routine; knowledge of habits and "the usual" only becomes visible when something unusual occurs. Jem's sudden disruption of his usual going-to-bed sounds, like Atticus's sudden refusal to walk, allows us to witness the young Scout moving from inside to outside a circle of meaning, an outsider position where she can view and translate Finch and Maycomb custom. We are watching called into being the narrator who can diagnose the closed Radley door as "alien to Maycomb ways." We are watching, in young Scout, the onset of comparative method for accumulating knowledge.

The child's growing realization of her intimate knowledge of familiar people is, in fact, the onset of double consciousness, defined as seeing the self and culture through the veil of how an outsider would see the self and culture. Frederick Douglass demonstrates the insider/outsider posture when he interprets the sorrow songs of the slaves that he did not understand *when he was a slave.* The flow of Scout's knowledge moves from her detection of something unusual in her environment to her questioning of it, to her recognition of familial and cultural norms, with the result of sudden isolation: being the one on the outside of a circle of meaning, or being in a privileged posture of insight.

Just as Maisie, as a child, is outside the social game and thus not "looking at it as through theories and associations," Stevenson's words for adult perspective, the lynch mob presents to Scout an inscrutable and illegible situation. It is a crucial detail that the journey to the jail has interrupted Scout in the process of reading a book, because it is the difficulty of scene-reading that confronts her. As we are taken into the scene, the older Scout gives us background on the Maycomb jail, a "miniature Gothic joke" (150): "Atticus said it was like something Cousin Joshua St. Clair might have designed" (150), a significant background that asks us to think like Scout—analogically. By analogy, the jail must harbor madness, and we must intuit that some sort of documented madness is likely before us. As we have now been trained to uncover, the scene quickly shifts from a masterful, Stowe-like narrator who can tell us what Atticus said earlier to the young Scout's raw perceptions of the events, a direct transcription of what she sees, dialogue that she hears, and actions of the children as they fly to Atticus. The older narrator, who might observe how Maycomb feels about taking a walk, or who might create irony by suggesting Scout's limitations—her "staying miserable for two days," for example—recedes and allows the young focalizer to take center stage. From outside the circle of meaning, from in the shadows, Scout can see the unusual aspects of the scene—the sleepy-eyed farmers "unused to late hours" out in the night; by virtue of her prior readings of Atticus and Jem in the pages before, we are accustomed to her increasing role as outside consciousness. It is a posture from which she can destabilize the scene by jumping in from the shadows.

What Scout mostly sees in the scene is a showdown between the two males she loves, Atticus and Jem. Her perspective dwells on their "mutual defiance" (152) and contrast in looks, as Atticus asks him to go home and Jem refuses. She thus sees the game in partial, seeing an Oedipal conflict and thus translating an incomprehensible scene to an analogical situation, just as she does in the porch scene by seizing upon the familiar checkerboard question "'do you really think so?'" Scout intervenes and changes the direction of the near-lynching scene largely because of her limited understanding and her flawed endeavors to apply Atticus's lessons in social politeness, which we have seen before in the school scene when she attempted to apply her knowledge of the Cunninghams to Miss Caroline. I discuss the full technique of the school scene in chapter 4, but here we must note that by this point in the novel, Lee has trained us to understand Scout's misfiring powers of reasoning. She engages Mr. Cunningham in conversation and tries various topics that she believes might interest him. Our sense that the older Scout has abandoned the young, which emerges in contrast to the school scene where the older narrator intrudes more, mirrors our sense that mastery and control of the scene are not fully possible.

To make the contrasting narrative styles more poignant, Scout again returns to narrative home ground on the way home, when she notes that Atticus gives Jem a rare gesture of affection—a detail again within her interpretive expertise because she so intimately knows the body languages of Atticus and Jem. The gesture surprises her, however, because she would have expected Atticus's anger at the father-son showdown; the result is complicated. By deploying the analogical reasoning of Scout as dependent on intimate body language, the reader is able to decipher far more than Scout can. Yet at the same time, the reader sees the posted presence of Lee's older narrator by seeing Scout's inevitably egocentric mind. The egocentricity of the human being is precisely what causes prejudice in the first place.

The near-lynching scene makes apparent the wide gap between reading and interpretation, just as it does in the various voices of Scout: the older Scout providing background; the young Scout who received Atticus's lesson about the Cunninghams earlier; the young Scout as focalizer who sees a showdown between Atticus and Jem rather than a showdown between the old Sarum crowd and the enlightened Atticus; and the actual character Scout who jumps head first into action without thinking it through and who is not quite adept at manipulating discourse to the situation. For example, Scout's use of the word "entailment" might not be appropriate. Such scenes convey the way in which the child mind selects partial, salient features of a situation rather than the whole, particularly when threatened with something new. For Maisie, focus tends to be on the most beautiful objects of a scene that seize her attention, in much the way developmental psychologists maintained child attention operated. For example, the scene of her father's mistress's home evokes an opulent beauty and suggests to her the tale of Arabian Nights, which functions quite ironically in the scene, given the gap between the tale and the actual fact that her father merely wants her permission to desert her. The gap between analogical reasoning and the actual situation can create extreme irony, just as Huck's focus on "stealing" Jim from the Widow gives readers a vision of how limited Huck's very thought process is. But while ironic, the technique of drawing a gap between seeing and interpreting can indicate far more. It can indicate gaps between national ideology and practice, which is to indicate, in fact, American double consciousness.

The implied gaps and indeterminacies, as theorized by Wolfgang Iser, comprise Lee's technique when Scout is seriously challenged with a new situation, such as when she journeys to Cal's church and obsessively records scents, smells, and raw data. This is a turning point of the novel, beginning part 2 and thereby taking us beyond Maycomb "background" in every sense of the word. Scout is quick to perceive a change in the usual speech of Cal, storing "sense memories" like Maisie does in her collection of "images and echoes," to attach meaning later. The scene of Cal's church embodies an important boundary-crossing, tantamount to Maisie's visit to her father's new residence, which shocks her other parents because her father's mistress, as Toni Morrison has discussed, is neither white nor of his class. Scout's journey shocks and even seems to conjure Aunt Alexandra, whom the young Scout humorously expects might actually be Boo Radley "sunning himself in the swing" (126). This is because Aunt Alexandra is a similar menace. The distinction between Aunt Alexandra, who closes the scene, and Cal, who opens it, is the difference between false and true civilization, or Twain's sense of civilization (nihilist) and a natural relationship between Cal and Scout "beneath" or "behind" Maycomb front porches. The distinction between Aunt Alexandra and Cal also bespeaks the difference between narrative styles; whereas the older, ironic narrator intrudes in the distancing representation of Aunt Alexandra, the young and impressionable child consciousness of Scout takes precedence in the focalization of the black church scene.

Aunt Alexandra's function—the importation of a self-righteous and inflated "civilization"—is the function of Mrs. Wix or the aunts of Twain's fiction. Like Mrs. Wix, Aunt Alexandra expresses indignation at "the horrors" to which the child is exposed. While these figures are comic, the comedy covers the most sinister and nihilist function of deadpan humor (see Bercovitch). Responding to the evolutionary theory driving child study, both James and Twain worried that the most civilized and most adapted people would hardly be the most moral. Adaptation and morality could be completely at odds with each other. What are horrors to Mrs. Wix are not horrors to Maisie, who adjusts to whatever *is*: "the natural way for a child to have her parents was separate and successive, like her mutton and her pudding or her bath and her nap" (26). The adaptable nature of the child is highly problematic, as we will explore with Huck, who can go along with Pap, the Widow, or Tom Sawyer, depending on whose worldviews are in front of him at the time. What becomes important in the scene of Cal's church is the technique by which Lee reveals the denaturalizing of Scout's prior "civilized" knowledge. Scout has to shift to sensory information because in the church scene her reading and interpretation skills fail. There is a reason Aunt Alexandra appears right after the journey, just as Tom Sawyer's aunt and Tom Sawyer himself appear in the final chapters of *Huck* to shut down the journey taken with Jim on the river. Aunt Alexandra bears an uncanny resemblance to James's self-righteous, pompous, and unattractive Mrs. Wix, who appoints herself Maisie's "saver" and is thus a parody of the child-savers in James's time. Mrs. Wix objects to

"the horrors" of what Maisie knew, which, to the adaptable and suggestive child, are not horrors at all. Aunt Alexandra objects to "the horrors" of
Scout's new knowledge, which, if we attend to narrative technique in the
church scene, is merely the de-evolution or denaturalization of all the prior
"civilized" assumptions Scout held.

Upon heading to Calpurnia's church, the young Scout emphasizes what
she sees and smells—raw impressions. The older Scout inserts background
intermittently, such as when she explains the origin of the name "First
Purchase," rather like she inserts background on the jail's architecture or on
the Ewell residence during the trial. With marginal insertions by the narrator and with a striking absence of ironic commentary, the excursion to the
church represents the very limits of what young Scout can read. Scout does
not understand why there are no hymn books. She needs to ask, but she de-
lays, showing that she is already in the stage of Maisie when Maisie delibe-
rates rather than blurts out her mother's message about her father—"'that he
lies and he knows he lies'" (26). Scout stores up her impressions in order to
query Cal privately, which then also reveals her blind spots and limitations.
She has never before thought to inquire about Cal! Cal's age, Cal's background, Cal's literacy, Cal's role in her own community, and Cal's family—all
are revealed to be new information to Scout, despite having spent each day
of her life with Cal.

Cal's "command of two languages" is a symbol not only for the insider/
outsider position that Scout herself comes to inhabit, but also an ironic lesson in young Scout's egocentrism: "The idea that she had a separate existence outside our household was a novel one, to say nothing of her having
command of two languages" (125). The moment echoes many moments in
children's literature when young characters realize their parents once had
lives that did not include them. In such moments, children are diminished
into awe-struck observers. In *Little House in the Big Woods,* for example, the
moment occurs when Laura looks in awe at her mother's strawberry delaine
from "the East," a remnant of the woman Caroline before she was ever Ma.
The sensory details of the delaine take precedence over the uninterpretable
reality that maybe Ma does not solely exist for the children. In this crucial
scene of *Mockingbird,* focalized to separate sensory impressions from skills
of reading, Cal takes a role equal to Atticus and gives Scout a lesson of civilization. She imparts her wisdom and answers things candidly and in a way a
child can understand.

Scout's close observation of Cal and her speech patterns at church is characteristic of the way that Scout *can* find a point of entry into adult and unfamiliar settings. Upon first arriving at the church and being confronted by Lula, Scout "sensed" rather than "saw" (119) the menacing stance; but the details that Scout notices tell us far more than narrator commentary would. The detail of how much Calpurnia scrubs the children for the day tells us about the status Calpurnia gains with her Finch guests. The description of the church cemetery littered by broken decorations tells us about the status and poverty of the black community, contradicting the narrator's odd conclusion, "It was a happy cemetery" (118). The scene culminates in a variety of significances, not least of which is Cal's lesson on double-voiced discourse and therefore writing. One significance to point out here is Scout's pattern of questioning "innocently," which, like Maisie's questions, implicitly challenges adults to reveal what they are hiding. For example, Scout asks why Helen cannot take her children to work with her, knowing that "field Negroes" typically take their babies to work with them. She then gets the real answer, which is that Helen faces the stigma of the rape case. Scout is penetrating with her analogical reasoning in the same way that Maisie is penetrating.

The trip to Calpurnia's church, where there are *no books,* is juxtaposed with the useless formal curriculum of school, which is stacked with books that do not apply to the real world at all. In the church scene, Scout finally learns more truth about the case of Tom and first hears of the word "rape." She has literally and symbolically crossed a boundary of knowledge, reading, and experience. The trip, of course, takes her beyond Atticus's world and philosophy, giving her a new perspective on Finch's Landing and Calpurnia's ties to the family. The person she previously called "the trash collector" is now Zeebo, Calpurnia's son, a detail somehow (remarkably) not important in her prior context. In this scene the very limited view of Scout's consciousness is exposed and shamed, much like Huck's is exposed and shamed with Jim's famous "trash" speech.

Of course, the point of James's "magic lanterns" and smoke-filled shadows dancing through Maisie's consciousness is their lack of substance—the impossibility of knowing what is true, given the problem of perspective and given that the strongest adults often shape reality. In the scene with Cal at church, it is impossible for Scout to know what is true; Cal's lesson about conforming to discourse communities and to the principle of adaptation as "ladylike" and civil actually bespeaks Cal's duplicity. Who knows the real Cal? Even Cal may not know the real Cal, her double consciousness always in the way. Atticus's information on Tom's character, fascinatingly, comes from Cal, and in the church scene Cal has not only evaded the question of rape but also confessed to the fact that *she* is a performance based on what her audience wants to hear, something perhaps intuited by the massive preparations for church. So while on the one hand the apparition of Aunt Alexandra seems to shut down Scout's exploration of the African American world, immediately reinscribing white supremacy when Aunt Alexandra, who "owned a bright green square Buick and a black chauffeur" (127), orders Cal to bring in her bags. But on the other hand Aunt Alexandra is an extension of the lesson Cal has imparted. Aunt Alexandra will throw at Scout books and background, but Scout now knows they are fictional. Scout will never again regard her known world as natural, like Maisie after seeing with her father a "vision of this vision of his, his vision of her vision, and her vision of his vision of her vision" (132). The scenes of Maisie's visit to her father's mistress and Scout's visit to Cal's church are the same turning points in the lives of "innocents." In effect, Scout has a vision of this vision of Cal's, Cal's vision of Scout's vision, and Scout's vision of Cal's vision of Finch's vision. No wonder Aunt Alexandra feels Scout needs a mother; at Cal's church Scout has very much lost one to the profound view of human duplicity. One of the first things Scout does when Atticus asks her if she would like Aunty to live with them is lie. Scout has learned her lesson in "linin'," lying, and ladylike behavior, or double-faced conformity, which will concern us further in other chapters.

The crux of what Lee appropriated from James and Twain should be apparent: the child's propensity to learn from the living bosom of nature rather than from books (or what adults want them to read) is a problem because the nature of nature is unclear. Huck has been championed in the tradition of American pioneers who reject the stifling conditions of (largely female) civilization and in the wilderness discover some sort of better self. This would be completely true if forces of civilization were not carried in mental life, which the story of Huck reveals. As I discuss the way Huck parallels Maisie's reasoning and mediated experience, it is important to keep in mind that while developmental psychologists of the period agreed that study of child nature would improve educational tools, they did not agree on whether a romantic or Darwinian view of nature prevailed. Educational theorists such as F. H.

Hayward grappled with the implications of child study and the vexed question of nature in theory:

> Why do I call Wordsworth's view "nonsensical"? For the reason that ever since Darwin's *Origin of Species* was published, thinking men have no longer been able to regard nature in herself as wholly wise or kind. There is a calmness, a callousness—one might almost say a cruelty and wastefulness—about her that precludes the reflective man from holding this view. There goes on everywhere in Nature a "struggle for existence," and the "fittest" who survive are not necessarily the most loveable creatures, but rather those that are strongest, or at any rate those that are most adapted to their special circumstances. (Hayward 26)

The question of whether child nature was inherently best or in need of regeneration would circulate in the educational application of child study. Twain exploits this critical crux by placing his child in between two father figures who exemplify learning from the natural world (primitive thinking, etc.) but also represent two contrasting views of nature—Pap a savage view, and Jim a kind one. Lee makes a similar move by putting Scout between a wise father who studies nature in the tradition of Emersonian romanticism and a savage father (Ewell) who brings the comic Pap back to life and, worse, gives him a daughter. Further, both novels of Twain and Lee give a benevolent black parent to the child inevitably heading for civilization. However, Jim interprets and is always associated with the book of nature, whereas Cal—a girl's role model, after all—teaches lessons implied by "civilization" and in many ways deconstructs it. Cal shows that civilization is a role that everyone plays.

Like Maisie and Scout, Twain's Huck also bases his moral reactions on the "living" book of nature—on how other people react, rather than on abstract notions of right and wrong. It is the Widow's face that makes him feel sorry in an early scene, and not his understanding of a wrong. He imagines the Widow's approval when he helps thieves (91) or disapproval when he considers how he is helping Jim. He measures himself against what he believes others might think of him, worrying that helping Jim would make others think him a "dirty abolitionist." He asks himself what Tom would do in certain situations and calls upon what he has learned from Pap as well; for example, he decides to follow Pap's lead and let the Duke and King imagine themselves as whomever they wish. This is very similar to Scout's importation of Atticus's lessons in a variety of scenes, which are sometimes applicable and sometimes not. Huck faces the limitations of the child's moral reasoning; he reacts morally when others respond to him in certain ways, but not on his own perceptions. When he tricks Jim into thinking that he dreamed the storm that parted them, and Jim gives him a moral lesson about what trash is, Huck maintains that he would not have played the trick if he thought it would make Jim *feel* that way. He cannot perceive the wrongness of an action or situation, only the wrongness of making someone *feel* a particular way. For example, although he readily plays along with the King and Duke, he changes his mind when Mary Jane is particularly kind to him; only then does he consider the consequence of the robbery and how it might change her face. This is very close to how Scout reacts to Cecil Jacobs's accusations, not because she understands them but because of the way he speaks. Similarly, Scout reads Miss Maudie's anger in the missionary society scene, unable to grasp the larger implications of Mrs. Merriweather's words. The responses of others, even internalized and imagined, tend to interfere with Huck's judgment continually, whereas alone in nature his judgments are better. In Twain's view, this was not an ideal situation for the human race. In Lee's view, which is a feminist one with a different relationship to civilization, the situation can yield insights and keys to female survival.

We can view modern women's revisions to Huck Finn and his descendent Holden Caulfield by looking at the focalizing twelve-year-old in Carson McCullers's novel *Member of the Wedding*, which influenced *Mockingbird*. Frankie of *Member* will concern us in later chapters more substantially. It is important to note here, however, that analogical reasoning permeates McCullers's representation of Frankie as focalizer, and that the associative mind of the child leads not to hurting people or to blindness but to intuited insights. For example, Frankie passes by an alleyway and catches a side glimpse of two boys together, "and because of this half-seen object, the quick flash in the corner of her eye, there had sprung up in her the sudden picture of her brother and the bride," which becomes such a strong association that it "brought back the wedding frame of mind" (69–70). In Frankie's case, the unconscious is trying to communicate something to her—something about why she is obsessed with her brother's wedding and what her own sexual orientation might be. Child characters read people for clues about the world, but they also read people for clues about themselves. Maisie, Scout, and Huck can only learn about themselves through reading aspects of scenes and connecting them to other mental images, but in deploying the comparative method they both arrive at insight and defamiliarize their prior ("old Frankie") position—their roots.

At issue in these novels with child focalizers is whether civilization is destined to absorb the young or not. At issue is adaptation. Just as Maisie quickly adjusts to various environments and forgets about prior ones, coming to view whatever is in front of her as "the natural" one, Twain's *Huck* parodies the process of adaptation, which is the goal of civilization. Although he is willing to stand apart from the tainted societies he encounters, Huck is equally willing to transform himself for the requirements of each new place. Huck is a humorous model of adaptability; unlike earlier child protagonists, such as Alice, who explicitly cannot adapt to Wonderland, Huck adapts his discourse, stories, and performance to every town. He epitomizes survival of the fittest and answers psychologists' claims that the human being's educability marks the species' adaptability and ability to make new environments (Drummond 6–7; Sully 79). Twain places Huck in particularly brutal settings to repeatedly demonstrate Huck's ingenuity. It is important to note that most of Huck's lies are not purely invented by him, but are suggested to him by others; he often "runs" with roles suggested to him, demonstrating what psychologists equated with the child. For example, Jim suggests that Huck become a girl to glean information from a woman; when this fails to trick the woman, he becomes the role that she ascribes to him—that of escaped apprentice. He becomes a master adapter, transforming himself into George Jackson in the Grangerford household, an English servant for Mary Jane, and Tom Sawyer for Aunt Sally. He is continually "born again" after passing through water, a symbol for his inconsistent character. For example, sometimes he treats Jim well and sometimes not; sometimes he, like the river, floats and plays along with immoral behavior, and sometimes he stands up for what is right. We should recognize this changeling behavior in young Scout, particularly in terms of voice, which is how Scout learns to adapt to discourse situations.

Whereas critics tend to oppose Huck with civilization and buy uncritically Huck's stated resistance, in reality Huck admits that he grows "sort of used to the widow's ways, too" (18). When Pap reclaims him, Huck fairly quickly becomes comfortable there, too: "it warn't long after that till I was used to being where I was, and liked it" (30). Huck is so adaptable that when he begins to live in the "fancy" Grangerford home, he completely forgets about Jim. In perhaps the most humorous instance in which Twain hyperbolizes the child's adaptability, Huck learns of the deceased Emmeline (the Grangerfords' daughter) and steps into her role, sketching graveyard poetry. This is as funny as Scout stepping into the "appointed" role of representing Walter Cunningham at school, which fails miserably. Twain expresses wonder at this quality in the child, but he also expresses concern. For example, the King and the Duke are thieves and shysters, but they only mirror Huck and Jim, who are similarly tricking others and, in Huck's understanding, engaging in a kind of theft (which he believes to be *his* crime). While adaptation is the very principle of childhood and survival, it is also the principle of thieves and shysters. What earns status in one community may be a lie or not permitted in the next. Scout may earn prestige by swearing with peers, but not with Uncle Jack. Fighting is certainly a way to settle accounts with other children, but apparently not with Mrs. Dubose; it might, however, have been the right way to settle Ewell. Importantly, a trial is one way to settle an account, but not the only way, Scout learns in the end—something she already knew with her case-by-case trials.

This points us to the real problem of the modern character's passivity. Both James and Twain are suggesting the essentially passive and imprintable nature of humanity. Huck and Maisie become studies in how experience is always heavily mediated by others. They are largely perceptive characters because they cannot forge their own destinies and thus presage the modern condition of a character like T. S. Eliot's J. Alfred Prufrock, who cannot enter the social scene but merely watches and records it, thus compensating for inaction with a rich interior life. Prufrock's question "Do I dare / Disturb the universe?" (lines 45–46) becomes an important intertext in adolescent literature such as Robert Cormier's *The Chocolate War*, as Roberta Trites observes when she traces a direct line of descent between modernism and novel studies of adolescence. In Maisie's "long habit" of "the sharpened sense of spectatorship" (83) involved in constantly scrutinizing brutal environments for clues about response and meaning, she cannot have an authentic experience, even of something as personal as pain. For example, in perhaps the most mediated moment of Maisie's, Maisie interprets being separated from Mrs. Wix through a memory, and the memory itself reveals her dependence on others to show her how to feel about something we would think natural:

> The second parting from Miss Overmore had been bad enough, but this first parting from Mrs. Wix was much worse. The child had lately been to the dentist's and had a term of comparison for the screwed-up intensity of the scene. It was dreadfully silent, as it had been when her tooth was taken out; Mrs. Wix had on that occasion grabbed her hand and they had clung to each other with the frenzy of their determination not to scream. Maisie, at the dentist's had been heroically still, but just when she felt most anguish had become aware of an audible shriek on the part of her companion, a spasm of stifled sympathy. (33)

The passage asks us to attend to the passivity of Maisie as an object mediated by the sentiments of others. An aspect of a situation suggests another, and the reaction of an adult suggests the way Maisie should feel about her own body. Even emotional response is mediated by environmental conditioning and analogy. In some ways, this signals the development of the sympathetic faculty voiced as an ideal by Atticus; the trouble with the commitment to always strive for seeing the perspectives of others is that it may lend itself to passivity—patience with even the racist sentiments of Mrs. Dubose, for example, or the inability to see Ewell as the threat he is. In Twain's *Huck,* the ability of Huck to mold himself into social roles so well translates into an inability to keep the character and needs of Jim foremost in his consciousness.

Lee conveys the convoluted state of processing adult worlds, not by obfuscating her syntax, like James does, but by evoking imagery to suggest the surreal manner Scout experiences certain events, such as the trial and its verdict. Scout senses the verdict before hearing it, using her past experience to read the jury's refusal to make eye contact, and then conveys the preconscious quality of the scene with imagery of being underwater:

> What happened after that had a dreamlike quality: in a dream I saw the jury return, moving like underwater swimmers, and . . . it was like watching Atticus walk into the street, raise a rifle to his shoulder and pull the trigger, but watching all the time knowing that the gun was empty. (210–11)

The dreamy, liquid experience conveyed in this passage is overtly linked to the unnatural stillness and slumber Scout has experienced throughout the trial and earlier in the street awaiting the arrival of the mad dog. The overwhelming mood of watching and waiting in *Mockingbird* is part of its modern artistic design as the posting of a spectator consciousness. The death of consciousness through immersion in dreamy water is all the more remarkable in a novel without any watery passage near the town. The imagery as symbol for Scout's consciousness conveys in a more accessible way what Twain only implies through Huck's naive consciousness and what Susan Honeyman describes as James's theory of "the elusive nature of childhood." The verdict streams across the brain just as the words of the men on the front porch, which Scout can only experience like Maisie, pressing her nose against a pane of glass. Scout shares with Maisie the sharpened sense of spectatorship that becomes a habit of her being, and her passivity becomes a universal symbol of how trapped we all are in our condemnation to process an unfathomable stream of human misery. Her role as spectator of something Atticus says "'is done again and again'" gives new meaning to there being "nowhere to go" in childhood. There is nowhere to go but toward civilization, Huck's fantasy notwithstanding.

The overwhelming passivity of the modern character is an artifact of regional writing's emphasis on the power of place, which Eudora Welty describes as the material of southern literature. But it is not limited to southern literature; in chapter 6 I discuss the anthropological language deployed by Lee and Edith Wharton's *The Age of Innocence,* in which the "tribal" rites and rituals of New York society overwhelm and entrap Newland Archer. The weightiness of place, kinship, and matriarchal lineage coalesces in the "formidable" queens common to both texts—Mrs. Mingott and Aunt Alexandra. We have to understand, however, that child consciousness in *Mockingbird* echoes William Faulkner's experimental views advanced by both his retarded narrator, Benji, who focuses on partial aspects of a scene rather than being able to name the whole, and his character Joe Christmas of *Light in August,* who lapses into sensory memory when he recalls a traumatic moment.

Benji of *The Sound and the Fury* has only sense memory, with no ability to piece together or give chronological framework to his impressions. The opening of the novel is disorienting because it provides the unmediated perspective of Benji on actions, and the simple syntax recording sensory perception masks the broader intent to disorient the reader:

Through the fence, between the curling flower spaces, I could see them hitting. They were coming toward where the flag was and I went along the fence. Luster was hunting in the grass by the flower tree. They took the flag out, and they were hitting. Then they put the flag back and they went to the table, and he hit and the other hit. (3)

Just as a child would narrate every action without providing context or naming the activity "golf," Benji's direct transcription nevertheless—by refusing us the orienting term "golf"—slants our focus to the extreme violence of the game, the repetitive "hitting." This is precisely the effect of Scout's subjective perception in the near-lynch scene. Like Scout, Benji has uncanny abilities beyond others in the novel—to read his environment closely and detect sensory changes, such as the smell of Caddy. He is perhaps the only character who knows she has changed.

Faulkner applies Jamesian theories of sense memory, to which the child later attaches meaning, to Joe's memory of discovering he is mixed race in *Light in August*. The chapter begins with sentences that divide the process of remembering from knowing, in the same way that seeing and understanding are distinguished in *Mockingbird:* "Memory believes before knowing remembers. Believes longer than recollects, longer than knowing even wonders." Faulkner continues with three words, "Knows remembers believes" (2), to show Joe regressing backward from knowledge to memory to raw and preconscious belief. The scene emphasizes the five-year-old Joe's sensory experience of the toothpaste he has stolen to eat: "He was watching the pink worm coil smooth and cool and slow onto his parchmentcolored finger" (120), "he contemplated the cool invisible worm" (121), "watching himself smear another worm of paste into his mouth" (122). The toothpaste, which is becoming less desirable and more sickening as the scene unfolds, is the child's way of deflecting the knowledge that while he is hiding two people have entered the room and are having sex. However, the toothpaste in all its wormlike splendor is actually the child's way to mask the trauma of identity that unfolds. Once discovered behind the curtain, he is called "'You little nigger bastard!'" Those words shift everything he thought he knew about himself, but it is the toothpaste and not the child that is impressed. Faulkner's technique of using unusual child focal points to partially mask and partially amplify trauma is similar to Lee's. The near-lynch scene comprises the intuition of fear without Scout's ability to name or control the scene, suggesting it as an uncontrollable matter and an intuition of raw violence in men. Additionally, Faulkner's theory of southern consciousness as fractured by race and the trauma of unspoken histories subtly underlies Lee's study of Scout, just as it prefigured a theory of rememory for Toni Morrison. As Lesley Marx says, *Mockingbird* is at root a story about memory. It is about the way traumatic memory works.

So is Willa Cather's novel *My Ántonia,* which in its frame offers its narrating character Jim Burden as racing by Nebraska in the "observation car," from which he can view childhood "buried in wheat and corn, under stimulating extremes of climate: burning summers when the world lies green and billowy beneath a brilliant sky, when one is fairly stifled in vegetation, in the color and smell of strong weeds and heavy harvests" (3). In modern regional writing, memory becomes a place because it is a sensory world "before knowing remembers." The movement of local color corresponded with alterations in late-Victorian and Edwardian children's literature, when separate fantasy worlds for children (Wonderland, Neverland, etc.) reflected a culture's sense that childhood was a place "inside" or "underneath" adulthood; that childhood was the historical past of Western man; and that child worlds were to be separate from adults worlds, such as the labor force. Jim Burden, who obviously influenced Capote's Collin of *The Grass Harp* and so probably Lee, chases the shadows of his past even though the landscape no longer registers his presence. After a two-hundred-page account of the mythic Ántonia, Jim concludes that the past is "incommunicable" (222), just as Lee never returns to the opening frame to tell us "how Scout grew." Instead, we learn how Scout slept, which in the end is likely hibernation from which she will leave her father's world and pass for a lady. "Lady" seems to be the endpoint of a passage through the traumatic memory of rape-that-never-was.

Conclusion: An Object of Subjectivity, A Subjective Object

Scout quickly detects environmental changes and unusual things in her environment because for a child this is an act of survival. To stress the unique narrative practice achieved by exploring the subjectivity of a child as a passive object whose "adaptation" depends on closely reading environment, we must understand that both Maisie and Scout, as well as Huck, are autonomous spectator-children because they are abandoned, neglected objects. The perspective of the older narrator-Scout draws both irony and sympathy for the younger Scout as an object foisted upon various caretakers, telling us the knowledge that young Scout intuits but protects herself from understanding (because it would be hurtful):

> Jem condescended to take me to school the first day, a job usually done by one's parents, but Atticus had said Jem would be delighted to show me where my room was. I think some money changed hands in this transaction, for . . . I heard an unfamiliar jingle in Jem's pockets. (15–16)

The voices, perspectives, and themes offered in this passage directly echo Maisie's experiences with her mother's bribe; she detects and does not detect it at the same time:

> [Maisie's] hand had for some moments been rendered free by a marked manoeuvre of both her mother's. One of these capricious members had fumbled with visible impatience in some backward depth of drapery and had presently reappeared with a small article in its grasp. The act had a significance for a little person trained, in that relation, from an early age, to keep an eye on manual motions, and its possible bearing was not darkened by the memory of the handful of gold that Susan Ash would never, never believe Mrs. Beale had sent back. (157)

James conveys the way the child mind works by attending to what it intimately knows (hands) for clues about significance, and yet "not darkened" by the actual significance. The liminality of consciousness, like the ham as symbol for the veil of regional consciousness, protects as much as pieces together significance. Maisie recalls an earlier passing of money regarding her but chooses not to absorb the full import of the comparison. Lee similarly explores the commodification of Scout as she enters the new world of school, where, Jem has explained, she is to leave him alone. The theme of the passage suggests her abandonment and the split between public and private now occurring; she can no longer acknowledge her brother in public.

But *Mockingbird*'s very form shows the split between self as abandoned object and interior subject by foregrounding what the young Scout perceives only in glimmers and then using the older narrator to either make fun of her or fill in gaps with "background." The immediate focalizer tells us what Atticus said and "reads" but cannot interpret the sound in Jem's pocket, for the young Scout, a good reader, intimately knows Jem, as she does Atticus. The understanding that "money changed hands," along with the vocabulary "condescended" and "this transaction," suggests an interpretation by the older narrator. But the phrase "a job usually done by one's parent," and the knowledge implied by the line, could be either of these Scouts. The irony derives from the older Scout's interpretation of what the young Scout could hear and suspect but could not put into a broader meaning—that she has been "dumped" on Jem, who, in turn, has been bribed. We laugh but feel sympathy because the two Scouts blend so smoothly and we feel simultaneously "with" and "beyond" the young Scout, just as we are privy to the unique training of Maisie into watching and becoming a passive witness to her abandonment.

The pageant scene in which Scout takes on the costume of ham similarly presupposes her abandoned status, as neither Aunt Alexandra nor Atticus wishes to escort her or watch her pageant, setting up her objectification in an exchange between adult power struggles (town and home, Ewell and Atticus, followed by a subsequent power struggle between Tate and Atticus regarding truth). Note how Lee takes consciousness itself as her subject when Scout is attacked in her shroud:

> One's mind works very slowly at times. Stunned, I stood there dumbly. The scuffling noises were dying; someone wheezed and the night was still again.
>
> Still but for a man breathing heavily, breathing heavily and staggering. (262)

Children who become pawns of adult games find compensatory value in become astute narrators and even poets, split into an acting self and an observing self. The latter observes the passive self being acted upon; the final sentence above could have come from Faulkner's dissociated characters whose pasts are felt and intuited rather than clearly described. We will explore this further when we analyze the missionary society scene; Scout watches herself pass as a lady. Thus "how Scout knows" derives from a legacy of modern investment in double consciousness, terms loosely circulating among early developmental psychologists and even Emerson before becoming linked to subaltern aesthetics by Du Bois.

In her book on the history of twentieth-century novel theory, Dorothy Hale shows how the posted presence of the artist, theorized by James as aesthetic vision, transformed over time to Bakhtinian voices as indicative of social views. In the next chapter I analyze the composition of voices that *Mockingbird* embodies. In *Mockingbird* we indeed feel the posted presence of an artist. But it is a female artist who is ultimately watching herself pass out cookies and seeing her old, uncultured self pass by Boo Radley's porch. We are seeing not only the posted presence of an artist but also the posted presence of a woman of civilization, speaking back to James and Twain in her own mocking style.

CHAPTER 4
MOCKINGBIRD AND MODERNIST POLYPHONY: HOW SCOUT TELLS, HOW LEE LAUGHS

There are particular continuities in the voices of all the Scouts identified in chapter 3—narrator, focalizer, and character. They all share an insider/outsider position in relation to their communities and, as such, speak a variety of tongues. In the same sentence, you might find the narrator using words like "synonymous" and "jackass" (5), or "unknown entity the mere description of whom" and "plain hell" (6). This vacillation parallels the diversity within the young character Scout, who says "pass the damn ham" yet is accustomed to her father's last-will-and-testament diction. The comic and often jarring effect of these language shifts demands analysis and background. The narration of *Mockingbird* highlights the multivocal quality of Scout and the need for different kinds of languages to apply to different encounters and subjects. The various Scouts put forth a picture of Scout as an example of heteroglossia, defined by Mikhail Bakhtin as a means for the novelist to import distinct voices and allow those contesting voices to coexist side by side. The overarching entity that we know variously by the name of "Scout" and "Jean Louise" is a synecdoche for the novel form: inherently social and, as James argues, a pierced aperture into the house of fiction or social scene. The character we call Scout is actually an architecture or even an archeology of Maycomb voices and social roles: she is a microcosm of Maycomb because of the diverse parenting she receives there.

Rather than follow the model of Atticus, who transcends the local by being and speaking the same at home as in public, Scout actually follows the model of the African American female character who speaks differently in different communal contexts. The "modest double life" (125) that Cal lives in her negotiation between worlds models for Scout a path to womanhood and writing; it is thus a meaningful detail in *Mockingbird* that Cal, in the Finch kitchen, historically the domestic's "most comfortable realm . . . the black town . . . of the white house" (Harris 15), has taught Scout to write.

The need to speak different voices is foundational to womanhood in the novel, a path apparent in the ladies that Scout comes to admire. In the missionary society scene, after Tom's death is revealed, Scout learns that both Miss Maudie and Aunt Alexandra can hide their inner worries and face the social scene with an undisturbed persona. The two women return to the room of grotesquely "laughing women" and calmly serve "as though their only regret was the temporary domestic disaster of losing Calpurnia" (237). As if a codified signal, Scout's Aunt looks at Scout and smilingly nods at her and a tray of cookies, indicating that Aunt Alexandra is now a body whose inside and outside can be read and interpreted by Scout. Picking up the torch of duplicity, the narrator reflects, "I carefully picked up the tray and watched myself walk to Mrs. Merriweather. With my best company manners, I asked her if she would have some. After all, if Aunty could be a lady at a time like this, so could I" (237). This is a scene of "passing" literally and figuratively. She is passing out treats and she is passing a crafted version of herself. In the scene, Scout has articulated her ambition to grow up and be a lady. Aunt Alexandra takes the express role of Cal here, both in serving the women and in teaching lessons of womanhood to Scout. Cal has already modeled the type of female narrator young and older Scout have embraced, with her instructive words: "'It's not ladylike [to tell all you know] . . . folks don't like to have somebody around knowin' more than they do. It aggravates 'em. You're not gonna change any of them by talkin' right, they've got to want to learn . . . there's nothing you can do but keep your mouth shut or talk their language'" (126). This Huck Finn–like lesson about social adaptation and "passing" is quite distinct from the transparency aspired to by our leading man of the novel, Atticus Finch. Critics such as Laura Fine in "The Narrator's Rebellion" have demonstrated the theme of resistance to socialization manifest in Scout's upbringing, but the polyphony of voices we glimpse in Scout's composite portraiture—in the focalization and in the telling—defines the way the novel's very narration critiques the unity that might be possible for a white nobleman. In "passing" around cookies, Scout experiences the Maisie-like split between her spectator self—"I watched myself"—and her acting self, the "passing" self that has learned to play the social game. Both James and Twain concerned themselves with how children learn to adapt and "pass" into various roles through the internalization of environmental voices—and at what costs to self. *Mockingbird* represents child consciousness for a similar purpose, but it also complicates the subject by incarnating the woman narrator as the harbinger of contesting discourses.

Oneness and continuity of public and private self are simply not workable if you are more socially defined, or a "body that matters" (Butler), a person that must perform certain narrative strategies for social acceptance. We see Cal's careful negotiation of social spaces among other characters of less privilege. Tom Robinson faces a particular predicament in his narrative strategies on the witness stand; he cannot claim Mayella is lying, so he uses the carefully crafted phrase of "[she is] 'mistaken in her mind.'" His predicament is also one of how to perform a scene that threatens to "stage" him and his future, and thus his predicament involves careful crafting of manners. The narrator specifically compares Tom and Atticus's manners, suggesting manners as a strategy to address "the subtlety" of a social "predicament" (195). In chapter 6 I reflect on the many ways Lee drew upon the novel of manners to explore social nuances and necessities. The issue of what sort of speech is permitted to whom is also important to those of the lower class. Ewell's "low" expressions are not permitted in court, but unlike Cal and Tom he has little ability as a changeling. Mayella's efforts aspire to a discourse of southern womanhood, yet her exclusion from that discourse is apparent when she feels mocked by Atticus's address. Her accusation that Atticus is *mocking* her, when the narrator certainly mocks her father several times, seems a carefully placed allusion to *Mockingbird*'s narrative strategy. In fact, it does not seem a stretch to consider that while offering Atticus as an old-fashioned instance of American romanticism, Lee's narrative strategy offers a feminist parody of his ideals of transparency, equality, and oneness. The mockingbird has a sharp ear for the speech patterns of others, and it replays them in extensive mocking songs.

The uniqueness of perspective and voices in *Mockingbird* as a whole derives from its composition of a wide variety of literary pasts. But, specifically, the older narrator, who is the present and future Scout, is more than adept at shifting her voice, diction, and tone, depending on what effect she desires. Often intruding her presence by manipulating a scene and articulating its meaning before it has unfolded for the young Scout, she is rather like Stowe's explicit stage-directing narrator. Close reading of scenes prior to and after the trial reveals her masterful presence and ironic direction of scenes. The narrator's intrusions and self-conscious manipulation of meanings direct us to laugh at the young Scout and her focalizations, as well as at Maycomb eccentricity and fussiness. The narrator's uniquely accomplished way of putting things is heightened in key scenes when Scout's six-year-old abilities at discourse fail, enabling the older narrator to compensate with her multivocal quality, humor, and irony, assuring us that Scout's discursive inexperience will not last. The older Scout's narration, like Stowe's, controls scenes with commentary, foreshadowing, flashback, prolepsis, and juxtaposition, all the more controlled in contrast with instances of Scout's immediate mental fragmentation, stream of consciousness, confusion, sleepiness, and obfuscation.

If Lee's deployment of child consciousness in the tradition of James and Twain enables her to focus on epistemology, thus the value of sensory experience, partial focus, analogical reasoning, and egocentricity, Lee's inclusion of a comic, multivoiced storyteller brings into her text what Twain only implies with his "deadpan Huck" (Bercovitch)—the child unaware that he is funny. Scout is unaware that she is funny, but the narrator provides her punch lines. In a moment tellingly revealing both a model for the narrator's womanhood and the narrator's comic project, Miss Maudie laughs at Scout's mimicry of her own word applied to the snowman—"morphodite." This mimicry is funny because Scout uses the word seriously, accepting it as a proper word for the snowman and using it casually. The scene is a condensation of the broader way that Scout and the narrator calmly appropriate and apply the dialect and colloquialisms of the region. Scout is a hybrid creature because she faces a diversity of "folks" who speak in a variety of tongues. Even as Scout identifies with her father and grows up ambivalent about being a lady (Shackelford 115, 122–23); even as Scout begins to emulate her father's stoicism (Seidel, "Growing Up" 81); and even as we can detect the legal metaphors and didactic technique of the law professor (Woodard 568); we can also view the narrator, who says, "Mrs. Dubose was plain hell," or "they were Haverfords, in Maycomb County a name synonymous with jackass," as polyphony if not cacophony.

The most significant moments for Maisie, Huck, and Scout involve moments of mimicry through which the authors explore the internalization of discourse and how the child can and cannot assert him- or herself in language. Maisie aspires to the gentlemanly discourse of Sir Claude by striking bargains with him, which is mirrored in Scout's bargains with Atticus. Maisie's father accuses Sir Claude and Ida of having "made" Maisie in their image, and their influences indeed become apparent when Maisie begins to act like Ida but sound like Sir Claude. She not only plays his games but also imitates his words and thoughts—even when she asserts her freedom in the final moments of the novel. Scout makes similar bargains with Atticus and in her final moment mimics his construction of reality—"the knife fell on [Ewell]." Lee's point in emulating Maisie is to communicate how growing up is a bargaining negotiation—a way of selecting models to mimic and, in that selection, bargain for the self as a linguistic agent. Mimicry defines Huck's journey as well, as I discuss by looking at how Twain demonstrates the internalization of voices and languages within Huck. Like Huck, Scout must adapt to survive; like Huck, she is very good at it. Like Huck, she tells us right at the beginning of her story that she will set the record straight.

With Huck, we are largely on our own in the activity of decoding layers of irony behind the "deadpan" mask. But Lee's narrator gives us far more assistance in demonstrating what voices apply in what situations; how Scout has to imitate and amend her language to adapt; and how Scout's specific path to womanhood and art relies upon bringing from the shadows what Twain only implied and then refused with his famous "notice," warning the reader against interpretation. While the narrator uses legal metaphors throughout the novel, she also utilizes anthropological languages and colloquial expressions, translating the eccentricities and "streaks" of her region as if she is forever liminal. Lee's anthropological approach is implied in John Carlos Rowe's discussion of a gift economy in Maycomb, and Lee's vision of "herself as a historian, a chronicler" (20) is noted by Jean Frantz Blackall in her comparison between Lee and Austen. But the discourses of this anthropologist or historian are not neutral, textbook accounts of Maycomb; rather, the languages, like young Scout's euphemisms, create surprises through incongruities, as analyzed by Jacqueline Tavernier-Courbin (42–43). Humor is always insightful, but Tavernier-Courbin's discussion of black humor that operates even during the trial suggests the "teaspoon of sugar" effect: "Thus what could be an unbearably painful story is relieved by a deep-seated humor that fosters perspective and a profound pity for, and eventual acceptance of, the human condition" (42). In fact, we can locate a "teaspoon of sugar"—or "large cup of sugar"—figure of humor, laughter, and social acceptance *in* the novel: in Miss Maudie, an obvious model for a person like Scout and the narrator—an odd mixture. She accepts the catastrophic loss of her house and laughs; she sees the trial as the Roman carnival it is, and she sees the children's Radley drama and "morphodite" as the mockery they are. With a wicked tongue and an uncanny ability to pass with the ladies although a chameleon herself, Miss Maudie is an obvious progenitor of Scout as well.

Lee's ability to build comic distance from the limited yet observant child consciousness of young Scout puts forth her writing as mocking laughter that we see incarnated in the novel in moments of laughter among closely connected characters: Miss Maudie, Boo, and Dill. All of these characters bend gender and sexual roles in significant ways, giving meaning to "morphodite"— the word that sends Miss Maudie into hysterics. Morphodite is a comic, mocking word for those neither male nor female—those in drag, which describes the role Dill vows to assume after the trial: the clown that laughs at people. As a character closely identified with an imaginative aesthetic, with sensitivity, and with Truman Capote, whose novels of Monroeville encompass gothic and comic, Dill and his assumption of the laughing clown symbolize the complex narrative stance taken in *Mockingbird*.

Mark Twain Unmasked

To some extent, as detailed in the last chapter about modern constructions of childhood as interior to adulthood, a child character's perspective is supposed to indicate some kind of heartfelt, presocial experience. The conveyance of an inner heart and even American goodness (see Arac) has been the ruling principle of criticism on *Huck Finn,* which Sacvan Bercovitch in "Deadpan Huck" demonstrates is Twain's joke on us as interpreters of his novel. Huck's deadpan style is revealed in Huck's delivery and claim to set Twain's story straight. Scout's self-conscious claim to tell her story as she likes is similar, except that she is battling not the author but the teen boy himself; in the opening of *Mockingbird,* Scout and Jem disagree over where the story really starts. Scout wants to start with the Ewells, while Jem asserts that Dill is the beginning. Scout humorously decides that the storyteller *could* go as far back in history as Andrew Jackson. The only reason their disagreement does not lead to a fistfight is because of their age; instead of fighting they go to Atticus, the mediator, who agrees with both of them (3).

Like in Twain's opening, Lee uses her narrator to humorously convey the fact that tale-telling involves choices and that the only real story is a matter of a fistfight, because there is no real truth to tell. Storytelling is power. Atticus's role as mediator is quite similar to Jim's role in Twain's novel; for example, when Huck debates about whether he can take people's food on his journey, he puts in dialogue Pap's perspective on "borrowing" and the Widow's perspective on "stealing," to which Jim responds that both Pap and the Widow are partly right. They are both right because the power to name things creates meaning. What seems particularly ironic in Lee's novel is that she does essentially begin her action, after some exposition, with Dill's entrance, thus accepting Jem's idea. But because she gives substantial background on the random mishap of Maycomb's birth and Finch's "landing" there, along with Finch "industry," the novel is in fact a settled fight.

Lee achieves Twain's ironic distance from Huck with her technique of co-narration by older and younger Scout and thus is gentler and more comprehensible to even a younger reader. From Twain's *Huck,* Lee derived a model of a southern child voice, able to tell things in its own colorful way and thus give a sharply humorous view of not only prejudice and accidents of circumstance, but also, Bercovitch argues of *Huck,* of *us* because we are duped into laughter. The young Scout emulates Huck's sense of disproportion but uses the older narrator's commentary to make explicit what the implied author behind Huck leaves unstated. For example, whereas the rules of deadpan style prevent Huck from acknowledging any amount of awareness over being funny when he emphasizes information usually subordinated or implicit, such as when he says he read "'Pilgrim's Progress,' about a man that left his family it didn't say why" (137), Lee more gently asks us to laugh when her focalizer exaggerates and emphasizes her unique, inflated conclusions:

> Calpurnia bent down and kissed me. I ran along, wondering what had come over her. She had wanted to make up with me, that was it. She had always been too hard on me, she had at last seen the error of her fractious ways . . . I was weary from the day's crimes.
>
> After supper, Atticus sat down with the paper and called "Scout, ready to read?" The Lord sent me more than I could bear. (29)

Like in *Huck,* the humor derives from the child's interpretation of an action that is neutrally stated. The relatively benign narration of Cal's kiss becomes, in Scout's mind, a story of repentance and crime, her father's innocent question a divinely sent trial of epic proportions. Just as Huck dismisses a pilgrimage that could not be more important to Western civilization, choosing instead to cut through the reverence with his practicality, the ironic narrator-Scout continually demonstrates the misplaced emphasis and interpretation of the young Scout. For example, following the trial, which bespeaks the scope of national trauma, young Scout's exhilaration comes not from the witnessed courtroom scenes but from Cal's treatment of Jem, as if it were the natural climax of a day of broad awakening: "I was exhilarated. So many things had happened . . . and now here was Calpurnia giving her precious Jem down the country—what new marvels would the evening bring?" (207) The implication is that if Cal can scold Jem, then the jury can perhaps see Tom's innocence. The flawed and humorous reasoning patterns of the children reveal preoccupations with self as center of the universe, which is why they are so funny.

Mockingbird is saturated with the self-irony of Twain's character Huck, with a similar purpose of social satire. They share the technique of misplaced emphasis. The Radley blanket receives more attention and emphasis than Miss Maudie's fire, and the presence of Arthur Radley receives greater emphasis at the end than the fact that Bob Ewell is dead and tried to kill the children. Only after Scout meets "Boo" does she admit to learning; only her encounter with Boo, a view from a close neighbor's porch, resolves the melodrama. However, upon reflection, it is easy to see Lee's point; skewed perspective is not a limitation of the child, but a problem of the human being. Tom dies and little changes in the town. Scout "stayed miserable for two days" about Dill's departure, just as the town is interested in the news of Tom's death for two days.

Lee wants to convey the Jamesian "perpetual present tense of a child's mind" that informs the entire town of her childhood. Scout's undue emphasis on certain things at the expense of others is only an instance of the broader limitations of Maycomb whites. For example, when Ewell spits on Atticus, the event receives more attention from the ladies than Tom's wrongful conviction. The novel thus continually emphasizes what counts in the white mind, with cues to the reader that what counts is delusional and that delusions are sinister when they continue beyond six years old. Scout self-aggrandizes in an endearing, humorous way: "what I would do if Atticus did not feel the necessity of my presence, help and advice. Why, he couldn't get along a day without me. Even Calpurnia couldn't get along unless I was there. They needed me" (143). The older Scout makes the young Scout's limitations a theme to distill the larger point of the novel, which is comic in the Flannery O'Connor fashion. J. P. Steed argues that O'Connor employs Bergsonian humor, which depends on character automaton-like inflexibility. Not only are white characters inflexible in *Mockingbird*, but they are convinced of their own self-importance. Mrs. Merriweather sees the problem with her maid's sour face as the problem of darkening her own day—not Sophy's. The Neverland mind of white Maycomb never grew up.

The Boo Radley plot, a relatively universal plot of the strange neighbor, is in many ways a means for Scout and young readers to understand the trial and an encounter with difference, the persecution of innocence. However, Boo is also a darker symbol for Scout and the closeted condition of human perception. From the beginning Scout is more sympathetic to Boo: she does not want the boys to mock him, she is the one who first discovers the gift in the tree, and she is the one rolled into his yard—the one to hear his laughter, which becomes her secret from Jem (38). She is intimately connected with the fate of Boo—she is the one covered by the blanket and the one to meet him at the end. She uses him as a point of comparison in understanding Mayella, a double for herself as a relatively constrained southern daughter. While Boo opens the world of Scout, he also serves as symbol of how growth can only occur so much; one can only cross the street in perspective, after all. This is the message of both James and Twain with their child voices: growth can occur, under certain conditions, but it is hardly freedom and hardly the possibility of rejecting society. Society is internal.

In *Huck,* too, Lee likely found a model for the child as a regional expert. Like Scout, Huck is a particular authority on local context, able to enter and "fit in" a wide variety of settings with a permeable voice and an infinite capacity for social adaptation. Like Huck, Scout voices folkloric beliefs, such as the Radley legend, and positions herself as an expert on southern mannerisms and ways, as well as on the "ethical culture" (35) of Maycomb children. Without Huck's mobility or access to water, a symbol for change and rebirth, Scout is even more fully rooted in a specific region. She even tells us she is an interpreter, translating for us phrases like "bought cotton" and thus presuming that we are outsiders to her landscape, the intimacies of which she and Jem know. Lee uses Dill, the outsider, as an excuse to establish the children's regional expertise. With Dill, in particular, the child-Scout establishes a "know-it-all" voice, which the older narrator echoes. Lee shares Twain's zest for narrating situations of "the backwoods" that become updated versions of Carrollian nonsense, ruthlessly pursuing absurd situations until their logical and nihilist ends. Perhaps the most slapstick scene involves the fiasco of the "northern" minty Miss Caroline attempting to teach a class of repeat first-graders, one of whom is hosting cooties, the sight of which makes her scream and rallies the class around her in chivalric defense. The scene deploys all the facets of Twain's Grangerford-Sanderson feud, complete with mock chivalry, absurdity, and physical comedy.

This sort of comedy in a broader romantic idyll can be found in an even closer artistic model, written by someone who admitted the influence of Twain (Capote, *Other* x). In Capote's *The Grass Harp*, published in 1945, a similar slapstick scene occurs. The townspeople attack the exiles in the tree house—figured as a raft in the sky in a nod to Twain—where the simple Dolly, her devotee Catherine, and young Collin have gone to escape Verena, who wishes to commercialize Dolly's herbal remedies. The attackers end up trying to climb the tree and falling down on one another in a heap. The classic comedy deployed by Capote in *The Grass Harp* coexists with the narrator's romantic longing for the stories that supposedly live in the grass, a nostalgic stance obviously influenced by Cather. Dolly is Capote's Ántonia, and Collin is condemned to become a lawyer like Jim Burden at the end, forever seeking "the incommunicable past" (200) found in childhood in "little towns." Lee, however, is careful not to expose romantic longing for childhood, not to create a mythic Dolly/Ántonia, and not to expose the narrator's current vulnerability, which Capote does even though he, too, deploys changes in vocal registers: "If some wizard would like to make me a present, let him give me a bottle filled with the voices of that kitchen, the ha ha ha and fire whispering, a bottle brimming with its buttery sugary bakery smells—though Catherine smelled like a sow in the spring" (18). Lee unconsciously echoes many of the distancing narrative strategies in Capote's *The Grass Harp*, but she is more Twain in her relentless satire of the past. The difference is a matter of *position;* Lee's narrator is paradoxically insider and outsider, whereas Capote's in both *Other Voices, Other Rooms* and *The Grass Harp* are outsiders "passing" through: "I felt exiled from the scene, again a spy peering from the attic" (83).

The artistic observer spies from the attic and bottles up the scene, just as Jim Burden writes of Ántonia from the transcendent outside, but Lee's narrator exploits her stance on "Maycomb's ways" and what is "alien" to them in the language of participant-observer. Her point is largely that place cannot be fully transcended at all.

The analogy between Huck and Scout in R. P. Blackmur's review of *Mockingbird,* titled "Scout in the Wilderness," inspired Horton Foote's approach to the screenplay and made him "feel at home in the material" (7). Huck and Scout are noteworthy child personalities who often act without thinking and with ingenuity; they are "innocents abroad" insofar as they imbibe local customs without thinking twice. Both Huck and Scout have been interpreted as instances of moral freedom, a discourse informing both *Maisie* and *Huck,* but in actuality both destabilize the possibilities of human freedom given environmental influences. Huck's racism mirrors Scout's, but because we see more than they do, we like to believe in them differently. Both Huck and Scout are engaged in understanding the plight of the black father and man, but both carry the languages of their environmental contexts and thus have limited means for understanding and describing that plight, posing to us the sense that a broader puzzle must be entangled. Even after witnessing the treatment of Tom on the witness stand, which makes Dill cry, Scout callously says to Dill, "after all, he's just a Negro," which is all too familiar to readers of Huck, who cringe when Huck tells Aunt Sally that no one was hurt on the riverboat explosion but it "killed a nigger." We must remember that these studies of modern children are specifically not studies of nineteenth-century possibilities for how individuals shape their own destinies. Rather, they are studies of environmental conditioning—how children "take up wickedness, being brought up to it," but occasionally, even if accidentally, learn something from their observer stances about what is "alien" to their world's "ways" and why.

Exploring the rhythms of child attention and epistemology enabled James and Twain to make implicit judgments about the inevitable alienation characterizing human relations, but it also allowed them to explore learning and therefore growth. Under what specific conditions can growth occur, and what type of growth can occur? The continual efforts of Miss Maudie to prune her yard, along with the association of *Mockingbird*'s children with yards and yard activity, at which Miss Maudie seems to be always looking, demonstrate the toughness of the charge. The very old Shakespearean metaphor of gardening and governance has always been applied in childrearing discussions. The working metaphor of the kindergarten is the provision of a garden in which the child will thrive; James and Twain give the child a kindergarten of perversity to explore early learning theory. Researchers were debating quite fiercely whether children learn through imitation or imagination, both of which would call attention to conditions of environments but in distinct ways. Some psychologists, such as British James Sully, were more inclined to regard human learning as imaginative, a theme explicit in the more continental Maisie, whereas some psychologists, such as American James Baldwin and G. Stanley Hall, were more inclined to discuss terms like "habituation and accommodation" or "biological instinct and evolution." Both James and Twain explore this question of imitation at length, particularly linguistic imitation, which gives us some background for decoding the unique aspects of the voices in *Mockingbird*. Environmental conditioning occurs primarily through a child's internalization of voice in all these novels, a theme that can only be revealed when voice is distinguished from consciousness.

Borrowing and Bargaining Voice

Like Victorian psychologists, Twain is concerned with the mechanism by which Huck adapts to whom he is with. It is important to analyze the voices inside Huck's head to understand Twain's legacy in the southern child-Scout, whom many forget dismiss Tom as "just a Negro." This parallels how many readers stress the "brotherhood" of Huck and Jim that occupies only a brief portion of Twain's novel and that never transcends the racist languages Huck is condemned to use. *Adventures of Huckleberry Finn* begins by positioning Huck between Tom, a symbol for ridiculous literacy and civilization, and Pap, a symbol for degraded and utterly "savage" nature. It then gives Huck two father figures, Pap and Jim, who represent two distinct views of the natural world. It then replaces Pap with Jim and positions Huck between Tom and Jim in the last third of the novel, when, unfortunately, Huck imitates Tom. These role models are important because through them Twain questions what moral sense is possible for Huck.

These living teachers are his only books. Tom is inside Huck's psyche when he rejects Pap and fakes his death: he "did wish Tom Sawyer was there,

I knowed he would take an interest in this kind of business, and throw in the fancy touches. Nobody could spread himself like Tom Sawyer in such a thing as that" (41). Yet Pap is inside Huck when he journeys into nature. Importantly, Huck has internalized Pap's voice and disregard for property law:

> Mornings, before daylight, I slipped into corn fields and borrowed a watermelon, or a mushmelon, or punkin, or some new corn, or things of that kind. Pap always said it warn't no harm to borrow things, if you was meaning to pay them back, sometime; but the widow said it warn't anything but a soft name for stealing, and no decent body would do it. Jim said he reckoned the widow was partly right and pap was partly right. (79–80)

The Widow and Tom are both embodiments of civilization. Like the Widow, Tom calls "borrowing" stealing at the end of the novel. What is funny is that Huck is perpetually stuck between impossibly inflexible perspectives. In his article on O'Connor, Steed applies comic theory: "The principal trait of the Bergsonian comic figure is inflexibility, a certain 'mechanical inelasticity' that surfaces 'just when one would expect to find the wide-awake adaptability and the living pliableness of a human being'" (301). Characters who act flexibly, like Atticus and Jim when they settle the inflexible positions by acceding to various views, are beyond laughter, although when Jim takes other minstrel roles Twain clearly suggests that his inflexibility is funny. What is crucial to note is that in Huck's head are inflexible viewpoints that he allows to argue their cases in mental life.

A discourse of stealing and "borrowing" recurs throughout the novel *Huck*, signifying an unresolved debate between nature and culture in Huck's head. In his final resolution to help Jim, he resolves to steal Jim out of slavery, a rhetorical embrace of thievery that demonstrates the total composition of his thoughts by others. The dilemma quoted above is subsequently presented to and resolved by Jim, who decides that they should make a list of things they can and cannot borrow, thereby lessening the offense. But lest we view Jim romantically, we also must remember that Jim defines himself in societal terms, claiming that he has $800 since he now owns himself. Huck continues to use the term "borrow" for stealing and for his connection to Pap: "We warn't going to borrow [a canoe] when there warn't anybody around, the way pap would do, for that might set people after us" (130). Even during the high point of Huck's moral reasoning, when Huck resolves to steal Jim, Twain demonstrates that Pap and Tom penetrate Huck's reasoning, which in turn affects Jim. So while it is funny to be trapped between limited perspectives internalized in the mind, humor turns sinister when it hurts.

It is not an accident that Huck is reborn as the bookish Tom Sawyer in the very last section when he allows Tom's elaborate and insensitive plans to consume his quest to steal Jim. Regarding Tom as better than himself, Huck aspires to imitation. The novel pits Pap's and Tom's definition of theft against one another, showing that the two characters compete for ascendancy in Huck's mind: "Along during that morning I borrowed a sheet and a white shirt off of the clothes line; and I found an old sack and put them in it, and we went down and got the fox-fire, and put that in, too. I called it borrowing, because that was what pap always called it; but Tom said it warn't borrowing, it was stealing" (303). Tom goes on to suggest that prisoners, which is their game, have a right to steal what they need; like Jim, he justifies the need for "borrowing," in similar terms to Pap. In fact, in the very beginning of the novel Tom organizes a band of robbers; although he is only pretending, he is, in fact, practicing for the "theft" that will free a man.

These terms of "stealing" and "borrowing" are more than Huck's endeavors to imitate his models and work out his conscience. They are Twain's playful terms for what a child "thieves" from the role models in his environment—how his identity and vision of himself come to be. We could substitute "select" and "adapt" and arrive at the same place, but Twain cleverly twists the terms to denote moral ambiguity. Even in the moment critics point to as the highest moral growth of the novel, Huck is not so much coming to any positive declaration as he is embracing Pap as a model (Bercovitch), blaming his early upbringing for his choice, just as Pap blames everyone else but himself for his own behaviors. Resolving to tear up his letter, Huck says "I would take up wickedness again, which was in my line, being brung up to it, and the other warn't" (271). Twain takes the new study of the child's environmental conditioning and parodies it; Huck only accidentally reasons in a way that leads him to a moral action, rather how Scout is only accidentally in the moral right when she punches Francis. The punch, like the destruction of Huck's letter, is satisfying for the reader, as it is intended to be; but these scenes of accidental morality do not earn these children any merit—

only shame. Huck is not a moral being because he is not, nor can he imagine himself, psychologically free. Rather, he weighs the voices and positions of others in his head. This method of learning is precisely both Maisie's and Scout's. They have to sort out contesting voices and pass tests by various discourse communities.

In *Maisie,* James is equally interested in the child's linguistic imitation, which comes across as even less intentional than Huck's reasoning through the voices of influential personalities. Without even being conscious of the words, Maisie imitates a message from her father to her mother, "'He said I was to tell you, from him,' she faithfully reported, 'that you're a nasty horrid pig!'" (24) Child psychologists believed imitation began before the child became conscious, but that consciousness was a transition between passive and active, as the child soon becomes conscious of imitating others. Consciousness eventually leads to a child's will. Only a few pages after Maisie parrots her father, James portrays Maisie's deliberations about whether or not to repeat her mother's message to her father—to say "that he lies and he knows he lies" (26). Already Maisie is experiencing the split between an internal and social self, which is also a split between subject and object.

However, Maisie most readily imitates the language of Sir Claude, whom she tends to mime, precisely how Scout tends to try out Atticus's discourse in social settings where he is not present. Maisie demonstrates how closely she resembles Sir Claude in speech when she separately says the same thing he does to Mrs. Wix. Maisie's imitation of Sir Claude seems to be the result of several factors. She admires his beauty and gentlemanliness, and he treats her like a conscious being. He "was liable in talking with her to take the tone of her being also a man of the world" (66), just like Jim treats Huck as an equal to be bargained with. Jim exacts Huck's promise not to tell on him when he first finds him on the island, thus negotiating a speech act with important assumptions. Sir Claude draws an economy of equality between him and Maisie when he bargains with her: "'If you'll help me [see Mrs. Beale], you know, I'll help *you*'" (66). This utterance functions like the promise from Huck exacted by Jim. Bargaining is a speech act that at once constructs the recipient as a free agent and paradoxically points out the consequences if he/she does not "freely" comply.

James's novel ends with the bargain that Maisie attempts to strike with Sir Claude, signifying the fact that she has fully become him linguistically, whereas she is also behaving like the women in terms of her manipulative skill. Her language becomes fully adult; for example, she says things like "'our affairs are involved'" (165). After Maisie realizes that the one thing Sir Claude fears is himself, she realizes that she is the same. Her upbringing becomes completely apparent to her; she realizes that she has been brought up on continental life (209), as effectively as Huck realizes he has been brought up to wickedness. To what has Scout been brought up? What bargains does she strike, and what voices does she embody?

The way this is echoed in *Mockingbird* is subtle; Scout is a fusion of confluences in her environment. Just as young Scout screams "'You take that back, boy!'" to a boy in the schoolyard and asserts "what the sam hill" (24) is Walter Cunningham doing with the syrup, she can adjust her tone and diction for Miss Maudie's porch or for her father's lap. She parallels the Huck who could enjoy Pap's ways yet find the Widow's comfortable too. The narrator has a solid command of legal languages, describing shared space with Miss Maudie as a "tacit treaty" (42), a message as cross-examination (51), a dog as "property of" Mr. Johnson (92), Aunt Alexandra as "the objective case" (129), childhood as a "code" of conduct (141), a phone call as a plea for a defendant (Dill) (144), and informal law as "finders were keepers unless title was proven" (35). But these metaphors to describe social customs emerge as frequently as her colloquial, colorful speech. Unlike Atticus, who speaks in standard English and uses the same language in the courthouse and at home, stating the same facts in front of Aunt Alexandra and Cal, despite Aunt Alexandra's objections, Scout speaks in different dialects, sometimes earthy and sometimes lofty. If this sounds a lot like a mockingbird, known for its remarkable ability to mimic a wide variety of tongues, the parallel is an apt description of the various vocal registers appearing sometimes in the same sentence.

For example, in describing the history of Atticus's practice, which she wishes to localize, she establishes her mocking voice, which will freely wander in and out of other people's viewpoints in parody fashion:

> Atticus had urged [his first clients] to accept the state's generosity in allowing them to plead Guilty to second-degree murder ... but they were Haverfords, in Maycomb County a name synonymous with jackass. The Haverfords had dispatched Maycomb's leading blacksmith in a misunderstanding arising from the alleged wrongful detention of a mare, were imprudent enough to

do it in the presence of three witnesses, and insisted that the-son-of-a-bitch-had-it-coming-to-him was a good enough defense for anybody. (4–5)

The older Scout combines colloquial language and legal concepts, establishing that she is both an insider to the local community and a transcendent being with more global knowledge. She establishes her insider and outside position in relation to the community, parodying how "the Haverfords" would view the matter (stupidly) versus her own legalese, "a misunderstanding arising from the alleged wrongful detention of a mare." She also establishes her authority to make claims about the sentiments of Maycomb County in an earthy language that parodies how she feels about the town and the stereotypes that she holds about backwoods folk. The hyphens in "the-son-of-a-bitch-had-it-coming-to-him" slur the phrase in the reader's mind but without misspelling; the long phrase is transformed into one noun as if the ten words are almost always heard in a string and therefore the narrator has learned the phrase as one noun. Many people develop characteristic phrases or swear combinations that emerge when they are upset; the humor here comes from the juxtaposition of the emotional outburst and the legal defense, which we equate with the unemotional and formal.

The narrator continually vacillates between these voices to show she is both a product of the environment she describes and has somehow transcended it, like Atticus has with his education and involvement in law. She tailors her language to match what she thinks of her subject; for example, she distinguishes the sophisticated way in which she and Jem view the Radleys and the way they view Mrs. Dubose: "The Radley Place was inhabited by an unknown entity the mere description of whom was enough to make us behave for days on end; Mrs. Dubose was plain hell" (6). We understand how to feel about the subject by whether she lends "high" or "low" language to it, and also whether she feels equal to those she mocks or above them. For example, when she describes the country crowd that is threatening Atticus at the courthouse, she makes observations in a way that "others" them as country folk unused to late hours. In the statement above, the description of the Radley Place emulates "high" literary language; people rarely use "whom" in oral discourse, much less "entity." This literary language accords with the literary imagination that the children bring to thinking about Boo and his haunted house—a product of gothic texts imported by Dill and filled with excessive artifice. Apparently, Mrs. Dubose is not worthy of highbrow language. The language is "plain," like her. But while we are to understand these boundaries of the Radleys and Mrs. Dubose as offering a variety of choices to Scout—between feminine male and masculine female, between being closeted and venomously "out," between a liberal silent majority and the spitfire racist—we are also supposed to understand that these are linguistic boundaries *in* Scout and therefore *in* the narrator. She can speak "high" (Radley) or "low" language (Dubose), use dignified or vicious words; she can calm dramas with Atticus-like dispassion or inflict wounds with her parody.

Both older and young Scout demonstrate that formative influences operate like a shifting kaleidoscope; environmental influences comprise character through an internal survival of the fittest. Which ascends is often a matter of expediency, as it is for Huck. In other words, the environmental struggles sketched by James and Twain are apparent in Scout because both older and young Scout present themselves to us. Various influences compete for ascendancy within the consciousness, embedded there as voices. The young Scout tries to imitate Atticus, just as the older Scout often uses legal metaphor and often quotes something he has said in the past, but we know from the colorful and sometimes "low" language of the narration that Scout is also "of" her region, just as she is quite literally dressed as a local ham toward the end—a local mask that allows her to sense some things and not others. In short, the story is not only about a character who says "pass the dam ham," but about a "dam ham" passing into various discourse communities.

Just as Maisie strikes two central bargains with Sir Claude as she becomes an equal player in the parlor game of social exchange, Scout makes two bargains with Atticus, each of which involves a process of mimicry. The first bargain of Sir Claude's with Maisie involves their agreement to help each other in battle against the women around them, which is strikingly similar to the first bargain struck between Scout and Atticus about how they can continue to read together at night if Scout does not tell her teacher. There are several things to note about this bargain. First, the equality and individuality of the bargainers are implicit, something James and Twain also suggest by positing the child as autonomous object, separate from the socializing worlds of women because not yet socialized. Maisie's freedom in the end is a question of her gradual assertion of her rights to emulate Sir Claude; in the very moment she asserts "I'm free," she is mimicking Sir Claude. He has just declared himself free from the machinations of the women fighting over him and over Maisie as objects. Then he articulates Maisie's freedom. She asserts her freedom only in mimicry, which tempers the thesis of her freedom.

The second thing to note about the reading bargain between Scout and Atticus is that it involves an implicit understanding that real reading occurs—real understanding takes place—beyond school as a socializing institution run by women. Atticus says that he would not want Miss Caroline to come after *him*. Third, Scout and Atticus are bending the law, despite Atticus's assertion that the truancy law remains firm for Scout. They are conspiring to do something Miss Caroline would not approve of, and insofar as Miss Caroline is in charge of Scout's education, they are rule-breaking. Atticus calls it a compromise and Scout "innocently" calls it what it is—bending the law. Her naming of the compromise looks even more innocent because she intones it as a question, after Atticus has asked her if she knows the meaning of the word "compromise." The fact that they *are* rule-breaking, even if the rule is silly, explains Atticus's refusal to "seal the deal with the usual formality" (spitting), a moment that seemingly reveals the difference between Atticus and Scout as not only adult and child in distinctly different "ethical cultures" but also with different subject positions; they have different responsibilities to different discourse groups. It is fairly significant that Atticus did not go to school at all, as school is the target of Lee's vicious irony against the state, just as he distances himself from "the ladies."

This initial bargain actually sets up the final moments of the novel, when they bargain again, this time overtly bending the law. Like the final scene of *Maisie*, which paradoxically articulates Maisie's freedom as an echo of Sir Claude's words, Scout's embrace of the mantra "he fell on his knife," circulated between men, raises the question of how this is an assertion of her choice. A long standoff between Atticus and the sheriff hinges upon Scout's acceptance of an obvious untruth:

> "Scout is eight years old," [Mr. Tate] said. "She was too scared to know exactly what went on. . . . "I may not be much, Mr. Finch, but I'm still sheriff of Maycomb County and Bob Ewell fell on his knife." . . . Atticus sat looking at the floor for a long time. Finally he raised his head. "Scout," he said, "Mr. Ewell fell on his knife. Can you possibly understand?"

Atticus looked like he needed cheering up. I ran to him and hugged him and kissed him with all my might. "Yes sir, I understand," I reassured him. "Mr. Tate was right. . . . it'd be sort of like shootin' a mockingbird, wouldn't it?" (274–76)

The scene suggests Scout's admission into a white gentleman's club that discusses, determines, and stages truth against "all the ladies" that might wish to recognize valor in their own ways ("knocking on [Boo's] door bringing. angel food cakes"). Tate even mentions that his wife would participate in the appalling action of celebrating Boo with cake, suggesting that his opinions are formed in defiance of her. Tate and Atticus are clearly using Scout as a pawn in their struggle for whose truth will prevail, a masculine struggle also contingent upon excluding from public the nonnormative male Boo—at once equating him with feminine angel food cake and protecting him from female exposure. Their struggle becomes a matter of what she might have seen and how competent a witness Scout is. Heck, an embodiment of local law enforcement who has in fact been implicated on the stand for not calling a doctor to assess Mayella's injuries, wins here, but by again not calling a doctor. For Scout to reject the final "truth" of the winning player would, in a very different way from that articulated in the novel, be like killing a mockingbird. Scout's survival is contingent upon mimicry—her acceptance of one sentence until it becomes undisputed truth. The sentence also evokes a convention of children's literature; "he fell on his knife" points to a tradition in which villains undo themselves with their own hand, thereby keeping the righteous pure.

Whether called law-bending or "a compromise," the scene directly echoes the initial bargain between Scout and Atticus about reading, which has always signified their physical connection: "I could not remember when the lines above Atticus's moving finger separated into words, but I had stared at them . . . when I crawled into his lap every night. Until I feared I would lose it, I never loved to read. One does not love breathing" (18). Reading is the breath of life from the father's body. In the closing scene, Scout reads her father's body to make her decision, seeing his need to be cheered because his day has passed. To deny the truth of his line, "he fell on his knife," would be tantamount to the panic of losing her only parent. Scout's understanding of her father's language is apparent in this scene. She meaningfully "understands" the power struggles going on, and she intuits that her admission to the club hinges upon acceptance. Here, her acceptance of her father's words is also acceptance of Heck's local authority: "'I may not be much, Mr. Finch, but I'm still sheriff of Maycomb County and Bob Ewell fell on his knife.'" This is in some ways Atticus's defeat from his seat of nobility, but Scout also selects her father over Heck by using his mockingbird metaphor, cleverly negotiating male demands for words. She retains some dignity by not exactly miming the fiction but by pledging allegiance to her father. Even while there is no possibility of asserting her own truth, she uses words to pass with both men.

The novel stresses this truth as a construction of local authority to emphasize the fact that Scout knows how to be a member of many clubs—not just her father's. She is a liminal figure that crosses "world[s]" (233) and "passes" more effectively than her father. Just as Maisie asserts her freedom, breathed into her by the father, and then marches off with Mrs. Wix, Scout asserts her "choice" to acquiesce to Heck and satisfy Atticus and then marches off with Boo. Prior scenes establish her struggles with miming Atticus given discourse situations that have different requirements. It thus makes sense that her final mime of Atticus would be an instance of actually miming a circulating idea from a regional representative. Heck's isn't the only regional point of view that Scout will make her own. In chapter 6 I analyze women's regional novels of manners that define aspects of Scout's journey as needing to "pass" into the life of ladies, "soft teacakes with frostings of sweat and sweet talcum" (5). A peculiar mesh of sweet and sour, they wilt in the heat and welcome the increasingly sleepy Scout like the successfully socialized of so many modern women's novels.

How Scout Tells: Narrative Interventions

The way in which the novel positions Scout as both insider and outside observer is by offering her as an anthropologist or folklore specialist on Maycomb and its residents. The older narrator gives us quite a bit of background on Maycomb "ways," of course, but she also establishes the young Scout as an authority on the county and its families. Readers tend to equate a child narrator such as Scout with innocence, but the young Scout is far from innocent. She, ironically like Aunt Alexandra, equates behavior with families; when she first attends school, we see her educating the teacher about the Cunninghams, based on lessons gleaned and somewhat simplistically applied from Atticus. Her first-grade class seems to recognize the young Scout as an eloquent authority on the community, one with Atticus-like skills who might be able to make clear to the teacher why Walter Cunningham will not accept the teacher's quarter for lunch. The teacher has just reprimanded her for knowing how to read, suggesting that her father does not know how to properly teach reading, so she must learn to read afresh. In retaliation, Scout establishes that the teacher from Winston County cannot read the community and that Scout can.

In the middle of the scene in which schoolmates are pleading with Scout to explain the predicament of Walter Cunningham, and in which she begins her explanation, the older narrator gives us background on how the young Scout knew about the Cunninghams from her father's lessons. Mr. Cunningham had been a client of Atticus's but had only been able to pay in "entailments" (20), which led to a discussion with Atticus about poverty. The narrator's flashback provides context to the immediate school situation, giving us background on how country folk are proud but have no money to pay, so they pay with things they have. The scene distances us from the young Scout by demonstrating her lack of eloquence:

> If I could have explained these things to Miss Caroline, I would have saved myself some inconvenience and Miss Caroline subsequent mortification, but it was beyond my ability to explain things as well as Atticus, so I said, "You're shamin' him, Miss Caroline. Walter hasn't got a quarter at home to bring you, and you can't use any stovewood." (21)

Scout promptly gets in trouble, and then we experience an inversion of her expertise. Like Maisie, Scout parodies her father's language and lessons without completely understanding or being able to fully articulate them. She does this later as well, when she directly asks Mr. Cunningham about his "entailments," a word he may not be familiar with.

After the scene of her disgrace in school, signifying a fall from her position of communal authority, Scout attacks Walter for getting her into trouble, and Jem invites Walter home for lunch. During that lunch, Walter and Atticus converse about matters that Scout cannot follow, speaking as male adults (24) in a way that excludes her, once again showing the limitations of her actual literacy. She tries to reestablish her place in the family and in Atticus's household by critiquing Walter's table manners. Presumably, she matches her peer discourse community by using the local dialect, "what the sam hill—." Scout embarrasses Walter and her family and is reprimanded by Calpurnia (sentenced to finish lunch with her) for not respecting social codes of entertaining. Scout thus shows her marginal position and desire for expertise on typifying and understanding people; she does not yet understand her own class position although she has tried to appropriate Atticus's voice and apply it for her own purposes. Like Calpurnia, who explicitly speaks different languages in different communities, Scout is marginal, and her future self already speaks both colloquial and legal, transcendent languages. It is more than appropriate that Scout would digest lessons in manners and writing in Cal's kitchen.

The co-narration by an older and younger Scout achieves a unique blend of local and transcendent, passionate and detached, that tests her father and brother's growing gentleman's club of courteous detachment. The older narrator continually mocks but also appreciates the way young Scout is the antithesis of the calm Atticus. She continually gets into trouble and loses her head, despite Atticus's repeated requests that she keep her head. The older Scout establishes a command of the story by calling attention to the way she orders its presentation and controls the flow of information, while the younger Scout disrupts the whole idea of control and command. For example, the beautiful transition of the older Scout's narration, "That was the summer Dill came to us" (6), greatly contrasts with the skills of the six-year-old, who is told to hush after prying Dill, "'Then if [your father's] not dead you've got one, haven't you?'" (8). The narrator offers background when she wishes us to have context, but she presumes that we are outsiders and that she has to translate for us: "The misery of that house began many years before Jem and I were born. . . . Jem said [Mr. Radley] 'bought cotton,' a polite term for doing nothing" (9). Her position as a translator demonstrates that she expects her reader to need her insider information—her expertise on local language.

In fact, in many ways both older and younger Scout establish themselves as folklorists, explaining what different groups will and will not do, given their belief systems. For example, she explains that Negroes avoid the dangerous Radley house and that children refuse pecans from the Radley tree because they would kill (9). Scout tells us what is part of children's "ethical culture" (35) and what its limits are. She uses legal language throughout the novel to describe the systems of informal law that govern particular social groups (see also Johnson, "Secret Courts"). The older narrator's role as a folklorist greatly contrasts with, but also echoes, the young Scout's prejudices and misunderstandings as she discovers truths about others.

The scene in which young Scout attempts to translate the meaning of "Cunningham" for her teacher also demonstrates Lee's unique narrative technique; the narrator can vacillate between the focalization of the child and older narrator at will, sometimes for comic effect and sometimes to render the confusing nature of adult assumptions. We cannot help but laugh at and yet feel badly for Scout's actions during lunch; Scout's thoughts after the lunch demonstrate that she has a child's tendency to blow things out of proportion. She suggests to Atticus that he "lose no time in packing [Calpurnia] off" (25), and she "returned to school and hated Calpurnia steadily until a sudden shriek shattered my resentments" (25). In other words, the strong emotion of hating "steadily" only lasts until something else intrudes upon her consciousness. The irony present in the sophisticated vocabulary and repetition of "s" sounds jars against the subject of Scout's impressionist and watery mind. It is this very Maisie-like liquidity, however, that allows various adults to make their marks in Scout.

The technique established in the school scene, interrupted by a flashback to Atticus's lessons on the Cunninghams, becomes a pattern for the early portion of the novel, and a symbol for the relationship between the child-Scout disrupted and complexified by her father's world. Lee manages information in the Cecil Jacobs scene similarly to the prior Cunningham scene, and she uses it to further her point that Scout is the antithesis to her father's philosophy and more akin to Calpurnia's context-based identity. The chapter begins with words and a no-named speaker, "'You can just take that back, boy!'" (74) We do not know who is speaking, but it sounds like someone establishing his or her superiority over another, and someone challenging someone else to a fight. However, the address of "boy" could be racially charged in such a novel; even Atticus refers to Tom as a boy at one point. The situation turns out to be the playground situation at school, a communal context in which the young Scout speaks in a particular way. We are supposed to hear later in the prosecutor's treatment of Tom an echo of young Scout's childish bullying. Distance from "'You can just take that back, boy!'" is immediately established by the passive voice that follows, "This order, given by me to Cecil Jacobs, was the beginning of a rather thin time for Jem and me. . . . Atticus had promised me he would wear me out if he ever heard of me fighting any more . . . the sooner I learned to hold in, the better off everybody would be. I soon forgot. Cecil Jacobs made me forget" (74). The older narrator, with analepsis (flashback) and prolepsis (flash forward) intrudes as a disciplinary future Scout, a controlling force that the prosecutor does not have. What follows is a flashback of an evening in which Scout consults with Atticus and tries to understand Cecil's words, "Scout Finch's daddy defended niggers," which she does not understand. In this scene she first learns from Atticus of the trial and has a very level-headed conversation with him, led by the discursive style of Atticus, which is *promptly* left behind in the schoolyard. The effect is hilarious because the older narrator asks us to consider how short-lived Atticus's lesson is when Cecil's challenge overrides it.

The child-Scout speaks many voices; her rational and innocent questions to Atticus, where she learns of his perspective on the trial and their need to be sensitive to the community, gives way when faced with school-yard challenges. While representing scenes of Atticus and Scout speaking, the older narrator presents the young Scout's dialogue and thoughts with little comment; however, when Scout observes that Atticus sounds like their war-obsessed Cousin Ike, the narrator inserts background on Cousin Ike to contrast Scout's knowledge with her present abilities. Then the narrator transitions back to the immediate scene with Cecil Jacobs to mock Scout: "With [Atticus's lesson] in mind, I faced Cecil Jacobs in the schoolyard next day: 'You gonna take that back, boy?'" (76). The young Scout misapplies Atticus's carefully worded lessons and heightens the gap between Scout's Emersonian training and passionate response to peers. The older narrator then puts further distance between us and the young Scout with a sentence about Scout's limited sense of time and the impending doom of a scene to come: "I felt extremely noble for having remembered [not to fight], and re-mained noble for three weeks. Then Christmas came and disaster struck" (77). The older Scout in effect foreshadows the importance and drama of the following Christmas scene, where Scout will strike her cousin.

This foreshadowing mirrors Stowe's command of the story when the narrator says things like "here, for the present, we take our leave of Tom, to pursue the fortunes of other characters in our story" (174), or "Here we must take our leave of [Eliza] for the present, to follow the course of her pursuers" (109), foregrounding the function and authority of the storyteller Scout, who achieves omniscience through comparison to the limited child-Scout. The technique pervades Capote's *The Grass Harp,* in which foreshadowing differentiates the narrator from the community: "The story that got around [about Verena and Dr. Ritz] was that they were up to something out in the old canning factory the other side of town. As it developed, they were; but not what the gang at the pool-hall thought" (Capote, *Grass* 19). The technique distinguishes the speaker from the limited views of those in the region, communicating a sense of missed options and opportunities: "Most people don't believe it when I tell about catching a catfish barehanded; I say well ask Riley Henderson. . . . Riley said it was one of the fattest catfish he'd ever seen: we would take it back to the tree and, since he'd bragged what a great hand he was at frying catfish, let the Judge fix it for breakfast. As it turned out, that fish never got eaten" (*Grass* 48). This fundamentally Jamesian technique is to summarize a scene before rendering it, telling the reader how to feel about it. Capote's novel shows how this technique communicates the feeling of missed opportunity—a sense of "if only" the scene could really be revised. This emerges in *The Grass Harp* in particular when Collin and Riley catch the fish, because Collin is attracted to Riley and when they go fishing they are sharing something far more than fishing. Lee's narrator is continually communicating Scout's missed opportunities of living up to Atticus's Emersonian standards. It is important to analyze this intrusive and controlling narrative technique in most major scenes of *Mockingbird* leading up to the trial because during the trial the pattern alters. The narrator does not summarize the trial in advance; she does not enter the action with a statement like "Then the trial started and disaster struck," just like she does not foreshadow Cal's church visit with anything like "Then Cal took us somewhere that opened our eyes." The narrator has trained us to expect the narrator's control, irony, and distance, but in scenes of immediate, unfolding experience she simply removes the narrator's intrusive narratological control.

In contrast to the tightly controlled flow of information by the narrator and the Twain-like irony employed in scenes of Scout's everyday world, scenes that take her beyond her everyday world are experienced more like Maisie. The more immediate and less ironic scenes of Cal's church and the jail set up Scout's transcription of the trial, where she acts as a quasi-objective filter, achieving the effects that Carol Clover equates with court-room fiction, the viewers of which become members of the jury. Scout is located beyond the all-white section and thus beyond the limited perspective of the prejudiced jury; she is thus a better juror, a more objective witness, and a model for the reader. The older narrator gives background on the judge, on the men who typically attend court, as well as on the courthouse, and on the Ewell yard and background, to develop sympathy for Mayella, but she leaves the young Scout as the primary filter (as opposed to focalizer) of how the trial unfolds. Scout gives raw impressions of those on the witness stand, but she also largely stands out of the way so the reader can have a more primary experience of the trial and its drama. Rather than our guide to understanding the trial, she remains our guide to understanding how to read Atticus—which of his behaviors are typical and which (such as taking off his coat) are atypical. The older narrator only points out the young Scout's limitations insofar as they affect her reading of the melodrama.

The fact that Lee wants us to feel differently about the trial than the rest of the novel becomes immediately apparent when distance between the young Scout and older narrator returns in a much fuller way outside the trial. After closing arguments, the intrusion of self-irony returns with full force. Scout dwells on hearing Calpurnia yell at Jem for taking her to the trial and then provides an ironic summary of the rape statute, as Jem becomes the expert: "we were subjected to a lengthy review of evidence with Jem's ideas on the law regarding rape: it wasn't rape if she let you, but she had to be eighteen—in Alabama, that is—and Mayella was nineteen. Apparently you had to kick and holler, you had to be overpowered and stomped on, preferably knocked stone cold. If you were under eighteen, you didn't have to go through all this" (208-9). The irony and colloquialism "kick and holler," usually deployed by the older narrator to mock the young Scout, are here turned toward the law and to Jem himself, whose impending adolescence has also been a site of challenge for the young Scout—as incomprehensible, and a mirror of, the illegible adult events of the town.

Ultimately, the satirical narrator that made us laugh at Scout, heightening the gap between Atticus's calm lesson and, "with this in mind, I faced Cecil Jacobs in the schoolyard next day: 'You gonna take that back, boy?'" (77), applies her technique more and more to social irony, creating hilarious incongruence:

Today Aunt Alexandra and her missionary circle were fighting the good fight all over the house. . . . [the Mrunas] were crawling with yaws and ear-worms, they chewed up and spat out the bark of a tree into a communal pot and then got drunk on it.

Immediately thereafter, the ladies adjourned for refreshments. (228)

Lee's vicious social satire seems disarming because she devotes much of the novel to irony against young Scout herself. When she turns the technique against Maycomb, the result resembles Twain's Huck, who can calmly and without awareness of humor point out discrepancies in culture. The incongruity between the Mrunas and the ladies, who use the Mrunas for pre-refreshment entertainment, becomes insightful congruity as we realize that the ladies themselves are enjoying a communal pot, chewing and spitting their various venoms, and crawling with yews in the form of the ugly things they say about others. Tavernier-Courbin reminds us that the mockingbird is actually a pretty vicious bird, just as Boo, supposedly the nonviolent "mockingbird," acts pretty violently, and that it may "also symbolize the satirist revealing the ugly underbelly of the South through humor" (59). Shackelford astutely observes that the two "mockingbirds" of the novel are ironically "unable to mock society's roles for them and as a result take the consequences of living on the margins—Tom, through his death; Boo, through his return to the protection of a desolate isolated existence" (125). Mocking is more than a "teaspoon of sugar" in *Mockingbird;* imitation, whether bargaining or scorning, is survival.

Clearly, Lee carefully controls the reader's reactions to various scenes through varying the narrator's treatment of the younger Scout and what she witnesses. Not only does Scout cross physical and symbolic boundaries in the novel; she also straddles narrative ones. She is both local and transcendent in voice and perspective, she is both passionate and detached through multivoiced narrative interplay, and she is both limited and omniscient in the roles she takes at different points—highlighting her limitations at points and her omniscience at others, often because of her acute senses rather than her developed sight. In short, her roots in Huck emerge most fully when she is in her comfortable everyday world, and thus more ironic, and her roots in Maisie emerge most fully when she is challenged by incomprehensible events streaming through her consciousness like the slide of a magic lantern.

The vacillations in narration are not at all the technical flaw that some reviewers initially thought, but a brilliant fusion of Victorian and modern narrative practices as they first took shape in a specific historical period studying the child as the index to unlocking the past.

Conclusion: How Lee Laughs

In literature with child characters, there are typically adults who mirror each child and serve as possible futures. For example, in the *Harry Potter* series, Harry is a mini-Dumbledore, Hermione a mini-Minerva McGonagall, and Ron a mini-Hagrid. In *Mockingbird,* Jem is clearly a mini-Atticus, overtly aspiring to be him ("He's a gentleman, just like me!" Jem exclaims). Dill is obsessed with Boo Radley, as I explore in the next chapter on homosexuality and Dill's obsessive desire to make Boo *come out.* Dill's disappearance and Boo's brief emergence, followed by a quick re-closeting, provides a clear vision of Lee's sense that Dill (and children like Dill) has no future in a small southern town like Maycomb. Scout's logical choice of future lies with the lady who is *only* a lady in the afternoon: Miss Maudie. In the spectrum of ladies who model for Scout ways to fit in and adapt discourse to social settings, there is one character who is both a lady and a rabble-rouser. Miss Maudie speaks various kinds of dialects, lending her high or low language to the subjects she believes those languages fit. She most closely resembles the narrator's mocking voice. Just as in chapter 3 we learned that ruptures in "what Scout knew" register our witnessing of the artist coming into being, Scout's slow gravitation toward Miss Maudie registers our witnessing of a woman's laughter and "morphodite" identity emerging.

In an important scene, Miss Maudie directly voices the way in which various social dialects combine in storytelling. Scout asks Miss Maudie if the Radley stories are true. Miss Maudie identifies in Scout's folklore a certain percentage of one community's influence and a certain percentage of another. She then follows her analysis of how narrative works with a story of how she used discourse against Miss Stephanie:

> "That is three-fourths colored folks and one-fourth Stephanie Crawford," said Miss Maudie grimly. "Stephanie Crawford even told me once she woke up in the middle of the night and found him looking in the

window at her. I said what did you do, Stephanie, move over in the bed and make room for him? That shut her up a while."

I was sure it did. Miss Maudie's voice was enough to shut anybody up. (45)

Miss Maudie models for Scout many eccentricities, including gender fluidity. Commenting on her as a "preferable model of southern womanhood for both Scout and readers," Richards discusses the way in which Miss Maudie constructs a public identity, and, "when she chooses, she can rival her neighbors in her successful enactment of white southern femininity" (132)—the key words being "when she chooses," because she transacts her business on her terms. But like the other female socialites, she models the power of voice and, more than other ladies, the power of the voice to mock and thereby lower the status of the mocked subject. She transforms a situation from gossip to an exposure of the petty gossiper. Most evidently, she is sharp to detect translation practices and serves as a translator herself, especially to the children about Atticus.

In a revealing moment that reflects on the hybrid liminality of Scout and her female neighbor, Miss Maudie models to Scout a way of coping with pain: laughter. After her house burns down and she shows to Jem and Scout that she has ruined her hands attempting to clean up her yard, the children offer assistance. She tells them they have work at home, and Scout's interpretation of this "work" results in Miss Maudie's laughter at Scout's unexpected mimicry of Miss Maudie's earlier words for the snowman:

> "You mean the Morphodite?" I asked. "Shoot, we can rake him up in a jiffy."
>
> Miss Maudie stared down at me, her lips moving silently. Suddenly she put her hands to her head and whooped. When we left her, she was still chuckling.
>
> Jem said he didn't know what was the matter with her—that was just Miss Maudie. (74)

This is an instance in which deadpan Scout is exposed to a reader. Scout has no idea that her mimicry of Miss Maudie's description of her snowman is funny, whereas Miss Maudie gives us a glimpse here of *Mockingbird* style and desired reception. Both involve laughter at the biting pain of humankind. Miss Maudie's laughter is unimaginable to Jem, the male and the mini-Atticus. Why? In his book *Rabelais and His World,* Bakhtin theorizes about the way in which laughter, both parody and bawdy humor, organized the times of festive carnival under feudal systems and helped the "folks" momentarily overturn the social order. Miss Maudie's allusion to sex in her comment to Miss Stephanie, along with her use of the word "morphodite" as an obvious reference to genitals, identifies her with the rare ability to use "low" humor even though she is a lady.

Lee uses low humor as well. In the scene of witnessing Mr. Avery's urination, the narrator mocks gender by exposing it for what it is—genitals that produce urine—and to create narrative distance from the "stream" with her "high" language. She describes his urine as a poetic "arc of water descending from the leaves and splashing in the yellow circle of the street light, some ten feet from source to earth." The intrigue results in "the ensuing contest to determine relative distances and respective prowess," in which Scout cannot participate because she is "untalented in this area" (50–51). Scout's talents lie elsewhere, within the art of burlesque. The scene sets up the humor of the snowman modeled on Mr. Avery and then disguised with a woman's hat, very subtly telling us about Miss Maudie's possible inner masculinity; the bawdy humor here mocks the street that is supposed to reflect "background" and instead models ways of being male that are worthy of the strutting rooster Mr. Ewell. The language "closer inspection revealed," "ensuing contest to determine relative distances and respective prowess," "untalented in this area"—like Maisie's sense that "our affairs are involved"—veils and cloaks the content of the humor, distinguishing the narrator from the sordid affair.

Nevertheless, the image of what Bakhtin calls "grotesque realism" aligns Lee's satire with folk festival:

Not only parody in its narrow sense but all the other forms of grotesque realism degrade, bring down to earth, turn their subject into flesh. This is the peculiar trait of this genre which differentiates it from all the forms of medieval high art and literature. The people's laughter which characterized all the forms of grotesque realism from immemorial times was linked with the bodily lower stratum. Laughter degrades and materializes. (Bakhtin 20)

Laughter brings down the Maycomb community with its pretensions at being superior to the Mrunas, but it also "kills by exposing the gangrene under the beautiful surface . . . one can hardly allow oneself to be controlled by what one is able to laugh at" (Tavernier-Courbin 59). Thus it is hardly likely that being "untalented" in the arena of projecting an arc of urine should make Scout or the narrator feel a lesser being.

The narrator's laughter is intimately intertwined with Miss Maudie's unusual insider/outsider position in regard to Maycomb ladies and "ways." What is really the matter with Miss Maudie is that she has lost everything but her unique way of saying things, which comes back to her in the form of a child who shares her ability to name things *and* the ability to recognize a "morphodite"—a figure neither male nor female. Miss Maudie is a liberal passing as a missionary society lady; somehow, like Mrs. Mingott of *The Age of Innocence,* who has the power to be blunt, Miss Maudie is free to voice the vicious "'His food doesn't stick going down, does it?'" (233) when Mrs. Merriweather alludes to Atticus's "misguided" defense of Tom. Similarly to how she silences Stephanie regarding Boo, Miss Maudie ends the insulting conversation with her icy anger, an image in contrast with the heat imagery usually applied to the ladies. We never see Atticus angry, but we certainly see angry ladies; we view the angry Miss Maudie here and the angry Cal earlier, both angry at misfiring hostess scenes and both falling into local dialects when challenged. Miss Maudie is an admirable hostess who "passes" in the world of ladies that makes Scout uncomfortable; Miss Maudie reassures her by gently touching her hand as if they are the same. Early in the novel we are told that others covet Miss Maudie's recipes, but the older narrator believes that they would be impossible to follow. The idea is that she is original; no *lady* could imitate her. A recipe unto herself, Miss Maudie is Scout's kindred insider/outsider who, like Cal, signifies "modest" double lives, mockingbird style.

Miss Maudie teaches us how intertwined anger and laughter are. In reaction to the trial and failed justice, Jem gets angry, whereas the future Scout-narrator deploys laughter. Laughter involves intrusion (Berger 6) and incongruity, which we can historicize by looking at its roots in the cult of Dionysus, as described by Peter Berger in *Redeeming Laughter: The Comic Dimension of Human Experience:*

Dionysus is the god who violates all ordinary boundaries, as do his devotees, who become satyr-like creatures, a grotesque hybrid of humans and animals. Comedy retains these Dionysian features, even when in later times they are toned down—domesticated or defanged, as it were. The comic experience is ecstatic, if not in the archaic sense of a frenzied trance, in a mellower form of *ek-statis*, "standing outside" the ordinary assumptions and habits of everyday life. The comic experience is orgiastic, if not in the old sense of sexual promiscuity, in the metaphorical sense of joining together what convention and morality would keep apart. It debunks all pretensions, including pretensions of the sacred. The comic, therefore, is dangerous to all established order. (16)

Comedy involves malice (Berger 18); laughter is always at someone's expense, even if it is intertwined with catharsis and redemption, or, for O'Connor, grace. Comedy, by pointing out discrepancy, enacts a "rupture in the fabric of reality" (Berger 18), which we can link to discrepancy between ideals and realities in *Mockingbird* and in Scout as the older narrator points out ruptures in young Scout's mind and behavior. Two other moments of laughter in *Mockingbird* connect laughing to something within Scout, to the idea that Scout is in drag, and to the function of art. Dill's memorable vow to become a laughing clown is voiced after his witnessing of the trial, at which his tears flow. He vows that he will remove himself from the human race and take on the comic mask of the clown, laughing at the world. In other words, he suggests we exchange the tragic mask for the comic mask. If this sounds like Twain, it should.

Dill's vow is essentially the assumption of an aesthetic stance that, my next chapter shows, echoes his role in the novel all along, enacting, as he does by pushing the Radley plot forward, what amounts to parody, opera, and camp. Clowns are typically found in circus pantomime, dumb show, masque, and even whiteface to emphasize grotesque features such as broad red permanent smiles. The smile is pure artifice, like camp, but it is also simultaneously sinister because stylized clowns mock the people who watch them. There are a wide variety of clowns, and the tradition of clowning has a complex history, but they seem to all exaggerate certain features of the human face, action, or social type to exploit the comic aspects of a situation when viewed from a distance. Their use of either makeup or props to heighten select features encodes the idea of distance between spectator and clown. Clowns can be deadpan like Huck; they can take on the role of the ringmaster manipulator; they can take on the role of the fool; they can clown any number of characters, as made famous by clowns like Emmett Kelly, Red Skelton, and Charlie Chaplin. Clowns, Bakhtin writes, "were the constant, accredited representatives of the carnival spirit," (8) and, as Seidel ("Growing Up") observed of Dill, clowns are somewhere between life and art since they remain clowns whenever they make their appearance. Dill is actually associated with parody and clowning much earlier in the novel when he gets the idea of making Boo come out and so enthusiastically performs the Radley tragedy throughout the summer. Dill's carnival presence and the early Radley camp performed for the neighbors is actually training us to view what Miss Maudie calls the "Roman carnival" of the trial as a feast of fools; the usual social order is indeed overturned there when Ewell and his daughter are treated like gentleman and lady. It is comic because they do not play those roles well, and the festival is incomplete with its clown.

Before he is laughing, Dill is continually acting out Boo's closeted condition, a symbol of homosexuality and drag, themes that preoccupied Capote in his fiction. However, an important laugh is heard by Scout when she inadvertently rolls into Boo's yard, telling us that the scene is both a comic escapade and a symbol of Dill's arts, which are simmering "inside" Scout: "I heard another sound, so low I could not have heard it from the sidewalk. Someone inside the house was laughing" (41). This laugh becomes her special secret, not told to Jem, although she usually loves to reveal knowledge to him of all people. These laughs add up to something significant. They suggest that people on the outside of the social world laugh at it, that laughter is a primal emotion from very deep within the soul, and that laughter is the only response one can have to human drama "out of the cradle endlessly rocking."

The connections between Miss Maudie, Dill, Boo, Scout, and "the Absolute Morphodite" are more significant, but here let us note that laughing suggests a shared emotion between outsiders and an aesthetic mask between writer and reader. Dill's clown, in particular, must be understood as an aesthetic stance, given his role throughout the novel as an imaginative author. Certainly Capote served this function for Lee. In her essay "The Laugh of the Medusa," French psychoanalytic feminist Hélène Cixous exhorts women to write and overturn the stereotypes men have perpetuated about women throughout Western literature: the angel and the demon, the Madonna and the whore, as explained by Virginia Woolf in *A Room of One's Own*:

> Indeed, if woman had no existence save in the fiction written by men, one would imagine her a person of the utmost importance; very various; heroic and mean; splendid and sordid; infinitely beautiful and hideous in the extreme; as great as a man, some think even greater. But this is woman in fiction. In fact, as Professor Trevelyan points out, she was locked up, beaten and flung about the room.

Cixous's idea is that women must write so we can find out what woman is. Cixous believes women can free themselves from how men have seen them if they take up the pen. Cixous takes the image of the Medusa as paradigmatic of an image circulating in male literature—an image that in chapter 1 I argued often manifested in American romantic literature as the female temptress. The Medusa is the "dark continent" of Freudian theory that women have internalized. Cixous says, "You only have to look at the Medusa straight on to see her. And she's not deadly. She's beautiful and she's laughing" (342). She is not scary, but she is joyous, celebratory, and privileged with insight. This is very much Boo's function: Scout believes he will be monstrous, but he is really laughing. That is what she is learning about herself—that someone "deep inside" the dark continent is beginning a low laugh.

Lee's *Mockingbird* is unique because it presents a woman's laugh alongside a story of American romance, melodrama, and modern dissatisfactions with older forms. Lee's critical view of Atticus and all he embodies emerges most fully in her deployment of an embedded narrative of homosexuality that encompasses Dill, Boo, and Scout, and in her embedding of modern women's regional writing in Scout's story. We turn now to some questions about Boo: why would it be so awful for Boo to receive cakes in recognition of his "child-saving"? Why is Scout one of "Boo's children"? Why is Jem really wounded and not caring so long as he can pass and punt? Why is Mrs. Dubose's camellia such an electric shock to him, as frightening as the Medusa's gaze itself?

With her ironic look at "a tired old town," the author laughs and we laugh with her. But to fully understand *Mockingbird*'s vision of the dispossessed, we have to look not at the relatively uncomplicated and melodramatic racial spectacle, but also at the discourse of homosexuality condensed into the laughing clown as the very inspiration for Lee's aesthetic enterprise. Dill is laughing, just as Boo, a projection from inside Scout, is laughing. And Miss Maudie is laughing and inviting Scout into a particular future: the laughter of "the Absolute Morphodite," whom Scout can "rig up in a jiffy" because she has plenty of folks to parody. In reference to the snowman, Atticus asks the children not to libel the neighbors and make caricatures of them (67); but this is precisely what his future Scout has done. In some ways, however, she has carried out his lesson to the letter. Just as she *drags* the snowman to make it *pass,* she in fact writes a story about how it takes dragging and passing to get along in the world. In the meanwhile, one can laugh.

CHAPTER 5

MOCKINGBIRD AND POST–WORLD WAR II SOUTHERN WRITING: DILL, CAPOTE, AND THE *DRAGGING OUT* OF BOO RADLEY

Mockingbird features an impressively long line of neglected children: Boo Radley; Mayella and her siblings; the lunchless Walter who craves sugary syrup; the motherless Scout, at whom the neighbors are shaking their heads; the mixed-race children, who sadly belong nowhere (says Jem); and the boy nicknamed Dill, perhaps the quintessential symbol of the child in perpetual exile. He is the wandering outsider of Capote's youth expressed in his fiction—Joel of *Other Voices, Other Rooms,* Collin of *The Grass Harp.* Dill's fatherless state confronts us right away as Jem and Scout readily ask about his patrimonial lineage. Despite his long name he proudly recites to introduce himself, his weighty name and his vivid lies about his family do not hide his self-conscious shame about being fatherless. His fatherlessness suggests he is somewhat removed from the patriarchy that overwhelms the novel as a whole, structured as it is around the idea that a good patriarch represents those without political voice.

Dill's fatherless state provides an inverse mirror of Scout and Jem's motherlessness. This mirroring suggests missing aspects of Dill and Scout; Dill is lacking an element of masculinity, whereas Scout is lacking proper femininity. These traits emerge in the trial. Dill sheds tears at the treatment of Tom as if Tom's disfiguration and victimization are somehow embodiments of self, whereas Scout saves her sympathy for Mayella, a motherless daughter like herself (see Fine, "Gender Conflicts" 124–25). Like the feminine Laurie of *Little Women,* interpreted as the counterpart to the masculine Jo since they share the same struggles against gender codes, Dill and Scout together comprise a "whole" androgynous person. In reference to *Little Women,* Elizabeth Keyser argues that the feminine boy and the masculine girl can only express the wholeness of androgyny prior to adolescent sexual development; thus the breakup of Jo and Laurie suggests limits in what nineteenth-century sexual codes can countenance in its individuals (66–67).

Mockingbird is similarly deeply concerned with the wounding process involved in gender development. Indeed, the opening segment about Jem being ever so slightly crippled, even while he can pass and punt, provides the reader with the thesis that the game of life is played upon, as Elaine Scarry titles her book, "the body in pain."

Earlier nineteenth-century audiences may or may not have equated gender inversion with homosexuality, but by the turn of the century, following the work of German Karl Heinrich Ulrichs and Havelock Ellis's book *Sexual Inversion* (Chauncey 49; Katz 51–52), scientists had begun to locate homosexuality as not only in a person's activities but also "in" the person him- or herself (see Bronski 34–39). It would take half a century before the binary opposition of homosexuality/heterosexuality would structure nonscientific thought patterns and the way men and women actually understood themselves (see Chauncey), but homosexuality would become an exclusive category of identity, and the trope of inversion or "the third sex" codified the essence of drag. Explorations of an awakening identity of homosexuality are more than apparent in Dill, a character obsessed with freakish monsters, aesthetic invention, and heterosexual normativity, the latter desperately sought in relations with Scout and Jem. His marital play with Scout quickly reaches a level of heterosexual parody (Fine, "Structuring" 69), and his longing for Jem to join him in games of making Boo "come out" become painful oscillations between expressing his gay identity and denying it by performing masculinity at another closeted individual's expense—Boo's. If we look closely at the preoccupations of drag in the fiction of Truman Capote, upon whom Dill was based, and how drag rears its head in *Mockingbird,* we can more sharply understand that, although *Mockingbird* participates in a relatively uncomplicated racial melodrama, it embodies a more complicated, sinister subtext of condemning gays to a life in the closet. *Mockingbird* opens up Dill's inner issues only to abandon him in the end. Whereas his vow to become a laughing clown inspires Lee's artistic enterprise, the only remnant of his presence in the novel that remains in the closing scene is his sacrificed book, *The Gray Ghost.*

Queer Couples at Summer Camp

In the opening of the novel we are told that the story's action begins with Dill. Actually, it is Jem's assertion that the events of the summer began the moment Dill entered the scene and "first gave us the idea of making Boo Radley come out" (3). The notion of coming out derives from an analogy to the debutante, and in the earlier years of the twentieth century it was used to signify not "*coming out of* what we call the 'gay closet' but rather of *coming out into* what [men] called 'homosexual society' or the 'gay world'" (Chauncey 7). A 1931 Baltimore article on a local pansy ball began by describing "'the coming out of new debutantes into homosexual society'" (Chauncey 7). In fact, in New York in the 1950s, the term "coming out" had a more particular meaning of first sexual experience with a man (Chauncey 8). Regardless of how Lee intended it, the phrase can hardly be divorced from homosexuality and Dill's desire for both acceptance and companionship in the novel. Although the narrator asserts her self-conscious authority in deciding where and when to begin her story, she does indeed accept Jem's opening, giving Dill's entry its own paragraph, "That was the summer Dill came to us" (6), a paragraph that turns the novel from expository background to an immediate scene. The immediacy of the line echoes the opening of Carson McCullers's novel about a girl intuiting her queerness and experiencing exile: "It happened that green and crazy summer when Frankie was twelve years old. This was the summer when for a long time she had not been a member. She belonged to no club and was a member of nothing in the world" (1). Lee thus gives to Dill the function of a threshold figure, which, in traditional myth, beckons protagonists across some kind of implicit or explicit boundary. The literal boundary will be Boo's yard, which immediately attracts him. The Finch household attracts him for different reasons. The former signifies an inner life and the latter social acceptance and patriarchy. Thus Dill seems to float between the boundaries of the hidden closet and secure, transparent patriarchy, both of which attract him. If Dill's machinations are the beginning of a story that ends with a "mock" trial about race, then we have to ask why.

Just why is Boo mythologized as a ghost? The background we get about Boo seems largely irrelevant to his closeted condition. Indeed, Scout wonders about it and Atticus explains with oddly cryptic language. Given his educational credence of clarity and non-evasion, stated to his brother, Atticus's mysterious description of the Radleys stands out. To his brother, whom Richards reads as prototype of the homosexual (138–39), Atticus lectures, "'When a child asks you something, answer him, for goodness' sake. . . . [Children] can spot an evasion quicker than adults, and evasion simply muddles 'em'" (87). In contrast, his response to Scout's imagination of the phantom Boo is the sort of nonresponse that muddles: "Nobody knew what form of intimidation Mr. Radley employed to keep Boo out of sight, but Jem figured that Mr. Radley kept him chained to the bed . . . Atticus said no, . . . there were other ways of making people into ghosts" (11). This is Atticus's unusually vague answer to how Boo has become synonymous with ghost. It would seem unlikely that Boo's abuse, agoraphobia, or legendary stereotype as a juvenile delinquent would be enough to make his situation parallel to Tom's, which the novel says it is. Boo's situation earns him the title of the novel; Scout maintains at the end that dragging Boo's heroics into the light would in fact be tantamount to killing a mockingbird. The parallel to the mockingbird seems extremely odd, given that the novel has advanced the mockingbird as a creature who sings solely for the pleasure of others, whereas Boo's great sin is to have shut his front door and recused himself from gentlemanly and neighborly social norms. I suppose the image alludes to his rescue of the children, but the image of singing exclusively for others hardly fits.

A much more compelling explanation for Boo as a symbol, particularly as used by Dill in his obsessive quest to make him "come out," is that he functions as the closet of sexual difference in a novel highly concerned with gender, inversion, and discourses of masculinity. Boo typifies the "everywhere and nowhere" invisibility of gays after the release of Kinsey's report and in the perpetual suspicion of McCarthy era hunts for them (Butt 9–10). Virtually the only way to account for why crossing the street with Boo at the end is so significant is to view him in a larger nexus of discriminatory practices that prohibit individuals from fully "coming out." When Scout looks back at her own street from the porch of the Radley's, she sees a spectacle of self and christens Scout and Jem "Boo's children" (279). It is an odd declaration of birth, given the novel's earlier emphasis on the gaping orifice of the Radley tree, which has, indeed, birthed various gifts for the children and even detailed images of them—in the form of soap. If the recognition of Scout and Dill as Boo's children indicates a familial relationship, it is also an unnatural and possibly anal image of procreation.

Clearly the subtle recognition of inner self occurring through unresolved persecutions of the freakish Boo Radley is foundational to the point of *Mockingbird*. The novel ends by asserting Boo's right to privacy and exclusion from the world of ladies, suggesting that sexual orientation is the one issue that simply cannot be openly addressed but must remain in the closet. In effect, Atticus's continual commands to leave Arthur alone are not really the liberal stance we equate with him; it is, rather, a sort of "don't ask, don't tell" policy that we recognize from our vantage point of the twenty-first century, when "don't ask, don't tell" has structured the most lenient of political tolerance toward the "heroic" military who save us when our lives are in jeopardy. The implication is that we need these heroes, but we do not need to know their secrets. It is not a kind position.

The vaguely defined resistance to "coming out" suggests not our lack of knowledge about why Boo selects celibacy, but a long history of gay shame in literature and culture, given the possibility of broad homosexual panic, as theorized by Sedgwick in her book *Epistemology of the Closet:*

> The closet is the defining structure for gay oppression in this century.... The image of coming out regularly interfaces the image of the closet.... Just so with coming out: it can bring about the revelation of a powerful unknowing *as* unknowing, not as a vacuum or as the blank it can pretend to be but as a weighty and occupied and consequential epistemological space. (77)

Could this be why the mad dog seems to "curve" (95) toward the Radley house? The path is not a straight one, and the dog stops right in front of the Radley gate as if a pointer of madness, or, perhaps its opposite, a limit because Boo is the most sane. The difference between discrimination against Tom and discrimination against Boo is perhaps a matter of visibility, which is fraught with weight in a novel about seeing with the right eye and shooting always "to the right": "Racism, for instance, is based on a stigma that is visible in all but exceptional cases ... so are the oppressions based on gender, age, size, physical handicap" (Sedgwick 75). We know that the freakish and vampiric "whiteness" of Boo demands the men's protection, but we really do not get an account of why. Richards writes of the odd silences surrounding Boo, "because Lee surrounds Boo with so many of the silences and absences that structure the frequent closetedness of same-sex desire, she invites readers to speculate that Boo's reclusiveness is comparable to closeted sexuality" (146). The suggestion of the closet is particularly strong when we consider that the metaphor was only coming into common usage in the period;

before the 1960s, gays who passed used the trope of the double or secret life (Chauncey 375), a trope Lee uses to describe other characters. Unlike them, Boo has no doubled existence, suggesting his status as closet or double for the younger characters. The novel acts as if Boo's emergence resolves the story of discrimination and of Dill's journey as he copes with neglect and difference, but Arthur's emergence is no "coming out." The powerful heterosexual men of the community ensure that his vampire existence continues where it must remain: beyond the social gaze of Maycomb. The "coming out" of Boo coincides with the disappearance of Dill. Lee makes no effort in the end of her story to explain how Dill fares at school, suggesting that Dill exceeds the limits of her narrative form.

While Boo's difference from others is obvious, and quite central to the novel's theme of tolerance, the precise nature of his difference occupies the space of the unknowable, which Sedgwick analyzes as a heavily burdened rather than "blank" space of the closet. It is all the more veiled because the Finch street is occupied by so many eccentric characters, most of whom are single or unmarriageable for some reason. If we trace the legacy of the laugh from deep "inside" Boo's house to Miss Maudie regarding Scout's use of "morphodite"—the word applied to the racially passing and "in drag" snowman—to Dill's vow of becoming the laughing clown, we find that the laugh circulates between and among characters who occupy various states of drag and mask in a broader gender farce.

The dual male-female aspects of Miss Maudie are revealed when we meet her:

> Miss Maudie hated her house: time spent indoors was time wasted. She was a widow, a chameleon lady who worked in her flower beds in an old straw hat and men's coveralls, but after her five o'clock bath she would appear on the porch and reign over the street in magisterial beauty. (42)

As the boys exclude Scout more and more from their games, Scout's relationship with Miss Maudie, which "was not clearly defined" (44) because it seems to have real potential for Scout's self-definition as "morphodite" herself, becomes more pronounced. They sit in twilight together as if lovers or mirrors of chameleon souls, in body and voice. They share liminality with the world of ladies. Whereas the pleasures Miss Maudie gleans from tending her garden seem part of the "polluting female" doctrine of the foot-washing Baptists, whom she despises, it is also seen by Scout as veiling violence: "If she found a blade of nut grass in her yard it was like the Second Battle of the Marne: she swooped down upon it with a tin tub and subjected it to blasts from beneath a poisonous substance she said was so powerful it'd kill us all if we didn't stand out of the way" (42). We are reminded of Boo, who uses seemingly benign tools like scissors and kitchen knives to inflict pain. Able to pass with the ladies yet free to speak her mind like the vicious addict Mrs. Dubose, whose masculinity is implied by her retention of the married name even though both she and Miss Maudie are widows, Miss Maudie is indeed some sort of embodied, vocal chameleon who can kill as well as nurture with cake. Her "large cup of sugar" seems overwhelming and overdetermined. It is significant that her hat is the one used to disguise the snowman modeled after Mr. Avery, as if made in the image of the town, akin to the mad dog as a symbol of racism. It is Miss Maudie who names the effect "absolute mor-phodite," suggesting her unique recognition of what one would look like. The "morphodite" embodies racial as well as gender drag, and it appears with the sudden snowfall, which embodies the winds of change.

This term of parody—"morphodite"—is quickly integrated into Scout's vocabulary, similarly to how she immediately recognizes Boo at the end ("'hey, Boo'"), although they have not been introduced. This is because the concept of gender inversion is familiar to her; the concept resides in her internal landscape. At the end of the prior chapter, I made the case that Miss Maudie's outrageous laughter at Scout's vocal parody is a code for the writing and reception of the novel's social irony. This assertion is supported by Miss Maudie's role as audience for the children's Radley tragedy enacted, like what we now recognize as camp, on their porch. At the children's performance, "her hedge clippers poised in midair" (40), her astonishment is expressed in the very tools used also to "drag" the snowman, as if she is part of the camp mosque. Like Boo, Miss Maudie recuses herself from the trial, choosing when and how she will enter public normative space on her own terms.

If Scout is pushed toward the porch of this "morphodite" for twilight experiences, a time on the threshold between day and night, Dill pushes himself further and further toward the porch of Boo, at which he gazes longingly, "I wondered how many times Dill had stood there hugging the fat pole, watching, waiting, hoping" (278). For what revelation is Dill watching, waiting, and hoping? It is as if Dill is in phallic prayer—either hoping to find it or already possessing it. We are being told that Boo is his personal Godot, for whom he is waiting, to uncover what being gay is—wholeness or lack. A chain of gazes in *Mockingbird* suggests a series of theatrical spaces in which gender play becomes parody or camp, the latter form identified with homosexual art and discourse, often used by Capote. It becomes apparent that Boo is also watching and waiting, performing various birth acts through the tree and witnessing the spectacle of the children's perverse summer camp as they perform his legendary influence back for his eyes. Boo and the children are engaged in a never-ending parody, a game of who can manipulate whom more. One of the pawns of the game is the more firmly masculine Jem, who seems to have little awareness that he circulates as a meaningful object between two laughers, Boo and Dill.

The theatricality of Dill is sharply related to his inner feelings of monstrosity. When we meet Dill, an imaginative "curiosity" (7) to the homegrown children, we learn that he has seen the now-classic 1931 *Dracula* starring Béla Lugosi. While this importation of "the monstrous" imagination signifies the seductive manner by which Dill will inspire Scout and Jem to author operas of the seemingly monstrous phantom of the opera Boo Radley, it also codifies the homosexual subtext of Dill and the Radley text he will inspire. Sedgwick writes in *Between Men* that "the Gothic was the first novelistic form in England to have close, relatively visible links to male homosexuality, at a time when styles of homosexuality, and even its visibility and distinctiveness, were markers of division and tension between classes as much as between genders" (91). In *Queer Gothic*, George E. Haggerty demonstrates the roots of sexual abnormalities in gothic fiction and shows how gothic themes have been continually updated to represent homosexuality. Contemporaneous with *Mockingbird*, Shirley Jackson's 1959 *The Haunting of Hill House* is a similar psychological gothic but more explicitly addressing lesbianism, and later Anne Rice rewrote the gothic as homosexual decadence.

Film critics have long recognized the intersections of "the queer" and "the monstrous" in cinema. In his book *Monsters in the Closet: Homosexuality and the Horror Film*, Harry Benshoff surveys the seemingly homophobic trope of "monster queers," but he also explains how queer viewers, like the monsters situated "outside a patriarchal, heterosexist order" (12), would be attuned to the homosexual undertones of the many queer couples we find in classic horror (*Dracula, Dracula's Daughter, Mark of the Vampire, Dr. Jekyll and Mr. Hyde, Werewolf of London, Frankenstein, Island of Lost Souls, Bride of Frankenstein*). Dill's story could be described as reveling in the fantastic and the gothic. He is a study in the creative reception of queer horror.

The homosexual subtext of Tod Browning's *Dracula* is not hard to find, given a long history of equating homosexuals with vampires and of looking at the Renfield-Dracula relationship as represented in the film. Explorations of "unnatural" or perverse "inversion" lie behind many gothic novels and films, of course, but *Dracula* is paradigmatic: "Critics almost universally agree that the vampire metaphor finds its definitive articulation in *Dracula*. Certainly the oscillation between homophilia and homophobia is more discernible there, and certainly the many recapitulations of Stoker's novel (print, film, television) confirm it as the most influential of all vampire texts" (Craft 928). With Joseph Sheridan Le Fanu's *Carmilla*, the lesbian content of the vampire becomes explicit. But Browning's *Dracula*, in particular, presaging his controversial *Freaks*, released in 1932, exposes the obsession of a young slave to an older, seductive and mysterious master. In his discussion of what he calls the "natural connection between horror films and gay audiences," William J. Mann discusses David Skal's description of the gay undercurrents of *Dracula*'s opening sequence, to which Carl Laemmle, head of Universal, objected. Browning insisted on including them, although unlike James Whale, who was comfortable with his homosexuality and whose *Bride of Frankenstein* has the clearest gay sensibility, "Browning himself held a good deal of antipathy for gay people" (Mann 64). Skal's sense that monsters are like drag queens fuels Mann's ruminations on their strange beauty: "As gays, we respond doubly to these films. They resonate deeper, entrancing us with their sense of alienation, of living on the edge, outside of accepted society. These movies repel us by their hideousness while intriguing us with their strange beauty. . . . It is a quintessential queer question: are we beautiful, or are we ugly?" (64) Dill's wish to see Boo, having seen the 1931 *Dracula*, replicates the structure of the slave-master in the film as well as the gay viewer entranced by the alterity represented on the screen.

As Gary Morris writes of it in "Queer Horror: Decoding Universal's Monsters," gay audiences would immediately see in the relationship between Renfield and Dracula a codified view of male homosexual pairing:

Dracula retains an awesome power, thanks largely to Bela Lugosi's hypnotic performance and Dwight Frye's energetically insane slavey Renfield. Gay audiences should find much to cheer in the relationship between the two. Drac's ruined castle, in spite of its vast size, looks every inch the s&m dungeon, lacking only a leather sling and a can of lube. His affair with the super-masochist Renfield begins with bloodsports and proceeds to various kinds of edgeplay, but the count, a typically fickle top, soon tires of the fun and wants to move on to women and children. But Renfield is a classic pushy bottom who refuses to vanish on cue: he continues to pester his master for attention even after Dracula makes him eat flies and rats. While the Count prefers to be elegantly aloof, only alighting to feed on a victim, Renfield's nagging forces Drac to drop his dignified pose, strangle his former slave, and throw him unceremoniously down one of the film's huge stone staircases. (2)

The obsession of the "slavey" with his aloof master mirrors the obsession of Dill with the aloof Boo that preoccupies every waking moment of his imagination. Dill's continual efforts to gain the cooperation of Jem in new Radley "coming out" plans could easily be interpreted as his own efforts at a relationship with Jem, complicated by his own internal sense of perversion and uncertainty about what might be revealed in a real "coming out." Dill succeeds in using Scout to get closer to Jem, excluding her based on gender when she is actually far more masculine than he is. Dill also succeeds in unsexing Jem, who loses his pants in the Radley yard and who is petted by Boo in the end, when unconscious and thus beyond consent. Wearing pants in *Mockingbird* is a clear symbol of masculinity; Aunt Alexandra, until the very end, when she brings Scout overalls, launches a continual campaign against Scout's proclivity for pants, asserting that she should not be doing anything that requires pants.

What remains fascinating about the pants lost in the Radley yard is that although Boo's domestic attentions heal the rip, the stitches are crooked and uneven, a distortion reminiscent of Jem's crippled left arm. Jem seems to intuit his invitation by Boo; he is certainly able to read the soap figures and the detailed attention of the boy-model to the very part of his hair, which the masculine Scout had never before noticed. One of the gifts—the pennies—comes in "the kind of box wedding rings came in, purple velvet with a minute catch" (34), patchworked from chewing-gum wrappers. Jem silently cries at the "filling in" of the "knot hole," intuiting the road not taken by him.

The theme of the homosexual seducing youth was an embedded aspect of many mid-century texts. Press campaigns of the 1950s linked homosexuality with child molestation (Benshoff 127): "This homosexuality-as-seductive-pederasty idea was becoming increasingly prevalent during the post-war period" (Benshoff 139). In many ways, however, *Mockingbird* presents Boo as a mythical child and Dill as the more sophisticated "pocket Merlin," who would therefore logically assist Boo (Merlin's Arthur) with the process of coming out. Given the plethora of queer monstrous couples that have attracted homosexual filmmakers, such as F. W. Murnau and James Whale, it is interesting that the selection in *Mockingbird* would be the vampire, a figure that parodies heterosexual relations in a method similar to *Mockingbird*'s other parodies of courtship rituals, which Richards has argued include Jack's shouting at Miss Maudie to marry him; Jem's reading to Mrs. Dubose; Scout's play-marriage to Dill; and Scout's escorting of Boo at the novel's end. Vampires have been interpreted as symbols of homosexuals because, argues Christopher Craft in *Gay Histories and Cultures: An Encyclopedia,* the vampire has signified perverse or disordered desire; desire for blood that cuts across all living beings, regardless of gender or even species; a seductive force that infuses a victim with the desire for penetration; an ambiguous gender identity and preference; and "a brutal parody of generative sexuality" (927). Sue Case, in her article "Tracking the Vampire," investigates the association between vampire and homosexuality as part of Western oppositional thinking between life and death, heterosexuality associated with producing life and homosexuality with the undead or unnatural (3).

Heterosexual parody, I agree with Fine ("Structuring" 69) and Richards, characterizes Dill's pretend play of heterosexuality with Scout:

> Dill was becoming something of a trial anyway, following Jem about. He had asked me earlier in the summer to marry him, then he promptly forgot about it. He staked me out, marked as his property, said I was the only girl he would ever love, then he neglected me. I beat him up twice but it did no good, he only grew closer to Jem. (41)

Capote includes a similar heterosexual parody between Lee and Capote in *Other Voices, Other Rooms*, in which the two friends appear as Idabel and Joel Knox, whom I discuss in detail below. Normally in plots of female Gothic, a genre underlying the entire Radley drama in *Mockingbird* (see Johnson), demonic or vampiric boys become juvenile-sized Byronic lovers for girls who are in some kind of transition. This is Heathcliff's role toward Cathy in Emily Brontë's *Wuthering Heights;* Peter Pan's role toward Wendy in J. M. Barrie's *Peter and Wendy;* and Laurie's role toward Jo in *Little Women.* Dill, along with the construction of the Boo drama he coauthors, *should* signify this function for Scout, but Scout takes the butch role here, parodying heterosexuality by mocking Dill's effort to "mark her as property." "The property" beats him up, thus undoing the terms of territorial agreement. It is clear that Dill wishes access to Jem (see also Fine, "Structuring" 69), and access to Jem can occur only through the repression of "female"—through "othering" Scout. No inherent access to Jem's masculinity seems possible without the ritualized exclusion of someone, such as theorized by Sedgwick in *Between Men.* Even if Boo is not explicitly homosexual, the least that can be said of him is that he stays out of the fray of Maycomb's trafficking of women, as on display in the trial, upon which heterosexual culture depends.

Dill repeatedly solicits Jem's cooperation in getting Boo to "come out," showing that he seeks community. For example, he bets Jem *The Gray Ghost* on condition that Jem cross the gate, and his logic is that Boo will come out if he spies Jem in his yard (14). Dill seems to think seeing Jem will make Boo desire to come out, which signals his own desires for Jem. Dill conspires with Jem to write to Boo a letter; the letter is a plea for knowledge, and it reflects Dill's theory that "coming out" would make anyone feel better: "Dill said 'It's my idea. I figure if he'd come out and sit a spell with us he might feel better'" (47). The Boo figure becomes a projective space for Dill in his desire to come out and to get closer to Jem. But the persecuting aspects of the attempts complexify the desire because it turns Boo into a pawn like Scout—a convenient figure to "other" and exclude, thereby seeming to participate in comparative masculinity. The older, football-playing Jem would respond to this attempt. Perhaps the finest example of Dill's goal of membership occurs when the children see Mr. Avery urinate in a long stream and then practice this, thereby excluding Scout, who remains "untalented in this area" (51) because she lacks the anatomy. The practice of measuring distance of urination directly leads to the plan of catching a glimpse of Boo at night, a plan from which Scout is initially excluded. Scout has all sorts of inner fantasies about seeing Boo herself, but she rarely transgresses the boundary of his yard unless literally thrown there by the boys. As much as Boo is a symbol for Scout's inner inversion, his role in *Mockingbird* is expressly an exploration of secrets in boys.

Sedgwick discusses the dilemma of homosociality in a homophobic culture. Whereas there is a continuum of feelings and practices for women-identified women and women-loving women, there is not the same continuum among men-identified men and men-loving men. It seems clear that Jem has to reject Radley games to earn Atticus's full respect; Atticus very meaningfully repeats that no one should come out if he does not wish to. Atticus continually admonishes the children against invading Boo's privacy and against making caricature of the neighbors. Although Atticus claims to "love everybody" in the most Emersonian sense of universal, theological affection for humanity, Atticus's identification with the role of gentleman hinges upon a certain "othering" of ladies, as revealed by his behaviors, by his immediate recognition of Mayella as a pawn of Bob Ewell, and by his commands to treat even the mean Mrs. Dubose with gentlemanliness. The long, drawn-out lesson that Jem has to learn is that masculinity quite simply depends upon disidentification with women, who are actually dangerous, polluting, and, like Mrs. Dubose's house, on the inside "dark and creepy."

The possible queerness within Scout, whose problems with femininity are overt in the novel, does not seem to present the same vexed emotions as Dill's need to come out and Jem's need to identify with his father. In the tradition of the tomboy, Scout is easily incorporated by critics as struggling with the limitations of her gender, like just about any other autobiographical account of a woman writer. The novel has been listed as a top lesbian literary choice (see Fine, "Structuring"), and Lee's possible homosexuality has been pondered quite casually; for example, in his biography of Lee, Charles Shields says that students often ask if Lee is gay: "I do not necessarily make a connection between being unmarried and being gay. I cannot say if she is homosexual (she was friends with Capote and other openly gay people)" (3). Sexual difference seems much more of a problem between male characters in the novel. In the scene of Dill's uncontrollable weeping at the trial, we first truly witness the differential treatment of Tom in court and Mr. Dolphus

Raymond's refusal to fully "come out" in his object choice; he prefers to wear the mask of alcoholic. Laura Fine interprets Dolphus Raymond as a potential model for Scout (73), whereas she views Boo as a model of the way in which any transgression would be severely punished. Coming out is simply not an option for men, even while Mayella's coming out with her desires is being aired in public. It is hard to say which is more punitive—Dolphus's donning of the mask or Mayella's unmasking. Dolphus owns property, whereas Mayella scrimps and saves nickels for a long while before she can steal her kiss.

The entire story seems geared to explaining why Jem is actually crippled for a very different reason, just as his crudely sewn pants will always look crudely sewn. Growing up requires that some parts of the self be denied. The gifts of "the knot hole" signify that Jem could be—and indeed Scout describes him as—one of "Boo's children" as well. Jem seems perfectly aware of the giver and the invitations implied, but Jem in fact receives another gift, as poisonous as the lock of hair that turns up for Simon Legree as a detached and thereby gothic symbol of the feminine. The wax camellia, sent from the grave by Mrs. Dubose as a symbol of the eternal expression of Jem's rage against female-identified polluting flowers, is a toxic object that he must keep in his box along with Boo's gifts. It is the final gift, a reminder that being a gentleman means rejecting all things female-identified, including all unnatural forms of reproduction and all opportunities for setting aside pants. At the filling of the knot-hole, Jem cries. But at the point of Mrs. Dubose's gift, Jem fully represses his femininity and becomes a creature Scout does not recognize—one who even betrays Dill by telling Atticus that Dill has run away and turned up under Scout's bed. At the trial, Jem is obsessed with winning; he has become the boy who cares little about being crippled "so long as he can pass and punt," which is parallel but not identical to the Scout who passes a lady in the missionary scene and who becomes more and more sleepy in the second portion of the novel. Atticus's final vigil at Jem's bedside is a crucial culmination of Jem's initiation and Atticus's approval, marking Boo as a missed opportunity even though Boo has killed for him. Jem will never see Boo. But so, too, will Boo be veiled from Dill's eyes. Boo replaces Dill for Scout, and thus "the closet" replaces the boy who comes out to her in a moving nighttime scene, which I analyze presently, in comparison with *Other Voices, Other Rooms.*

Jem is the unconscious target of Boo's affection, which Scout knows, just as she intimately knows Boo and can more easily accept the closet he embodies. She encourages him to cross the taboo of touching Jem, who functions as the boyhood inaccessible to Boo:

> An expression of timid curiosity was on his face, as though [Boo] had never seen a boy before. His mouth was slightly open, and he looked at Jem from head to foot. Boo's hand came up, but he let it drop to his side.
>
> "You can pet him, Mr. Arthur, he's asleep. You couldn't if he was awake, though, he wouldn't let you . . . " I found myself explaining. "Go ahead."
>
> Boo's hand hovered over Jem's head.
>
> "Go on, sir, he's asleep."
>
> His hand came down lightly on Jem's hair. (277–78)

Scout has a growing recognition that the circulation of desires between Dill, Jem, and Boo do not include her, just as, argues Bram Dijkstra, same-sex male attachments of the nineteenth century were bound up with notions of female inferiority (205). Later Scout mourns the fact that Boo will never gaze at her, showing her slow recognition that her connection to him is not one in which he desires her, but something altogether different. In the scene above, Jem is clearly no longer open to these advances, just as he is not immediately open to the chewing gum, whereas the accepting and open Scout immediately, impulsively, and swiftly devours the gum (33). Yet he grows more than curious about Boo. There are very important differences in the journeys of Dill and Jem toward the Radleys. For example, whereas Jem will conclude that Boo wants to stay inside (227), Dill concludes that he stays inside because he has nowhere to go—in other words, no place tolerant of him. Whereas Dill desperately wants Boo to come out, Jem gets the idea of staging the Radley drama as spectacle, thereby making fun of him. Dill quickly joins in the operatic staging as a "villain's villain" to Jem, "a born hero" (39), as if enacting in camp his difference from masculine heroes who steal the spotlight.

Camp and double entendre have historically structured gay interactions as codes that could escape nongay eyes, but many critics source camp to Oscar Wilde, who, Moe Meyer argues, derived his use of gestures and poses from the nineteenth-century French system of actor training known as Delsarte (76). Harold Beaver's discussion of camp in "Homosexual Signs" contributes to my conclusion that Dill is both enacting and differentiating himself from the Radley drama of the exiled child:

> To be natural, as Wilde observed, is such a very difficult pose to keep up. The result is camp: the whole gay masquerade of men and women who self-consciously act; who flaunt incongruous allusions, parodies, transvestite travesties; who are still sanely aware of the gap between their feelings and their roles. . . . At its worst, camp is a joke aimed at the "straight" who make the same or similar gestures unconsciously. . . . Camp is the desire for the subject never to let itself be defined as object by others but to reach for a protective transcendence, which, however, exposes more than it protects. Camp is withdrawal into inverted commas, a flaunting *self*-definition, a leap-frog of distancing. The delights of camp come from the call to interpretation that it issues. It was Wilde's most paradoxical pose to mask his homosexuality by outbidding W. S. Gilbert's caricature, outbunthorning Bunthorne in velvets and lilies and bows, to suggest that he could not be what he seemed to be, when that is exactly what he was. (106–7)

Simply put, camp is queer parody, and as an aesthetic mode it has leaked into popular culture as "Camp Trace" (Meyer, "Introduction" 9, 20). In her "Notes on 'Camp,'" Susan Sontag discusses the indulgence of camp in the unnatural, in artifice, and in exaggeration: "The whole point of Camp is to dethrone the serious. Camp is playful, anti-serious. . . . Camp is the consistently aesthetic experience of the world. It incarnates a victory of 'style' over 'content,' 'aesthetics' over 'morality,' of irony over tragedy" (7). Camp is the good taste of bad taste, which defines the Radley drama and the playful way that Dill's "worst" performances are all the more perfect for it.

Bronski, responding to Sontag, says that homosexuals have sought authenticity in culture through artistic contribution (12), which is clearly Dill's ticket to the Finch children, but Sontag says that although homosexuals have been the vanguard of camp, "camp taste is much more than homosexual taste. Obviously, its metaphor of life as theater is peculiarly suited as a justification and projection of a certain aspect of the situation of homosexuals. . . . Camp is (to repeat) the relation to style in a time in which the adoption of style—as such—has become altogether questionable" (9). The sensibility of camp fits these monstrous Radley performances in an even more ludicrous manner because this is quite literally summer for the children, and Scout's name at the time of the setting would be inseparable from the Girl Scout summer camp movement.

Summer camps in the early part of the twentieth century staged elaborate local pageants that featured people enacting local histories and impersonating abstractions like "The Spirit of Pageantry." The pageants of summer camps were based on William Chancy Langdon's appropriation of the English model of the pageant, which had updated the older masque. Langdon pioneered the pageant for Thetford summer camp, but pageants were soon professionalized and in demand everywhere. Some members of the American Pageant Association felt that "the fantastic flights of symbolic dancers also disrupted the serious historical message of the community pageant," whereas "Frank Chocteau Brown cited the precedent of abstract symbolism's persuasive power in the allegorical masques and miracle and mystery plays of the Renaissance and Middle Ages" (Glassberg 120). I discuss changes in the early twentieth-century pageantry movement in chapter 6, when I discuss the difference between the community pageant in Edith Wharton's *Summer* and in Lee's *Mockingbird*. Like critic Kathryn Kent, who identifies Girl Scout camp as a queer space of "camp," I find the intersection of camp and childhood in the masque-styled camp pageants. They had become the fashion in summer camps and regional festivals by the time of Scout's childhood, when Girl Scouts, summer camps, and indigenous celebrations had become in the American mind pretty much synonymous. A thorough history of pageants can be found in David Glassberg's *American Historical Pageantry: The Uses of Tradition in the Early Twentieth Century*. The "fantastic flight" enacted by Lee's girl Scout and her cohorts all summer long are likely parodies of the pageants in which wealthier children would be participating at camp. The tendency to find childhood inspirations for camp can be seen in the art of Larry Rivers, for example, who when he did *Washington Crossing the Delaware* was thinking of the patriotic grade school plays in which he participated as a child; he even used illustrations in a children's book as a basis for sketching (Butt 90–91). Historical pageants for children are inherently campy, ripe for becoming enacted fun with embedded critiques of official civic narratives.

Dill's liminality and shape-shifting, rather like Dracula's, allow him to play any role: "he could get into any character part assigned him, and appear tall if height was part of the devilry required. He was as good as his worst performance; his worst performance was Gothic" (39). The Radley drama is a parody of gothic, much like *Other Voices, Other Rooms* ends up a camp parody of Gothic, as argued by Brian Mitchell-Peters. Just like Catherine of Austen's *Northanger Abbey,* however, Scout will discover in *Mockingbird* that evil does exist, silencing the parody. The Radley drama, with its campy Dill, is an instance of "the worst performance" becoming good because it is so dreadfully bad. Dill sounds a lot like the children's imaginations of Boo, who alters with each description. Lee is clearly poking fun at Capote's gothic writing, although she, too, deploys gothic in a parody and carnival form.

The Radley "play" is indeed play in the Bakhtinian sense of carnival and in the sense of Jean Baudrillard, that play indicates "endless play of simulation or parody . . . because each image is an imitation or exaggeration of some other image. There is no point of origin, no authentic beginning or authentic end point" (Sutton-Smith 146). With no authentic facts behind the legend, the staged Radley opera is an instance of farce performing for the street a subtext of Maycomb: there are no happily married couples or unconditionally loving families on the street, as discussed by Fine ("Structuring" 61). Richards observes that normative gender and heterosexuality are the exception rather than the norm in *Mockingbird;* that only the most unsympathetic characters police the children's gender; and that Scout and Jem are actually growing up "within a community whose instabilities of gender and sexuality mark it as, in the broadest sense, queer" (145). By perpetually performing the Radley farce that hides and victimizes a child, the children are camping the heritage that no one can name. The opera prepares us for the "carnival" trial as ritual enactment of the community's farce; it pretends to be one thing and is actually quite another. At one point of the trial, the community "camping out" for "the fun" of the spectacular play turns into the subject of black humor.

In a very poignant moment of emerging difference between Dill and Jem, which the Radley drama has rehearsed, the two disagree on the figure of the clown, which Dill has vowed to become in response to the "mock" trial:

> "I think I'll be a clown when I get grown," said Dill.
> Jem and I stopped in our tracks.

"Yes sir, a clown," he said. "There ain't one thing in this world I can do about folks except laugh, so I'm gonna join the circus and laugh my head off."

"You got it backwards, Dill," said Jem. "Clowns are sad, it's folks that laugh at them."

"Well I'm gonna be a new kind of clown. I'm gonna stand in the middle of the ring and laugh at the folks." (216)

In this scene, Dill is claiming an aesthetic mask is one's only choice, something he has already claimed by theorizing that maybe Boo is the symbol of "nowhere to go" and by meeting, through his tears, Dolphus Raymond (whom he immediately *outs* to Scout and Jem). The futility expressed here is just like Wharton's Madame Olenska's sense that there is nowhere for she and Newland to go. But here Dill is taking his aesthetic stance to a new level and explaining to us the very purpose of mocking art. He will become the mode of comic farce, a godlike figure that will laugh at, and point out to others, the human farce unfolding in front of him. Jem disagrees and feels he "got it backwards"—that recusing oneself from social life is tragic rather than a deliberate statement or choice. Jem has not understood the message of Mr. Raymond (he didn't drink the Coca-Cola)—that masks are parodies of *passing* rather than tragedies.

It is clear that the narrator affirms Dill's stance on the aesthetic function, which accords with the influence that Capote had on Lee's writing life and with the 1950s' equation of homosexuality with aesthetics and genius (Butt 56–57). I view the mockery implied in the laughing clown as an inspiration to Lee's own style of mocking the voices of Maycomb in the farce she writes. Dill's conclusion that all you can do is stand in the ring and laugh at folks resonates with Scout's conclusion, voiced to Jem, that there are not really differences between people—that there are "just folks." If we consider the structure of the novel, in which the spectacle of the Radley drama in the first half parallels the spectacle of racial melodrama in the second half, then we can consider the Radley opera as authorial practice for the humorous novel Scout/Lee ends up writing. The comic mask must be assumed because the world is simply intolerant. Dill, however, has revealed the function of art.

Capote's Drag Characters behind Lee's Clown

To remove oneself from "folks" and laugh at them from behind a mask is a meaningful image when we consider the man behind Dill, Truman Capote, who indeed inspired Lee to write and who brought his active and outrageous imagination to their childhood sport. In his essay "Truman Capote: Harper Lee's Fictional Portrait of the Artist as an Alabama Child," Going accepts Lee's portrait of young Capote as accurate in light of how few trustworthy accounts of his childhood exist. Dill's vow to be the clown is poignant to those familiar with Capote: "There are those who would say that Capote did join the circus of life. In his search to belong somewhere Capote seemed to seek throughout his career for a unique place among writers of fiction, among Broadway dramatists, among in-depth journalists, among party givers and jet setters" (Going, "Truman" 148). As distinct from Lee, Capote reveled in the limelight of difference: "His famous statement which appeared as a headline in the *Village Voice*, 'I'm an alcoholic. I'm a drug addict. I'm a homosexual. I'm a genius,' established his outsider credentials and contributed to the notoriety of his public persona" (Waldmeir 2). His symbolism-infused writings and his eccentric characters and landscapes, however, "midwifed the birth of the anti-hero into the fiction of the 1950s," argues Joseph Waldmeir (2), who discusses his congruence with Faulkner, Welty, McCullers, and O'Connor—but not Lee. Yet Capote's influence on Lee's youthful writing life is well known; the two would work together on an old typewriter perched in Lee's tree house as an office, a yard where there were apparently twin Chinaberry trees that seem related to the world created in *The Grass Harp*. If Capote's famously lonely characters who desire escape and who "simply climb defiantly into a tree, and wait" (Waldmier 2) took root in Lee's yard, then Lee is as much part of Capote's vision as Capote is the root of her aesthetic stance.

In her book *A Bridge of Childhood: Truman Capote's Southern Years*, Marianne Moates publishes reminiscences of Truman's cousin Jennings Faulk Carter, upon whom, she argues, Jem was based. Truman, Nelle (Harper Lee's nickname), and "Big Boy" (Jennings Faulk Carter) participated in Truman's elaborate games and activities, such as making up a freak show with animal displays, one of which was a two-headed chicken that they engineered. The freak show seems to have permeated Capote's consciousness as a vision of eccentricity and a possible environment to convey both homosexuality and drag; writing of the carnival scene that ends *Other Voices, Other*

Rooms, Mitchell-Peters identifies it as the camp that overturns the gothic trappings of the novel, which sheds light on possible ways to understand the two spectacles of *Mockingbird*—the Radley drama and "roman carnival" of the trial, both of which foreground grotesque features, disabilities, violence, and bodily impairments.

Capote seems to have understood his gifts as a writer early on, carrying around notebooks for observations from a very young age, which, along with his voice, likely distinguished him from normative masculine codes in the rural town. Capote has become something like the tragic aesthete in literary circles—Butt compares him to Wilde and shows how his friend Andy Warhol aspired to be him but paled in comparison (116)—a homosexual figure of enormous talent who went through various stages of writing and eventually pioneered, with Lee's help in research, the nonfiction novel *In Cold Blood.* With a thriving career at the time of Lee's writing of *Mockingbird,* he was an inspirational colleague as well as childhood friend to Lee—someone whose aesthetic style must have been in the forefront of her mind as both model and emblem of a writing stance on small-town life. He, too, featured eccentricity and drag as masks that characters wear for the world and even for themselves.

Capote's mother, Lillie Mae Faulk Persons, knew little about raising a child and apparently neglected him, locking him alone in hotel rooms while she would continue to go out: "In later years he remembered being abandoned there, desperately banging on the door to get out, all the while screaming at the top of his lungs" (Moates 27). She brought him to live with relatives and remarried Joseph Capote, but Truman never really grew close to him. It is this remarriage that Dill apparently alludes to in *Mockingbird.* Moates notes that "'Home' to [Truman] was the comfortable Carter farmhouse on Drewry Road, about two miles from Monroeville" (7), which he reflected on in several of his short stories, such as "A Christmas Memory," "The Thanksgiving Visitor," and "Guests." There he lived with his aunt Mary Ida Carter, with whom he was very close. He moved to Monroeville at the age of four in 1928, and Monroeville became the fictional Noon City of his first novel, *Other Voices, Other Rooms.* The difference is that whereas Lee depicts Monroeville as a "tired old town" with a sagging courthouse and a stagnant economy—"nowhere to go, nothing to buy and no money to buy it with" (5), Capote's boy protagonist is the outsider who finds no way *in:* "Now a traveler must make his way to Noon City by the best means he can, for there are no buses or trains heading in that direction . . . It's a rough trip no matter how you come . . . this is lonesome country" (3).

The relatives in and around Monroeville, "the rural atmosphere, and isolation left indelible marks on Truman" (Moates 19); Monroeville became the setting for both *Other Voices, Other Rooms* and *The Grass Harp*. Both explore drag through perspective on characters that were clearly inspired by relatives, such as Jenny Faulk, a spinster who had earned her money from a millinery shop and inheritance; she became Verena of *The Grass Harp*. There are numerous references to the inverted nature of Verena, who, in the course of the story, tries to commercially exploit the herbal medicines of her sister Dolly. Dolly, with whom the narrator says he fell in love, was based on Jenny's eldest sister, Sook, "a childlike woman who probably suffered from agoraphobia" (Moates 28) and who did indeed have secret recipes for herbal medicines. Truman's closeness to Sook was nostalgically expressed in "A Christmas Memory," and Moates relays that the rejection of these relatives (particularly Sook) because of his homosexuality must have been more than hurtful. The only adult male in Capote's Monroeville household, Bud, who was fifty-nine, smoked medicinal cigarettes and appears as Cousin Randolph in *Other Voices, Other Rooms*. This novel, which features the quest of a young boy for his father, also features a phantom lady that the young protagonist keeps glimpsing in his father's house; the mysterious lady that he glimpses at windows preoccupies him, just as the phantom presence of Boo preoccupies Dill. This lady turns out to be Cousin Randolph as a transvestite, giving us meaningful background on why Lee might have made the Radley story the central focus of Dill in *Mockingbird*.

In case the meaning of Boo for Dill is in doubt, we can clarify it by comparing the phantom haunting Joel's father's house. Joel keeps glimpsing a strange lady from outside the house—someone who should not be there yet who seems to belong. He longs to know about her. She is, in fact, a transvestite, and she is teaching him about himself. Whereas Joel senses the beauty of the hidden lady inside his house (67), Idabel bears all the ugliness of the invert. The masculine Idabel is all he abjects, while the queer lady is his unconscious before full awakening. She lives just beyond the veil of his more cultural consciousness:

Rising, he glanced up at the yellow wall of the house, and speculated as to which of the top-floor windows belonged to him, his father, Cousin Randolph. It was at this point that he saw the queer lady. She was holding aside the curtains of the left corner window, and smiling and nodding at him, as if in greeting or approval; but she was no one Joel had ever known: the hazy substance of her face, the suffused marshmallow features, brought to mind his own vaporish reflection in the wavy chamber mirror. And her white hair was like the wig of a character from history: a towering pale pompadour with fat dribbling curls. Whoever she was, and Joel could not imagine, her sudden appearance seemed to throw a trance across the garden: a butterfly, poised on a dahlia stem, ceased winking its wings, and the rasping F of the bumblebees droned into nothing. (67)

The queer lady takes the express role of Boo Radley in *Mockingbird*; she is the phantom within, a hazy reflection of the young boy who intuits his metamorphosis. The passage has a very similar feel to the mad dog scene when even the mockingbirds were still, as if waiting judgment of nature, and we must remember that the dog pauses before the Radley gate as if an almost-moment of either penetration or recognition. With this reading, Atticus's straight shot has a meaning not of social justice but of preventing gay exposure. In comparison with Capote's representation of a vicious rape of Zoo, Joel's African American caretaker and friend, who tries to escape and finds "nowhere to go" quite violently, the vision of the queer lady beckoning Joel across the curtain of consciousness takes on innocence and imagery of nature, even while suggesting the aesthete, in Capote's insistent equation of effeminacy and homosexuality (Richards 31).

The general environment of decay in Capote's novel, manifest in the decayed hotel, the decayed portion of what used to be a grand house, the decay of the father's body, and the decay of Randolph as he pines for his lost love Pepe, links gender inversion with the undead in a way Case would recognize. But the lady embodies the splendor and beauty of the drag queen—the gay embrace of the hyperfeminine icon. Capote's lady is not one of the society ladies sketched by Lee in *Mockingbird*, the lady world in which Scout must learn to "pass." This is because she is not a means for passing per se, but a means for escape and integration of the homosexual self. Idabel will not see her, just as Dill will not see Boo. Critics agree that Joel accepts his homosexuality at the end; he comfortably answers the lady's summons at the end and views his old child self from the outside. This resolution is definitely not allowed in *Mockingbird,* which returns Capote to a younger preadolescent age and points to a quandary in regard to the queer child:

> This queer child, whatever its conscious grasp of itself, cannot unfold itself according to the category of "the homosexual"—a category culturally deemed too adult, since it is sexual. And yet to refuse a child this designation actually reveals our culture's contradictions over childhood sexual orientation: the tendency to treat all children as straight while we culturally consider them asexual. The effect for the child who already feels queer (different, odd, out-of-sync, and attracted to same-sex peers) is an asynchronicity. (Stockton 283)

Similarly, as Sedgwick writes in her article "How to Bring Your Kids up Gay," healthy homosexuals are viewed as adults, and there is simply no support for effeminate boys. As Mark Simpson observes in his foreword to Tim Bergling's *Sissyphobia: Gay Men and Effeminate Behavior,* even "modern gay culture is actually built upon the disavowal of sissiness" (xi). In *Other Voices, Other Rooms,* Capote has written for himself such support. He certainly did not find support for his homosexuality from his mother, who, in her efforts to reform him, sent him to military school, where he became sexual prey (Clarke 45). The phantom lady of Capote's *Other Voices* explains the wondrous attraction of Dill for Boo as a desire to glimpse inner truth; the tales about Boo as menace—the fear of him—primarily reside in Scout and Jem, not Dill, who is entranced by the idea of him, just as the butterflies and bumblebees stop in their flights for the phantom lady. And if butterflies and bumblebees, who enjoy flights of fancy, do not describe Dill, I do not know what does.

The parallels between *Other Voices* and *Mockingbird* are revealing. In Capote's novel Joel Knox enters Noon City in the same way that Dill enters Scout's world. Joel gives his name in full, "Jo-el Harr-ri-son Knox," with careful, clear articulation and an "uncommonly soft" (5) voice, similarly to Dill's announcement of his weighty name, "Charles Baker Harris," along with the pronouncement of his literary skills. In *Other Voices,* it is an adult who defends Joel's feminine appearance by calling attention to his dexterity with language; he uses "'words you and me never heard of,'" says Sydney Katz to Radclif, when he wishes Radclif to drive Joel to Skully's Landing, where Joel believes his father expects him. The eager search to meet his father and "be loved" results in a Hawthorne-styled gothic easily recognizable as Capote's own sense of being abandoned, which also, Moates argues, drew Capote to Amasa Lee (37). Moates argues that Capote's "writings and interviews reflect an eternal quest for his parents' love and acceptance. He became the Joel Knox of *Other Voices, Other Rooms*, "'crazy with the questions he wanted answered,' as he searched for his father" (33). Joel's search for his father leads only to the increasing exposure of the "queer lady" within.

Joel's actual father falls into the "grotesque aspects" of southern fiction famously discussed and contributed to by O'Connor. He is paralyzed and speechless, thus a symbol of impotence and gothic decay, imagery of declining southern patriarchy evident in literature as early as Edgar Allen Poe's "Fall of the House of Usher." The ineffectual father contrasts a vibrant, colorful though tragic cousin in drag. Randolph moves "in a queer way" (119) and often wears a kimono and nail polish; he is the "strange lady" Joel keeps glimpsing in the house. The phantom lady within the house seems to keep him from his father, as if the boy's missing masculinity means he does not deserve a father, or perhaps that he will never be a father; either he will never resolve an Oedipal complex or he does not even get one. Joel's girlishness is explained very early in the novel:

> Radclif eyed the boy over the rim of his beer glass, not caring much for the looks of him. He had his notions of what a "real" boy should look like, and this kid somehow offended them. He was too pretty, too delicate and fair-skinned; each of his features was shaped with a sensitive accuracy, and a girlish tenderness softened his eyes, which were brown and very large. His brown hair, cut short, was streaked with pure yellow strands. A kind of tired, imploring expression masked his thin face, and there was an unyouthful sag about his shoulders. He wore long, wrinkled white linen breeches, a limp blue shirt, the collar of which was open at the throat, and rather scuffed tan shoes. (4–5)

The view here is external, but the tone is confessional. The trope of the young Capote seeking acceptance and even blessing by the patriarch emerges in *Mockingbird*, in a crucial confessional scene between Dill and Scout. But whereas Capote's scene features Idabel's violent sexual initiation of Joel, sort of like Scout's efforts to beat up Dill for love, Lee's nighttime confession scene of Dill's, as he comes out to Scout, is a profound rewriting of Capote's scene.

Before we deconstruct Lee's scene of Dill's nighttime confession to Scout, reflecting how much the abandoned gay child lies at the very core of *Mockingbird*, we need to discuss how Lee appears in Capote's *Other Voices* as well, as Idabel. Joel initially detests her for her tomboyishness, but subsequently they become inseparable. In an important scene in which they bathe in the river naked and even kiss, but afterward fight for a reason unknown to them, it becomes clear that Capote, too, viewed Lee as the complementary "invert" to himself, but his mood about their complementary wholeness differs.

Tellingly, Idabel in Capote's novel is not a vehicle for Joel's confession, as Scout is for Dill in Lee's *Mockingbird*, because she herself has something to hide. Critics, such as Pugh and Mitchell-Peters, feel Idabel accepts her homosexuality even before Joel, but I cannot agree. I feel that Capote sacrifices Idabel, just as Lee sacrifices Dill in the end. It is Idabel and not Joel with the secret, largely because Joel's transvestite side is now embodied in a parent figure. Idabel's early ferocity veils her longing for women, which emerges most when she falls for Miss Wisteria. But Miss Wisteria is not a positive resolution, just as Boo is not a positive ending for Dill. Both Miss Wisteria and Boo are vulnerable, afraid, longing, and firmly kept in their places. Early in the novel, a female proprietor describes Idabel as a freak because she does not wear dresses (21); more important, she is mean, like Verena of *The Grass Harp* is mean to Dolly. Joel's introduction to her is from a one-armed barber, suggesting his victimization and Idabel's incompleteness, at whom she is throwing rocks, "thumbing her nose at the barber and twisting her face into evil shapes" (20). She initially repels Joel. Her unattractive masculinity is all the more pronounced in contrast to her twin sister, Florabel, the ultra-feminine of the pair. Joel dislikes tomboys because one used to pick on him at his prior residence in New Orleans, stripping off his pants and hanging them from a tree. The tomboy causes in him feelings of shame and exposure rather than wholeness, initially. Really, it is Ida who must "come out" to Joel, whereas it is the other way around in *Mockingbird*.

Homosexuality as a particular spectacle is conveyed in *Other Voices* by recurrent imagery and various characters. For example, Joel has seen in New Orleans "two grown men standing in an ugly little room kissing each other" (65), much like McCullers's Frankie sees the glimpse of it in an alley she passes. Joel's memory of another strange vision—a naked woman dancing alone—does not contain the word "ugly." *Other Voices* seeks to transform the ugliness of homosexuality to an aesthetic, even "magisterial beauty"— the words used to describe Miss Maudie after her bath, which explicitly do not say "feminine" beauty. *Other Voices* makes the transformation occur through the surrealism of the circus sequence and the dizzying stream-of-consciousness Ferris wheel, which both Joel and Idabel ride at different times with the midget woman Miss Wisteria. Sexual identity is fluid and even bi- for the children, although not for the tragic Miss Wisteria, who weeps because "little boys must grow tall."

I wish to compare the two confessional scenes of Lee and Capote because each reflects on the other. Both occur in the very center of the two novels, and both serve as spiritual and physical moments of complete connection between the two young inverts. But whereas Lee's ends in Dill's fantasy of producing a baby, Capote's ends in the shattering of Idabel's glasses, won at the traveling circus, and the bleeding of Joel's buttocks—a loss of his virginity. Lee's confession scene is actually speaking back to the violence of Capote's initiation scene, in which it is Idabel who confesses her desire to be a boy. Dill confesses his fear that he is not a real boy. And while to Lee it is primarily Dill's obsession to make "the phantom" Boo emerge, to Capote it is Idabel who falls in love with a circus freak, a midget woman whose perfect, feminine appearance in miniature suggests Idabel's inner vulnerability, stagnation, and wounding. It suggests undevelopment rather than the beauty that Joel sees in the Diva, although it is evident they are both competing for the miniature Miss Wisteria in an odd way.

Just like the nighttime scene that occurs between Scout and Dill in *Mockingbird* after Dill runs away, Capote's river scene features the trope of wholeness between the twins of boyish girl and girlish boy. For a brief moment, unity seems imminent. But it does not last, and in Capote's novel the scene embodies *her* confession followed by *his* transgression. Idabel suggests that they bathe naked, and he hesitates because she is female. She immediately convinces him that she is exempt: "'Son,' she said, and spit between her fingers, 'what you've got in your britches is no news to me, and no concern of mine: hell, I've fooled around with nobody but boys since first grade. I never think like I'm a girl; you've got to remember that, or we can't never be friends. ... I want so much to be a boy: I would be a sailor, I would ... '" (132). Naked, she is even "more boyish" (133), and she surprises him with being "funny and gay" while she washes his hair. Significantly echoing Lee's scene in which Dill proposes that Dill and Scout have a baby, although it is clear they do not know how that occurs, Idabel tells a crude sexual joke but neither character understands it. Thus they are poised on the threshold of knowledge, but not yet over it (about her hips "a mild suggestion of approaching width" [133]). The sentimental Joel (as read by Pugh) kisses Idabel because, I believe, he has more than accepted her identity as a boy. This, however, contradicts her desire and she fights him. In the process, Idabel's special "dark glasses" from the traveling show, which are green lenses that color perspective and thus allude to L. Frank Baum's *The Wonderful Wizard of Oz,* break, "and Joel, falling back, felt them crush beneath and cut his buttocks. 'Stop,' he panted, 'please stop, I'm bleeding'" (135). He has to repeat the plea for her to stop attacking him.

We would expect the breaking of the glasses to signify a breakthrough in seeing true selves. The scene is a thinly veiled initiation into gay sexuality and *his* femininity; his transgression for initiating desire has been punished, but although her "glasses" have come off, it is not at all clear that she has actually been illuminated. Rather, she casually says the broken glasses were not his fault and that she can win another pair. In other words, she can cover her own vulnerability and truth perpetually, while he never will be the same virginal boy again. The ease with which Idabel says she can replace her glasses suggests, as in *Mockingbird,* that the tomboy can more easily pass than the effeminate boy. She believes she can see things as she wishes, just like the people of Baum's Emerald City. At the beginning of the chapter is a clue to its meaning. Zoo (Missouri) tells Joel about the old lady she cared for just before death; the old lady quickly grew a beard each day. The bearded lady is informing us that people in drag who do not realize they are in drag are empty and dying, like Miss Amy herself. The only healthy state is to unveil the lady within and accept her beckoning, even if it means bleeding buttocks for Joel. Capote's perspective on Lee, at least as revealed in the "touching" "futility" (132) of Idabel's desire to be a boy rather than accepting being gay, fuels his sense that her unfulfilled and unfulfillable love will end with Miss Wisteria, a symbol of stunted growth with whom Idabel is "in love" (193). Miss Wisteria is the one who earns the novel title; she is left wandering around looking for "other rooms."

A crucial scene of Dill's defilement occurs in the core of *Mockingbird*, not coincidentally at the very moment that Scout feels abandoned by her father because Aunt Alexandra is living with them, the trial has taken over their lives, and Atticus is acting as ambassador to Aunt Alexandra. The context of the scene in which Dill runs away, appears under Scout's bed, and movingly confesses to Scout his parents' distaste for his girlishness is crucial. The issue at hand is the proper mother for Scout. Aunt Alexandra has debated with Atticus about keeping Cal, and Atticus has defended Cal as a tough and therefore excellent caregiver. Jem and Scout have been fighting because Scout believes Jem has transgressed child boundaries by threatening to spank her; the scene will demonstrate Jem's movement into patriarchy when he subsequently breaks the "remaining code of childhood" by reporting to Atticus Dill's presence. In the middle of the chapter, however, we hear Dill's voice in the night, a voice of the dark that mirrors the dusky aspect of Tom Robinson's voice in the jail and Boo's laugh in the hidden recesses of his house. Clearly a secret is emerging.

The secret is Dill's pain at being rejected by parents; but in a deeper way, through symbolism, the scene communicates the abjection of culture's equation between homosexuality and waste. Disturbingly, Atticus reifies the idea that the gay is defiled, telling Dill to put the country (the dirt) back where it belongs because soil erosion is bad enough. While the line could signify acceptance, given his insistence on Boo's privacy and choice, he is telling Dill to hide the dirt. Dill in this scene has also been betrayed by Jem, and he is pushed back to Scout because of it.

Initially, Scout believes there is a snake under her bed, which is a traditional symbol for something seducing, and which Idabel slays in Capote's novel, but rather than a phallic snake, it is "a filthy brown package shot from under the bed" (139). The description calls to mind human waste and anal imagery, echoing the packages emanating from the Radley "knot-hole." This is a demented coming-out scene in the form of monstrous birth; the usually overly clean and well-dressed Dill is here filthy. Jem becomes the divine witness to this abject birth, petitioning God twice, which will culminate in his summons of Atticus as the God figure who may or may not give Dill a blessing for being different:

> Suddenly a filthy brown package shot from under the bed. . . . "God Almighty." Jem's voice was reverent.
> We watched Dill emerge by degrees. He was a tight fit. He stood up and eased his shoulders, turned his feet in their ankle sockets, rubbed the back of his neck. His circulation restored, he said, "Hey."
> Jem petitioned God again. I was speechless. (139–40)

This is a birth and coming-out scene, which is dangerous and stuns Scout into silence and the dreamlike state ("in a dream") that often results from her witnessing abject actions. As the "reverent" and thereby orthodox male, Jem summons Atticus to specify what this coming out means. The exile or acceptance of this filth has yet to be determined. The meaning of this desire for Atticus's blessing becomes clear when Dill later whispers to Scout in the night that his mother and her new husband reject him because he is not like other boys: "Dill tried to deepen his voice. 'You're not a boy'" (143), he says, mocking the voices used against him, just as Scout's mocks words like "Absolute Morphodite," which imply a social judgment.

The difference between Scout and Dill emerge in this crucial scene, for we know that Atticus "doesn't mind *much* the way Scout was," whereas Dill is not accepted for the curiosity he is. Dill's rich imagination seems compensation for "not belonging," rather like Anne of *Anne of Green Gables* compensates for her state of orphanhood by spinning stories, or perhaps the way the motherless Tom Sawyer compensates by emulating romantic literature. Dill's attraction to Scout and Jem's house implies, like the passage above, that he seeks the blessing of divine patriarch and the missing masculinity within, just as, conversely, Scout seeks information about "being a girl" where she can extract it—from Miss Maudie, from Cal, from Mayella Ewell.

The passage in which Dill shares his innermost pain at being rejected by his parents occurs in the context of a larger conversation about childrearing practices. In fact, the conversation between Scout and Dill mimics the conversation between Aunt Alexandra and Atticus about the "right" way to parent—to rule with formidable interference (Aunt Alexandra) or detached, contemplative, Socratic "Do you really think so?" (Atticus). The two embody very different teaching methods—one lectures, as exemplified when Aunt Alexandra gets Atticus, "but a man," to lecture the children on family, and the other democratically offers questions, clarifications, and meditations. As Scout and Dill express their feelings about being children, Scout embraces independence, telling Dill that he really does not wish too much attention, which would lessen independence. She thus reifies the position taken in the beginning of the novel when she says Atticus's detachment is courteous and satisfactory. She tells Dill, "'Atticus's gone all day and sometimes half the night and off in the legislature and I don't know what—you don't want 'em around all the time, Dill, you couldn't do anything if they were'" (143). Scout values a patriarchal and public style of independence, whereas Dill, who has more material things, values connection. His parents expect him to do his own thing, but he, instead, "worries" them:

> As Dill explained, I found myself wondering what life would be if Jem were different . . . what I would do if Atticus did not feel the necessity of my presence, help and advice. . . . "Dill, you ain't telling me right—your folks couldn't do without you. They must be just mean to you. Tell you what to do about that—"
>
> Dill's voice went on steadily in the darkness. "The thing is . . . they *do* get on a lot better without me . . . They ain't mean. They buy me everything . . . but it's now-you've-got-it-go-play-with-it." . . . Dill tried to deepen his voice. "You're not a boy. Boys get out and play baseball with other boys, they don't hang around the house worryin' their folks."
>
> Dill's voice was his own again: "Oh, they ain't mean. They kiss you and hug you good night . . . and tell you they love you—Scout, let's get us a baby."
> (143)

Scout wonders how it would be if "Jem were different" because here she is faced with the plea of difference. The difficulty of "not being a boy" is that others' revulsion is deep beneath the surface—so very closeted. He intuits his parents' revulsion, but it is largely unseen. His parents are not mean, and they give him everything, but he knows his queerness stands in the way of real connection. Rather than really listening at all, Scout deploys a more masculine strategy of counsel—telling him how to take action and assuming, though the older narrator is mocking the young Scout in the scene, that she is the center of Atticus's universe and Dill must be wrong.

It is clear that Dill is part of a nonrepresented group when Jem pleads to Atticus on his behalf (144), followed by Atticus pleading "on the part of the defendant" to Miss Rachel, just as Scout offers to Walter mock-legal counsel when in school. In *Mockingbird* it is always the duty of the more powerful to represent the less powerful. This confession of Dill's is placed pivotally on the fringe of the novel's descent into "nightmare" (144), as the external world is impinging more and more on Scout's everyday life with Atticus and Jem. The changes are just as internal as they are external. The significance of Dill's confession, voiced at precisely the moment the trial exerts pressure on Scout, suggests that the disabled male body (Tom) and the inordinately aggressive female body (Mayella) are as much on trial as black and white.

This inevitably queer artifact of Lee's desire to overturn sexual panic about potent black men responds to what Somerville has uncovered in the historical intersection of interracial and same-sex desire. He cites a 1913 article by Margaret Otis titled "A Perversion Not Commonly Noted," in which she analyzes "love making between white and colored girls" at an all-girls school (qtd. in Somerville 34). Somerville demonstrates how Otis is tangled in a simple analogy that "black was to white as masculine to feminine" (35) when she cites how a white girl in such a relationship describes the colored girl as the man. The tendency to model same-sex on cross-gendered pairings shows how dominant ideologies pervasively inform people's thinking about the unexpected. Marking something similar in Capote's *Other Voices, Other Rooms,* Richards discusses Randolph's fetishizing of the racial other; not only does he lust for Pepe's "Indian skin" and flat eyes, but he also reveals his attraction to African American men when he describes Zoo's lover Keg as a "strapping young buck, splendidly proportioned, and with skin the color of swamp honey" (qtd. in Richards 34). In *Mockingbird,* Scout's imaginative identification with Mayella (she imagines her life, her loneliness) is definitely stronger than her identification with Tom, whose body she admires with an objectifying gaze, whereas Dill's identification with Tom is so strong that it sickens him to see Tom's mistreatment. At the end of chapter 1, I offered multiple possibilities of the trial as spectacle for Scout's awakening ideas about sexuality; the strongest identification, however, is Scout's identification with Mayella's aggressive desire for the "velvet" black body (to me, a female metaphor that evokes plush, sensory rarity, as famously desired by Morrison's Amy Denver in *Beloved*). In contrast, Dill's identification with Tom bespeaks his identification with the ravished body, doubly ravished by Mayella and by the prosecutor. It is significant that the narrator says in the beginning of *Mockingbird* that Dill "had seen" (7) *Dracula*. Because Dill replicates the posture of Renfield toward Boo, and "the result of [Dracula mesmerizing and biting Renfield's throat] is every gay man's nightmare of being seduced by the trick from hell" (Mann 64), Dill fears victimization.

Astonishingly, the feminization and ravishing of Tom reveal his innocence, and the feminization of Atticus reveals his universal love. But Dill's voice about the subtlety of rejecting gay people implies quite another message. The abrupt shift to "'let's get us a baby'" is an expression of desire for a natural birth and an opportunity to have a second birth without shame. But all Dill really can do is mock masculinity with his voice; he deepens his voice to say "'You're not like other boys,'" and his voice only becomes his own again when he turns away from the painful subject. The desire to "get" a baby rather than birth his "improper body" is a painful wish, but at least Scout emerges as someone to whom he could come out. This seems to be why she, and only she, sees Boo and Boo's children in the end. She, like Whitman's narrator, is the witness.

Dill and Scout's discussion of unifying to make a baby is meaningful because of their potential wholeness and balance together, but it is also parody of adult sexuality because, quite fortuitously, the two children lack knowledge about heterosexuality and reproduction. Scout wants to know where to get a baby, interested more in the pragmatics than the concept. Interestingly, in hypothesizing about getting a baby, Dill voices the myth informing Peter Pan, the myth of Solomon articulated in *Peter Pan in Kensington Gardens*, where Peter works for Solomon on the island, helping select souls for women who wish for babies. Dill seems to identify with the fairy leader, who takes responsibility for lost children: "There was a man Dill had heard of who had a boat that he rowed across to a foggy island where all these babies were; you could order one—" (143–44). Dill's fantasy depends on exclusively male reproduction, which is also a dominant theme in queer couples of horror films like *Island of Lost Souls* (1933). However, Dill's fantasy is also consumer oriented, which Rachel Adams has explored in McCullers's likely homosexual character Sherman, who compensates for a freakish body by buying things that only exaggerate his unusual body (569–70). When Scout admits really false knowledge of how babies are made, Dill answers with some truth—"'you get babies from each other. But there's this man, too—he has all these babies just waitin' to wake up, he breathes life into 'em...,'" which suggests his reluctance to give up the myth of maleness as complete and divine, encompassing nurturance and reproduction. The myth is also one of community and potential; there are a whole lot of babies waiting for the breath of life, and they are hardly discriminated against yet.

Paradoxically and persistently reaching out for community even while he prefers fantasy to the real world, Dill is intrinsically linked to the reclusive Boo, who intermittently reaches out to the children with his own artistic gifts. But unlike the drag queen Cousin Randolph, whom Capote authors to exorcise demons and who summons Joel to the south, Boo embodies the protective closet of exile that Lee feels necessary for protection from a violent town. Lee has Dill float off like the artistic Pan to Neverland. Exile is always double-edged as tragic lonesomeness, like Capote's Noon City, and a chosen freedom from conformity. Scout is quite clear in her view of Dill as a dreamer, a writer, and a twilight luminary:

> Dill was off again. Beautiful things floated around in his dreamy head.
> ... He could read two books to my one, but he preferred the magic of his own
> inventions. He could add and subtract faster than lightning, but he preferred
> his own twilight world, a world where babies slept, waiting to be gathered
> like morning lilies. ... but in the quietness of his foggy island there rose the
> faded image of a gray house with sad brown doors. ... "Why do you reckon
> Boo Radley's never run off?"
> Dill sighed a long sigh and turned away from me.
> "Maybe he doesn't have anywhere to run off to ... " (144)

The reality of Dill's homosexuality, its circulating projection onto Boo Radley, and the aesthetic stance that the exiled gay dreamer embodies are all linked here, meaningfully encapsulated by "the gray house" prefiguring the gray ghost or "ghostly 'gay' child" of which Stockton writes. Jem explicitly equates femininity and imagination: "Jem told me I was being a girl, that girls always imagined things, that's why other people hated them so" (41). A chain of associations in *Mockingbird* thus equates feminine with monstrous imagination, as if Dill's *embrace* of Dracula sheds some light on Lee's portrait of the artist in herself as a young girl.

While Lee offers this poignant moment of meditating about difference that cannot even be brought to trial, Capote refuses even the opportunity of connection. When Idabel and Joel decide to run away together, an old rickety house falls on them and thus punishes them for their brief belief in freedom. It is evident that their freedom would mean the collapse of the South. The house that falls, like Lee's rape trial, bears a legend of violent rape and murder, the violence implied by either self-masking to "pass" or repressing desires. In both novels, heterosexuality seems to mean rape, and normative masculinity seems to mean crippled.

Capote's second novel about small-town Monroeville, *The Grass Harp,* is a likely intertext to the relationship between Dill and Jem in *Mockingbird.* In it, Capote turns a comic rather than gothic-camp lens on issues of drag, exile, and wounds that will not heal. Just like it is Lee's masculine boy Jem who is wounded by the experience the novel represents, it is Riley, the manly boy whom the effeminate Collin admires, who ends up wounded in the arm. The boy-focalizer named Collin longs for, admires, and wishes to be the boy two years his senior—Riley, gun-shooting, fishing, hunting, disciplinarian, tough boy:

> He said, "You build [the tree house], Collin?" and it was with a happy shock that I realized he'd called my name: I hadn't thought Riley Henderson knew me from dust. But I knew him, all right.
>
> No one in our town ever had themselves so much talked about as Riley Henderson. Older people spoke of him with sighing voices, and those nearer his own age, like myself, were glad to call him mean and hard: that was because he would only let us envy him, would not let us love him, be his friend. . . . How I longed for him to be my friend! And it seemed possible, he was just two years older. But I could remember the only time he ever spoke to me. (26–27)

The masculinity of Riley draws Collin, even though Collin will supposedly turn from him when Riley begins dating. Importantly, the masculinity of Riley makes him an object of longing for "older people," as if he provides a vision a prior generation would admire. Capote's idealization of masculine prowess prefigures the body ideal that later gay culture would similarly admire: "Gay liberation in the 1970s was about the masculinization of the faggot body, so that gay men could find one another—and themselves—desirable" (Simpson xi). The relationship that unfolds between Riley and Collin *only* when living in the tree house, a relationship that includes nakedness and tenderness, is very similar to Dill's thirst for the admired Jem, also just a few years older and also a figure of wounding upon normative development. It is symbolic that Riley's wound is also the result of falling from the tree house, conceived as a temporary place of freedom against the town, a raft in the sky reminiscent of Huck's raft. It is at the point that Riley begins dating that Collin fixes his gaze on Riley's "limp hands" (80), once strong enough to catch fish without tools. Like Dill, Collin is an artist figure who is inspired by Dolly's romantic definition of the grass as a harp that sings stories of the past, a theme that gestures to Cather's *My Ántonia;* like Dill, Collin sees his status as wanderer and outsider, linking his artistic distance to the fact that he never really belonged; he was always spying on this world from the attic, unwanted (81).

Capote therefore foregrounds in *The Grass Harp* love of one adolescent boy for a slightly older and more masculine one, linking the relationship to a Whitmanesque romance; in contrast, the character in *The Grass Harp* who has few redeeming qualities is Verena, the man-woman perpetually grieving for her lost love, Maudie, like the transvestite Randolph in *Other Voices* is grieving his lost love. The appearance of Miss Maudie in *Mockingbird* seems more than a coincidence, given that Verena's lost Maudie left Verena to get married. We learn about Verena as an inverted individual right away in the novel: "she was too like a lone man in a house full of women and children, and the only way she could make contact with us was through assertive outbursts" (15). She mourns for "a blonde jolly girl called Maudie Lara Murphy" (12), and "one of the stories [Papa] spread, that Verena was a morphodyte, has never stopped going around" (10). Her status as unconnected is only heightened when she forges an alliance with a Jewish man who wishes to, with her help, exploit Dolly's medicinal recipes. In Capote's fiction, the man-woman has little appeal, whereas adolescent boys are a thing of beauty and a joy forever, contextualizing the persistent theme of Scout's exclusion from Jem and Dill in *Mockingbird.*

But if love between adolescent boys has a romantic beauty and communicates longing for what might have been, the character who ends up being the most in exile and the most tragic is Verena, the man-woman. The relationship between Dolly and Verena is represented as a marriage, with Verena in the role of neglectful husband, like Scout and Idabel in roles of inverted "wife" beater; African American character Catherine expresses the outrage Dolly should feel after they have left the house to live in the tree house. Dolly, the feminine character who is romanticized and fought over by everyone, would never assert herself. Catherine functions as all Dolly has repressed, especially since no one else can understand Catherine's speech:

> But, as Dolly pointed out, the house belonged to Verena, and was therefore not ours to haul away. Catherine answered: "You wrong, sugar. If you feed a man, and wash his clothes, and born his children, you and that man are married, that man is yours. If you sweep a house, and tend its fires and fill its stove, and there is love in you all the years you are doing this, then you and that house are married, that house is yours. The way I see it, both those houses up there belong to us: in the eyes of God, we could put That One right out." (30)

Dolly comes to inhabit a power struggle between Judge Cool, who wishes to marry her, and her sister Verena, who needs her "wife" or she will have nothing left. Indeed, she is left with nothing financially, as Dr. Morris takes all her money. Not only is Capote harsh about marriage between two women, but he also seems to symbolically show that any relationship modeled on traditional sex roles (Verena man, Dolly woman) is destined to exploit.

Like the blinded Rochester of *Jane Eyre,* Verena must be shamed before she can become sympathetic. Capote's view of the man-woman simply isn't pretty. It is she who is like Miss Wisteria, condemned to exile in her search for "other rooms"—in this case, Dolly's pink room:

> Successive strokes of lightning throbbed like veins of fire, and Verena, illuminated in that sustained glare, was not anyone I knew; but some woman woebegone, wasted—with eyes once more drawn toward each other, their

stare settled on an inner territory, a withered country; as the lightning lessened, as the hum of rain sealed us in its multiple sounds, she spoke, and her
voice came so weakly from so very far, not expecting, it seemed, to be heard
at all. "Envied you, Dolly. Your pink room. I've only knocked at the doors of
such rooms, but not often—enough to know that now there is no one but you
to let me in. Because little Morris, little Morris—help me, I loved him, I did.
Not in a womanly way; it was, oh I admit it, that we were kindred spirits.
We looked each other in the eye, we saw the same devil, we weren't afraid;
it was—merry. But he outsmarted me; I'd known he could, and hoped he
wouldn't, and he did, and now: it's too long to be alone, a lifetime. I walk
through the house, nothing is mine: your pink room, your kitchen, the house
is yours, and Catherine's too, I think. Only don't leave me, let me live with
you. I'm feeling old, I want my sister." (84)

The fall of Verena is uncannily similar to the fall of Amelia in McCullers's
Ballad of the Safe Café; she inhabits empty rooms after the hunchback leaves
her. While the tomboy child figure Idabel is initially unsympathetic but re-
deemable, the manly woman in Capote's work longs for the pink room and has
no place except in exile, like the stereotype deployed by Capote in the wandering Jew whom Verena recognizes as a kindred spirit. Collin bids farewell
to the town and moves on to bigger and better things, but after Dolly's death,
Verena has nothing left. The final glimpse of her is her thought of travel in
response to a postcard from Morris asking, tellingly, "do you miss me?" (97),
which suggests the internal, greedy masculinity that once sustained her even
if it prevented real connection with others. With this masculine component
now shamed and missing, her eyes are left with "an uneven cast, an inward
and agonized gaze" (97), which is then antithetical to the eye of the writer
that Collin has developed from his role as feminine outsider, fueled by his
connection with and overwhelming appreciation for Dolly. Therefore, while
Lee writes Dill into the role of muse, Capote's muses were the most feminine
characters—Dolly (based on Sook) and the drag queen Randolph, later Holly
Golightly, a master of feminine illusion who is seemingly based on Capote's
mother.

In my view, Capote's portraits of female inverts denote the monstrous
because they are associated with mercantilism, commercialism, marketplace aggression, and everything unromantic. The detail that Idabel can buy

another pair of green glasses is actually crucial, just like the fact of Miss Wisteria's ability to exploit herself for the show (whereas Joel's father's house is falling apart). In *The Grass Harp* it is Verena and not Dolly who obtains the town's support; the townspeople object to Dolly leaving "that good woman" Verena. The social world is always limited in these novels, and so they see things with green glasses, too—the color of money and success. They cannot see through the mask, whereas Collin can; and what he sees is truly disturbing, despite the comic context of the novel. Verena's shipwrecked old age is very similar to McCullers's queer characters who experience tragic loss, not only Miss Amelia of *Ballad of the Sad Café,* but also Singer of *The Heart Is a Lonely Hunter,* Frankie of *Member of the Wedding,* Captain Penderton of *Reflections in a Golden Eye,* and Jester of *Clock without Hands.*

To these and Capote's fictions of southern inverts, Lee and her novel speak in return. Lee reclaims the man-woman in Miss Maudie and her narrator, depicts an uneasy negotiation between Jem and Dill for Boo, and telegraphs her sympathetic yet realistic view of Dill's condemnation to other voices, other rooms, because he simply will not pass in Maycomb society. The two writers had different relationships to the south. Yet another literary intertext explains how Lee softens the exile of the effeminate boy. Lee's *Mockingbird* embeds the veiled drag of McCullers's Frankie in *Member of the Wedding,* in which effeminate six-year-old John Henry—likely based on Capote, whom McCullers was promoting at the time (V. Carr 261)—meets a brutal and freakish end.

Dragging out F. Jasmine

Member of the Wedding is a clear intertext to *Mockingbird,* as McCullers and various reviewers noticed. The novel's central protagonist is a tomboy like Scout, with both feminine names (Frances, F. Jasmine) and a masculine nickname (Frankie). Frankie spends her time in the kitchen with African American Berenice, a woman whose one blue and one brown eye signifies a double life like Cal's, and six-year-old cousin John Henry, a girlish "curiosity" just like Dill. His fate sheds light on Dill, just as the fate of Capote's female inverts illuminate Lee's reversal of his tropes. McCullers helped to promote Capote's career until she became frustrated with his "poaching" tendencies (Long 12). Paired with Capote's writings of Monroeville, McCullers's overt concern with gender inversion and latent queerness draws out aspects of the *Mockingbird* children that Lee only implied as subtexts.

Just as Mayella bears the brunt of sexual knowledge in *Mockingbird*, about which Scout is curious and which seems to reflect on Scout's own feelings of isolation, as reflected by Scout's deep sympathy for Mayella and her lonely life, Frankie actively denies knowledge of sex. Just as Scout does not know what "their time" means in reference to Mruna women, Frankie does not know what menstruating is when Berenice says she still is, but this is remarkable because she is twelve, not six. A character whom Lee has divided into Scout and Mayella, the adolescent Frankie represents extreme fear of sex and growth. Frankie is pretending to be grown up without understanding the responsibility, which is why becoming a member of the wedding, rather than becoming sexually active herself, appeals to her. She is obsessed with some unnamed sin committed with a boy, but we are never told what. She seems to have no idea what the soldier who invites her to his hotel room wants, although she has vague feelings of disturbance. She has directly witnessed boarders in her father's house actually having sex, but she has no understanding of the action except as an awful fit. She wishes she could continue to sleep alongside her father, just as Scout wants to climb in Atticus's lap, but her father has tossed her out. She is "too big," a theme that transforms into Frankie's concern with being a freak: "This summer she was grown so tall that she was almost a big freak, ... The reflection in the glass was warped and crooked" (2). At the freak show, corresponding to the traveling show of curiosities in *Other Voices, Other Rooms*, "She was afraid of all the Freaks, for it seemed to her that they had looked at her in a secret way and tried to connect their eyes with hers, as though to say: we know you" (18). Not surprisingly, it is the Half-Man Half-Woman "morphodite" that earns her attention, a word that connects several inverted chameleons to one another in *Mockingbird*.

We can understand Frankie's obsession with her brother's wedding as an index of her interest in, and wish to belong to, institutions of normative heterosexuality. The proper "we" she seeks would emerge in the classic romance narrative. The fact that "they" are "the we of me" suggests the inner split of male and female—an inner wedding, if you will, that she has yet to understand. Frankie's inverted cousin John Henry functions as Dill to Scout: the feminine boy as counterpart to masculine girl. Frankie desires more than anything else connection to other people, which Lee has echoed in her representation of the country girl Mayella Ewell as the loneliest person in the world. It is a future state of spiritual isolation, perhaps, for Scout, if we view the stories of isolated children like Boo, Dill, Mayella, and mixed-race children as important to Scout for some inner reason.

Frankie cannot hide her rough elbows, cropped hair, and tough feet, no matter what dress she wears; her feet are so infamously tough that she can cut out invasive objects with a knife and not suffer. In fact, she uses a knife several times in *Member*. Her sudden feelings of isolation at "being a member of nothing in the world" the summer she turns twelve signifies a sudden discontentedness with her masculinity. Presumably, she has become discontent because her brother's wedding has given her a glimpse of what the dominant culture views as the proper end to female adolescence, as argued by Barbara White (46–51). In view of this ending to a typical girl's story, Frankie feels in a perpetual state of being unfinished; this feeling of being unfinished is expressed in imagery of unfinished tunes, such as a piano being tuned "across the August afternoon. A chord was struck. Then in a dreaming way a chain of chords climbed slowly upward like a flight of castle stairs: but just at the end, when the eighth chord should have sounded and the scale made complete, there was a stop. This next to last chord was repeated. The seventh chord, which seems to echo all of the unfinished scale, struck and insisted again and again. And finally there was a silence" (81). The metaphor is partly autobiographical, since McCullers began her artistic life as a musician and felt deserted when her music teacher (Mary Tucker) moved away (V. Carr 35). A similar occurrence repeats when she and John Henry hear a horn play and then break off, unfinished. Another mirror character is Honey Camden Brown (B. White 98), whom Berenice said "was a boy God had not finished. The Creator had withdrawn His hand from him too soon. God had not finished him, . . . The Creator, Big Mama said, had withdrawn His hand from him too soon, so that he was left eternally unsatisfied" (122). The sense of being unfinished points to the wedding as a looming endpoint of normative heterosexuality; in speaking to others about her dream of being a member of the wedding, Frankie feels connection (50, 55), precisely what Mayella seeks in the already married Tom, whom she might have thought she could approach with less risk than a white man.

A discussion of *Member* clarifies the boundaries of identity surrounding Scout. If Frankie has two main influences, John Henry and Berenice, we can similarly view Scout as being in an unfinished state between Dill, an emblem of John Henry and thus gay, and Cal, related to Berenice and thus a symbol of passing—a symbol of lady. Dill will not pass, just as John Henry will not pass in these girls' stories of growth; black women such as Berenice and Cal, in contrast, show how to pass with duplicity. Cal is doubled with her socially adaptive voice, whereas Berenice remains an odd symbol of doubleness with her one blue eye. In terms of drag, however, it is important that Berenice differs from John Henry on many matters, including her vision of gender as sacred, her lessons to Frankie about the importance of obtaining a beau, and her stories of heterosexuality. Married many times and the first time at thirteen, Berenice is as heterosexual as they come. She is one path for Frankie, John Henry another. The integration that Frankie perhaps achieves at the end, as Frances, participating in a female relationship with Mary Littlejohn and inclined toward the arts, suggests a revised way to wed conflicted self-aspects; this is perhaps Scout's path as well. She grows up to clown Maycomb with her novel but abandons Dill, like McCullers abandons John Henry, because Frankie is determined to pass in social life.

The specter of homosexuality surrounds Frankie. Passing by an alleyway, Frankie as F. Jasmine sees two boys whose postures distinctly remind her of her brother and his fiancé. She "did not look at directly" because she was afraid; nevertheless, her consciousness analogically processes how "something about the angle or the way they stood, or the pose of their shapes, had reflected the sudden picture of her brother and the bride that had so shocked her" (69–70). The word "pose" evokes the trial of Oscar Wilde in which he was accused of "posing sodomite." Wilde maintained, "I do not know whether you use the word 'pose' in any particular sense," and even punned, "I have no pose in this matter" (Meyer, "Under" 93). The passage communicates the knowledge of homosexuality Frankie intuits, only glimpsed in sideways glances and analogies but never addressed openly, just as Scout's sympathy for Mayella and for Boo suggests self-aspects without overt acknowledgment of her own issues. Unlike in the glimpse of real sex that Frankie views as "a fit," in the double shapes of two boys she sees love. She sees connection, the "they" of her yearning for "we."

This alleyway vision absorbs her interest and "queer" feelings so much that she speaks to Berenice about it; the scene seems to evoke "the shiver" that Berenice associates with love and sexual desire. A man to marry is one who makes you shiver, Berenice argues, which goes along with images of cold, snow, Alaska, and Winter Hill that the novel in general associates with romance and the opposite of Frankie's endless August, which resonates with the wilting and sagging heat of Maycomb. Berenice addresses gender inversion when she discusses the queer love she has seen; "'I have knew boys to take it into their heads to fall in love with other boys. You know Lily Mae Jenkins? . . . He prisses around with a pink satin blouse and one arm akimbo. Now this Lily Mae fell in love with a man named Juney Jones. A man, mind you. And Lily Mae turned into a girl. He changed his nature and his sex and turned into a girl'" (76). John Henry is most interested in how that is done, but Berenice does not know. This is because John Henry and Berenice have distinct differences in regard to inversion, much like Cal becomes an emblem of passing and Dill its refusal.

McCullers positions Frankie in between John Henry and Berenice to place her in between one character representing gender inversion and the other heterosexuality. When the three characters fantasize about the perfectly created worlds that they would create were they God, John Henry and Berenice disagree about gender. Frankie believes that people should be able to change back and forth from boys to girls, but John Henry believes that "people ought to be half boy and half girl, and when the old Frankie threatened to take him to the Fair and sell him to the Freak Pavilion, he would only close his eyes and smile" (92). Berenice, whose fantasy of a perfect world includes a homogenous race and no divisions at all, believes firmly in male and female natures. This difference is telling because John Henry represents the inverted part of Frankie—the part that would be out and smiling about it—whereas Berenice represents the potential heterosexuality of Frankie, a heterosexuality that could result in the freakish sense of having different colored eyes. A figure of precocious and hypersexuality, Berenice speaks often of love and heterosexual longing, having chased her first love through various male partners. Of course, her first love was wounded; he had a smashed thumb, which mirrors the fact that a few of Berenice's own fingers are inoperable, in a pattern of heterosexual wounding that by now we should recognize across these southern writers.

Where John Henry differs from Dill is his comfort with himself. He is queer and alien to Frankie because *she* is uncomfortable with latent possibilities of inversion, but he is not queer and alien to himself. He is more than happy to have the doll she rejects; he loves to dress in female clothing such as Berenice's plumed pink hat and high heels; he loves the smell of perfume, he loves to do detailed artwork, he steals the kings and queens from their cards, and he is sweet to Frankie in spite of her meanness. He falls in love with the Pin Head from the freak show, naming her the cutest thing he ever saw, which suggests his absolute comfort with freakishness as adorable. His Pin Head is not Miss Wisteria in her loneliness, complicit with how he, unlike Frankie, always says "'less play out'" (9, 111). This accords with Mitchell-Peters's reading of how *Other Voices, Other Rooms* deconstructs the concept of "freak" by locating it more with social figures who name Joel and Idabel "freakish," rather than with how the queer characters think of themselves.

Frankie, in contrast, views John Henry and his drawings as alien and queer; they make her uncomfortable because to her they are always slightly warped, much like her sense of herself. For example, John Henry draws pictures on the walls, and what Frankie sees as "queer drawings" and "freak soldiers" bothers her (7); when he draws a man in profile climbing a telephone pole, it disconcerts Frankie that the man's two eyes are showing. It is John Henry's sight in general that makes her uncomfortable; at the beginning of the novel, she takes off his glasses and wishes he would do without them, just as she worries the Freaks will look at her and recognize her. Frankie very overtly uses John Henry as a means for projecting her fears and her sense of isolation, even though he occasionally rejects her projections, saying, for example, that he is not lonely at all. When Berenice allows John Henry to make a biscuit man, he makes an aesthetic dandy but shows no worry that Berenice's cooking makes it look like any other biscuit and undoes his uniqueness. Berenice's socialization embedded in her cooking is no threat to him. In contrast to John Henry, Frankie is struggling with her sense of being unfinished; the unfinished tune that John Henry and Frankie hear together drives her crazy but does not affect him much. In this way, we can locate queer angst in the girl and not the boy in *Member,* whereas *Mockingbird* reverses the angst. Scout does not worry about not being the ray of sunshine her Aunt Alexandra believes she should be for her father; Dill bears all the grief of gender inversion.

Frankie's feelings of being unfinished create her efforts in part 2 to perform a heightened femininity through drag. She christens herself F. Jasmine, and her first decision is to make calling cards, demonstrating the social transvestite. She then purchases an outlandish orange evening gown for a simple summer wedding; she wears silver slippers in what is continually described as a gray landscape, suggesting an intertextuality of *The Wonderful Wizard of Oz*, which has been appropriated as the colorful signification of gay drag.

Frankie's sense that she is a member of nothing in the world, and her consequent obsession with who might be the "we" of "me," because everyone needs a "we," mirrors Whitman's speaker's sentiments in *Calamus* when he wonders if there are other men in the world like him. The question is the question of every vampire or monster; the immediate question about "who am I" is "who is like me." In the scene of Dill confessing to Scout, we are seeing him ask that question, as best he can. He is trying to see if Scout has similar questions about herself, or if she faces similar rejections from adults who wish her to be another way. Scout is not receptive to being similarly classed, just like Idabel in Capote's fiction, who suggests she can always don more green-colored glasses. Just as Idabel very firmly denies being a girl at all, and Scout has to participate in the boys' games when they accuse her of being a girl, Frankie initially longs to be a boy to fight the war, which is why her "F. Jasmine" performance can best be understood as drag.

Berenice signals her disapproval of Frankie's drag when she condescendingly says, "'I'm not accustomed to human Christmas trees in August'" (85) and "It don't do. . . . It just don't do. . . . You had all your hair shaved off like a convict, and now you tie a silver ribbon around this head without any hair. It just looks peculiar. . . . And look at them elbows . . . Here you got on this grown woman's evening dress. Orange satin. And that brown crust on your elbows. The two things just don't mix'" (84). Drag does not hide because it is camp—it parodies a particular vision of heterosexual normativity. The drag section of *Member* is similar to the hopeless isolation of Miss Wisteria; it is bound to be tragic as we see Frankie invest her hopes and dreams in what we understand to be a delusion. The image of a hyperfemininity doomed to miniaturization and vulnerability comes to a crux when Frankie wanders into "other voices, other rooms" of the soldier; she thinks she will touch the world, but we know the truth.

The innate doubleness within McCullers's protagonist is discussed further at the end of chapter 6, along with discussion of the novel's highly ambiguous ending and its potential relevance to the ambiguous ending of *Mockingbird*. There are many possibilities to understanding Frankie's mantra, "they are the we of me," in Scout: the recognition that Dill and Boo are a "they" within Scout; the sinister recognition that "they" of Maycomb, who convict Tom and what he embodies, are the "we" of Scout and her future as a lady; the parody recognition that Atticus's creed of dual perspective—seeing from another's eyes—is always "they" within the "me." To conclude this chapter, however, we have to take into account that John Henry dies a gruesome, horrible death; his torture by meningitis always bothers my students, even as Lee's Dill only quietly slips out of the novel to perhaps become the laughing clown, we do not know. The desertion of the gay boy unites both McCullers's and Lee's novels; it is the part of the female protagonists that have to be put away for them to pass. And passing is precisely what the newly named Frances—not Frankie, not the dragged-out F. Jasmine—is doing. Frances has not the beau that Berenice thought would answer all her problems, but a bosom girlfriend who shares her aesthetic interests and who possibly makes her shiver. The final line of the novel, "with an instant shock of happiness, she heard the ringing of the bell" (153) as Mary arrives, suggests Wharton's ghost story "The Lady's Maid's Bell," in which the quivering bell of the lesbian Emma Saxon gives the servant Hartley several instant shocks.

Frances and Mary Littlejohn, who is tellingly *not* liked by Berenice and who is certainly not a dainty feminine being, are planning to see the world together, the world an important symbol throughout *Member* as something, like the time embodied by her father's watches, of which Frankie wants to be a part. One line Frances keeps repeating, in anticipation of Mary's arrival, is how she is mad about Michelangelo; the reference to T. S. Eliot's Prufrock echoes what Eliot meant to be an image of modern passivity, alienation, and utter isolation. But Frances shares her madness with another girl, so while they look like friends it could be that what passes as friendship is possibly a very fulfilling lesbianism.

John Henry is another story that provides a specific way of understanding why Dill's book *The Gray Ghost* might be haunting the margins of *Mockingbird*. *Member* continually evokes images of ghosts and shadows as symbols for the nonmembership Frankie feels: "She could not name the feeling in her, and she stood there until dark shadows made her think of ghosts" (38). John Henry, when she sees him race by, "was quick as a shadow and F. Jasmine did not see his face—his white shirttails flapped loose behind him like queer wings" (110–11). When she sees him on his porch, he looks like a "little black paper doll on a piece of yellow paper" (38). Dressed in Berenice's clothing, "John Henry stood like a little old woman dwarf, wearing the pink hat with the plume, and the high-heel shoes. The walls of the kitchen were crazy drawn and very bright. The three of them blinked at each other in the light as though they were three strangers or three ghosts" (117). The ghost-grayness of John Henry is narrated twice, along with the specter of death he represents to Frankie if she does not learn to pass: "The kitchen, done over and almost modern, had nothing that would bring to mind John Henry West. But nevertheless there were times when Frances felt his presence there, solemn and hovering and ghost-gray" (149). Similar to the "faded image of a gray house" that Scout associates with Dill, the second repetition of John Henry's ghost-grayness further renders him a freak in the same way that Frankie threatened to send him to the freak show earlier:

> [John Henry] came to her once or twice in nightmare dreams, like an escaped child dummy from the window of a department store, the wax legs moving stiffly only at joints, and the wax face wizened and faintly painted, coming toward her until terror snatched her awake. . . . it was seldom now that she felt his presence—solemn, hovering, and ghost-gray. Only occasionally at twilight time. (153)

Of course the season of his death is the very season of the fair, as if the fair is for Frankie unimaginable horror but for him a place of resurrection. We must remember that he smiled when she threatened to send him there. Perhaps the circus for Dill as laughing clown functions similarly, with "Dill" as possible slang for "dilly boy," a well-known shorthand for male prostitutes of Piccadilly, whose clients were called "punters" (see M. Harris).

In his article on freakish boy bodies in Louisa May Alcott's *Under the Lilacs*, critic Hugh McElaney demonstrates the political use of disability in Alcott's fiction; disability and freakish male bodies exempt boys from the discourses of manhood that Alcott associated with vehicles of oppressing women: "such exploitation [of male bodies], set within the backdrop of the American circus, renders masculine status in general as an indeterminate, sometimes freakish, commodity" (1), which "renders them less than fully human or androgynous—in either case, less fit for competition in the marketplace with, among others, young women of ambition" (3). The politics of women writers Lee and McCullers look similar. If we ponder the image of John Henry as the painted dummy and Dill as the laughing clown, we have to understand Lee's abandonment of Dill as a symbolic sacrifice of the muse that paves the way for Scout to pass. These male freaks shall not *pass*. For Scout and Frankie's stories are ultimately stories of the need to *pass* into social worlds that will accept them, however that can be achieved. John Henry and Dill, unlike Jem, are forever rendered grotesque art because they refuse to heal their wounds "so they can pass and punt."

Conclusion: The Lady and the Monster of *Mockingbird*

In her lecture on the grotesque of southern writers after standards set by Faulkner, O'Connor says that Southerners can still recognize the grotesque, because to do so one has to have a sense of the whole man, which, she argues, is theological. In the South, she continues, the definition of man remains a theological one (4). *Mockingbird*'s use of the word "whole" in its description of Tom attests to the fact that a theological wholeness can be glimpsed from wounds. O'Connor views the freak of southern literature as a sign of "our essential displacement":

> Whenever I'm asked why Southern writers particularly have a penchant for writing about freaks, I say it is because we are still able to recognize one. To be able to recognize a freak, you have to have some conception of the whole man, and in the South the general conception of man is still, in the main, theological. That is a large statement, and it is dangerous to make it, for almost anything you say about Southern belief can be denied in the next breath with equal propriety. But approaching the subject from the standpoint of the writer, I think it is safe to say that while the South is hardly Christ-centered, it is most certainly Christ-haunted. The Southerner, who isn't convinced of it, is very much afraid that he may have been formed in the image and likeness of God. Ghosts can be very fierce and instructive. They cast strange shadows, particularly in our literature. In any case, it is when the freak can be sensed as a figure for our essential displacement that he attains some depth in literature. (4)

Are the many freaks—Boo, Dill the clown, the Pin Head, Miss Wisteria, Tom, the half man half woman who continually appears—grotesque or actually whole? Wholeness becomes visible when something is missing; thus it is quite possible that the wounded or the freakish figure, such as Boo, complete the one entranced by looking at them. It is the narrator of *Mockingbird* that recognizes how fine Tom would have been if he had been whole, and it is Scout who seems most connected to the phantom Boo even though the connection is one of fear rather than desire.

To consider the function of Boo as freakish phantom for Scout, we have to turn to film theory. In her famous essay "When the Woman Looks," Linda Williams discusses the peculiar repetition of scenes in which women look at "the horrible body of the monster" (85), which recurs in such films as *Nosferatu, The Phantom of the Opera, Vampyr, Dracula, Freaks, Dr. Jekyll and Mr. Hyde, King Kong,* and *Beauty and the Beast.* The woman's stare is a paralyzing stare: "the monster or the freak's own spectacular trance holds her originally active, curious look in a trance-like passivity that allows him to master her though *her* look" (86). Williams argues that the monster's power results from his body's difference from the normal male and thus bears a resemblance to the woman's sense that the monster is actually a double for the woman in a patriarchal culture. The sense of the double also involves the monster and the woman's status as threats to male power, which is quite explicit in *Mockingbird,* as argued by Laura Fine in "Dark Double." The Boo who legendarily thrusts scissors in his father's leg expresses rage against patriarchy that neither Scout nor Mayella can express. He also, as parodied in the children's opera, symbolizes the "backstabbing" town citizens beneath a calm exterior.

However, whether the woman's gaze at the monster is sympathetic identification or queer desire is a matter of debate. Sue-Ellen Case critiques Williams for being trapped in a heterosexual paradigm; vampire literature since *Carmilla* has always sung the lesbian's thirst. In his discussion of *Carmilla* and *Dracula,* Dijkstra historicizes the monsters and shows that women were thought to be particularly blood-thirsty because they periodically lose blood and because their blood was thought to be thinner than men's, as articulated by Havelock Ellis in *Man and Women* (Dijkstra 336). Although Dracula is male, he signifies a world of women, associated with

Eve, the East, and effeminacy (343). The monster *could* denote a flash of recognition between woman and monster, not because of their monstrous difference from the normal male, but because of their complete rejection of the male as an object of desire.

Scout is always looking at and for her monster, but all she has is male stories of his monstrous body. Jem's "reasonable description" of the phantom includes enormous height, deduced from bigfoot tracks, traces of eating raw animals (unwashable blood, rotting teeth, permanent scars, and perpetual salivation) (13). She is not inclined to coax him out unless forced, but she lives in wait of him, expecting him to emerge at any time. She is paralyzed by the thought of him, more so because of his invisibility and dispersal: "Every night-sound I heard from my cot on the back porch was . . . Boo Radley . . . loose and after us . . . insane fingers picking the wire to pieces . . . I lingered between sleep and wakefulness" (55). This seems to mean that whether Scout identifies as a girl or "morphodite," she is equally, when young, an object of shame. The refrain of shame at simply being a girl, sung by Jem, makes the point. It is clear that Atticus wants this play of looking "at and for" the monster to end, for recognition of the parallel between daughter and monster must be prevented. How does Scout's fantasy of Boo fit with the drag aspects of *Mockingbird*? What is her view of the closet "when you finally see him"? The trial reveals the castrating agent as Mayella and the castrat*ed*—shot seventeen times and therefore less and less whole—as the disabled black man, signifying the novel's drag and its potential misogyny, a connection between queer and disability readings that critic Robert McRuer has applied to *As Good as It Gets*, suggesting we ask how "able-bodied sexual subjects" are narratively constructed.

In *Mockingbird*, as we have discussed, it is mostly Dill who gazes at Boo's house, hugging the pole in his desire for a glimpse, whereas as much as Scout desires the gifts from the tree, it is clear that "the monster" wants Jem, not her. Her posture is like Collin's in the tree house when he realizes nobody wants him. This is a freeing posture because it allows the young character to pass into another world, which is precisely what Scout is in the process of doing. In fact, her fantasy of Boo is radically changing in the last chapters of the novel; she still imagines seeing him, but she mourns her new knowledge that "he would never gaze at us" (242). Whereas earlier she expects his appearance at any time and imagines all the horrid things he might be, now she imagines social contact:

> But I still looked for him. . . . Maybe someday we would see him. I imagined how it would be: . . . he'd just be sitting in the swing when I came along. "Hidy do, Mr. Arthur," I would say, as if I had said it every afternoon of my life. "Evening, Jean Louise," he would say, as if he had said it every afternoon of my life, "right pretty spell we're having, isn't it?" "Yes, sir, right pretty," I would say, and go on.
>
> It was only a fantasy. We would never see him. He probably did go out . . . and gaze upon Miss Stephanie Crawford. . . . He would never gaze at us. (242)

This passage echoes the earlier appearance of Aunt Alexandra, who rises in the place that Scout expects Boo to inhabit on the porch. The phantom inner monster and the social world of socialization are two ends of the spectrum for Scout; they are choices. To calmly socialize with the monster and discuss the weather is not to confront an inner monster. Miss Stephanie is in the passage as a new object of envy, and she will feature in the final scene of escorting Boo home. This reinterpretation of Miss Stephanie, heretofore a gossip after Miss Maudie's recipes, is crucial. Scout's fantasy above is not so much of a ghost as it is of a social encounter with a gentleman in the most mundane and regular fashion; this is not so much her Boo as it is Mr. Arthur, who is indeed the person she meets and whom she transforms into a gentleman in the final pages. She is the lady she is destined to be, completely aware of the system of social gazes in Maycomb.

The final appearance of Boo is complicated because he evokes: the vampire in his whiteness, repeated five times (270); the anorexic or consumptive, which in the nineteenth century marked not the vampire but the kiss of the vampire (Dijkstra 348); the lame with his "sickly white hands"; the ill with his awful cough and sweat (277); the dead with his return to the coffin; the homosexual who keeps looking at Jem (277–78), and who will only appear the gentleman if Scout positions his hands on her arm correctly (278); the misunderstood pedophile; the potentially mentally disabled or autistic; and, in the end, Scout's mother, as noted by Amy Laurence (183), for he has given life. Atticus thanks him for his children, the narrator notes that he had given them various presents "and our lives" (278), and she christens them "Boo's children" as she looks back at the past two years from his porch (279). We should have a presentiment of his maternal nurturing role when Scout looks at the tree, "the trunk was swelling around its cement patch. The patch itself was turning yellow" (242). It is as if Boo's principle as mother (even diseased one) is about to burst through, which makes sense because Atticus is "all father" in his courteous detachment.

The connections between the monster that the woman sees in classic cinema and the intrauterine mother are well established. In the "home" aspect of Freud's *unheimlich,* the uncanny that literally means both unhome-like and homelike, "is the desire for what Freud calls intra-uterine existence . . . the lustful pleasure of being buried alive and dead—her intra-uterine re-creation. . . . And the feminist psychoanalytic theorists carry on his tradition: his intra-uterine pleasure, this *jouissance,* can only be enjoyed as a pre-Oedipal *jouissance* with the mother" (Case 14). Mr. Arthur's familiarity and unfamiliarity, furthered by his nonspeech "body English" (278) and his immediate expulsion to the porch, where other bargains are made between the federally minded Atticus and Maycomb representatives, accords with the way he evokes the dead mother of the novel. The late Mrs. Finch, from the beginning, retains a more special role for Jem than Scout. Boo thus signifies, simultaneously and paradoxically, the wounded man condemned to the closet and a woman who did not survive Maycomb society.

And survive Scout will. Her interactions with Boo demonstrate that she has already made her choice and rendered him the path not taken. The closet is not for her. What stands out in the scene between Scout and "Mr. Arthur" is her perfect manners; she is the perfect social hostess, leading him to the porch, asking him to take the comfortable seat in the rocking chair, asking him if he would like to see Jem, and then leading him home but maintaining the farce of him as a gentleman: "if Miss Stephanie Crawford was watching from her upstairs window, she would see Arthur Radley escorting me down the sidewalk, as any gentleman would do" (278). Since when is the approval of Miss Stephanie foremost in Scout's mind?

The emergence of Scout's mother, as both a deserved treat and a warning to her, signifies the extent to which Scout has learned to "pass" as a lady, which is her own way of coping with drag. As a lady, Scout has learned to pass and set aside queer considerations and perspectives. We do not see Dill in the novel again, once Boo "comes out," but if we consider the parallel between Boo and the "strange lady" of Capote's *Other Voices,* as well as the integrated "Frances" of *Member,* we have to understand that drag is a stage of life for a girl growing into a woman, if she wishes to survive. Scout is indeed Boo's child in terms of learning that drag can actually be a social advantage for her, in a way it could not be for the males. Boo's difference from the normal male body, which is the typical monster's plight, is apparent in his sickly femininity, but it is also masked by the fact that he is not monstrous. Although he turns out to be a regular person after all, it is the very illegibility of his identity that unsettles us and excludes him from Scout's story.

Like Scout's mother, Boo is an example of the consequences of not passing, which is not an option for Scout. Just as Aunt Alexandra brings to Scout clean overalls in the end, Scout has already proven her ability to pass in the missionary society scene, and it is Miss Maudie whose gentle yet strong hand has guided her into the room and conversation of ladies. The missionary society scene and the sophisticated social manners of Scout when she meets Boo demonstrate that a lady's genre has emerged to define Scout's story. Scout has entered the novel of manners that rules female society in Maycomb. Lee's deployment of women's regional writing as modeled by Kate Chopin, Edith Wharton, Nella Larsen, and Carson McCullers needs to be addressed to fully understand Scout's story. Analyzing the modern aspects of women's writing in the earlier part of the twentieth century explains both Scout's success at passing and the peculiar way she keeps passing out. Not only does she keep dropping off to sleep in a poetics of overwhelming exhaustion, for it is tiring to falsify nature and adapt femininity, but when she experiences Boo as a point of view rather than an (invisible) object of the gaze, she looks back at her own life and sees the events of it pass before her eyes. The view from Boo's porch fits the convention of seeing one's life before death. And thus we are subtly told that seeing from the mother's gaze is also to understand the close linkage between death and coming-of-age female in modern women's novels. Falling asleep upon Atticus's reading of *The Gray Ghost* at the end, Scout, who knows that story already, has indeed given up the ghost.

CHAPTER 6

MOCKINGBIRD AND MODERN WOMEN'S REGIONAL WRITING: AWAKENING, PASSING, AND PASSING OUT

To be awake is to be alive. I have never yet met a man who was quite awake.

—Henry David Thoreau, *Walden*

If the ending image of Atticus's bedside vigil shows him in a posture of both "Waiting for Godot" and of reading, thus echoing the politically charged closing of Frederick Douglass's first slave narrative, the ending image of Scout distills the feelings of sleepiness and stillness that have been increasingly overwhelming her in the final third of the novel. The unnatural stillness of awaiting judgment at the trial; the surreal way in which the jury's decision passes through her sluggish consciousness; her sense that the communal "oversoul" is too tired to work; her slumber upon being caged as a ham; and her exhaustion at the end of the novel: all evoke a poetics of sleepiness as poignant as the poetics of reading that informs Atticus's stance and her connection to him. If reading embodies a form of studying the world and human nature, sleeping is its exact opposite. It is withdrawal and escape. In some ways, it is a movement within the self; Chura demonstrates how Scout makes her most astute connections and associations when she is in fact drifting off to sleep. But sleeping can be opposed to awakening. It involves retreat into habit and comfort zones, echoing the "sleepy-eyed men" who approach the jail for ill intent.

Going to sleep in American literature is fraught with meaning. *Mockingbird* evokes a legacy of modern women's writing in which characters who awaken to social repression have "nowhere to go," so they languish in passive acts of suicidal sleep or even madness. At the turn of the twentieth century and the "awakening" of feminist awareness, Kate Chopin's languishing Edna Pontellier, Charlotte Perkins Gilman's unnamed narrator of "The Yellow

Wallpaper," Nella Larsen's Helga Crane of *Quicksand,* Edith Wharton's Charity Royall of *Summer,* and Lily Bart of *The House of Mirth* all succumb to the modern world's exclusion of them, to the frustration of many female readers. Barbara White argues that although McCullers's Frankie neither goes mad nor commits suicide, she is both crippled and deadened at the end after the queer walls have been repainted; in her view, this is McCullers's point—that adjusting to growing up female involves sacrifice of self (106–7). Perhaps we can read the repetition of how Frankie is mad about Michelangelo in that light. Chopin establishes the essential framework in her 1899 novel of Louisianan social rituals that are slowly rejected by native Kentuckian Edna Pontellier. The trope of heat exhaustion offsets the internal occurrence of *The Awakening.*

The ending of *Mockingbird* parallels the ending of Chopin's *The Awakening,* which, like *Mockingbird,* occupies the cusp of a new era for women's rights. The character Edna Pontellier has awakened to her trapped condition as a woman: "An indescribable oppression, which seemed to generate in some unfamiliar part of her consciousness, filled her whole being with a vague anguish. It was like a shadow, like a mist passing across her soul's summer day" (8). In the wake of chaos that follows her dim early recognition of "her position in the universe as a human being" (14), she vacillates between awakenings, such as her reading of Emerson, and narcotic states of sleep. Once fully aware of indescribable oppression, her only escape path is eternal sleep in the soothing embrace of the sea, which is not dissimilar to the soothing tuck-in by Atticus and which therefore counterpoints the two novels' relationships to patriarchy:

> The foamy wavelets curled up to her white feet, and coiled like serpents about her ankles. She walked out. The water was chill, but she walked on. The water was deep, but she lifted her white body and reached out with a long, sweeping stroke. The touch of the sea is sensuous, enfolding the body in its soft, close embrace.
>
> She went on and on . . . thinking of the blue-grass meadow that she had traversed when a little child, believing that it had no beginning and no end.
>
> Her arms and legs were growing tired.
>
> [. . .]
>
> Exhaustion was pressing upon and over-powering her. (109)

The imagery of Edna's suicide is actually maternal and tied to the novel's emphasis on the female body and its introduction of a variety of women as possible role models for Edna, who is figured as a child in contradistinction to the "mother-women" of Grand Isle. In contrast, *Mockingbird* isolates its young sleeping/wakeful character in a generally unchallenged patriarchy. But if Boo is a surrogate mother whom she has glimpsed, albeit briefly, then perhaps the ending's allusion to death is both death and not death. What we can draw from the parallels between the novels' ending sleepiness is the political nature of choosing sleep and being overwhelmed by the exhaustion that fighting injustice requires. The state of awakening is ultimately transferred to the reader, who remains uncomfortable and restless in place of the numbed character.

Many turn-of-the-century feminist works, such as Charlotte Perkins Gilman's "The Yellow Wallpaper" and Doris Lessing's "To Room Nineteen," end with some sort of regression or descent into an earlier state of being because there is no place for awakened characters in the present social order. The stillness and the reading of *The Gray Ghost* in *Mockingbird* suggest there is indeed "nowhere to go" for anyone enlightened to injustice and a broader consciousness of exclusionary democracy. *The Awakening* uses as its intertext Washington Irving's "Rip Van Winkle," an American parable published in 1819 about sleeping, waking, and viewing national transformation. In other words, the connections between democracy, independence, and awakening provide us with an intertext to decoding the ending of *The Awakening*. This ending is echoed with an image of the consuming state of pregnancy in Larsen's similar story, *Quicksand,* which ends with the depressing lines, "And hardly had she left her bed and become able to walk again without pain, hardly had the children returned from the homes of the neighbors, when she began to have her fifth child" (135). Larsen deploys tropes of sleeping and awakening similarly to Chopin, showing the spiral of descent into which her mulatto character descends because her composite, hybrid self cannot find satisfaction in any communities, all of which have specific expectations for her and hypocrisies to which she "awakens."

Larsen's novel, like Chopin's and Lee's, documents a woman's struggle between social worlds that initially look progressive for various reasons and into which the liminal protagonist can *pass* if she can bear the cost to self. However, each world ushers in discontent for different reasons; the point is that *passing* is dissatisfactory, but it is the unfortunate essence of coming of age. Emulating Chopin, Larsen features her motherless character suddenly awakening to her discontent at the platform of submission embraced by the southern school in which she teaches: "Naxos Negroes knew what was expected of them. They had good sense and they had good taste. They knew enough to stay in their places, and that, said the preacher, showed good taste" (3). Suddenly realizing that the school is actually a machine "cutting all to a pattern, the white man's pattern" (4), she, reminiscent of Edna's refusal to accept callers, leaves her room untidy "for the first time" (9) and stays in bed, where a more docile teacher "came in the morning to awaken Helga Crane" (9). The rhetoric of awakening and its necessary opposite of falling into various states of vertigo, unconsciousness, and childish tempestuousness peppers Helga's subsequent attempts to find where she might fit, given her awakening to the fact that she—who loves color, beautiful objects, etc.— does not blend with "the drab colors" of Naxos (17). When head of the school Dr. Anderson asks her to stay because she is a "lady," she refuses to pass as a lady and rather childishly lashes out at him, saying she was born in a slum. Like Edna, who takes toward her husband the persona of a lost child because she has never really developed herself, Helga later does not even know why she lost her temper with him. She goes to sleep wondering why she "lost her temper" and burst out with "angry half-truths" (26).

The scene echoes Edna's childish refusal to go to bed when her husband orders her to, "her will had blazed up, stubborn and resistant" (31); after a stand-off between them that lasts all night long, she "began to feel like one who awakens gradually out of a dream, a delicious, grotesque, impossible dream, to feel again the realities pressing into her soul. The physical need for sleep began to overtake her" (31). This suggests that the life she has been living is the dream, and retreat into unconsciousness is the capacity for real awakening; similarly, Scout returns from the grotesque scene of the near-lynching in a state of sleepiness that enables awakening: "I was very tired, and was drifting off to sleep when the memory of Atticus calmly folding his newspaper and pushing back his hat became Atticus standing in the middle of an empty waiting street, pushing up his glasses. The full meaning of the night's events hit me, and I began crying" (156). Like Edna and Helga, Scout has acted in the near-lynch scene without thinking, and only in the state of suspended consciousness do the sinister connections and risks become apparent. Chopin and Larsen are using the trope to express the repression of female sexuality required by political institutions at the time—marriage and motherhood for Edna, Naxos's training for Helga; the feelings within Edna are "the first-felt throbbings of desire" (30); for Helga, "a long-hidden, half-understood desire welled up in her with the suddenness of a dream" (104; see Lewis). Lee appropriates the trope to define Scout's "indescribable oppression" or "indefinite discontent. Not clear, but vague, like a storm gathering far on the horizon" (Larsen 81). The trope defines not sexual desire but the vague and gradual shifts in Scout as she intuits but cannot consciously name the sense that her environment is not protective but sinister.

Attempting to pass into a new society, Helga experiences borderline unconsciousness on the train when she is surrounded by a crowd of people, akin to Edna's voyage to Grand Terre, where a church service causes Edna the "feeling of oppression and drowsiness" (34), after which she retreats to a cottage, disrobes, and awakens after a long sleep, a scene narrated with imagery of fairytale transformation, Rip Van Winkle, and the Garden of Eden. Likewise, Helga retreats from the crowded car to a private quarter, after which she awakens to gray, cold Chicago. Her languishing of consciousness on the train is hardly an isolated occurrence:

> Throughout the novel, such moments of vertigo mark Helga's abandonment of a specific social identity—her sensation before she has located a new social role. Cut free from social restrictions, Helga experiences not liberation but fear and a sensation of falling. Indeed, she may be falling into a void of nothingness—the nothingness of identity stripped from all its social moorings. (Cutter 78)

This is precisely the story of Edna, who one by one peels away social expectations and ends with nothing left. Identically to Edna, who "never realized that the reserve of her own character had much, perhaps everything, to do with" the fact that she had only had a few "self-contained" friends (17), Helga "was herself unconscious of that faint hint of offishness which hung about her and repelled advances" (34). Helga begins working for women who give speeches on race, and she is welcomed into circles of Harlem, circles in which she must veil the fact that her mother was white. Her Harlem is Edna's Grand

Isle, where Edna encounters women happy in their roles as mother-women or artists. Helga experiences at first tremendous happiness, "but it didn't last, this happiness of Helga Crane's," and she is "filled . . . only with restlessness," a need "she could not put a name to" again (47). Her restlessness is meaningfully linked to her increasing abilities to see hypocrisy in the social world. "A sensation of estrangement and isolation encompassed her" (47–48) as she starts to notice that the women hate whites but "aped their clothes, their manners, and their gracious ways of living" (48). The onset of suffocation, "as if she were shut up, boxed up, with hundreds of her race" (54), and alienation from "uplift"-women parallels Edna's alienation from mother-women and Scout's elongated experience of the trial closing in on her until she nods off and hears the jury's decision from underwater, immersion in which Edna indulges while she awakens to suffocating environments.

The hypocrisy Helga marks in uplift-women leads to her "awakening" to "the realization of a dream" (67) in Denmark, where she sojourns with her deceased mother's family and where she is immediately dressed and displayed as an exotic black object. She becomes more and more resistant to this, just as Edna in New Orleans becomes more and more resistant to social mores, longing for her Grand Isle (and Robert), like Helga is soon longing for Harlem (for Negroes and for Anderson). The equivalence of this in *Mockingbird* is Scout's entry into the world of ladies and her objectification in Mrs. Merriweather's pageant, where she nods off and misses her entrance. Restless again because Helga sees hypocrisy in her relatives' commodification of her, she returns to Harlem and has "riotous and colorful dreams" (105) of Dr. Anderson, who has married her friend. In a moment of passion, they kiss, much like Robert returns to Edna. But collapses and final descents are immanent, just like they are for Scout the very moment she dons the ham, accepts objectification, and experiences suffocation and loss of vision. Robert bids Edna farewell, Helga collapses when Dr. Anderson explains that the kiss was a mistake, and Ewell comes out of the shadows to attack the ham.

Just as Edna finally returns to the sea in complete exhaustion, Helga experiences two final states of unconsciousness; in the first, much like Scout, she becomes vulnerable to a local community that alters her life. In Helga's case it is a religious revival meeting, and she wakes to find herself married to Reverend Pleasant Green: "she still felt a little dizzy and much exhausted. So great had been this physical weariness . . . she had been seized with a hateful feeling of vertigo and obliged to lay firm hold on his arm to keep herself from falling" (115). She finds herself trying to pass as a proper preacher's wife in Alabama, but the destiny of perpetual pregnancy and care of small children leads into the vortex of utter unconsciousness:

> Nothing reached her. Nothing penetrated the kind darkness into which her bruised spirit had retreated. . . . While she had gone down into that appalling blackness of pain, the ballast of her brain had got loose and she hovered for a long time somewhere in that delightful borderland on the edge of unconsciousness, an enchanted and blissful place where peace and incredible quiet encompassed her. . . . Helga did sleep. She found it surprisingly easy to sleep. Aided by Miss Hartley's rather masterful discernment, she took advantage of the ease with which this blessed enchantment stole over her. From her husband's praisings, prayers, and caresses she sought refuge in sleep, and from the neighbors' gifts, advice, and sympathy. (128, 131)

Just as Scout makes her most penetrating connections in such a state, during this unconsciousness Helga "awakens" to the realization that her people have accepted their downtrodden condition because they have pledged faith to "the white man's God" (130). Analogously, before Scout processes with a "dreamlike quality" the final verdict, she "receive[s] the impression" in partial unconsciousness that the silent courtroom is only replaying the mad dog scene (210).

Passing into an endless reproductive role that has already half-deadened her, killed her fourth child, and will likely kill her, Helga Crane is claimed by the female body in the same way that Madame Ratignolle's delivery and the sea itself claims Edna Pontellier from trespassing against the South. Scout is paradoxically sleepy and "suddenly awake" (280) in the final scene at the reading of *The Gray Ghost,* which, I have shown, reflects the plot of the many dispossessed by a suffocating environment. Scout mumbles the story to Atticus in the style of earlier stream-of-consciousness scenes, her phrases separated by ellipses and her "grammar erratic." By the end of the novel, we are conditioned to understand the astute analytical abilities of Scout while in such trances. Comparison with Edna and Helga reveals sleepwalking as the fate of the analytical, detached female.

Readers of *Mockingbird* need to understand Scout's final "passing out" as an ironic consequence of her success at learning to "pass" as a lady. In Scout's negotiations with Maycomb ladies, particularly the imported Aunt Alexandra, and in the anthropological language the narrator uses to mark "Maycomb ways" throughout the novel, we have to recognize the genre of the novel of manners informing Scout's story. It is a genre that emerges to "take in" Scout in a crucial scene: the missionary society scene. This scene reveals the kinship between Lee and Wharton, particularly in Lee's importation of Wharton's social metaphor, perspective, and royal matriarch in *The Age of Innocence*. If Aunt Alexandra seems imported from a different land and time, reflecting the weighty burden of Finch's Landing and tradition, she is also an import from a specific genre. The representation of Aunt Alexandra echoes Wharton's humorous depiction of the matriarchal head of the New York tribe—Mrs. Catherine Mingott—whose ample body and royal dominion provide a clear precedent for the formidable, corpulent Alexandra, also a name reminiscent of Russian royalty.

The Age of Innocence is, like *Mockingbird,* a novel about social entrapment and the way in which a tightly knit society ritualizes the exclusion of whatever seems foreign to it. The anthropological language deployed by Lee to depict her insider/outsider's view of Maycomb parallels Newland Archer's slow yet hopeless alienation from New York society such that he can see the primitive rites of it through the lens of anthropology and even archeology, fields established in the early twentieth century and increasingly important in midcentury, particularly because the popularized work of Margaret Mead had raised questions about the naturalness of childhood, adolescence, and gender roles in American culture. Wharton repeatedly characterized herself as an ethnologist in her novels, a role she assumed because of her wide reading in ethnography, sociology, and anthropology (Gibson 57, 58). In *The Age of Innocence* she explicitly drew upon James Frazer's *The Golden Bough* to describe social rites and tribal customs of New York, a novel she set back in time fifty years, not to mark the changing of her contemporary generation (as in her other novels), but to pose "a challenge to the old order that comes not from without but from within, from men and women who share the dominant values of the old society" (Gibson 58).

Lee's efforts to mark the challenge to "tribal" Maycomb from *within* is equivalent, explaining the same paradoxical stance of irony and "nostalgic longing, for what one would not wholly have wished to have," that Gibson describes in Wharton's *The Age of Innocence* (67). *The Age of Innocence* simultaneously constructs nostalgia for tradition and emphasizes the constrictions of Wharton's girlhood New York, which Wharton said surprised her because it "'would fifty years later be as much a vanished city as Atlantis or the lowest lawyer of Schliemann's Troy'" (Gibson 57). Lee's desire to mark the richness of the small-town social world, which she felt to be disappearing, with her anthropological stance on its customs, gives the reader the same effect. Aunt Alexandra and scenes that include her seem to directly allude to *The Age of Innocence*, suggesting that Lee's depiction of her childhood past was her equally ironic view of an "age of innocence" that was only innocent insofar as a web of deception could be maintained in social rituals.

If we look at *Mockingbird* as Scout's story of compromise with "Aunty," we can also view her compromise as Newland's compromise with May, or his grooming *by* May, which similarly ends with retreat and lost illusions: "Newland's solution is one many a female character has taken: retreat to the interior," because "there is no place for [Newland and Ellen] in this world" (Chandler 177, 178). Newland may be a man in a world of matriarchs, but in many ways he has as feminine a sensibility toward social nuance as Scout has a masculine one, at home in her father's world and ironic toward ruling matriarchs. The Jane Austen-styled social irony of Lee and Wharton provides us with visions of how individuals become products of overwhelming social systems, which is how Newland views May. Wharton was an obvious model for a novel of regional modernism, and Wharton had, earlier in her career, applied her regional modernism to female coming of age with her short novel *Summer;* like Chopin's *Awakening,* Lee's *Mockingbird,* and McCullers's *Member of the Wedding,* the trope of awakening to vague discontent in the context of endless, stifling summer communicates the hopelessness of development in consuming environments.

In my chapter on child consciousness, I demonstrated how young Scout's mental limitations, such as her ability to mourn for only "two days," echo the limits of white Maycomb and thus of regional consciousness in the novel. Scout's increasing exhaustion, which suggests a passivity shared with many modern female protagonists who long to belong but who feel alien and freakish in whatever world they try to belong to, is actually a book-length study in how young Scout comes to mirror a "tired old town" that is sagging and wilting from heat. Scout is destined to be one of those sweet and sour ladies "like soft teacakes with frostings of sweat and sweet talcum" (5), as much as she prefers the transparent world of men: "I was more at home in my father's world. People like Mr. Heck Tate did not trap you with innocent questions to make fun of you; . . . there was something about [men] that I instinctively liked . . . they weren't—'Hypocrites, Mrs. Perkins, born hypocrites,' Mrs. Merriweather was saying" (233–34). Scout's perspective on the female-ruled social world of Maycomb deepens with the narrator's analysis of Maycomb tribes, clans, and kinships, just as Newland's perspective deepens on matriarchal New York.

Yet Scout's entrapment in the ritualized, cyclical force of social inclusions and exclusions parallels the young women of modern writing. Characters like Charity Royall and Frankie of *Member* are trapped in the anguish of inaction even as they long for modernity because they become a synecdoche for environmental reproduction. This is why pregnancy is a particularly strong symbol of "confinement," both because pregnancy does alter the course of a woman's life, but also because it suggests cultural and environmental reproduction. Chopin directly ties sleeping and awakening to childbirth when she witnesses Madame Ratignolle give birth: "[Edna] recalled faintly an ecstasy of pain, the heavy odor of chloroform, a stupor which had deadened sensation, and an awakening to find a little new life to which she had given being, added to the great unnumbered multitude of souls that come and go" (104). Similarly, Helga does not wish to have children and be "'responsible for the giving of life to creatures doomed to endure such wounds . . . as Negroes have to endure'" (103), but not long after, "the fourth little dab of amber humanity which Helga had contributed to a despised race was held before her . . . she failed entirely to respond properly" (127). It is as if Larsen rewrites Edna's story from the perspective of a combined Adèle (on her fourth child) and "the octoroon" who cares for Edna's children.

The language of uncertainty about whether confinement is change or painful continuity inflects the final rest in *Mockingbird* with similar uncertainty. Presumably, the ending sleep is the cocoon before transformation. As Fine points out, we have no real conclusion to Scout's story as an adult—no information about whether this descent into sleep is hibernation before metamorphosis or giving up ("Structuring"). We are left only with deadened sensation and Atticus's bedside vigil. However, we can apply the intertexts of modern women's regional writing to arrive at an understanding of Scout's sense that she must soon pass into the world of ladies. The narrator has, after all, carefully weighed Aunt Alexandra's theory of family streaks, and she finds in the ladies multitudes of "mother-women" that teach her deployment of gossip and mockery through voice, suggestion, and innuendo.

As Maria Nikolajeva has anatomized, the difference between childhood and adolescence in literature is synonymous with the distinction between mythic and linear time; mythic time is cyclical and repetitive, corresponding with the seasons, while linear time is chronological and historical. Even as Jem has access to Atticus's watch, even as Frankie loves to watch her father fix watches, even as Charity listens to the modern Lucius Harney mark the history of architecture around her, modern female protagonists become aware of time passing only in the cyclical sense of needing to *pass* into womanhood. Women are literally vehicles of cultural and social reproduction. Edna's return to the mythic, maternal sea; the pregnancy of Helga; the half-dead state of the pregnant Charity in her sleepwalking wedding to Royall; the allusion to Eliot's J. Alfred Prufrock in the final pages of McCullers's Frankie, "'I am just mad about Michelangelo,' [Frankie] said" (150): these are women writers looking at Darwin's insights about survival of the fittest. The fittest "fit" because they *pass*, but *passing* is perilously close to *passing out* from the heat of the anguish.

Ages of Innocence

Like *Mockingbird, The Age of Innocence* parodies the "innocence" of a past American age by focusing on a lawyer who, like Atticus, has one overriding passion; the legal case that confronts Newland Archer affects him personally, albeit for a different reason. The detached contemplation by which Newland encourages the reader to regard his wife May and "her set" is perilously close to the way Atticus dryly and sarcastically copes with his sister's emphasis on social matters. The parallel makes it clear that although men in *Mockingbird* occupy positions of authority in court and law, Atticus also inhabits a matriarchal tribe where his power is very limited. The missionary society scene, where the death of Tom becomes ironic "background," a word fraught with meaning in Maycomb, echoes the carefully crafted farewell dinner Wharton's May "tribe" performs for Countess Olenska, structured as it is to reify social rites by exorcising and "othering" foreigners. If we regard the missionary society scene through the lens of one of Wharton's famous, elaborately described dinner parties, some crucial insights emerge.

It is in this missionary society scene that Lee's comic social mask becomes most vivid. It is in this scene that the ladies we know best—Miss Maudie and Aunt Alexandra—are wearing their masks for the ball. The scene depends on a shared understanding of the camouflage required by the ritual; as a missionary society meeting, the scene suggests for the ladies a summons to rescue and Christianize the unenlightened as long as they are far, far away from Maycomb. Wharton's dinner party reveals how the dinner guests and host conspire to excise "the other" in what is really a primitive rallying of the New York tribe, which becomes apparent to Newland Archer:

> Archer, who seemed to be assisting at the scene in a state of odd imponderability, as if he floated somewhere between chandelier and ceiling, wondered at nothing so much as his own share in the proceedings. . . . And then it came over him, in a vast flash made up of many broken gleams, that to all of them he and Madame Olenska were lovers, lovers in the extreme sense peculiar to "foreign" vocabularies. He guessed himself to have been, for months, the centre of countless silently observing eyes and patiently listening ears; he understood that, by means as yet unknown to him, the separation between himself and the partner of his guilt had been achieved, and that now the whole tribe had rallied about his wife on the tacit assumption that nobody knew anything, or had ever imagined anything, and that the occasion of the entertainment was simply May Archer's natural desire to take an affectionate leave of her friend and cousin.
>
> It was the old New York way of taking life "without effusion of blood": the way people who dreaded scandal more than disease, who placed decency above courage, and who considered that nothing was more ill-bred than "scenes," except the behaviour of those who gave rise to them. (283)

The "tribal rally around a kinswoman about to be eliminated from the tribe" (281) celebrates shared values through revealing who is different and who must be excluded, ritualistically, and it all occurs with a deception participated in by all the players, betrayed by no one who wants to be on the inside. The innocence is ironic because innocence requires a careful social performance—a taking of sides. Newland understands the scene as a warning. As he listens to discussion of the newly exiled Beauforts, discussed "over the asparagus" (282), he understands or at least interprets the cannibalistic excision of the disgraced as showing him "'what would happen to *me*—' and a deathly sense of the superiority of implication and analogy over direct action, and of silence over rash words, closed in on him like the doors of the family vault" (282–83). This same sense of enclosure is occurring to Scout as she watches the missionary society ladies and begins to observe her own "share in the proceedings," watching herself serve the ladies cookies as she responds to Aunt Alexandra's silent nod to do so.

Throughout *The Age of Innocence*, Ellen Olenska has been shunned for her difference, her foreignness, her refusal of convention. The way the dinner party scene "others" and thereby solidifies the clan becomes all the more apparent when the gentlemen separate from the ladies, and Lawrence Lefferts "others" Beaufort, who has recently scandalized New York with dishonorable financial investments:

> The talk, as usual, had veered around to the Beauforts.... Never had Lefferts so abounded in the sentiments that adorn Christian manhood and exalt the sanctity of the home. Indignation lent him a scathing eloquence, and it was clear that if others had followed his example, and acted as he talked, society would never have been weak enough to receive a foreign upstart like Beaufort ... once [society] got in the way of tolerating men of obscure origin and tainted wealth the end was total disintegration—and at no distant date. (284–85)

The double-voiced discourse in Lee's scene is similar; Mrs. Merriweather begins:

> "Gertrude," she said. "I tell you there are some good but misguided people in this town. Good, but misguided. Folks in this town who think they're doing right, I mean. Now far be it from me to say who, but some of 'em in this town thought they were doing the right thing a while back, but all they did was stir 'em up. That's all they did. Might've looked like the right thing to do at the time, I'm sure I don't know, I'm not read in that field, but sulky ...

dissatisfied . . . I tell you if my Sophy'd kept up another day I'd have let her go." (232–33)

Wharton's understanding of a social world's primitive tribalism, thinly veiled by civilization, indicates the "tissue of elaborate mutual dissimulation" (286) characterizing Maycomb matriarchy. Scout's lack of biological mother indicates what Madame Olenska indicates for Newland: the possibility of an escape valve and the complete existence of the social world as an unnatural and thereby an entirely artificial world. However, there is "nowhere to go" outside of it, and thus Scout watches herself escorted into it by many mother figures.

Archer Newland's dissociated reaction to the ritual is similar to Scout's numbed view of herself entering the scene, which echoes her trancelike view of the jury ritualizing exclusion of the black man from citizenship and justice. Wharton's New York and Lee's Maycomb are similar in that they exclude people based on paranoid views of sexuality and kinship acceptability. On top of the sleepwalking experience of participating in such scenes, however, both novels emphasize the response of laughter to what is in the scene itself "even mirth" (284). No reader can see the word "mirth" without contemplating Lily Bart, the most extreme victim of mirth in *The House of Mirth*. Lily stands in a long line of hopeless awakenings of female characters who spiral into an endless cycle of decline, as I believe Scout does in the last third of the novel. But Newland's reaction to the scene's mirth corresponds to his own mad laughter that he lets out on several occasions in *Age of Innocence,* just as extreme laughter erupts in *Mockingbird* in punctuating moments of entrapment. In fact, there are three major moments of mad laughter in Wharton's *Age of Innocence* that we can parallel to *Mockingbird.*

The first time Newland laughs, he startles his sister, rather like Miss Maudie startles Scout and Jem. Newland laughs at the irony of the turn of the screw that he himself has occasioned. He has hastened his wedding by talking the women into a shortened engagement, even as he has become slowly aware of his reluctance. The telegram from May comes precisely after his discovery that Ellen returns his passion (148). The laughter comes not only because of the situational irony, but also because entrapment is the result of his own actions. Similarly, Miss Maudie laughs because the source of the joke is herself. Her words, "absolute morphodite," have returned to haunt her, just as Newland's own words have returned to haunt him, and Miss Maudie has started her own fire by trying to save her plants. She has carried out a punishment that her enemies, the foot-washing Baptists, would like to see occur, punishing herself for her indulgence in flowers just like Mayella, who tends her geraniums as carefully as Miss Maudie does her flowers, is punished for blooming in the only way she believes she can. Wharton's intertext sheds light on the fact that laughter is a response to the awareness of taking on a social lens toward the self.

In such moments of laughter, irony toward the self as a vehicle of self-incarceration overflows. These moments teach us how to theorize laughter as the "mad" response to one's own participation in a system that sickens. Newland laughs again and even recalls his first laugh as "incomprehensible mirth" (274) when he hears, from May, Ellen's letter, stating her intent to return to Europe. The laughter is again a result of ironic timing; the very moment he is about to come clean to May and confess his love for Ellen is interrupted by the female tribe's interference. His "laughter of inner devils that reverberated through all his efforts to discuss the Martha Washington ball with Mrs. Reggie Chivers" (286) parallels both Dill's reaction to the trial (his vow to be the laughing clown) and the inner laughter Scout hears from "inner devils" in the Radley house. The laughter is a response to the "clan/ Klan" closing in like the "doors of the family vault." As the most different and most unrecognized homosexual characters, Dill and Boo would seem to be laughing in response to their own participation in hiding themselves from an intolerant world. Newland's "inner devils" laughing enable us to read the laughter in the "morphodite" characters of *Mockingbird* as madness engendered by environments that use primitive hostilities to trap modern characters who, unfortunately, have full knowledge of the trap.

Wharton's dinner parties, where lessons can be taught and vicious alliances made or unmade, underlie Lee's strategic placement of her missionary society scene, particularly because the host of the scene could not be more related to Wharton's novel. The matriarchal corpulence of Mrs. Catherine Mingott is reincarnated in Aunt Alexandra. And "Aunty" makes everyone laugh because she is fully intended to be comic. The narrator calls up all her comic arts to level them against Aunt Alexandra as a ridiculous and weighty embodiment of the social South that at once suggests nostalgia for a sagging past and a fleeting quality called on the surface Christian southern womanhood:

Today was Sunday, and Aunt Alexandra was positively irritable on the Lord's Day. I guess it was her Sunday corset. She was not fat, but solid, and she chose protective garments that drew up her bosom to giddy heights, pinched in her waist, flared out her rear, and managed to suggest that Aunt Alexandra's was once an hour-glass figure. From any angle, it was formidable. (128)

The weight of Finch's Landing is architected on her very body. The "gentle gloom that descends when relatives appear" (128) is reminiscent of Mrs. Mingott's "immense accretion of flesh which had descended on her in middle life like a flood of lava on a doomed city" (Wharton 23), which similarly suggests a comic archeology of past society doomed and pronounced on the bodies of women. Aunt Alexandra must have conceived her one child "long ago, in a burst of friendliness" (77), because "Uncle Jimmy present or Uncle Jimmy absent made not much difference" (128) in Aunt Alexandra's abundant existence. She "was fanatical on the subject of my attire . . . furthermore, I should be a ray of sunshine in my father's lonely life" (81), and her campaign for Scout to be a lady is part and parcel of her interpretation of the world as a system of kinships, family streaks, and "tribal groups" (129), anthropological discourse imported from Wharton's view of regional "clans" and their rallying rituals around kinswomen. The excision of Aunt Alexandra from the film only bespeaks its refusal to accommodate comedy and caricature. Where this art comes from reveals Lee's stance on regional irony.

Named after the empress Catherine the Great, Mrs. Catherine Mingott and her abundant flesh signify the need to excavate societal power in the bodies of women, who, when excavated, are actually quite small. But they grow with their social power, particularly when revered by the tribe. Mrs. Mingott's flesh accumulation "had changed her from a plump, active little woman with a neatly turned foot and ankle into something as vast and august as a natural phenomenon":

She had accepted this submergence as philosophically as all her other trials, and now, in extreme old age, was rewarded by presenting to her mirror an almost unwrinkled expanse of firm pink-and-white flesh, in the centre of which the traces of a small face survived as if awaiting excavation. A flight of smooth double chins led down to the dizzy depths of a still-snowy bosom veiled in snowy muslins that were held in place by a miniature portrait of the late Mr. Mingott; and around and below, wave after wave of black silk surged away over the edges of a capacious armchair, with two tiny white hands poised like gulls on the surface of the billows. (23)

A "formidable" caste system like that of Maycomb or New York piles social significance onto tiny faces and hands; but if women are originally miniature, men are more so. Mr. Mingott is the tiniest of miniatures in a massive matriarchy that relies on codes of dress, domestic detail, dinner rites, guests and balls, engagements, and family alliances that men in general would find incomprehensible. This is similar to the nonrole of Aunt Alexandra's husband and the nonroles of pretty much any husbands in Maycomb when it comes to social life. Men are unnecessary appendages who have a prescribed role in the "Gothic joke" of a courthouse. From this "formidable angle," Atticus's efficacy in changing one hundred years of Maycomb tradition is pretty futile. The fact that both Catherine and Alexandra share royal names is more than coincidence.

The "giddy heights" of Aunt Alexandra's bosom finds its sister in the "prodigious projection of [Mrs. Mingott's] bosom" (179), and the great bulk of Catherine means that she is "enthroned" in as a queen; all must answer to her "imperial summons" (236) by coming to her for an understanding of their place. Mrs. Mingott has the power to place Ellen and the weighty means to convey financial and social independence. The unconventional Ellen means something to Mrs. Mingott, just as the unconventional and motherless Scout means something to Aunt Alexandra, for some mysterious reason. It seems that integrating these wayward girls would solidify their reign: "[Aunt Alexandra] never let a chance escape her to point out the shortcomings of other tribal groups to the greater glory of our own" (129). The analogy between royalty and the way these women rule is quite obvious in Lee's novel. The narrator comments on how Aunt Alexandra "would exercise her royal prerogative: she would arrange, advise, caution, and warn" (129). She is immediately enthroned by the community and a member of the missionary society, as well as a ruling officer of the Maycomb Amanuensis Club: "To all parties present and participating in the life of the county, Aunt Alexandra was one of the last of her kind: she had river-boat, boarding-school manners; let any moral come along and she would uphold it; she was born in the objective case; she was an incurable gossip" (129). This is precisely Mrs. Mingott's function in the formidable kinship structure of New York; like her, Aunt Alexandra immediately anchors the social world around her. In the process, she profoundly alters the genre of Scout's life to an imported novel of *manners*.

The archeological metaphor implied by the description of Mrs. Mingott's body, veils, and waves upon waves of silk is crucial because the sense of a social world as past, but unaware of itself as past, recurs in *The Age of Innocence*. This is rather like the point of returning to the Depression era on the brink of the Civil Rights era. A society that does not understand its doom is doomed indeed. Significantly, Newland can begin to excavate how power operates in his world because he once studied anthropology (57), a field peppering New York civilization to suggest that civilization is not at all civilization but raw primitivism deceiving itself. Like the metaphor of the game that James uses to define social relations throughout *What Maisie Knew*, underlying the checkerboard metaphor that surfaces in *Mockingbird* and that complements the book of Alabama law in Atticus's office, the metaphor of primitivism recurs in both Wharton's and Lee's novels. The narrator of *Age of Innocence* compares New York's awareness of what is "the thing" and "not the thing" to "the inscrutable totem terrors that had ruled the destinies of [Newland's] forefathers thousands of years ago" (4). What Aunt Alexandra names family streaks are such things as "the Mingottian aplomb which old Catherine had inculcated in all her tribe" (12). Two ruling "clans" (28) of kinship networks rule New York. Mrs. Welland's simulation of reluctance at announcing her daughter's engagement is compared to the ritual of "primitive man" (38) in dragging the shrieking "savage bride" from her parents' tent. Archer feels that in his courtship ritual he has been "rolled from one tribal doorstep to another" (57), that he "had been shown off like a wild animal cunningly trapped." The wedding is compared to a primeval rite, where the groom is a ritualized object of the communal gaze (151); the rite of female wardrobe is, Newland perceives, women's armor (167); Newland has "some deep tribal instinct" (212) that the family has left him out in an effort to silence any opposition when it comes to Ellen; and the final dinner party becomes the cleanest blood sacrifice of an ancient rallying right (282). The language resonates with Lee's discussion of the Ewells as an "exclusive society" (30); Scout's special knowledge of "the Cunningham tribe" (20); poor eyesight as the "tribal curse of the Finches" (89); and various "tribal" discourses and family "streaks" articulated by Aunt Alexandra but, importantly, both analyzed and verified by *Mockingbird*'s anthropologist narrator. In "Colonizing Children: Dramas of Transformation," Melanie Eckford-Prossor demonstrates that childhood narratives are modeled on imperialist ones in which "native" informants describe a colonial culture so that it can be understood and controlled by those foreign to it, which explains both Atticus's lessons to Scout on Cunninghams and Ewells, as well as Lee's shaping of her novel at a cultural moment when federal forces were acting against Alabama. Actually, Lee shows this in the novel when Scout is able to change the mob outside the jail by applying lessons in the culture of "the Cunningham tribe."

Newland is resigned to the fact that May is not responsible for the "curtain of emptiness" she is, in his view, because she is a product of the kinship system; like Atticus, he is resigned to it in the most passive manner. Just as Atticus had hoped to get through life without a case like Tom's, before Newland comes to know Ellen Olenska and her situation, "few things seemed to Newland Archer more awful than an offence against 'taste,'" (13) even though he considers himself above others:

> In matters intellectual and artistic Newland Archer felt himself distinctly the superior of these chosen specimens of old New York gentility; he had probably read more, thought more, and even seen a good deal more of the world than any other man of the number. Singly they betrayed their inferiority, but grouped together they represented "New York," and the habit of masculine solidarity made him accept their doctrine on all the issues called moral. He instinctively felt that in this respect it would be troublesome—and also rather bad form—to strike out for himself. (7)

The alteration engendered by the legal case that comes to affect him personally, however, makes him more passive and more discontent than Atticus. For example, when he decides to go get Madame Olenska from the beach, he sets arbitrary criteria for himself; he will summon her only if her head turns before "that sail crosses the Lime Rock light" (182). In other words, Newland allows the environment to overshadow his personal choice, preferring instead Prufrock-like inaction that enables him to compensate with an analytic stance toward the kinship rites. This role in *Mockingbird* is bequeathed to Scout and her future role as narrator, whereas Atticus takes the active role in striking out for himself against what he views as "his friends."

With her narrator who excavates the tight caste system of Maycomb with anthropological discourse and vicious humor about matriarchal tribal society, but who also questions it with the device of young Scout trying to figure out the meaning of "background," Lee brings to us her version of an age of innocence. Literally, she is using what we perceive as the innocence of childhood and a small town's "nothing happening" existence, which upon closer examination is merely the complex mutual dissimulation of innocence. The Missionary Society ladies have no awareness that they regard others as primitive (the Mrunas) when their own town has participated in a "Roman carnival" ritually exorcising difference and reifying their preferred kinship networks. In fact, the news of Ewell having spit at a gentleman seems more scandalous to them than the "mock" trial. And since the ritual exclusion of poor white society is the main intent of their overwhelming rituals, since the inclusion of blacks isn't even a question, a man will really die "for no reason" because he is not really a threat to white Maycomb self-definition.

Immediately upon Aunt Alexandra's entry into the Maycomb social scene, webs of deception enfold Scout in a complex tissue. The narrator admits that one must lie to live within the system: "one must lie under certain circumstances and at all times when one can't do anything about them" (128). In other words, Scout's initiation into tissues of mutual dissimulation begins the very moment Atticus says Aunt Alexandra is here to stay because the summer is going to be "a hot one." The trope of endlessly stifling summer will become important in our comparison of regional coming-of-age texts. The particularly "hot" quality of the summer is largely a matter of the stifling society novel Aunt Alexandra has brought to Scout's doorstep.

Aunt Alexandra's propensity to be "fanatical" about Scout's clothing takes on a new light when we view her as an imported Mrs. Mingott, from a novel in which Newland has figured out that women's clothing is their armor. In fact, we first encounter Aunt Alexandra at a dinner party, where Scout is isolated from "the big table" (81) because of her improper manners and because space defines her status under Alexandra's royal reign. Even Atticus begs that he has no influence on her, so he cannot change Scout's seat. The plenty of food that she provides is ironically read as "a modest Christmas dinner" (82), when it is really social and corpulent excess. Passages on Aunt Alexandra's interpretations of inherited family streaks, which the narrator echoes two pages later, seem directly transposed from Wharton's novel:

> Aunt Alexandra, in underlining the moral of young Sam Merriweather's suicide, said it was caused by a morbid streak in the family. Let a sixteen-year-old girl giggle in the choir and Aunty would say, "It just goes to show you, all the Penfield women are flighty." Everybody in Maycomb, it seemed, had a Streak: a Drinking Streak, a Gambling Streak, a Mean Streak, a Funny Streak. . . . Aunt Alexandra's theory had something behind it, though. . . . There was indeed a caste system in Maycomb, but to my mind it worked this way: the older citizens . . . took for granted attitudes, character shadings, even gestures, as having been repeated in each generation and refined by time. Thus the dicta No Crawford Minds His Own Business, Every Third Merriweather Is Morbid, The Truth Is Not in the Delafields, All the Bufords Walk Like That, were simply guides to daily living: never take a check from a Delafield without a discreet call to the bank; Miss Maudie Atkinson's shoulder stoops because she was a Buford; if Mrs. Grace Merriweather sips gin out of Lydia E. Pinkham bottles it's nothing unusual—her mother did the same. (*Mockingbird* 129–131)

> [Mr. Sillerton Jackson] could also enumerate the leading characteristics of each family: as, for instance, the fabulous stinginess of the younger lines of Leffertses (the Long Island ones); or the fatal tendency of the Rushworths to make foolish matches; or the insanity recurring in every second generation of the Albany Chiverses, with whom New York cousins had always refused to intermarry—with the disastrous exception of poor Medora Manson, who, as everybody knew . . . but then her mother was a Rushworth. (*Age of Innocence* 8–9)

The similarity of the Beauforts and Bufords is deliberate. The sense that this "inside" knowledge is a shortcut, "guides to daily living," appears in *Age of Innocence*. When May Archer wants to easily explain to her mother why Newland "doesn't look ahead," she simply says that he reads when he has little to do, and her mother immediately recognizes the resemblance to his father. "Like his father!" (187) explains any oddity or dissatisfaction. It does so by relieving any particular individual from having made a choice or exercised agency. The phrase above "everybody knew" finds its counterpart in *Mockingbird,* even among the children when they hear of Miss Caroline from Winston County, which seceded from Alabama in 1861 "and every child in Maycomb County knew it" (16). From Wharton's modern view of how individuals are hopelessly trapped in Darwinian social environments, Lee derived her own portrait of a world in which there is "nothing beyond the boundaries of Maycomb county" because the world looks inward.

In fact, the narrator inserts herself to carefully weigh Aunt Alexandra's "preoccupation with heredity" (130) and to oddly reify it, analyze it, and ultimately reveal her allegiance with ladies, even though she is, like Newland, far enough on its margins to also diagnose its anthropological value to the tribe. The narrator gives us "background" on Maycomb's "inward" growth and tendency for families to marry into families, such that she appears a lot like Wharton's Mr. Sillerton Jackson, who is practically the only authority who knows "all the ramifications of New York's cousinships, and could not only elucidate such complicated questions as that of the connection between the Mingotts (through the Thorleys) with the Dallases of South Carolina, and that of the relationship of the elder branch of Philadelphia Thorleys to the Albany Chiverses (on no account to be confused with the Manson Chiverses of University Place)" (8). The reader is expected to feel dizzy in trying to keep these Chiverses or Cunninghams straight. His opera glass in hand to scrutinize who is sitting with whom at the event, Sillerton Jackson is humorously akin to the narrator of *Mockingbird* and even to both Scout and Jem. They enumerate a Who's Who column to Dill as each eclectic community member rolls by and heads for the trial, Lee's ironic equivalent to Wharton's opera.

Lee even puts in a kinship joke when she writes of the Cunninghams and Conninghams, whose dispute over a property title and authority to a landholding hinges solely upon someone's misspelling at some point. Kinships paradoxically gesture toward stability and confusion; they are at once unreadable and familiar. These are like the "tangled skeins of genealogy" that Harriet Jacobs references on the first pages of her narrative as she attempts to sort out who is related to whom, who took care of whom, and who "belongs" to whom in the South. Capote's commentary on Noon City in his novel is similar; he says that there are no newcomers, but he also shows that few leave, depicting the place as a sort of inward-looking vortex. Similarly, John Berendt ends his novel of Savannah with a poignant description of the eccentricity bred and paradoxically tolerated by inward-looking towns:

> For me, Savannah's resistance to change was its saving grace. The city looked inward, sealed off from the noises and distractions of the world at large. It *grew* inward, too, and in such a way that its people flourished like hothouse plants tended by an indulgent gardener. The ordinary became extraordinary. Eccentricities thrived. Every nuance and quirk of personality achieved greater brilliance in that lush enclosure than would have been possible anywhere else in the world. (386)

Lee's *Mockingbird,* like Wharton's regional writing, analyzes the small town's paradoxical tolerance for eccentricity, if the eccentricity is inherited and thus "inward," and intolerance for outsiders—its need to other someone, however it finds that someone, for its sense of insider/outsider boundaries. Greene's trial novel *Death in the Deep South* marks these boundaries by casting a Northerner in the role of accused rapist and releasing the black man originally arrested. If there were not Madame Olenskas, Toms, and Mrunas to make foreign, how else could streaks be mapped? Berendt's metaphor of plant roots and mutations sharply concretize the Darwinism of Lee's study, a Darwinism ideologically behind both child consciousness and anthropological study driving the early modern novels. It is perhaps not surprising that the most eccentric *Mockingbird* character spends most of her time gardening and thus engineering "natural" selection.

The irony unfolding in the narrator is the way she (Scout), like Maisie, has been "made" in Aunt Alexandra's image; she, too, is an incurable gossip, and just as Newland develops an outsider anthropologist lens, the narrator of *Mockingbird* verifies Aunty's position on tribes and streaks by concluding that these beliefs and practices have a function: they help people get along. They are social shortcuts, both convenient and expedient. To analyze the function of these beliefs in streaks is not necessarily to challenge them, as Newland proves. The narrator asserts that faith in streaks relieves the community from concern about neighbors; one need not be concerned about someone like Mrs. Merriweather sipping gin. If these thought patterns are "guides to daily living," the narrator inserts herself as our guide to the various tribes and clans that rule a young girl's upbringing. When her father comes into her room to more intimately import Aunt Alexandra's insistence on developing appreciation for Finch background and family, Scout becomes upset and restates, "There was nowhere to go" (134), the words of our initial introduction to Maycomb life. For Scout, there is no way to escape "a living-room overrun with Maycomb ladies, sipping, whispering, fanning" (132), which begins to stream across Scout's consciousness in the missionary society scene as incomprehensible snippets of conversation pour through the door at her, mirroring the time when she eavesdropped on Atticus's porch conversation with men. Ladies are Scout's final frontier.

It is when Aunt Alexandra arrives that Atticus becomes "only a man. It takes a woman to do that kind of work" (134)—the work of socialization. Although we are initially supposed to reject Aunt Alexandra's socialization strategies, like Atticus does, the narrator comes to accept the novel of manners as the strategy of those dispossessed from law and white male positions of authority. She calls attention to Tom's manners, Cal's mannerisms, and her own passing in the missionary society scene to demonstrate that unless Scout wishes to stay isolated at her own dinner table, she must learn to participate in Wharton-elucidated "tissues of mutual dissimulation." Close analysis of the complex and strategically placed missionary society scene makes it clear that it is not only Atticus who is "passin'" and must therefore be respected. It is also Scout who is passin', and it is Cal, Miss Maudie, and Aunty who teach her how.

Mockingbird's Maycomb Mission

Lee's missionary society scene is a complex farewell party for Tom, for Atticus, and for Scout, who has been mostly immersed in her father's world. These farewells are thus strategically interconnected. The scene is a harbinger of death and slumber, on the brink of the novel's expression of eternal rest for Tom and, in the end, Scout. Irony unfolds in it because the social organization has multiple missions. Its overt mission is to civilize those far away, with no recognition of trouble at home, and with no awareness of the

Western bias involved in viewing other cultures as primitive, "to the greater glory of our own [tribal group]" (129). This mission is ironic because, as Wharton's intertextual novel shows, a society organizing itself in a ritual is not helping another group but is "othering" difference to reify its own caste system. Therefore, its mission is to celebrate itself as a portrait of civilization. Another mission that becomes apparent in the scene is the celebration of whiteness and the exorcism not only of blackness but of liberalism, and of maleness. Its last and final mission is the socialization of girlhood into Maycomb lady, which carries Scout across the threshold into its deceptive tissue and masque.

Chapter 24 is uniquely set entirely among female members of Maycomb society, and therefore the "drama of beset manhood" is off stage. Yet this is the scene in which Lee chooses to reveal the death of Tom and the sacrifice of "the other" in an Uncle Tom–like repetition of tears. Even Aunt Alexandra is shaken at the news, and Scout is literally shaking. But one can only shake in the kitchen, behind the scenes. Miss Maudie will command Scout to stop so she, too, can pass as a lady. In the beginning of the chapter, it is actually Cal who takes us into the scene; for Scout, she is the first symbol of the double life a lady takes on when she crosses a threshold, even though she does not conform to white Maycomb's vision of lady: "I admired the ease and grace with which [Cal] handled heavy loads of dainty things" (227). The characteristic ambiguity of the phrase "heavy loads of dainty things" that Cal "handles" gracefully has double meaning; it could mean the ladies themselves, who appear dainty but are in reality heavy in significance and tradition, and it could bear the much larger meaning of the heavy load coming in the chapter— the death, news of which Cal must deliver in her role as boundary-crosser, shape-shifter, handmaiden to a man so often involved in moments of death. The scene is important as foreground to Tom's death because it suggests an exclusively female-dominated world that Atticus cannot even enter; he hides in the kitchen, unable to interrupt the proceedings of "the civilizing mission." This is a limit to Atticus's ability to pass. It is a place he cannot go and a place he cannot really help Scout go. It is therefore also his death as adviser to Scout, for she is sentenced beyond reasonable doubt, too: "There was no doubt about it, I must soon enter this world, where on its surface fragrant ladies rocked slowly, fanned gently, and drank cool water" (233). The analogy to water is an old one, and the feeling of drowning evoked in response to the jury is relevant here. Margaret Atwood, in *The Edible Woman,* calls the office virgins a Sargasso-sea of femininity, which again echoes Edna Pontellier's suicide. Clearly, the world of Maycomb ladies comprises a parallel court to the one that excludes ladies, a separatist court in which statements are deemed admissible or not, and in which judgment is always occurring.

Lee's irony, like Wharton's on clothing as women's armor, derives from the juxtaposition between the society the ladies are discussing and the Maycomb ladies "fighting the good fight all over the house"—contained in their own view, their own vault. Each thing deplored about the Mrunas could be applied to recent Maycomb events:

> They put the women out in huts when their time came . . . they had no sense of family . . . they subjected children to terrible ordeals when they were thirteen; they were crawling with yaws and earworms, they chewed up and spat out the bark of a tree into a communal pot and then got drunk on it.
>
> Immediately thereafter, the ladies adjourned for refreshments. (228)

The final sentence, a paragraph unto itself like many other single-sentence paragraphs that Lee has trained us to read as transitions from exposition to action, is funny because the paragraph before it suddenly seems like entertainment. The word "immediately" suggests that the story of the Mrunas is nothing more than an appetizer; although the image of the communal pot of spit is hardly mouthwatering, it is made parallel to the social society enjoying refreshments together. Yet the language "adjourned" also suggests court. Judgment upon others is easily, lightly, and gracefully passed in this court. Irony unfolds in each line. The Mrunas separate women from co-ed society, and so does this scene. The Mrunas have no sense of family, while a black man has just been taken from his by a white "family" that appears to be incestuous; the Mruna children were subjected to "terrible ordeals when they were thirteen," which is about Jem's age when he was subjected to the trial and to ugly treatment by the town; "crawling with yaws and earworms" suggests the initial scene of cooties crawling out to greet Miss Caroline; spitting suggests the scandalous treatment of Atticus by Ewell; and getting drunk suggests the ruse of Dolphus Raymond, and Mrs. Merriweather herself, who we know sips gin, and thus is something Maycomb tolerates far more than miscegenation. The language cannot help but make the reader laugh, which is all the more remarkable because we are about to learn of Tom's murder.

Initially Scout stays in the kitchen, and the ladies' conversation mirrors the moment when Scout earlier heard the men on the porch allude to threats to Tom:

> The gentle hum of ladies' voices grew louder as [Cal] opened the door: "Why Alexandra, I never saw such charlotte . . . just lovely . . . I never can get my crust like this, never can . . . [. . .] anybody tell you that the preacher's wife's . . . nooo, well she is, and that other one not walkin' yet . . ." (228)

The stream-of-consciousness style connects the moment to the conversation on the porch about lynching, with similar menace for Scout as her future penetrates her consciousness. The reader understands that young Scout is not yet proficient in this discourse, which fluently though unaccountably flows from female prowess in the kitchen to pregnancy and gossip. A reader familiar with *The Awakening* is reminded of Edna's confusion at the Louisiana ladies' tendency to be discursively open about their bodies, about reproduction, and about flirtation, a paradox for a culture that rigidly expects one to adhere to, for example, Tuesday calling days. Symbolically, Scout is in the kitchen, but she then takes up her mother's coffee pitcher, a position awaiting her, and serves it to the ladies. She is invited to stay, and it is clear that her destiny is to decode matriarchal lineage.

The reader sees that older Scout, narrator Scout, is proficient with the language of femininity and is as much inside it as she is outside it, for purposes of contemplation and analysis. The narrator communicates Scout's fear and vague attraction to the ladies, just as she once did sympathy for Miss Caroline, "she was a pretty little thing": "The ladies were cool in fragile pastel prints: most of them were heavily powdered but unrouged; the only lipstick in the room was Tangee Natural. Cutex Natural sparkled on their fingernails, but some of the younger ladies wore Rose. They smelled heavenly" (229). While the communication of a lesbian eye view is up for debate, the emphasis on scents and colors echoes the crossing into Cal's church, suggesting liminality; the narrator reveals her intimate knowledge of the ladies' lipstick colors and nail polish. It would not be likely that someone who is not a lady would know Tangee Natural, Cutex Natural, and Rose. The colors appear "Natural," as befits a social performance seeking to naturalize what is really a masque. It would be unlikely for someone not proficient in the language of femininity to know not only color but also the distinction between powder and rouge, all at a quick glance. The vague sense of being attracted coupled with the intimate knowledge of femininity distinguishes this reading of the ladies as alien territory yet "heavenly" and "inviting" with the scent of "the other."

We have to pursue, once again, the symbolism of the inverted Scout as we analyze the intimacy between Miss Maudie and Scout that emerges in the scene. In fact, it is Miss Maudie that touches Scout and guides her across the threshold of this foreign space, modeling for her the way a dragged-out figure can pass, yet, like the Van der Luydens, give a lesson when she wishes. Scout is immediately teased by Miss Maudie for passing and inversion when she asks where Scout's britches are. It is unclear whether Miss Maudie means this kindly or not, given her bent for exposing what should be hidden. When Scout admits the britches hide beneath her dress, she becomes the subject of communal laughter. Scout is embarrassed at what she perceives as her mistaken response, but really the mistake is Miss Maudie's, and Scout immediately notices that Miss Maudie is the only one not to laugh. Perhaps she does not laugh because she, too, wears britches and dresses every day, as we have discussed in chapter 5. What follows is a negotiation of whether Scout will be a mini-Atticus or a mini-lady. The ladies ask whether Scout will be a lawyer and tease her about going to court already; after their laughter, and the significant touch of Miss Maudie, Scout declares her intent to be "just" a lady, which is ironic because the scene is teaching her about the complexity of the role. Upon being further prodded about needing to wear more dresses, "Miss Maudie's hand closed tightly on mine, and I said nothing. Its warmth was enough" (230). Miss Maudie initially teases and resents Scout for her betrayal of britches, although she likes the freedom pants afford a motherless child. The ladies' laughter, however, pushes Miss Maudie into a new direction. She realizes that she has to invite Scout to pass—that passing allows people to do some good in the world.

Miss Maudie subsequently assumes Cal's place in passing out the tarts, taking over the role of teaching Scout about leading a double life. The leading of a double life as chameleon lady/morphodite, whichever way you want to put it, allows Miss Maudie to chastise Mrs. Merriweather, just as she once did Miss Stephanie about Boo, when Mrs. Merriweather begins attacking Atticus with words that are not successfully veiled. The vocal shift engendered by Miss Maudie when she becomes angry and lapses into colloquial, plain speech, sort of how Cal's voice changes when she is angry at Scout, is important because throughout the scene of ladies gossip Scout has attended more to how voices sound than to what is actually said. Importantly, Scout pictures the ladies as singing the song of "the ancient little organ in the chapel at Finch's Landing" (232) by analogy to how the organ works on air and replenishment. The image suggests that the women perpetually affect airs of Christian womanhood, which would end if they ever stopped speaking. Scout notes the elongated "s" sounds of one woman, the "clink of coffee cups" and "soft bovine sounds of the ladies munching their dainties" (232), caught up in a symphony revealing its affinity with the southern plantation of the Finch's "background" and the ritual of the ancient chapel. This is yet another song marked by the concept of the mockingbird; the narrator is mocking this performance of the female "organ." The duplicity of someone like Mrs. Merriweather becomes apparent to Scout not so much in what she says, although Scout intuits confusion when she mistakenly believes Mrs. Merriweather to be speaking of forgiving Mayella rather than Helen Robinson, but in how she speaks, noting that the childless Mrs. Merriweather is the type of adult who shifts vocal tone when addressing children (231). As we discussed in chapter 4, the very concept of womanhood in *Mockingbird* is shape-shifting and adapting discourse to social context.

The scene, in emphasizing the racism implied by discussing the Mrunas— "'Not a white person'll go near 'em but that saintly J. Grimes Everett'" (288) —and the deceptive belief that Maycomb in contrast is a Christian town, has everything to do with the real reason behind Tom's death. Claudia Johnson writes of the gap in this scene between surface and depth:

> Their expression of sympathy for the Mrundas is charitable, public formality. It is apparent, however, in a scene as primitive and tribal in its way as the Mrundas could ever be, that a greater countermanding force lies beneath the surface, one neither Christlike nor charitable nor gentle. . . . The meeting of the missionary society undercuts Atticus' and Miss Maudie's attempts to reassure the children that Maycomb is not as bad as the jury that convicted Tom Robinson. ("Secret Courts" 137)

Scout's discomfort with the way ladies "trap you with innocent questions" is nothing less than Wharton's point in depicting an age that believed itself innocent. Scout, Miss Maudie, and Aunt Alexandra are all utterly shaken by the news of Tom's death, but all cross the threshold and act the part of being a lady; they serve, or watch themselves serve, "with my best company manners" (237): "After all, if Aunty could be a lady at a time like this, so could I." Lee's novel actually ends up admiring Aunt Alexandra, who brings Scout the very garments she despises—overalls—after Ewell's attack.

Wharton's novel admires Catherine Mingott all along, of course, and it is Mrs. Mingott who suffers a stroke and finds herself with useless limbs after the Beaufort scandal. But both Wharton and Lee have a complicated relationship with the past. Wharton's novel, through Newland, who may or may not be the most trustworthy authority, concludes that there is "good" in both old ways and new ways. Both novels are marking the cusp of social change. With Wharton, the major changes take place at the turn of the twentieth century; with Lee, the winds of change occur in a postwar culture where small towns, caste systems, and civil rights undergo major transformations. Blackall argues that in contrast to Jane Austen's sparse details about setting, Lee "sees herself as a historian, a chronicler" (20). Lee herself articulated her desire to chronicle:

> "I would like to leave some record of the kind of life that existed in a very small world. . . . to chronicle something that seems to be very quickly going down the drain. . . . There is a very definite social pattern in these [tiny southern] towns that fascinates me. I would simply like to put down all I know about this because I believe that is . . . something to lament in its passing." (qtd. in Blackall 19)

Johnson comments that *Mockingbird* and its reader become enthralled with past innocence (*Threatening* 112), but the mood of passing, a trope accenting many characters as well as the social pattern, creates the paradox that can be found at the end of *Age of Innocence,* when Newland reflects on the next generation—how different his children are, how different their concerns, how irrelevant the details that were so important just twenty years earlier. These careful attentions to what one ought and ought not to do—what is "the thing" and what "not the thing"—may likely not matter in another few decades, as Countess Olenska makes explicit when in the museum she ponders the remnants of other cultures and the way the very things important in one time and place become, in just a short while, unidentifiable scraps to future generations.

Endless Summer before Fall

The missionary society scene and Tom's death occur in a meaningful month: "August was on the brink of September" (228). To fully understand Lee's representation of Scout's "passing" in this scene and the ending's allusion to the death almost always occurring when girls transform into young women, we have to look back at a novel Wharton published before *Age of Innocence*. In many ways a rewriting of Rowson's *Charlotte Temple,* Wharton's 1917 novel, *Summer,* openly represents a young girl's sexual awakening only to demonstrate how regional boundaries close in on her, in the same way that the "primal horde" of *Age of Innocence* closes in on Newland but cloaks itself with fine lace. The imagery in *Summer* echoes for an adolescent Chopin's summer of inner awakening and sets up the imagery in McCullers's *Member of the Wedding,* which also focuses on the adolescent awakening of a southern girl clearly struggling with her sexual orientation. She spends her summer, like Scout, experiencing her feelings of freakish "doubleness" with two mirror characters, a precociously sexual African American woman, Berenice, and a "queer" girlish boy, John Henry, her younger cousin. McCullers even points to Wharton's *Summer* by naming Frankie's father Royal Addams. Read as intertexts to *Mockingbird,* which, as Laura Fine establishes ("Gender Conflicts"), deploys Mayella as Scout's dark sexual double and, as Natalie Hess discusses, uses Cal's doubled identity (just as McCullers uses Berenice's and Honey's), they shed light on how Lee's story enters the tradition of regional modernism in which girls awaken but are forced to succumb to a small town's reproduction of itself.

Wharton's regionalism in *Summer* influenced later writers who would explore female development in overwhelming environments through imagery of intense heat, stasis, and stagnation. The trope of exhaustion continually featured in Chopin's meaningfully titled *The Awakening* haunts these novels. Just as Lee introduces Maycomb as a "tired old town" that "was hotter then," a place of "sweltering shade," "wilting" collars, sweating ladies, and people moving very slowly (5), Wharton introduces Charity's view of North Dormer as an isolated inward-looking place left out of modern life; her description of it emphasizes the negative, "It had no shops, no theatres, no lectures, no 'business block'" (3). This mirrors the negativity of Maycomb, where there was "no hurry, for there was nowhere to go, nothing to buy and no money to buy it with, nothing to see outside the boundaries of Maycomb County" (5). Like the sudden and swift appearance of Dill in the line "That was the summer Dill came to us," and the opening of McCullers's *Member,* "It happened that green and crazy summer . . . when for a long time she had not been a member . . . she was a member of nothing in the world" (1), the appearance of a summer stranger in Wharton's *Summer* makes the stasis of the small town suddenly visible:

> The sight of the stranger [Lucius Harney] once more revived memories of Nettleton, and North Dormer shrank to its real size. As she looked up and down it, from lawyer Royall's faded red house at one end to the white church at the other, she pitilessly took its measure. There it lay, a weather-beaten sunburnt village of the hills, abandoned of men, left apart by railway, trolley, telegraph, and all the forces that link life to life in modern communities. It had no shops, no theatres, no lectures, no "business block"; only a church that was opened every other Sunday if the state of the roads permitted, and a library for which no new books had been bought for twenty years, and where the old ones mouldered undisturbed on the damp shelves. Yet Charity Royall had always been told that she ought to consider it a privilege that her lot had been cast in North Dormer. She knew that, compared to the place she had come from, North Dormer represented all the blessings of the most refined civilization. Everyone in the village had told her so ever since she had been brought there as a child. Even old Miss Hatchard had said to her, on a terrible occasion in her life: "My child, you must never cease to remember that it was Mr. Royall who brought you down from the Mountain." (3–4)

This passage serves as a synecdoche for Wharton's story, which is intended to show the bleakness of the modern female condition. Like the towns, girls are left out of modernity and yet they are told that towns with stable traditions embody the blessings of the most refined civilization. If the passage on Maycomb cues us in to the story of Scout, who will also have "nowhere to go" beyond the boundaries of Maycomb County, this passage describes the story of Charity, who will be romanced and then abandoned by this stranger from the city, emblematic of modern technology that has left behind North Dormer. Upon closer examination, the above passage exemplifies the irony that Charity believes herself opposed to North Dormer (she claims to be sick of it and to hate it), when she has really internalized the discourse of its inhabitants. Town residents have repeatedly told her that she owes a debt to Mr. Royall for "bringing her down from the Mountain," where she was born. It is a debt that she eventually comes to pay by marrying him and accepting his funds to pay the city doctor, whom she has consulted about her pregnancy with Harney. By then, she is, like Scout, sleepy and trancelike, following Royall "as passively as a tired child" and accepting herself as an economic commodity.

As argued by Carol J. Singley, *Summer* contains the tensions that Wharton experienced during the first world war, when she organized relief efforts in France for French and Belgian citizens who lost their homes. Charity is depicted as a war-torn refugee, mirroring the many displaced children Wharton encountered; however, Charity's rebelliousness toward her "savior" reflects Wharton's struggle with maintaining control when the Red Cross and the United States became involved in relief efforts. However, "Charity is overcome with exhaustion by the time Royall reaches her. Wharton similarly felt so fatigued just before the government-sponsored relief agency arrived that she said she was willing 'to give our whole planet' to the American Red Cross" (Singley 170). Giving up control is a double-edged sword.

Like Maycomb, "determined to preserve every physical scrap of the past" (162), North Dormer is synonymous with the past rather than the modern present, left out of historical time. Symbols of its past-tense status can be found in its musty library where Charity works and in the historical architecture that draws Harney as researcher. It is as if the city dweller returns to the small town as tourist to mark it as a quaint object—the childhood of America—which is how Harney appears to view Charity. He can view her this way because she herself has no appreciation for the past or for reading, which distinguishes her from reflective characters or Victorian heroines that might forge their own paths and which signals Wharton's rewriting of a modern Charlotte Temple (see B. White 46–51). What becomes apparent in Charity's sense of the small size of North Dormer and the way it embeds both childhood and American history is that by the twentieth century small towns had become synecdoche for the childhood of America. The romantic association between childhood and country was so strong that rural farm labor was one of the last fields to enact any child labor laws (Zelizer), so strong a belief did people have that rural and childhood went together. Wharton is suggesting that the old concept of American faith in virgin land is highly problematic when it comes to developing female subjectivity.

Charity feels new feelings and passions brewing inside her, and, like Lee, she associates those feelings with the backwoods—the Mountain, where she was born and where the mother whom she does not know lives a wild life. In her comparison of Charity Royall to Charlotte Temple, White demonstrates that while both Charity and Charlotte are unreflective characters, Wharton gives free reign to Charity's feelings, which emerge in oceanic waves and overwhelm her with their intensity (B. White 49); the eruption of feelings and preconscious intuitions link Charity and Scout, as well as McCullers's Frankie, who has no name to describe her vague feelings and fears that unaccountably arise from deep inside. Although fifteen miles away, the Mountain "seemed almost to cast its shadow over North Dormer" (4). Charity is seeking to understand this shadow of the primitive always lurking just beyond or even within "the blessings of the most refined civilization," just as Scout is seeking to understand the passions located in the characters beyond town boundaries. The topography of wilderness, middle landscape, and celestial cities has always been meaningful in American literature; these topographies are spiritual, the wilderness embodying the chaos of potential self-dissolution. The fact that the wilderness is within becomes apparent when Charity, now heavy with pregnancy after her summer with Harney, crosses into the Mountain for her pilgrimage, only to find the abject dead body of her mother there, much like the unruly abjections that Scout associates with the backwoods folks make her accept Maycomb as "refined civilization" into which she must pass, even though she, like Wharton, understands that the shadow of the Mountain is actually present in the town. The symbolism of Charity's wild mother of the Mountain and civilized guardian of the town, lawyer Mr. Royall, is an obvious symbol of the coparenting necessary to reproduce a girl's cyclical acceptance of the boundaries civilization draws between civilized and primitive. In fact, White compellingly argues that Charity's initial abhorrence of Mr. Royall is merely her attraction for him and fear of sex (58–60); Charity's suspicion of him as a Rochester-figure, along with her glimpse of his desire for her on one night, signals her intuition, if not her acceptance, of the fact that shadows of "the Mountain" are always in the civilized landscape; otherwise, no definition of civilization is possible.

The ritualized acceptance of the small-town community and how it views itself occurs in a pivotal chapter of historical pageantry, which functions like Maycomb's pageant in the closing chapters of the novel. In the late nineteenth century, historical pageants were highly fashionable. Old Home Weeks were structured around the reunion principle to show "continuity between the town of the past and the present" (Glassberg 18), even as railroads altered the dynamics and isolation of towns. Early pageants were structured around a prominent citizen's oration, which we can distinguish from the sort of later pageant mocked by Lee as an excessive, ridiculous exercise in a new kind of pageantry that emerged in England as Renaissance revival and soon migrated to American summer camps and small towns.

Several important things are revealed at the pageant called "Old Home Week" in *Summer*. In that celebration Charity's guardian, Royall, gives an eloquent public speech, his one moment of public passion in oratory that parallels moments of public eloquence in Atticus and in Hawthorne's Dimmesdale. Whereas Charity has viewed Royall as a washed-up lawyer with little business, pathetic because he settled for North Dormer rather than staying in the city of his training, Charity sees his brilliance in this Old Home Week speech. His speech concerns the "there's no place like home" intent of the historical pageant. He discourses on how many young people will leave North Dormer for city life, but they will return as he did and see the eternal value in the grace of the small town. In other words, he articulates the fact that youthful urges (aka modernity) will "pass" and home-grown values will triumph.

During the course of his electrifying speech, Charity sees Harney with another girl and realizes her abandonment. She also literally passes out from the heat, she says, but she is actually in the early stages of pregnancy. Thus in many ways, the pageant has done its office, transforming her body into a reproductive bearer of North Dormer. This precedent in Wharton's novel explains the centrality of Scout dressed as a ham and in reality passing out at Maycomb's pageant. The overwhelming heat of the scenes is deliberate;

Wharton discussed her novel as a "hot" *Ethan Frome* (B. White 49–50), reversing the melodramatic image of Charlotte Temple fleeing into the icy snow. The hot, pregnant Charity and the hot, womb-enclosed ham-Scout are the same—children of these historical pageants through which communities ritualize their reproductive prowess.

The unconsciousness of Charity in this scene mirrors her trance at the end of the short novel, when her guardian marries her. The words of the preacher echo, in Charity's mind, the words of the sermon upon her mother's burial. The resonance of marriage as both incest and death is an overwhelming communication of the marriage's meaning for Charity (B. White 54). Having followed Royall "as passively as a tired child" (194), Charity "no longer heard what was being said" (197) at her own wedding. She "felt a ring that was too big for her being slipped on her thin finger. She understood then that she was married . . . " (197), and "for a while the long turmoil of the night and day had slipped away from her and she sat with closed eyes, surrendering herself to the spell of warmth and silence" (197). This "merciful apathy" gives way to her posture of being "motionless and inert" (199). The marriage is really marriage to the embodiment of Old Home: to North Dormer itself, the house to which she must return and bear its legacy.

Like Lee, Wharton asks us to understand Old Home Week as ironic because it is a fashionable imposition from outsiders, just as the embrace of indigenous landscapes in the 1920s and 1930s Girl Scouts summer camp movement was an outsider viewpoint on "natives" that preferred a romantic view rather than a realistic one (Miller):

> North Dormer was preparing for its Old Home Week. That form of sentimental decentralization was still in its early stages, and, precedents being few, and the desire to set an example contagious, the matter had become a subject of prolonged and passionate discussion under Miss Hatchard's roof. The incentive to the celebration had come rather from those who had left North Dormer than from those who had been obliged to stay there, and there was some difficulty in rousing the village to the proper state of enthusiasm. (122)

The irony of Old Home week as a ritual of confinement also stems from a prior scene in Nettleton. Charity has gone to Nettleton with Harney to celebrate the Fourth of July, thus independence, and there she sees her guardian with Julia, a character whose story surfaces throughout the novel as a warning of a ruined woman. Julia, from North Dormer, had become pregnant and went to Nettleton for an abortion; it is Julia who exclaims, upon seeing Charity, "if this ain't like Old Home Week." The implication is that for girls there is no escape from North Dormer, except through becoming a ruined soul, one also glimpsed in the female doctor who betrays, cheats, and blackmails Charity. Modern city women are soulless, just as Charity is essentially as dead as Charlotte Temple in her condition in 1791. In fact, the name of the girl who got an abortion and moved on is not a coincidence, since it is Julia Franklin who lures away Charlotte's seducer with her independent spirit in Rowson's seduction novel.

Wharton's 1917 novel merely changes around the numbers of Rowson's original publication date; the final trancelike descent of women who try to challenge patriarchy and forge an independent path actually has a very long history. White points out that the protagonist of *St. Elmo*, also named Edna, passes out from the intensity of her wedding (63), but Wharton's *Summer* transitions the nineteenth-century novel to modern novel by focusing on what happens inside the protagonist. Her discussion of the outward story of growth as distinct from the inner story of regression is applicable to *Mockingbird*, which also has an outside and inside story—a surface story of Atticus's small step in getting the jury to deliberate and in teaching his children, as distinct from an inside story of Scout's increasing understanding of what it means to pass into the social world of Maycomb ladies:

> In the twentieth century, as the heroine's inner life is opened up, the underside of the essentially optimistic nineteenth-century plot is plainly exposed. Edith Wharton elevates this "underplot"—the shrinkage of the girl, the unchanging corruption of the social order—to parallel importance with the main plot, the positive growth as described by Baym. In novels of adolescence after *Summer*, the underplot will come to overshadow the basic nineteenth-century story altogether.
>
> *Summer* is a transitional novel in other ways. If Wharton uses nineteenth-century plot conventions, transforming them in the process, she adopts a narrative stance midway between Louisa May Alcott, with her hand on the little women's shoulders, and the modern novelist of adolescence whose

presence is markedly unobtrusive. As we have observed, Wharton creates distance from Charity Royall and occasionally provides ironic commentary on her character and situation; however, the focus is on Charity's consciousness and we mainly see from her point of view. (63)

The distance that Lee creates from Scout's point of view as her future ladyhood streams across her consciousness comes from the way in which Chopin and Wharton turned inward for an account of awakenings and slumbering in response to the social plot. Wharton alludes to Chopin's ending in *The Awakening* when Charity feels an instant of rebellion: "For an instant the old impulse of flight swept through her; but it was only the lift of a broken wing" (198). Mademoiselle Reisz in *The Awakening* tells Edna that birds who wish freedom must have very strong wings; Edna sees the bird with a broken wing while putting on her bathing suit for her final descent into a long rest: "A bird with a broken wing was beating the air above, reeling, fluttering, circling disabled down, down to the water" (108). These broken birds give us yet another way of understanding the slaying of the mockingbird, since the image of the mockingbird introduces *The Awakening* as well.

Throughout Chopin's novel, the image of birds taking flight stands for an image of freedom, but we know from the opening pages that birds, associated with women, are not only in cages; they also speak solely in parody, and their "maddening persistence" of chatter does not express much, although it annoys the patriarch Mr. Pontellier:

> A green and yellow parrot, which hung in a cage outside the door, kept repeating over and over:
>
> "*Allez vous-en! Allez vous-en! Sapristi!* That's all right!"
>
> He could speak a little Spanish, and also a language which nobody understood, unless it was the mocking-bird that hung on the other side of the door, whistling his fluty notes out upon the breeze with maddening persistence.
>
> Mr. Pontellier, unable to read his newspaper with any degree of comfort, arose with an expression and an exclamation of disgust. He walked down the gallery and across the narrator "bridges" which connected the

Lebrun cottages one with the other. He had been seated before the door of the main house. The parrot and the mocking-bird were the property of Madame Lebrun, and they had the right to make all the noise they wished. Mr. Pontellier had the privilege of quitting their society when they ceased to be entertaining. (3)

The birds actually belong to a character Edna never considers as a role model, which is unfortunate because she exemplifies both independence and economic freedom. Significantly, the caged bird that picks up snippets of languages but never can self-determine is a symbol for Edna, and only the mockingbird can possibly understand. Maya Angelou famously uses the image of the caged bird in her autobiographical novel *I Know Why the Caged Bird Sings*. The reason Chopin suggests the mockingbird's understanding, however, has to do with her idea, similar to the one articulated by Cixous in "The Laugh of the Medusa," that a woman cannot even know what she wants or how to intuit a self because she has only been trained in mimicry. The last lines of dialogue in *Summer* are tellingly similar moments of mimicry that we have discussed in James's *Maisie* and in Lee's bargain between Scout, Heck Tate, and Atticus regarding "mutual dissimulation." Royall tells Charity she is a good girl, as if she were six, and Charity returns the compliment by saying he is good, too.

The strong presence of Old Home Week and its confinement of girls calls our attention to the brains behind the pageant in *Mockingbird;* the idea is Mrs. Grace Merriweather's. She is "not only the author, but the narrator" (253) of *Maycomb County: Ad Astra Per Aspera,* and we are well acquainted with her politics from the prior missionary society scene, where she is also author and narrator of the Mrunas as tragic black "other." The pageant reproduces town values through the children. Mrs. Merriweather transforms children into cows, butterbeans, peanuts, and pork, until "the supply of children were exhausted" (252). In fact, exhaustion is precisely Scout's condition upon donning her costume. Scout's cue is supposed to be the word "pork," uttered by Mrs. Merriweather. Even in voicing the plan, the narrator observes, "there were several discomforts, though: it was hot, it was a close fit; if my nose itched I couldn't scratch, and once inside I could not get out of it alone" (252–53). Not only is transforming children into "the supply" of a market tantamount to exhaustion, but also enclosing them into tight assembly lines confines them and robs them of independence. Lee makes it clear that taking on the role of staging a local festival has some costs; one must live with discomfort, similarly to how one must put manners before things like itching, and one must give up independence for the veil. When we view Charity as an instance of North Dormer seeking to reproduce itself and its values—whom it excludes (the Mountain people) and whom it includes (virtuous women)—we then can understand the various discourses that define Charity as an object, something embedded in her very name. Harney clearly sees Charity as a sexual object, an exhibit of a quaint old-home town, and a ticket to gaining access to rural houses. Royall (North Dormer) competes with Harney (Nettleton City) over Charity, and North Dormer elders have told Charity she "owes" a debt to Royall, so she becomes the object of repayment in the end. Like *Charlotte Temple, Summer* points to the novel as an exercise in female education—how warped views warp children's views of themselves. This calls attention to children as objects of Maycomb, especially if the novel continues a long line of novels exploring female education as a vision of what America is and is not. Children are objects in power struggles between adults. Scout is an object between ladies, Cal (and her community), Atticus, Ewell, and Boo, just as Mayella is an object between Ewell and Maycomb. Just as Maisie is so clearly an object between male and female parents, children become pawns in community power struggles.

The equation of children with local production is an ideology found throughout the historical pageantry movement and in association with the Girl Scout summer camp movement. The name "Scout" would, in both the time of *Mockingbird*'s setting and publication, have evoked the popular and growing organization of the Girl Scouts, which by the 1930s had become synonymous with summer camp and with fervor for celebrating indigenous landscapes. Some background on how the name Scout embeds a national embrace of a children's organization will point toward further irony in *Mockingbird*.

The history of organizations like the Girl Scouts, Campfire Girls, Girl Pioneers, and Girl Reserves is documented by Susan A. Miller in *Growing Girls: The Natural Origins of Girls' Organizations in America*. Although their ideologies differed, all were formed to restore to girls the sense of the simple and "primitive" pioneer experience that, leaders felt, modern girls had lost. Although Girl Scouts and Campfire Girls were founded in 1912, by 1935 they had become largely associated with the American summer camp movement, and America was identified as practically "camp crazy" by that period (Miller 4). They were viewed as a way to get girls closer to nature, and the movement idealized country life and became associated with the celebration of indigenous landscapes, which resulted in the use of camp girls in performances of historical pageants like the kind staged in *Mockingbird*. Some profound changes in the ideology of the pageant between the Old Home type of the late nineteenth century and the masque of the twentieth century illustrate the irony involved in having a girl nicknamed Scout perform the role of ham and thus personify the allegorical spirit of harvest at the end of *Mockingbird*, when she is indeed attacked by the backwoods environment personified by Ewell, supposedly an unforeseen player in the masque. However, Ewell only makes the sinister quality of the masque apparent.

Since Turner had theorized in 1893 that the American pioneer experience had uniquely shaped vital American identity, Americans worried about their future vitalities with the closing of the frontier and the onset of modernity. Girls' organizations in the modern period sought to translate this vital identity to girls. Although the Campfire leaders focused on Native American imagery as a vision of "primitive" domesticity, Girl Scout founder Juliette Low took a different route. She named her organization after the British program founded in 1907 by Robert Laden-Powel, who founded the Boy Scouts and named them after the British army scouts in the Boer War. He named his girls' organization Girl Guides to remove the aura of military ambitions encoded into the boys' program. Low, a friend of Laden-Powel's, imported Guiding into the United States in 1912, but she also secured his endorsement and "borrowed heavily from Boy Scout materials" (Miller 30) to organize the same type of movement for girls. What became known as "the scouting method" is certainly applicable to the outdoorsy Scout of *Mockingbird*. In 1956 Martin Luther King Jr. called the Girl Scouts a force for desegregation because the first desegregated troop had been established earlier that year.

During the First World War, summer camps run by these organizations used a rhetorical philosophy recognizable to any scholar of transcendentalism; as believed by Luther Gulick, Campfire founder, "Democracy, conveyed through lessons of self-reliance and teamwork, was inherent to the 'wilderness' in which camps were situated" (69). Miller quotes Gulick's vision at length to demonstrate the American project explicit in the Campfire movement:

If girls could be persuaded to endure the hardships that would give them an unvarnished look at themselves, they could develop into true unsentimental patriots and citizens. "When girls are away from places where money can buy ease and are in places where family prestige means nothing if it does not help them to swim, to endure on a hike, to cook a good meal and to make a neat pack, they stand on their own merits and they unconsciously learn to judge other girls by what the girls can do and by what they themselves are." This clear-eyed self-sufficiency would help girls to appreciate the lessons of democracy all citizens had to learn. "I have never seen anything which tended to bring out the personal character, develop independence, grip, courage, self-reliance and democracy, as much as camping." Properly run, a camp could encourage the creation of democratic girls in a democratic environment. "The democracy of the wilderness is the greatest democracy the world knows," concluded Luther Gulick. (71–73)

The camps in the 1920s began to espouse attention to the indigenous qualities of camp landscapes, complicit with regional celebrations that had been sweeping the country in the late nineteenth and early twentieth century. Miller argues that the word "indigenous," referring to the physical attributes and natural resources native to a region (97), achieved mythic proportions in the first decades of the twentieth century because rural places sought to stay afloat and thus romanticized their legacy. The rhetoric celebrating place found its way into camp design, architecture, activities, and programs. Of course, the machine in the garden paradox was forever apparent in the camping movements; as camps became more elaborate and larger, signs of civilized life began to predominate, and leaders always found disjunction between their idealization of country life and the real people encountered in outback places. This discrepancy is precisely what we find in Ewell's attack on "the ham" as idealized indigenous value in the pageant.

It was apparent from the camping movement that the transcendental study of nature was to be made available to girls. For example, in a training manual for Girl Scout leaders (1922), the theory is voiced that girls should study nature so they would realize their own partial role in divine creation. Even more fascinating was the movement's emphasis on direct, scientific observation of nature, a method that would allow girls to become more intimate with it: "Natural camps were supposed to be transcendent, the embodiment of a youthful imagination set free to discover its own powers and potential. Girls were meant to lose themselves in the mystical experiences inherent to camp's physical landscape and, in doing so, come to recognize the contours of their own souls" (Miller 228). Achieving unprecedented popularity in the twentieth century and aligned with transcendentalism, appreciation of the American legacy and landscape, and girls' skills of observation and boyish scouting activity, the Girl Scout inertia that was often noted and even mocked in popular iconography of Lee's childhood opens up the possibility of a very specific history to Scout's tomboyism as the type of activity modeled on Boy Scouts and certainly seeking membership with boys. It also opens up the idea that Lee focused on self-reliant summer activities to mock the tradition of organized, middle-class summer camping. With Jem and Dill, Scout executes and organizes her own summer camp, indigenous as one's own landscape always is.

The sort of aesthetic pageant of the Radleys inspired by Dill, the outsider obsessed with Boo, is counterpoint to the reunion model of the late nineteenth-century pageant, because a shift occurred in 1907 when George Turnbull recommended for purposes of civic enthusiasm that Americans import the English historical pageant, which Louis Napoleon Parker had been staging in England since 1905 (Glassberg 43–44). The community historical pageant in England was motivated by "members of the British arts and crafts societies [who] had been fascinated with revivals of Medieval and Renaissance imagery and handicrafts":

> Staging costumed historical revels and allegorical masques seemed a logical extension of these interests; indeed, John Ruskin had called for a revival of Renaissance "pageantry" in England in 1882. These revivals began as private affairs, offering the membership of arts and crafts societies evenings of entertainment and propaganda. In 1899, the Art Workers Guild of London presented the allegory *Beauty's Awakening,* in which symbolic figures representing the spirits of Renaissance town planning and Ruskin's "Seven Lamps of Architecture" triumphed over crass and tasteless modern sprawl. (Glassberg 44)

The form took off in public celebrations and migrated to summer camp when in 1910 William Chauncy Langdon orchestrated a pageant for Charlotte Farnsworth, who managed a summer camp near Thetford, Vermont, and wished to commemorate the town's 150th anniversary (74). Langdon proved the civic value of the elaborately staged and symbolism-infused pageant; he became the pageant master by writing about pageants, organizing pageant associations, and spreading his model by directing several in New England and the Midwest, such as "the five 'Pageants of the New Country Life' that he staged in rural New England between 1911 and 1914" (Glassberg 71). America's playground movement was anxious to support the pageants because play advocates believed that America's recreation life needed to be encouraged and that Americans needed to learn how to play together. By 1920 forty-eight states held such pageants. The highly symbolic enactments of the masque thus migrated to America and held a peculiar hold on communities, youth, and campers, who would enact and watch highly idealized and "fantastic flights of symbolic dancers" (120) such as the sort usually seen in experimental theater.

Viewing these pageants now and seeing images of, for example, performer Virginia Tanner as "The Spirit of Pageantry" in a graceful outdoor tableau (Glassberg 90), it is hard not to understand these pageants as an early form of "Camp trace," as well as the inculcation of summer camp ideology. The difference between Charity's awakening and passing out during Old Home Week, where she sees and hears citizens, and Scout's parody of the masque by falling asleep and missing her entrance as ham is precisely this historical shift in the civic festival as teaching tool and as outrageous and elaborate deception of abstract values juxtaposed with the Ewell farmer who indeed treats people as hams. Lee takes the scene and in her mocking manner points out not only its confinement but also its ridiculousness at idealizing the harvest when the result is dehumanization and not fantastic flight of the dance. Just before the pageant, Scout has encountered all sorts of ridiculous Halloween pretend play, attesting to the pageant as parody. The real symbolic pageant is the two we have already witnessed—the Radley drama symbolically incarnating Maycomb's hostility toward the American family, and the courtroom drama organized along the same theme. What distinguishes Lee from Wharton is her transcendent older narrator, who watches the pageant and laughs, even as she offers up young Scout to be sliced, diced, and left to stew. If nothing else, however, cross-dressing as a ham does help her pass, which seems to be why Aunt Alexandra accepts her need to cross-dress, bringing her clean overalls in the end.

Conclusion: "A Jail You Could Not See"

The trope of endless summer to explore regional confinement evokes traditional imagery of the seasons that equates summer with a woman's blossoming and fall with, well, a woman's "fall." Summer in *The Awakening, Summer, Member of the Wedding,* and *Mockingbird* takes on the cadence of the time just before the fall or just before the winds of change. The idea of heat before a fall has a wide variety of meanings in *Mockingbird* for a wide variety of characters who fall or "pass" at the end of the novel. Even the detail that "summer meant Dill," but that fall with Dill is never possible, is meaningful, given his status as unable to "come out." Indeed, we find the pattern of his character in the endless summer of McCullers's *Member of the Wedding,* in which the Dill character, here named John Henry, will not live to see fall, when the repainting of the kitchen will wash almost all traces of him away. Comfortable with his freakishness, John Henry cannot live. John Henry has seen snow, which Frankie wishes to see, and yet he is content to "play out" in summer. The long summer of McCullers's novel signifies the ennui of Frankie, just as it signifies the Madame Bovary–like ennui of Edna—an inner and restless emptiness that the characters do not understand. If we understand Frankie's anguish as "the feeling she could not name," we can view her as Edna, who experiences "days when she was happy without knowing why" and "days when she was unhappy, she did not know why" (56). Edna turns into a child with her various temper tantrums, whereas Frankie tests the waters of lady in her hyperbolic drag play. Quite possibly, McCullers has excavated a subtext of Chopin's novel, for it is quite possible that the sleek-bodied and not handsome Edna, who sees herself in mental images of a naked man on the beach, is in drag and is attracted to Madame Ratignolle and Mademoiselle Reisz (see LeBlanc). Robert, ostensibly her desired lover, is actually introduced as a mirror character; they physically resemble one another, and they are the same age. As a codified lesbian artist, Mademoiselle Reisz functions much as John Henry for Frankie and Dill for Scout; the freak of false nature, signified by her artificial violets and fear of water, is somehow not a satisfactory model for the protagonist despite her artistic pretensions. Passing and avoiding the "well of loneliness" (title of Radclyffe Hall's 1928 novel on the female invert) are too important to the female protagonists, even if it means, as McCullers puts it, "a jail you could not see" (148).

Frankie experiences her memberless summer as a state of being trapped in cyclical time, which she experiences as the *unheimlich* (uncanny), the familiar made strange: "The three of them sat at the kitchen table, saying the same things over and over, so that by August the words began to rhyme with each other and sound strange" (1). In the background is forever the hum of the radio, which is never turned off, and the sound of dissonance. The walls of the kitchen become akin to the oddity of the yellow wallpaper in Gilman's feminist parable:

> After the darkening yard the kitchen was hot and bright and queer. The walls of the kitchen bothered Frankie—the queer drawings of Christmas trees, airplanes, freak soldiers, flowers. John Henry had started the first pictures one long afternoon in June, and having already ruined the wall, he went on and drew whenever he wished. Sometimes Frankie had drawn also. At first her father had been furious about the walls, but later he said for them to draw all the pictures out of their systems, and he would have the kitchen painted in the fall. But as the summer lasted, and would not end, the walls had begun to bother Frankie. That evening the kitchen looked strange to her, and she was afraid. (7)

The queerness of John Henry suggests that the writing on the wall is homosexuality, and her father's sentiments suggest that he wishes the children to get these feelings out of their systems by fall. Although Frankie has outgrown herself and her walls, she is in the August period of not yet knowing herself or what she wants. Her obsession with the wedding, however, also bespeaks her roots in modern female characters. Whereas an earlier, more Victorian character might wish to be married, Frankie can only imagine being married to the wedding ritual itself, which is a clear symbol of passing, just as the missionary society is.

If the trial of *Mockingbird* is a representation of "inappropriate" female desire on trial, Frankie's inappropriate feelings and performances of drag, as discussed in chapter 5, indicate her membership on trial. Just as Atticus and Jem are associated with time and watches in *Mockingbird,* symbols of linear and chronological time as theorized by Julia Kristeva in "Women's Time," Frankie loves to watch her father fix watches: "There was a strong streak of watchmaker's blood in her and always the old Frankie had loved to sit at her father's bench" (60). Frankie listens to the ticking of John Henry's heart, which "felt as though a little clock was ticking inside him" (13), just as Scout listens to the clock striking while she awaits the verdict and Jem to the mortal time of Mrs. Dubose's alarm clock. These images of looming mortality, like the crocodile in Barrie's Neverland, suggest they are on the brink of falling into time, which would signify the end of mythic childhood. McCullers seems to have first fleshed out the trope of a daughter's fixation on father time in her first novel, *The Heart Is a Lonely Hunter,* in which Mick is a precursor to Frankie, and she, too, likes to watch her father fix watches. The symbolism of Frankie's yearning to join the world and her sense that the "cracked globe" of the world is changing, but that it does not include her, bespeaks entrapment and fear of eternal condemnation to small-town summer where the streets and the light are always gray, like Kansas for Dorothy.

The (to her) inexplicable fact that Frankie's childhood summer monotonously carries on despite the backdrop of the war, and her attraction to it, parallels the way in which Scout's life journeys on despite the trial and its significance. Just as Scout recognizes Atticus's gestures with his watch makes the world turn, Frankie is obsessed with the world turning and believes it must do so at thousands of miles per hour. The way she imagines the world mirrors the various fractures permeating the novel:

> It was the year when Frankie thought about the world. And she did not see it as a round school globe, with the countries neat and different-colored. She thought of the world as huge and cracked and loose and turning a thousand miles an hour. The geography book at school was out of date; the countries of the world had changed. Frankie read the war news in the paper, but there were so many foreign places, and the war was happening so fast, that sometimes she did not understand. (20)

Both she and Scout are beginning to feel the rupture between the mythic, cyclical time of childhood and the linear, developmental time of adulthood. With the latter comes an understanding of sex and death, Roberta Trites argues, because they are the biological imperatives that give boundaries to an individual existence. When Frankie meets the soldier, she feels that "the world had never been so close to her" (66). Just like Charity Royall, Frankie views the soldier as a manifestation of global landscapes, a way out of the repetitive, provincial region through tourism: "The soldier was joining with her like a traveler who meets another traveler in a tourist town" (63). The modern relationship of anonymity looks attractive and equal, for both Charity and Frankie, but it is only a new enclosure, as quickly seen by a glimpse at the soldier's dingy quarters. Both Lee and McCullers draw attention to the "tired" towns that defy clocks; Lee's Greek courthouse columns "clashed with a big nineteenth-century clock tower housing a rusty unreliable instrument" (162), and McCullers's Frankie notices, "The clock in the tower of the First Baptist Church clanged twelve, the mill whistle wailed. There was a drowsing quietness about the street, and even the very cars, parked slantwise with their noses toward the center aisle of grass, were like exhausted cars that have all gone to sleep" (61). The affinity of *Mockingbird* with *Member* and other incarnations of female characters on the brink of "falling" is closely tied to the period of publication. Just as *Member* is concerned with postwar changes, *Mockingbird* is the last stand of summer before fall and before the characters, now sagging from heat, will, in literary terms, see snow.

It is the not so modest "double life" character of Berenice who finally articulates, clearly and poetically, the fact of life as entrapment for Frankie: "'We all of us somehow caught. We born this way or that way and we don't know why. But we caught anyhow. I born Berenice. You born Frankie. John Henry born John Henry. And maybe we wants to widen and bust free. But no matter what we do we sill caught. Me is me and you is you and he is he'" (113). Berenice sees Frankie—not F. Jasmine, not Frances—as her nature. Berenice views the trappings of birth as particularly poignant to the black community, because "'they done squeezed us off in one corner by ourself'" (114). Berenice implies that the double consciousness required for African Americans to get along in the world is particularly dangerous for a character like Honey, who might possibly go mad. Both Berenice and Honey embody the double life that for Frankie is a matter of double consciousness required for gender and sexual development.

Just as Cal signifies a double life, revealed when Scout hears her speak at the black church and for the first time realizes how little of Cal's history she knows, Berenice's eyes suggest her double life:

There was only one thing wrong about Berenice—her left eye was bright blue glass. It stared out fixed and wild from her quiet, colored face, and why she had wanted a blue eye nobody human would ever know. Her right eye was dark and sad. (3)

The blue eye, recurrent in *Clock without Hands* and presaging Toni Morrison's point in *The Bluest Eye,* seems to embody Berenice's self split because of white standards of beauty. Significantly, it is her left eye that cannot see; this bothers Frankie: "Her dark eye looked up as Frankie spoke, but, since Berenice did not raise her head, the blue glass eye seemed to go on reading the magazine. This two-sighted expression bothered Frankie" (25). The blue eye seems, whereas the dark eye sees. It "seems" to be reading a magazine, as if facing its (cultural) maker. While the doubleness is disconcerting, it is also a duality of male-female that attracts and symbolizes Frankie. Berenice's mannerisms, such as her card playing and smoking, often seem masculine, although, as Barbara White writes, Berenice is a man-oriented woman (94), and thus her journey can be understood as parallel to Frankie's (95). We have already analyzed the duality of gender inversion represented in *Member,* but significantly Frankie is not effective at doubling: "She would have liked for her expression to be split into two parts, so that one eye stared at Berenice in an accusing way, and the other eye thanked her with a grateful look. But the human face does not divide like this, and the two expressions canceled out each other" (105). She cannot mirror Berenice's face. The duality of Berenice and the failure of Frankie suggest, too, that Berenice has successfully established herself as a hyperfeminine figure with beaus and husbands, but that she paradoxically models a kind of independence in doing so.

The blue eye has a slight suggestion of freakishness or madness—Frankie finds it inexplicable that she chose a fake blue eye—like in *The Bluest Eye,* in which an African American girl's desire for blue eyes is granted when she goes completely mad at the end. The blue eye is, of course, Berenice's left and not her "right" eye, politics that are similar in *Mockingbird,* as argued by Laura Champion. The blue eye on the left side of Berenice is a vapid, unseeing eye, which could signify how conforming to white culture causes blindness. Additionally, it may symbolize the fact that neither white nor black can see Frankie if she is queer, although Berenice's sense that she was born *Frankie* retains the slight suggestion of sympathy for the invert that pervaded texts at the time. The eye is also a representation of Berenice's wounding at the hands of a bad husband—heterosexuality gone awry and violent.

The suggestion of an inner madness that double consciousness engenders becomes explicit in the character of Honey, who represents heteroglossia as well as the embedded violence in Frankie:

> The Creator had withdrawn His hand from him too soon.... When she had first heard this remark, the old Frankie did not understand the hidden meaning. Such a remark put her in mind of a peculiar half-boy—one arm, one leg, half a face—a half-person hopping in the gloomy summer sun around the corners of town. But later she understood it a little better. Honey played the horn, and had been first in his studies at the colored high school. He ordered a French book from Atlanta and learned himself from French. At the same time he would suddenly run hog-wild all over Sugarville and tear around for several days, until his friends would bring him home more dead than living. His lips could move as light as butterflies and he could talk as well as any human she had ever heard—but other times he would answer with a colored jumble that even his own family could not follow. (122)

With him, Frankie shares an inner propensity to steal and be violent (B. White 98). She is similarly liminal, neither fully adult nor child; she is neither tomboy, as emblematized in her rough elbows, nor woman, as glimpsed in the evening gown she buys for the wedding. She is neither lover nor friend, not ready for the soldier and not decent to John Henry. Like the many girls we have discussed, she is neither simply experiencing nor intellectually reflecting. Frankie tells Honey that he should go to Mexico and *pass.* Importantly, it is Honey, whom Berenice predicted would "break something or break himself," who winds up in jail at the end of the novel. Frankie, now turning into Frances, understands the end to his story as commenting on herself when she says it is at least best to be in a jail you can see rather than in a jail you cannot. Is Scout at the end of *Mockingbird* in a jail you cannot see, since Lee uses Tom Robinson and Cal as similar commentary on who can pass and who cannot?

Berenice, the voice of insight Frankie does not have and Scout only has when half-asleep, connects the two tragedies of Honey and John Henry as divine retribution: "'I don't know what I've done,' she kept saying. 'Honey in this fix and now John Henry'" (152). Berenice dislikes Mary Littlejohn and thus dislikes the end of these journeys. Berenice's fantasy of a better world included one race of "light brown" people "with blue eyes and black hair" (91). She suggests that her ideas of wholeness have not been realized in Frankie's final identity of Frances. In *Mockingbird,* the tragedies of Tom Robinson and Boo Radley forever mingle, and Lee, too, ends her novel with a girl implicitly committed to *passing* despite the costs.

Barbara White reads Frankie's ending as imprisonment in an invisible jail in the same way as Charity's trancelike death in marriage to Royall. This reading corresponds to a long line of drowning Ophelias, to use Mary Pipher's word, in modern women's regional writings. If we compare the ending of *Member* to McCullers's other works, the ending actually looks almost cheerful. In *Ballad of the Safe Café,* the queer leading lady, who has no idea why she shunned her husband, has lost everything, including the freakish Cousin Lymon; in *Reflections in a Golden Eye,* the female hysteric is dead, and Private Williams, a character to project on rather like Singer in *The Heart Is a Lonely Hunter,* has been shot by Captain Penderton, who is obviously gay and wanted Private Williams to come to *his* room; in *Heart,* Singer has shot himself and everyone is missing him. At the end of *Member,* Frances is waiting to see the world with Mary Littlejohn, because she is "'just mad about Michelangelo'" (150, 153), she repeats twice, the second time cut off after "about" to signify that she just might be mad about Mary. At any rate, Frankie's allusion to Eliot's Prufrock is complicated by the fact that she seems to share her passion with another person, which seems a lot more positive than Mick's dead-end job as a clerk. McCullers communicates the lesbianism of she and Mary Littlejohn by telling us they collect pictures and that Frances wants to be a poet; the equation of homosexuality and the arts in the postwar period suggests that the interests of Mary and Frances are coded gay but that interest in high culture, like for other homosexuals, can codify shared homosexuality and yet pass for nonhomosexual aestheticism. It is not likely that they can fool Berenice, although the final line of the novel seems to allude to Wharton's story "The Lady's Maid's Bell," in which lesbian women elude men. Girls can pass as best friends.

Both *Mockingbird* and *Member* suggest that it is only a matter of time before each individual must face the double consciousness required to live in a state of social performance. Just as Scout dissociates herself into an observer and participant as she "watched" herself pass out cookies with her best company manners, "a lady at a time like this" (237), Frankie continually sees signs of impending double consciousness:

> Her father went back behind the gray sour velvet curtain that divided the store into two parts, the larger public part in front and behind a small dusty private part . . . she settled herself carefully at the workbench before the front window. A watch, already taken apart, was laid out on the green blotter. (60)

It is only a matter of time before someone like Frankie, like the boys for whom Capote's Miss Wisteria weeps, grows tall and thus sees the division between the private and public parts. For a brief moment at the end of *Mockingbird* Scout has tamed her father, and he gives her not courteous detachment but sonorous attentions. She has in some sense awakened to the intolerance of the larger world and the double consciousness required to pass as a lady, which makes her father's world a new world of childhood and slumber.

But, tellingly, the novel's long lineage of modern women writing regional novels about consuming environments and endings in which characters descend into deathlike trances tell us that this slumber is not safe. It is the numbness of Chopin's mockingbird, anaesthetized like the patient laid out on the table of Eliot's journey with Prufrock. McCullers shows us that passing is a prison you cannot see, a theme loud and clear in Chopin's *The Awakening* and Wharton's *Summer* and *Age of Innocence.* Just as six-year-old Maisie experiences the awakening of her consciousness as dividing her forever from her experience of herself, the narrator of *Mockingbird* incarnates the complexity of consciousness implied in the journey of development. It is always to be inside and outside the self at once, always the self as iterative performance, as theorized by Judith Butler, and thus always the mockingbird.

Emerson defined double consciousness as human necessity in "Fate":

> One key, one solution to the mysteries of human condition, one solution to the old knots of fate, freedom, and foreknowledge, exists, the propounding, namely of the double consciousness. A man must ride alternatively on the horses of his private and his public nature, as the equestrians in the circus throw themselves nimbly from horse to horse, or plant one foot on the back of one, and the other foot on the back of the other. ("Fate" 32)

It is perhaps more than coincidence that Emerson compares the individual's divided nature to the circus acts that feature so prominently in southern literature, worlds in which everyone is cracked, maimed, or missing a crucial limb. Just like in Flannery O'Connor's stories of club feet and disabled migrants, "the southern grotesque aligns itself with a gloomy vision of modernity . . . the grotesque worlds of southern literature, it is argued, allegorize the human condition itself as existential alienation and angst" (Gleeson-White 108).

The following passage from Emerson's "Experience" reifies the theme of *Member of the Wedding* and could have been found there if the narration were not limited third person:

> Never can love make consciousness and ascription equal in force. There will be the same gulf between every me and thee, as between the original and the picture. The universe is the bride of the soul. All private sympathy is partial. Two human beings are like globes, which can touch only in a point, and whilst they remain in contact, all other points of each of the spheres are inert; their turn must also come, and the longer a particular union lasts, the more energy of appetency the parts not in union acquire. ("Experience" 289)

Emerson writes in "Experience," "I am a fragment, and this is a fragment of me" (293), in a very similar manner to Frankie's fantasy that *they are the we of me.* Focus on child consciousness, racial exclusion, social passing, and individuals in the closet uniquely allows *Mockingbird* to unite the various crusades for rights burgeoning throughout the 1950s in a more inclusive way than the activists could because to do so would have lessened their rhetorical powers. There is always a "they" in the "we" of "me," and *Mockingbird* shows precisely how the insider/outsider posture takes hold of us.

Perhaps just as Edna Pontellier struggles with what solitude means and therefore reads Emerson to try to understand the shadows within herself, Atticus's reading of *The Gray Ghost* ironically brings us back to the romantic who found he could not escape the divisive nature of experience and reflection. Perhaps *The Gray Ghost* is the shadow of himself that Emerson became in the end, along with the shadow he cast over American literature as writers sought in him answers and found in him only questions. Indeed, the looming presence of Atticus, as if he *is* the gray ghost, is the final line: "He turned out the light and went into Jem's room. He would be there all night, and he would be there when Jem waked up in the morning" (281). Jem's waking to Atticus is promised, although Scout's is not. This is the last image readers have in a series of awakenings and sleepings. Atticus is not even reading; he has turned out the light. Perhaps, like Berenice, who desires oneness, the man who more than anything else desires transparency is, in the end, split into a private and a public man. By joining the many gray ghosts of the novel, he really does walk in the shoes of others. He walks into the shadows that many characters, ghosts, and literary canons have cast before him.

WORKS CITED

Abate, Michelle Ann. "Launching a Gender B(l)acklash: E. D. E. N. Southworth's *The Hidden Hand* and the Emergence of (Racialized) White Tomboyism." *Children's Literature Association Quarterly* 31.1 (2006): 40–64.

———. "Topsy and Topsy-Turvy Jo: Harriet Beecher Stowe's *Uncle Tom's Cabin* and/ in Louisa May Alcott's *Little Women*." *Children's Literature* 34 (2006): 59–82.

Abrams, M. H. *A Glossary of Literary Terms.* 5th ed. New York: Holt, Rinehart & Winston, 1998.

Adams, Rachel. "'A Mixture of Delicious and Freak': The Queer Fiction of Carson McCullers." *American Literature* 71.3 (Sept. 1999): 551–83.

Arac, Jonathan. *Huckleberry Finn as Idol and Target: The Functions of Criticism in Our Time.* Madison: U of Wisconsin P, 1997.

Atwood, Margaret. *Negotiating with the Dead: A Writer on Writing.* New York: Cambridge UP, 2002.

Baecker, Diann L. "Telling It in Black and White: The Importance of the Africanist Presence in *To Kill a Mockingbird*." *Southern Quarterly* 36.3 (1998): 124–32.

Bakhtin, Mikhail. *The Dialogic Imagination: Four Essays.* Ed. Michael Holquist and Vadim Liapunov. Trans. Kenneth Brostrom and Vadim Liapunov. Austin: U of Texas P, 1982.

———. *Rabelais and His World.* Bloomington: Indiana UP, 1984.

Baldwin, James. *Notes of a Native Son.* New York: Dial, 1963.

Baldwin, James Mark. *Mental Development in the Child and the Race.* 1894. New York: Augustus M. Kelley Publishers, 1969.

Barthes, Roland. "The Death of the Author." *Image Music Text.* 1977. Trans. Richard Howard. 23 May 2010 <http://evans-experientialism.freewebspace.com/barthes06.htm>.

Baym, Nina. "Melodramas of Beset Manhood: How Theories of American Fiction Exclude Women Authors." *American Quarterly* 33.2 (Summer 1981): 123–39.

Beacker, Diann L. "Telling It in Black and White: The Importance of the Africanist Presence in *To Kill a Mockingbird*." *Southern Quarterly* 36.3 (Spring 1998): 124–32.

Beaver, Harold. "Homosexual Signs (In Memory of Roland Barthes)." *Critical Inquiry* 8.1 (Autumn 1981): 99–119.

Beckett, Samuel. *Waiting for Godot: A Tragicomedy in Two Acts.* New York: Grove, 1954.

Benshoff, Harry M. *Monsters in the Closet: Homosexuality and the Horror Film.* Manchester: Manchester UP, 1997.

Bercovitch, Sacvan. "Deadpan Huck: Or, What's Funny about Interpretation." *Kenyon Review* 24.3–4 (2002): 90–134.

Berendt, John. *Midnight in the Garden of Good and Evil.* New York: Vintage, 1994.

Berger, Peter L. *Redeeming Laughter: The Comic Dimension of Human Experience.* New York: Walter De Gruyter, 1997.

Bérubé, Allan. *Coming out under Fire: The History of Gay Men and Women in World War Two.* New York: Macmillan, 1990.

Betts, Doris. "The Mockingbird's Throat: A Personal Reflection." *On Harper Lee: Essays and Reflections.* Ed. Alice Hall Petry. Knoxville: U of Tennessee P, 2007. 135–42.

Bishop, John Peale. *Act of Darkness.* New York: Avon, 1935.

Blackall, Jean Frantz. "Valorizing the Commonplace: Harper Lee's Response to Jane Austen." *On Harper Lee: Essays and Reflections.* Ed. Alice Hall Petry. Knoxville: U of Tennessee P, 2007. 19–34.

Blackford, Holly. "Apertures into the House of Fiction: Novel Methods and Child Study, 1870–1910." *Children's Literature Association Quarterly* 32.4 (2007): 368–89.

——. "Child Consciousness in the American Novel: *Adventures of Huckleberry Finn* (1885), *What Maisie Knew* (1897), and the Birth of Child Psychology." *Enterprising Youth: Social Values and Acculturation in Nineteenth-Century American Children's Literature.* Ed. Monika Elbert. New York: Routledge, 2008. 245–58.

Bronski, Michael. *Culture Clash: The Making of Gay Sensibility.* Boston: South End, 1984.

Brooks, Peter. *The Melodramatic Imagination: Balzac, Henry James, Melodrama, and Mode of Excess.* New Haven: Yale UP, 1995.

Brown, Gillian. *Domestic Individualism: Imagining Self in Nineteenth-Century America.* Berkeley: U of California P, 1990.

Butler, Judith. *Bodies that Matter: On the Discursive Limits of "Sex."* New York: Routledge, 1993.

——. *Gender Trouble: Feminism and the Subversion of Identity.* New York: Routledge, 2006.

Butler, Robert. "The Religious Vision of *To Kill a Mockingbird.*" *On Harper Lee: Essays and Reflections.* Ed. Alice Hall Petry. Knoxville: U of Tennessee P, 2007. 121–34.

Butt, Gavin. *Between You and Me: Queer Disclosures in the New York Art World, 1948–1963.* Durham, NC: Duke UP, 2005.

Cadden, Mike. "The Irony of Narration in the Young Adult Novel." *Children's Literature Association Quarterly* 25.3 (Fall 2000): 146–54.

Capote, Truman. The Grass Harp *and* A Tree of Night. New York: Signet, 1945.

——. *Other Voices, Other Rooms.* New York: Random, 1948.

Carr, Brian. "Paranoid Interpretation, Desire's Nonobject, and Nella Larsen's 'Passing.'" *PMLA* 119.2 (March 2004): 282–95.

Carr, Virginia Spencer. *The Lonely Hunter: A Biography of Carson McCullers.* Athens: U of Georgia P, 1975.

Case, Sue-Ellen. "Tracking the Vampire." *Differences: A Journal of Feminist Cultural Studies* 3.2 (Summer 1991): 1–20.

Cather, Willa. *My Ántonia.* New York: Barnes and Noble, 2003.

Cauthen, Cramer R. "The Gift Refused: The Southern Lawyer in *Mockingbird, The Client,* and *Cape Fear.*" *Studies in Popular Culture* 19.2 (October 1996): 257–75.

Champion, Laurie. "Lee's *To Kill a Mockingbird.*" *Explicator* 61.4 (Summer 2003): 234–36.

——. "'When You Finally See Them': The Unconquered Eye in *To Kill a Mockingbird.*" *Southern Quarterly* 37.2 (Winter 1999): 127–36.

Chandler, Marilyn R. *Dwelling in the Text: Houses in American Fiction.* Berkeley: U of California P, 1991.

Chappell, Charles. "The Unity of *To Kill a Mockingbird.*" *Alabama Review* 42 (1989): 32–48.

Chase, Richard. *The American Novel and Its Tradition.* Baltimore: Johns Hopkins UP, 1980.

Chatman, Seymour. *Coming to Terms: The Rhetoric of Narrative in Fiction and Film.* Ithaca: Cornell UP, 1990.

Chauncey, George. *Gay New York: Gender, Urban Culture, and the Making of the Gay World, 1890–1940*. New York: Basic, 1994.

Chopin, Kate. *The Awakening: An Authoritative Text, Biographical and Historical Context, Criticism*. 2nd ed. Ed. Margo Culley. New York: Norton, 1976.

Chura, Patrick. "Prolepsis and Anachronism: Emmet Till and the Historicity of *Mockingbird*." *Southern Literary Journal* 32.2 (Spring 2000): 1–26.

Cixous, Hélène. "The Laugh of the Medusa." *Feminisms: An Anthology of Literary Theory and Criticism*. Ed. Robyn Warhol and Diane Price Herndl. New Brunswick, NJ: Rutgers UP, 1993. 334–49.

Clarke, Gerald. *Capote: A Biography*. New York: Carroll & Graf, 1988.

Clover, Carol. "'God Bless Juries!' *Refiguring American Film Genres: History and Theory*. Ed. Nick Browne. Berkeley: University of California Press, 1998. 255–77.

Corber, Robert. *Homosexuality in Cold War America: Resistance and the Crisis of Masculinity*. Durham: Duke UP, 1997.

Cutter, Martha J. "Sliding Significations: Passing as a Narrative and Textual Strategy in Nella Larsen's Fiction." *Passing and the Fictions of Identity*. Ed. Elaine K. Ginsberg. Durham: Duke UP, 1996. 75–100.

Craft, Christopher. "Vampires." *Gay Histories and Cultures: An Encyclopedia. The Encyclopedia of Lesbian and Gay Histories and Cultures. Vol II*. Ed. George Haggerty, John Beynon, and Douglas Eisner. New York: Garland, 2000. 927–29.

Crespino, Joseph. "The Strange Career of Atticus Finch." *Southern Cultures* 6.2 (Summer 2000): 9–30.

Darwin, Charles. "A Biographical Sketch of an Infant." 1877. *Classics in the History of Psychology*. Ed. Christopher D. Green. Toronto: York University. 7 July 2006. <http://psychclassics.yorku.ca/Darwin/infant.htm>.

Dave, R. A. "*To Kill a Mockingbird*: Harper Lee's Tragic Vision." *Harper Lee's* To Kill a Mockingbird. *Modern Critical Interpretations*. Ed. Harold Bloom. Philadelphia: Chelsea House, 1999. 49–59.

Davidson, Cathy. *Revolution and the Word: The Rise of the Novel in America*. New York: Oxford UP, 1986.

Dewey, John. "The New Psychology." *Andover Review* 2 (1884): 278–89.

Dijkstra, Bram. *Idols of Perversity: Fantasies of Feminine Evil in Fin-de-Siècle Culture*. New York: Oxford UP, 1986.

Douglas, Ann. "Introduction." *Charlotte Temple and Lucy Temple*. Ed. Ann Douglas. New York: Penguin, 1991. vii–xliii.

Douglass, Frederick. *Narrative of the Life of Frederick Douglass, an American Slave*. 1845. Ed. Houston A. Baker Jr. New York: Penguin, 1986.

Drummond, W. B. *The Child, His Nature and Nurture*. London: J. M. Dent, 1901.

Du Bois, W. E. B. 1903. *The Souls of Black Folk*. 9 March 2009 <http://www.duboislc. org/html/DoubleConsciousness.html>.

Dusinberre, Juliet. *Alice to the Lighthouse: Children's Books and Radical Experiments in Art*. New York: St. Martin's Press, 1987.

Early, Gerald. "The Madness in the American Haunted House: The New Southern Gothic, and the Young Adult Novel of the 1960s: A Personal Reflection." *On Harper Lee: Essays and Reflections*. Ed. Alice Hall Petry. Knoxville: U of Tennessee P, 2007. 93–104.

Eckford-Prossor, Melanie. "Colonizing Children: Dramas of Transformation." *JNT: Journal of Narrative Theory* 30.2 (Summer 2000): 237–62.

Eliot, T. S. "The Love Song of J. Alfred Prufrock." 1917. Ed. Ian Lancashire. Toronto: University of Toronto Libraries, 2006. <http://www.prufrock.org/poem/ fulltext.php>.

——. "Tradition and the Individual Talent." 1920. *Quotidiana*. Ed. Patrick Madden. 23 January 2008. <http://essays.quotidiana.org/eliot/tradition_and_the_ individual>.

Emerson, Ralph Waldo. "The American Scholar." *Nature: Addresses and Lectures. Ralph Waldo Emerson—Texts*. Ed. Jone Johnson Lewis. 1–12. 12 January 2009. <http://www.emersoncentral.com/amscholar.htm>.

——. "Experience." *The Works of Ralph Waldo Emerson: Second Series*. Vol. 1. New York: Heart's International Library, 1914. 267–95.

——. "Fate." *Conduct of Life. The Works of Ralph Waldo Emerson*. Vol. 3. New York: Heart's International Library, 1914. 1–33.

——. "Heroism." *The Works of Ralph Waldo Emerson: First Series*. Vol. 1. New York: Heart's International Library, 1914. 157–70.

——. "Nature." *The Works of Ralph Waldo Emerson*. Vol. 1. New York: Heart's International Library, 1914. 346–65.

——. "The Over-Soul." *The Works of Ralph Waldo Emerson*. Vol. 1. New York: Heart's International Library, 1914. 171–92.

———. "The Poet." *The Works of Ralph Waldo Emerson.* Vol. 1. New York: Heart's International Library, 1914. 239–66.

———. *Representative Men. The Works of Ralph Waldo Emerson.* Vol. 2. New York: Heart's International Library, 1914.

———. "Self-Reliance." *The Works of Ralph Waldo Emerson.* Vol. 1. New York: Heart's International Library, 1914. 30–60.

Entzminger, Betina. *The Belle Gone Bad: White Southern Writers and the Dark Seductress.* Baton Rouge: Louisiana State UP, 2002.

Erkkila, Betsy. *Whitman and the Political Poet.* New York: Oxford UP, 1996. Excerpted, "On 'Out of the Cradle Endlessly Rocking.'" *Modern American Poetry.* University of Illinois at Urbana-Champaign. 1 September 2008. <http://www.english.uiuc.edu/maps/poets/s_z/whitman/cradle.htm>.

Erisman, Fred. "The Romantic Regionalism of Harper Lee." *Harper Lee's* To Kill a Mockingbird: *Modern Critical Interpretations.* Ed. Harold Bloom. Philadelphia: Chelsea, 1999. 39–48.

Faulkner, William. *Light in August.* New York: Vintage, 1932.

———. *Requiem for a Nun.* New York: Random, 1950.

———. *The Sound and the Fury.* 1929. New York: Vintage, 1984.

Felluga, Dino. "Terms Used by Narratology and Film Theory." *Introductory Guide to Critical Theory.* 26 March 2009 <http://www.cla.prudue.edu/english/theory/narratology/terms/narrativetermsmainframe.html>.

Fiedler, Leslie. "Afterword: John Bishop Peale and the Other Thirties." *Act of Darkness by John Peale Bishop.* New York: Avon, 1935. 305–19.

———. *Love and Death in the American Novel.* Champaign, IL: Dalkey Archive, 1998.

Fine, Laura. "Gender Conflicts and Their 'Dark' Projections in Coming of Age White Female Southern Novels." *Southern Quarterly* 36.4 (1998): 121–29.

———. "Structuring the Narrator's Rebellion in *To Kill a Mockingbird.*" *On Harper Lee: Essays and Reflections.* Ed. Alice Hall Petry. Knoxville: U of Tennessee P, 2007. 61–78.

Forte, Horton. "Writing for Film." *Film and Literature: A Comparative Approach to Adaptation.* Austin: Texas Tech UP, 1988. 5–20.

Freedman, Monroe. "Atticus Finch Does Nothing to Advance Social Justice." *Readings on* To Kill A Mockingbird. Ed. Terry O'Neill. San Diego: Greenhaven, 2000. 117–20.

Gammel, Irene. *Looking for Anne of Green Gables: The Story of L. M. Montgomery and Her Literary Classic*. New York: St. Martin's, 2008.

Gentry, Lee. "Whitman, Emerson, and the Song of Sex." *American Transcendental Web*. Virginia Commonwealth University. Psymon. 1 September 2008. <http://www.vcu.edu/engweb/transcendentalism/roots/legacy/whitman/ww-rwe-sex.html>.

——. "Whitman and Transcendentalism." *American Transcendental Web*. Virginia Commonwealth University. Psymon. 1 September 2008. <http://www.vcu.edu/engweb/transendentalism/roots/legacy/whitman/index.html>.

Gibson, Mary Ellis. "Edith Wharton and the Ethnography of Old New York." *Studies in American Fiction* 13.1 (Spring 1985): 57–69.

Gillman, Susan. *Blood Talk: American Race Melodrama and the Culture of the Occult*. Chicago: U of Chicago P, 2003.

Ginsberg, Elaine. "Introduction: The Politics of Passing." *Passing and the Fictions of Identity*. Ed. Elaine K. Ginsberg. Durham: Duke UP, 1996. 1–18.

Glassberg, David. *American Historical Pageantry: The Uses of Tradition in the Early Twentieth Century*. Chapter Hill: U of North Carolina P, 1990.

Gleeson-White, Sarah. "Revisiting the Southern Grotesque: Mikhail Bakhtin and the Case of Carson McCullers." *Southern Literary Journal* 33.2 (2001): 108–23.

Going, William T. Foreword. *On Harper Lee: Essays and Reflections*. Ed. Alice Hall Petry. Knoxville: U of Tennessee P, 2007. ix–xi.

——. *Essays on Alabama Literature. Studies in the Humanities* 4. Tuscaloosa: U of Alabama P, 1975.

——. "Truman Capote: Harper Lee's Fictional Portrait of the Artist as an Alabama Child." *Alabama Review* 42 (1989): 136–49.

Grant, Julia. "'A Thought a Mother Can Hardly Face': Sissy Boys, Parents, and Professionals in Mid-Twentieth-Century America." *Modern American Queer History*. Ed. Allida M. Black. Philadelphia: Temple UP, 2001. 117–30.

Greene, Ward. *Death in the Deep South: A Novel about Murder*. New York: Stackpole Sons, 1936.

Haggerty, George E. *Queer Gothic*. Urbana: U of Illinois P, 2006.

Hale, Dorothy. *Social Formalism: The Novel in Theory from Henry James to the Present*. Palo Alto, CA: Stanford UP, 1998.

Harris, Mervyn. *The Dilly Boys: Male Prostitution in Piccadilly*. London: Croom Helm, 1973.

Harris, Trudier. *From Mammies to Militants: Domestics in Black American Literature*. Philadelphia: Temple UP, 1982.

———. "Preface." *The House of the Seven Gables*. NY: Bantam, 1981. vii–viii.

Hawthorne, Nathaniel. *The Scarlet Letter: An Authoritative Text, Essays in Criticism and Scholarship*. 3rd ed. Ed. Seymour Gross, Sculley Bradley, Richmond Croom Beatty, and E. Hudson Long. New York: Norton, 1988.

Hayward, F. H. *The Educational Ideas of Pestalozzi and Fröbel*. 1904. Westport, CT: Greenwood, 1979.

Hébert, Kimberly G. "Acting the Nigger: Topsy, Shirley Temple, and Toni Morrison's Pecola." *Approaches to Teaching* Uncle Tom's Cabin. Ed. Elizabeth Ammons and Susan Belasco. New York: MLA, 2000. 184–98.

Heilman, Robert Bechtold. *Tragedy and Melodrama: Versions of Experience*. Seattle: U of Washington P, 1968.

Hess, Natalie. "Code Switching and Style Shifting as Markers of Liminality in Literature." *Language and Literature* 5.1 (1996): 5–18.

Honeyman, Susan. *Elusive Childhood: Impossible Representations in Modern Fiction*. Columbus: Ohio State UP, 2005.

Irigaray, Luce. "This Sex Which Is Not One." *Feminisms: An Anthology of Literary Theory and Criticism*. Ed. Robyn Warhol and Diane Price Herndl. New Brunswick, NJ: Rutgers UP, 1993. 350–56.

Iser, Wolfgang. "Indeterminacy and the Reader's Response in Prose Fiction." *Aspects of Narrative: Selected Papers from the English Institute*. Ed. J. Hillis Miller. New York: Columbia UP, 1971. 1–46.

Jacobs, Harriet. *Incidents in the Life of a Slave Girl: Written by Herself*. Ed. Lydia Maria Child. *Narrative of the Life of Frederick Douglass, an American Slave* and *Incidents in the Life of a Slave Girl*. New York: Modern Library, 2004. 121–371.

James, Henry. *Portrait of a Lady*. 2nd ed. Ed. Robert Bamberg: New York: Norton, 1995.

———. *What Maisie Knew*. New York: Penguin, 1986.

James, William. "The Stream of Consciousness." *Psychology*. New York: World, 1892. Reprinted in *Classics in the History of Psychology*. Ed. Christopher D. Green. Toronto: York University. 1 April 2009. <http://psychclassics.yorku.ca/James/jimmy11.htm>.

Jameson, Fredric. *The Political Unconscious: Narrative as a Socially Symbolic Act*. New York: Routledge, 2006.

Johnson, Claudia Durst. *To Kill a Mockingbird: Threatening Boundaries.* New York: Twayne, 1994.

———. "The Secret Courts of Men's Hearts: Code and Law in Harper Lee's *To Kill a Mockingbird.*" *Studies in American Fiction* 19 (1991): 129–39.

———. *Understanding* To Kill a Mockingbird: *A Student Casebook to Issues, Sources, and Historic Documents.* Westport, CT: Greenwood, 1994.

Jones, Carolyn. "Atticus Finch and the Mad Dog: Harper Lee's *To Kill a Mockingbird.*" *Southern Quarterly* 34.4 (Summer 1996): 53–63.

———. "Harper Lee." *The History of Southern Women's Literature.* Ed. Carolyn Perry, Mary Louise Weaks, and Doris Betts. Baton Rouge: Louisiana State UP, 2002. 413–18.

Kaiser, Charles. *The Gay Metropolis: 1940–1996.* Boston: Houghton Mifflin, 1997.

Katz, Jonathan Ned. *The Invention of Heterosexuality.* Chicago: U of Chicago P, 2007.

Kent, Kathryn R. "'No Trespassing': Girl Scout Camp and the Limits of the Counterpublic Sphere." *Curiouser: On the Queerness of Children.* Ed. Steven Bruhm and Nataha Hurley. Minneapolis: U of Minnesota P, 2004. 173–90.

Keyser, Elizabeth. *Whispers in the Dark: The Fiction of Louisa May Alcott.* Knoxville: University of Tennessee Press, 1993.

Killingsworth, M. Jimmie. "Whitman's 'Calamus': A Rhetorical Prehistory of the First Gay American." Paper presented at the Modern Language Association Convention, San Francisco, December 1998. 29 January 2009. <http://www.english.tamu.edu/pubs/body/calamus.html>.

Kristeva, Julia. "Women's Time." *Feminisms: An Anthology of Literary Theory and Criticism.* Ed. Robyn Warhol and Diane Herndl. New Brunswick, NJ: Rutgers UP, 1997. 860–79.

Larsen, Nella. Quicksand *and* Passing. Ed. Deborah E. McDowell. New Brunswick, NJ: Rutgers UP, 1986.

Laurence, Amy. *Echo and Narcissus: Women's Voices in Classical Hollywood Cinema.* Berkeley: U of California P, 1991.

LeBlanc, Elizabeth. "The Metaphorical Lesbian: Edna Pontellier in *The Awakening.*" *Tulsa Studies in Women's Literature* 15.2 (Fall 1996): 289–307.

Lee, Harper. *To Kill a Mockingbird.* 1960. New York: Warner, 1982.

Lejeune, Philippe. *On Autobiography. Theory and History of Literature.* Vol. 52. Ed. Paul John Eakin. Trans. Katherine Leary. Minneapolis: U of Minnesota P, 1989.

Lewis, Jenene. "Women as Commodity: Confronting Female Sexuality in *Quicksand* and *The Awakening*." *MAWA Review* 12.2 (1997): 51–62.

Long, Robert Emmet. *Truman Capote—Enfant Terrible*. New York: Continuum, 2008.

Loving, Jerome. *Emerson, Whitman, and the American Muse*. Chapel Hill: U of North Carolina P, 1982.

Lynch, Michael. "Walt Whitman in Ontario." *The Continuing Presence of Walt Whitman: The Life after the Life*. Ed. Robert K. Martin. Iowa City: U of Iowa P, 1992. 141–51.

MacGregor, Robert M. "The Eva and Topsy Dichotomy in Advertising." *Images of the Child*. Ed. Harry Eiss. Bowling Green, OH: Bowling Green State UP, 1994. 287–306.

Makman, Lisa Hermine. "Child's Work Is Child's Play: The Value of George MacDonald's Diamond." *Children's Literature Association Quarterly* 24.3 (Fall 1999): 119–29.

Mann, William J. "Children of the Night: The Natural Connection between Horror Films and Gay Audiences." *Frontiers* 14 (3 November 1995): 62–68.

Marx, Leo. *The Machine in the Garden: Technology and the Pastoral Ideal in America*. New York: Oxford UP, 2000.

Marx, Lesley. "Mockingbirds in the Land of Hadedahs: The South African Response to Harper Lee." *On Harper Lee: Essays and Reflections*. Ed. Alice Hall Petry. Knoxville: U of Tennessee P, 2007. 105–20.

Matthews, Brander. *Introduction to American Literature*. American Book Co., 1896.

McCullers, Carson. *The Member of the Wedding*. Boston: Houghton Mifflin, 1946.

McDowell, Deborah E. "Introduction." Quicksand *and* Passing *by Nella Larsen*. Ed. Deborah McDowell. New Brunswick: Rutgers UP, 1996. ix–xxxv.

McElaney, Hugh. "Alcott's Freaking of Boyhood: The Perplex of Gender and Disability in *Under the Lilacs*." *Children's Literature* 34 (2006): 139–60. *Literature Online*, 1–9. 4 December 2007. <http://lion.chadwyck.com>.

McRuer, Robert. "As Good as It Gets: Queer Theory and Critical Disability." *GLQ: A Journal of Lesbian and Gay Studies* 9.1–2 (2003): 79–105.

Meer, Sarah. *Uncle Tom Mania: Slavery, Minstrelsy, and Transatlantic Culture in the 1850s*. Athens: U of Georgia P, 2005.

Mercer, John, and Martin Shingler. *Melodrama: Genre, Style, Sensibility*. New York: Wallflower, 2004.

Meyer, Moe. "Introduction: Reclaiming the Discourse of Camp." *The Politics and Poetics of Camp*. Ed. Moe Meyer. New York: Routledge, 1994. 1–22.

——. "Under the Sign of Wilde: An Archeology of Posing." *The Politics and Poetics of Camp*. Ed. Moe Meyer. New York: Routledge, 1994. 75–109.

Mitchell-Peters, Brian. "Camping the Gothic: Que(e)ring Sexuality in Truman Capote's *Other Voices, Other Rooms*." *Journal of Homosexuality* 39.1 (2000): 107–38.

Miller, Susan A. *Growing Girls: The Natural Origins of Girls' Organizations in America*. New Brunswick, NJ: Rutgers UP, 2007.

Minter, Shannon. "Diagnosis and Treatment of Gender Identity Disorder in Children." *Sissies and Tomboys: Gender Nonconformity and Homosexual Childhood*. Ed. Matthew Rottnek. New York: New York UP, 1999. 9–33.

Mirkin, Harris. "The Pattern of Sexual Politics: Feminism, Homosexuality and Pedophilia." *Journal of Homosexuality* 37.2 (1999): 1–24.

Moates, Marianne. *A Bridge of Childhood: Truman Capote's Southern Years*. New York: Henry Holt, 1989.

Monroe, Will S. "Status of Child Study in Europe." *Pedagogical Seminary* 6 (1898/1899): 372–81.

Morgan, Jo-Ann. "Picturing Uncle Tom with Little Eva-Reproduction as Legacy." *Journal of American Culture* 27.1 (March 2004): 1–24.

Morris, Gary. "Queer Horror: Decoding Universal's Monsters." *Bright Lights Film Journal* 23. 23 September 2008. <http://www.brightlightsfilm.com/23/universalhorror.html>.

Morrison, Toni. *Playing in the Dark: Whiteness and the Literary Imagination*. New York: Vintage, 1993.

Nikolajeva, Maria. *From Mythic to Linear: Time in Children's Literature*. Lanham, MD: Scarecrow Press, 2000.

Noble, Marianne. "Sentimental Epistemologies in *Uncle Tom's Cabin* and *The House of the Seven Gables*." *Separate Spheres No More: Gender Convergence in American Literature, 1830–1930*. Ed. Monika M. Elbert. Tuscaloosa: U of Alabama P, 2000. 261–81.

O'Connor, Flannery. "Some Aspects of the Grotesque in Southern Fiction." 1960. 14 February 2009. <http://en.utexas/edu/amlit/amlitprivate/scans/grotesque.html>.

Parker, Hershel. "The Real 'Live Oak, with Moss': Straight Talk about Whitman's 'Gay Manifesto.'" *Walt Whitman Archive.* 29 January 2009. <http://www.whitmanarchive.org/criticism/current/anc.00157.html>.

Perez, Bernard. *The First Three Years of Childhood.* New York: E. L. Kellogg & Co., 1894.

Petry, Alice Hall. "Introduction." *On Harper Lee: Essays and Reflections.* Knoxville: U of Tennessee P, 2007. xv–xxxix.

Pipher, Mary. *Reviving Ophelia: Saving the Selves of Adolescent Girls.* New York: Riverhead, 2005.

Preyer, William. *The Mind of the Child: Parts I and II.* New York: Arno, 1973.

Price, Kenneth. "Whitman on Emerson: New Light on the 1856 Open Letter." *American Literature* 56.1 (March 1984): 83–87.

Pugh, William White Tison. "Boundless Hearts in a Nightmare World: Queer Sentimentalism and the Southern Gothicism in Truman Capote's *Other Voices, Other Rooms.*" *Mississippi Quarterly* 51.4 (1998): 663–82.

Rahill, Franik. *The World of Melodrama.* University Park: Pennsylvania State UP, 1967.

Rampersad, Arnold. "Introduction." *Native Son.* New York: Harper, 1993. xi–xxviii.

Reynolds, David S. *Beneath the American Renaissance: The Subversive Imagination in the Age of Emerson and Melville.* New York: Alfred A. Knopf, 1988.

Richards, Gary. *Lovers and Beloveds: Sexual Otherness in Southern Fiction, 1936–1961.* Baton Rouge: Louisiana State UP, 2005.

Rowe, John Carlos. "Racism, Fetishism, and the Gift Economy in *To Kill a Mockingbird.*" *On Harper Lee: Essays and Reflections.* Ed. Alice Hall Petry. Knoxville: U of Tennessee P, 2007. 1–18.

Rust, Marion. "The Subaltern as Imperialist: Speaking of Olaudah Equiano." *Passing and the Fictions of Identity.* Ed. Elaine K. Ginsberg. Durham: Duke UP, 1996. 21–36.

Saney, Isaac. "The Case against *Mockingbird.*" *Race and Class* 45.1 (2003): 99–110.

Scarry, Elaine. *The Body in Pain: The Making and Unmaking of the World.* New York: Oxford UP, 1987.

Sedgwick, Eve. *Between Men: English Literature and Male Homosocial Desire.* New York: Columbia UP, 1985.

——. *Epistemology of the Closet.* Berkeley: U of California P, 2008.

———. "How to Bring Your Kids up Gay." *Social Text* 29 (1991): 18–27.

Seidel, Kathryn Lee. "Growing up Southern: Resisting the Code for Southerners in *To Kill a Mockingbird.*" *On Harper Lee: Essays and Reflections.* Ed. Alice Hall Petry. Knoxville: U of Tennessee P, 2007. 79–92.

———. *The Southern Belle in the American Novel.* Tampa: U of South Florida P, 1985.

Shackelford, Dean. "The Female Voice in *To Kill a Mockingbird:* Narrative Strategies in Film and Novel." *Mississippi Quarterly* 50.1 (Winter 1996–97): 115–25.

Shields, Charles J. *Mockingbird: A Portrait of Harper Lee.* New York: Holt, 2007.

Simpson, Mark. Foreword. *Sissyphobia: Gay Men and Effeminate Behavior.* By Tim Bergling. New York: Harrington Park, 2001. ix–xii.

Singley, Carol J. *Adopting America: Childhood, Kinship, and National Identity in Literature.* New York: Oxford UP, 2011.

Smith, Elizabeth Oakes. *The Sinless Child.* 1846. 3 October 2007. <http://www.iath.virginia.edu>.

Smith, Rita. "Harriet Beecher Stowe." *Recess! The World of Children's Culture Every Day.* University of Florida's Center for the Study of Children's Literature and Media, WUFT-FM, "Classic 89," 2001. 2 November 2006 <http://www.recess.ufl.edu/transcripts/2001/0613.shtml>.

Somerville, Siobhan B. *Queering the Color Line: Race and the Invention of Homosexuality in American Culture.* Durham: Duke UP, 2000.

Sontag, Susan. "Notes on 'Camp.'" 1964. 25 March 2009. <http://interglacial.com/~sburke/pub/prose/Susan_Sontag_-_Notes_on_Camp.html>.

Spenser, Stuart. "Horton Foote." *BOMB* 15 (1986). <http://www.bombsite.com/issues/15/articles/764>.

Steed, J. P. "'Through Our Laughter We Are Involved': Bergsonian Humor in Flannery O'Connor's Fiction." *Midwest Quarterly* 46.3 (Spring 2005): 299–313.

Steedman, Carolyn. *Strange Dislocations: Childhood and the Idea of Human Interiority, 1780–1930.* Cambridge: Harvard UP, 1995.

Stern, Julia. "Spanish Masquerade and the Drama of Racial Identity in *Uncle Tom's Cabin.*" *Passing and the Fictions of Identity.* Ed. Elaine K. Ginsberg. Durham: Duke UP, 1996. 103–30.

Stevenson, Robert Louis. "Child's Play." *Virginibus Puerisque.* 1881. <http://www.gutenberg.org/dirs/etext96/virpr10.txt>.

Stockton, Kathryn Bond. "Growing Sideways, or Versions of the Queer Child: The Ghost, the Homosexual, the Freudian, the Innocent, and the Interval of Animal." *Curiouser: On the Queerness of Children*. Ed. Steven Bruhm and Nataha Hurley. Minneapolis: U of Minnesota P, 2004. 277–316.

Stokes, Mason. *The Color of Sex: Whiteness, Heterosexuality, and the Fictions of White Supremacy*. Durham: Duke UP, 2001.

Stowe, Harriet Beecher. *Uncle Tom's Cabin or, Life among the Lowly*. New York: Penguin Classics, 1986.

Sully, James. *Studies of Childhood. Significant Contributions to the History of Psychology 1750–1920*. Ed. Daniel Robinson. Washington, DC: University Publications of America, 1977.

Sutton-Smith, Brian. *The Ambiguity of Play*. Cambridge: Harvard UP, 1997.

Taine, M. "On the Acquisition of Language by Children." *Mind* 2 (1877): 252–59.

Tavernier-Courbin, Jacqueline. "Humor and Humanity in *To Kill a Mockingbird*." *On Harper Lee: Essays and Reflections*. Ed. Alice Hall Petry. Knoxville: U of Tennessee P, 2007. 41–60.

Taylor, Jenny Bourne. "Between Atavism and Altruism: The Child on the Threshold in Victorian Psychology and Edwardian Children's Fiction." *Children in Culture: Approaches to Childhood*. Ed. Karin Lesnik-Oberstein. New York: Routledge, 1998. 89–121.

Thoreau, Henry David. Walden *and* Civil Disobedience. New York: Penguin, 1986.

Thorndike, Edward Lee. 1901. *Notes on Child Study*. New York: Arno, 1974.

Tiedemann, Dieterich. *Record of Infant-Life*. Trans. Bernard Perez. Syracuse, NY: C. W. Bardeen, 1890.

Tompkins, Jane. *Sensational Designs: The Cultural Work of American Fiction, 1790–1860*. New York: Oxford UP, 1985.

Tracy, Frederick. *The Psychology of Childhood*. Boston: Heath, 1909.

"Transcendental Legacy in Literature: Walt Whitman, 1819–1892, Whitman and Transcendentalism." *American Transcendentalism Web*. Virginia Commonwealth University. Psymon. 10 May 2010 <http://www.vcu.edu/engweb/transcendentalism/roots/legacy/whitman/index.html>.

Trites, Roberta. *Disturbing the Universe: Power and Repression in the Adolescent Literature*. Iowa City: U of Iowa P, 2004.

Twain, Mark. *Adventures of Huckleberry Finn*. 1884. New York: Bantam Books, 1981.

———. *Pudd'nhead Wilson*. 1894. New York: Bantam, 1959.

Wald, Gayle. *Crossing the Line: Racial Passing in Twentieth-Century U.S. Literature and Culture*. Durham: Duke UP, 2000.

Waldmeir, Joseph J. "Introduction." *The Critical Response to Truman Capote*. Ed. Joseph J. Waldmeir and John C. Waldmeir. Westport, CT: Greenwood, 1999. 1–30.

Wallace, Maurice O. *Constructing the Black Masculine: Identity and Ideality in African American Men's Literature and Culture, 1775–1995*. Durham: Duke UP, 2002.

Warhol, Robyn R. "Poetics and Persuasion: *Uncle Tom's Cabin* as a Realist Novel." *Essays in Literature* 13.2 (1986): 283–98.

Wharton, Edith. *The Age of Innocence*. 1920. New York: Signet, 2008.

———. *Summer*. 1917. New York: Bantam, 1993.

Welty, Eudora. *Place in Fiction*. New York: House of Books, 1957.

White, Barbara. *Growing up Female: Adolescent Girlhood in American Fiction*. Greenwood, CT: Greenwood, 1985.

White, Sheldon. "G. Stanley Hall: From Philosophy to Developmental Psychology." *A Century of Developmental Psychology*. Ed. Ross D. Parke, Peter A. Ornstein, John J. Rieser, and Carolyn Zahn-Waxler. Washington, DC: APA, 1994. 103–26.

Whitman, Walt. "A Child's Reminiscence." Poems in Periodicals. *The Walt Whitman Archive*. 2 September 2008. <http://www.whitmanarchive.org/published/periodical/poems/per.00071>.

———. "All about a Mocking-Bird." Review of "A Child's Reminiscence." Published anonymously. *Walt Whitman Archive*. 2 September 2008. <http://www.whitmanarchive.org/criticism/reviews/a_child/anc.00140.html>.

———. "A Word Out of the Sea." *Leaves of Grass*. 1860. *The Walt Whitman Archive*. 29 January 2009. <http://www.whitmanarchive.org/published/LG1860/poems/53>.

———. "Out of the Cradle Endlessly Rocking." *Legacy: Walt Whitman. American Transcendentalism Web*. Virginia Commonwealth University. 26 August 2008. <http://www.vcu.edu/engweb/transcendentalism/roots/legacy/whitman/cradleweb.html>.

Wilder, Laura Ingalls. *Little House in the Big Woods*. New York: Scholastic, 1963.

Williams, Linda. *Playing the Race Card: Melodramas of Black and White from Uncle Tom to O. J. Simpson*. Princeton: Princeton UP, 2001.

——. "When the Woman Looks." *Re-Vision: Essays in Feminist Film Criticism*. Ed. Mary Ann Doane, Patricia Mellencamp, and Linda Williams. Los Angeles: University Publications of America, 1984. 83–97.

Woodard, Calvin. "Listening to the Mockingbird." *Alabama Law Review* 45.2 (Winter 1994): 563–84.

Woolf, Virginia. *A Room of One's Own*. 1929. 20 April 2009 <http://ebooks.adelaide.edu.au/w/woolf/virginia/w91r/chapter3.html>.

Wordsworth, William. "Preface to the Second Edition of *Lyrical Ballads*." 1800. *Critical Theory since Plato*. Ed. Hazard Adams. New York: Harcourt Brace Jovanovich, 1971. 437–47.

Wright, Richard. *Native Son*. 1940. New York: Harper, 1993.

Wyile, Andrea Schwenke. "Expanding the View of First-Person Narration." *Children's Literature in Education* 30.3 (1999): 185–202.

Zelizer, Viviana. *Pricing the Priceless Child: The Changing Social Value of Children*. Princeton: Princeton UP, 1985.

INDEX

Atticus, Titus Pomponius, 60

Atwood, Margaret, 3–4, 286

Augustine St. Clare, of *Uncle Tom's Cabin,* 17, 71, 100, 109, 119, 136; compared to Atticus Finch of *Mockingbird,* 120–25

Aunt Sally, of *Adventures of Huckleberry Finn,* 161

Awakening, The, by Kate Chopin, 10, 16, 26, 40, 261–68, 269, 287, 291, 298–99, 312

Austen, Jane, 8, 10, 12, 141, 142, 175, 224, 269, 290

Autobiography of Benjamin Franklin, The, 59

Avery, Mr., of *Mockingbird,* 34, 201, 218. *See* snowman

Bacon, Sir Frances, 81

Baecker, Diann, 46

Bakhtin, Mikhail, 2, 140, 169, 171, 201, 204

Baldwin, James, 17, 32, 36, 40, 90, 98, 104, 105, 127–28

Baldwin, James Mark, 140, 182

Ballad of the Sad Café, The, by Carson McCullers, 244, 311

Barrie, J. M., 218, 307

Barthes, Roland, 2–3

Baudrillard, Jean, 224

Baum, L. Frank, 234

Baym, Nina, 21, 45, 46, 297

Beale, Mrs., 146, 167, 174–75, 185

Beauty and the Beast (film), 255

Beauty's Awakening, 303

Beaufort(s), of *The Age of Innocence,* 273, 281, 290

Beaver, Harold, 49, 222

Beckett, Samuel, 1, 29

Beecher, Catherine, 122

belle, in southern literature, 35, 73, 116

Beloved, by Toni Morrison, 12, 239

Benji, of *The Sound and the Fury,* 98, 164–65

Benshoff, Harry, 32, 214, 217

Bercovitch, Sacvan, 20, 155, 174, 176, 177, 184

Berendt, John, 1, 283

Berenice, of *The Member of the Wedding,* 25, 37, 69, 245–53, 291, 308–12

Berger, Peter, 202–3

Bergling, Tim, 230

Bergsonian humor, 179, 183

Bérubé, Allen, 32

Betts, Doris, 29

Between Men, by Eve Sedgwick, 9, 35, 73, 81, 82, 139, 214, 218

Bigger Thomas, of *Native Son,* 17, 72, 93, 104–5, 128, 129

Binet, Alfred, 140

"Biographical Sketch of an Infant, A," by Charles Darwin, 139

Bird, Senator, of *Uncle Tom's Cabin,* 112

Birth of a Nation (film), 95

Bishop, John Peale, 36, 84, 85

"Black Boy Looks at the White Boy, The," by James Baldwin, 36

Blackall, Jean Frantz, 8, 10, 175

Blackmur, R. P., 181

Blood Talk: American Racial Melodrama and the Culture of the Occult, by Susan Gillman, 95

blues, 34

Bluest Eye, The, by Toni Morrison, 309

Bob Ewell. *See* Ewell, Bob

Bodies that Matter, by Judith Butler, 16, 48, 173

Body, 16, 34, 71; of Aunt Alexandra and Mrs. Mingott, 268, 276–78; black male, 36, 104–7, 111; freakish, 211, 240, 246, 253–59, 309; maternal, 263, 267, 270, 291–92; monstrous female, 255–59; nonwhite 48, 173; in pantomime, 98–99; queer, 37, 235–39, 246–47, 255–59; shame of, 65; on trial, 73, 92–94, 238–39; in Whitman's poetry, 49–50, 73–75. *See* disability, freakishness

Body in Pain, The, by Elaine Scarry, 208

Boo Radley, 5, 6, 8, 10, 12, 13, 19, 21, 22, 23, 26, 28, 29, 33, 50, 61, 63, 67, 73, 79, 81, 116, 127, 141, 155, 169, 176, 178, 179, 187, 190, 191, 198, 199, 203–6, 263, 300;

as analogous to homosexual closet, 208–45, 254–59, 275, 289, 303, 311

Boular, Sonny, 28

Boy Scouts, 301, 303

Bride of Frankenstein (film), 215

Bridge of Childhood, A, by Marianne Moates, 4, 27, 266

Bronski, Michael, 34, 81, 208, 222

Brontë, Emily, 218

Brooks, Peter, 92

Brown, Frank Chocteau, 223

Brown, Gillian, 94, 112, 115, 122

Brown, Sterling, 105

Brown v Board of Education, 28, 30, 31

Browning, Tod, 215

Bud (John Byron Faulk), 228

Bufords, of *Mockingbird,* 281

Bunyan, John, 114

Bush, President, 2, 15

Butler, Judith, 16, 38, 39, 48, 173, 313

Butler, Robert, 45, 63

Butt, Gavin, 31, 33, 210, 223, 225, 227

cabin, as symbol, 110–11, 114

Caddy, of *The Sound and the Fury,* 165

Calamus, by Walt Whitman, 16, 49, 77, 251

Calpurnia, of *Mockingbird,* 16, 20, 24, 47, 50, 64, 69, 73, 77, 91, 100, 106, 107, 113, 116, 120, 123, 137, 142, 146, 154, 155–59, 171–73, 178, 186, 193, 194, 202, 235, 236; lessons of, 171–72, 193; as model for Scout, 118, 119, 127, 133, 156–58, 159, 284–91, 300, 309, 311

camp, style, 21, 203–4, 213, 221–25, 227, 251, 304

Camp movement. *See* summer camp movement

Campfire Girls, 43, 300–305

Capote, Joseph, 227

Capote, Truman, 4, 5, 9, 10, 12, 13, 14, 21–23, 27–28, 33, 36, 49, 50, 64, 67, 80, 81, 87, 95, 196, 207, 218, 225, 226–45, 283; literary influences on, 13, 166, 180; relationship with Harper Lee, 12–13, 22, 27–28, 87, 204, 226–27

Captain Penderton, of *Reflections in a Golden Eye,* 245, 311

Carlyle, Thomas, 51

Carmilla (film), 215, 255

carnival, 21–23, 37, 201–6, 224, 226–27, 233, 313. *See* clown, freakishness

Caroline (Ma), of *Little House in the Big Woods,* 156

Caroline, Miss, of *Mockingbird,* 64, 85, 148, 153, 180, 189, 191–93, 282, 286, 287

Carpenter, Edward, 49, 82

Carr, Brian, 39

Carr, Virginia, 245, 247

Carroll, Lewis, 141, 144

Carter, Jennings Faulk, 27–28, 226

Carter, Mary Ida, 227

Case, Sue-Ellen, 217, 229, 255, 258

Cassy, of *Uncle Tom's Cabin,* 17, 107, 114; compared to Mayella of *Mockingbird,* 115

Cather, Willa, 13, 166, 180, 242

Catherine, of *The Grass Harp,* 243

Catherine, of *Wuthering Heights,* 218

Catherine the Great, 276

Catherine Mingott, Mrs., in *The Age of Innocence,* 14, 24, 202, 268; compared to Aunt Alexandra of *Mockingbird,* 268, 275–84, 209

Catherine Morland, of *Northanger Abbey,* 8, 141, 224

Cauthen, Cramer, 62, 112

Cecil Jacobs, of *Mockingbird,* 133, 146, 160, 194–95

Cézanne, 144

Champion, Laura, 67, 310

Chandler, Marilyn, 269

Chaplin, Charlie, 204

Chappell, Charles, 8

Charity Royall, of *Summer,* 8, 24–25, 262, 270, 271, 291–300, 308, 311

Charlie, of *Act of Darkness,* 84

Charlotte Temple, by Susanna Rowson, 17, 24, 90, 92, 101–2, 108, 110, 130, 131, 291, 294, 296, 297, 300

Chase, Richard, 45, 46, 94

Chatman, Seymour, 14

Chauncey, George, 21, 31, 33, 35, 39, 40, 49, 81, 208, 209, 212

checkerboard game, as symbol, 65, 148–49, 150, 278

child study, 14, 19, 283. *See* developmental psychology

"Child's Play," *Virginibus Puerisque*, by R. L. Stevenson, 144, 149

"Child's Reminiscence, A" by Walt Whitman, 28, 75–78, 89

"Children of Adam," by Walt Whitman, 74

Chillingsworth, of *The Scarlet Letter*, 99

chivalry, 67, 73, 91, 180. *See* class

Chopin, Kate, 5, 10, 11, 16, 23, 26, 259, 261–68, 291, 298–99

Christianity, 55, 98–103, 107, 108, 110, 112, 289; black church, 64, 107, 108, 116, 124, 134, 154–58, 196, 287, 309; crucifixion symbol, 96, 107–8, 109, 115. *See* sin

"Christmas Memory, A," by Truman Capote, 95, 227, 228

Chloe, Aunt, of *Uncle Tom's Cabin*, 109, 110, 111, 112

Chocolate War, The, by Robert Cormier, 162

Chura, Patrick, 28, 62, 83, 143, 261

Cicero, 60

"Civil Disobedience," by Henry David Thoreau, 51

Civil Rights era, 12, 26–37, 79, 278, 279, 290

Civil War, 50, 79

Cixous, Hélèn, 21, 204–5, 299

Clare, of *Passing*, 39–40

Clarke, Gerald, 230

class, social, 67–68, 70–71, 116, 120–21, 124–25, 172–73, 185, 190, 191, 204, 219, 220, 257–59, 277–84

Claude, Sir, of *What Maisie Knew*, 18, 19, 136, 143, 147, 150, 174–75, 185–86, 188–89

Clock Without Hands, by Carson McCullers, 37, 245, 309

closet (homosexual), 5, 12, 13, 31–35, 37, 40, 248; Boo Radley as, 199, 204, 208–25, 248, 258; Idabel in, 232–35; monsters in, 214–17; as trope in African American literature, 36

Clover, Carol, 97, 197

clown, Dill as, 224–26, 176, 203–6, 252–54

Cold War America, 31–36

Collin, of *The Grass Harp*, 166, 180, 196, 207, 241–45, 256

"Colonizing Children: Dramas of Transformation," by Melanie Eckford-Prossor, 279

Color of Sex, The, by Mason Stokes, 35, 73

comedy, 10, 20–21, 24, 132–33, 134, 146, 155, 162, 173–82, 183, 192, 194, 199–206, 272, 275–76. *See also* humor

coming out (homosexual), 13, 21, 22, 28, 220, 305; of Boo, 255–59; in Dill's games, 204, 216, 218, 219, 232–41; history of term, 209

comparative literature methodology, 2–5

Compayré, M. Gabriel, 140

Concord, Massachusetts, 46, 51

confessional scenes, 233–41

conscience, 51, 52

consciousness, 10, 11, 12, 14, 17, 18–19, 24, 48, 84, 131–69, 228, 248, 262, 265, 267, 287, 294, 297–98, 310; limits of, 50, 78, 86, 132–69, 178, 179, 188, 194, 198, 269. *See* double consciousness

Constructing the Black Masculine, by Maurice O. Wallace, 72

Continuing Presence of Walt Whitman, The, by Robert Martin (ed.), 82

Cool, Judge, of *The Grass Harp*, 243

Cooper, James Fenimore, 72

Coquette, The, by Hannah Smith Foster, 90

Corber, Robert, 32, 34

Countess (Ellen) Olenska, of *The Age of Innocence*, 24, 225, 269, 271, 272, 273, 274, 279, 291

courtroom drama, 17, 90, 92–94, 97, 99–101, 197; as queer space, 84–85, 128–29

Cousin Ike, of *Mockingbird*, 195

Cousin Randolph, of *Other Voices, Other Rooms*, 228, 231, 238, 240, 242, 244

Craft, Christopher, 215, 217

Crespino, Joseph, 51, 72

Crevecoeur, John de, 46
Cummins, Maria, 8
Cunningham, Mr., of *Mockingbird*, 32, 153, 192
Cunninghams, of *Mockingbird*, 112, 153, 154, 191–94, 278, 279, 282
Cutter, Martha, 23, 40, 265

Dalton, Mr., of *Native Son*, 128
Darwin, Charles, 19, 130, 137, 139, 140, 145, 159, 283
Daughters of Bilitis, 34
Daughters of the Revolution, 30
Dave, R. A., 4, 49, 89, 90, 91, 99
David, by Michelangelo, 33, 82
Davidson, Cathy, 101
deadpan humor, 10, 20, 155, 174–76, 177, 200–201, 204
"Death of the Author, The" by Roland Barthes, 2–3
Death in the Deep South, by Ward Greene, 35, 97, 283
Delsarte, 222
democracy, 12, 28, 45–46, 57, 72, 101–2, 130, 263, 301
Depression era, 26, 28, 30, 31–32, 278
detachment: in Atticus, 48, 68, 71, 79, 100, 107, 109, 112, 119–20, 237; in Atticus and Augustine St. Clare, 109, 112, 119–26; in narration, 17–19, 20–21, 76, 93, 96, 98, 132–34, 146, 155, 162, 191–99, 267, 280, 298; in work of Emerson and Whitman, 76–77. *See also* narration
developmental psychology, 19, 135, 138–44, 159, 182, 185
Dewey, John, 140
Dialogic Imagination, The, by Mikhail Bakhtin, 2
didactic literature, 102
Diderot, 90
Dijkstra, Bram, 221, 255, 257
Dill (Charles Baker) Harris, of *Mockingbird*, 6, 7, 8, 9, 10, 13, 21–23, 26, 33, 41, 50, 67, 73, 79, 86, 87, 108, 122, 146, 176, 177, 180, 186, 187, 199, 203–6; as feminine, 117, 207, 219; as queer

outsider, 207–25, 228, 235–41, 245, 256, 275, 292
dilly boys, 253
Dimmesdale, of *The Scarlet Letter*, 92, 94, 99, 100, 119, 295
Dinah, of *Uncle Tom's Cabin*, 112
Dionysus, 202–3
disability, as symbol, 11, 17, 21, 28, 36, 37, 46, 66, 72, 73, 77–78, 92–94, 99, 104, 105–6, 107, 108, 111, 118, 208, 216, 220, 227, 231, 238, 249, 253–54, 256–59, 290, 313
discourses, in *Mockingbird*. *See* voice(s)
distancing effects of narrator. *See* narration
Dixon, Thomas, Jr., 17, 35, 73
Dolly, of *The Grass Harp*, 180, 228, 232, 242–45
Dolphus Raymond, of *Mockingbird*, 34, 40, 73, 80, 101, 219–20, 225, 286
domesticity, 110–14, 122–24
double consciousness, 135, 140, 152, 154, 169, 171–73, 308–14. *See also* double life, consciousness
double life, in *Mockingbird*,16, 20, 40–41, 156–58, 167–69, 202, 212, 245, 248, 251–52, 275, 285, 288–89, 291, 308–14; in African Americans, 135, 156–58, 171–73, 185, 202; in Emerson, 75, 135, 313–14; in Whitman, 77. *See also* consciousness, double consciousness
Douglas, Ann, 102
Douglass, Frederick, 26, 36, 86, 152
Dr. Jekyll and Mr. Hyde (film), 215, 255
Dracula (film), 214–17, 223, 239, 255
Dracula's Daughter (film), 215
drag, 13, 20, 21, 31, 38, 40, 80, 81, 86, 203–6, 208, 212, 215, 226, 227, 229, 231, 234, 241, 248, 250–51, 253, 259, 288, 305; balls, 31; shows, 34
Drame sérieux, 90
Driscoll, Judge, of *Pudd'nhead Wilson*, 58, 62
Drummond, W. B., 144, 161
Du Bois, W. E. B., 135, 140
Dubose, Mrs., of *Mockingbird*, 21, 26, 58, 65, 68, 77, 86, 112, 122, 124, 162, 163, 187–88, 217, 219, 220

Mary Clay, of *Death in the Deep South*, 35, 97–98, 129

Mary Dalton, of *Native Son*, 105

Mary Jane, of *Adventures of Huckleberry Finn*, 160, 161

Mary Littlejohn, of *The Member of the Wedding*, 25, 248, 252, 311–12

masculinity, 21, 31–37, 46–87

matriarchy, 275–90

Mattachine Society, 34

Matthews, Brander, 53

Matthiessen, F. O., 45

Maudie, of *The Grass Harp*, 22, 242

Maudie, Miss, 4, 15, 20, 22, 24, 31, 47, 51, 52, 53, 56, 57, 60, 66, 80, 110, 120, 123, 129, 133, 160, 175, 177, 178, 179, 181, 186, 191, 198, 199–206; 257, 259, 274, 281; as invert, 212–13, 233, 236, 242, 288–90; as model for Scout, 174–76, 199–206, 285–90

May Archer, of *The Age of Innocence*, 24, 271, 274, 275, 281

Maycomb, 16, 21, 24, 26, 27, 30, 49, 53, 58, 59, 64, 66, 83, 91, 107, 114, 119, 126, 139, 151, 152, 153, 154, 186, 187, 189, 191, 218, 249, 259, 291–92; compared to New York in *The Age of Innocence*, 164, 268–91; compared to North Dormer in *Summer*, 292–305

Maycomb Tribune, The, 9

Mayella Ewell, 17, 24, 34, 35, 41, 46, 73, 79, 81, 84, 92, 100, 106, 108, 114, 115, 124, 139, 173, 179, 197, 202, 207, 219, 238, 247, 255, 258, 275; compared to Cassy of *Uncle Tom's Cabin*, 114–15; as double for Scout, 116, 117, 179, 291

McCullers, Carson, 5, 10, 11, 13, 21–23, 25, 36–37, 80, 98, 160, 209, 226, 244, 259, 291, 311

McDowell, Deborah, 39

McElaney, Hugh, 253

McGonagall, Minerva, of *Harry Potter*, 199

McRuer, Robert, 256

Mead, Margaret, 268

Medusa, 21, 205

Meer, Sarah, 91

melodrama, 8–9, 10, 16–18, 89–128, 134; and children, 117–18; court as, 128–29; emotions in, 101–2; history of, 90–91; as social theater, 102–3, 106, 109, 126

"Melodramas of Beset Manhood," by Nina Baym, 21, 45

Melodramatic Imagination: Balzac, Henry James, Melodrama, and the Mode of Excess, The, by Peter Brooks, 92

Melville, Herman, 45

Member of the Wedding, The, by Carson McCullers, 13, 22, 25, 37, 68, 69, 80, 86, 245–59, 269, 262, 291, 292, 305–14

memory, 130, 163–66; limits of, 11, 19, 76. *See also* reminiscence

Mercer, John, 91, 92, 94, 97

Merriweather, Mrs., 20, 160, 172, 179, 202, 266, 270, 273, 281, 286, 288, 289, 299–300

methodology, 2–5; of modernist novel, 18–19, 131–69

Meyer, Moe, 221, 222, 248

Mick, of *The Heart is a Lonely Hunter*, 307

Michelangelo, 33, 82, 252, 262, 271

Midnight in the Garden of Good and Evil, by John Berendt, 1, 38, 283

Miller, Susan, 25, 300, 301, 302, 303

mimicry, of child characters, 19, 150, 174–75, 182–91, 198, 200–201, 299

Mingott, Mrs., of *The Age of Innocence*. *See* Catherine Mingott

minstrel shows, 95; minstrelsy in Topsy of *Uncle Tom's Cabin*, 119

Minter, Shannon, 33

Mirkin, Harris, 33

miscegenation, 96, 100, 101, 124, 287; Cassy and Mayella as symbols of, 115

missionary society scene, 14, 20, 23, 24, 30, 55, 59, 85, 118, 148, 160, 169, 202, 259, 268, 270, 271, 273, 275, 281, 284–91, 299

Mitchell, Margaret, 69, 71

Mitchell-Peters, Brian, 224, 227, 232

"Mixture of Delicious and Freak, A," by Rachel Adams, 37

World War I, 301

World War II, 30, 307–8

wounds, as symbol, 11, 21–22, 146, 208, 241–42, 249, 310. *See also* disability

Wright, Richard, 5, 17, 40, 72, 90, 93, 104–5, 127–28

writing, Cal as teacher of, 171, 193

Wyile, Andrea, 132

Yellow Wallpaper, The, by Charlotte Perkins Gilman, 262, 263, 306

youth culture, 34

Zeebo, of *Mockingbird*, 157

Zelizer, Viviana, 294

Zoo, of *Other Voices, Other Rooms,* 229, 234, 238